Women and Credit in Pre-Industrial Europe

EARLY EUROPEAN RESEARCH

Series founded by the Australian Research Council Network for Early European Research, and now directed by The University of Western Australia Centre for Medieval and Early Modern Studies.

Previously published volumes in this series are listed at the back of the book

Volume 12

Women and Credit in Pre-Industrial Europe

Edited by

Elise M. Dermineur

BREPOLS

British Library Cataloguing in Publication Data

A catalogue record for this book is available from the British Library.

D/2018/0095/143
ISBN 978-2-503-57052-5
E-ISBN 978-2-503-57053-2
DOI 10.1484/M.EER-EB.5.111944

Printed in the EU on acid-free paper.

Contents

List of Illustrations

Figures

Tables

Acknowledgements

I would like to thank the contributors to this volume for their diligence and support. Their enthusiasm helped to bring this project to a successful conclusion. This volume originated from an international symposium organized at Umeå University, Sweden, 30–31 May 2016. We would like to acknowledge the generous support of Riksbankens Jubileumsfond, Handelsbankens Stifelserna, and Umeå University. Riksbankens Jubileumsfond funded our symposium in Umeå, while Handelsbanken Stiferlserna made the availability of this volume in an open access repository possible. I am grateful to Linda Edlund who took care of all the administration and finances of this project at Umeå University. Finally, and as always, thanks to Alyson and Emelie who helped with the editorial process in many ways.

Women and Credit in Pre-Industrial Europe: An Overview

Elise M. Dermineur

Across Europe and throughout various periods, women have played a significant role in formal and informal financial exchange. They borrowed money to make ends meet and provide for their households, or to invest in their shops, businesses, or farms. They placed their capital and savings in credit markets to overcome the death of a husband, secure a decent retirement pension, or to provide for a dowry. We also often find them acting as intermediaries and giving pledges, key roles in the circulation of credit. Here and there, women were active agents in credit exchanges and credit networks.

To date, however, their role in these markets has been under-examined and underestimated. We still know very little regarding the extent of their participation, its significance and impact on their households and communities. What was the role of women in pre-industrial credit markets? What was the extent of female credit capacity in terms of lending and borrowing? How did women participate in credit exchange in practice? This collection of essays, therefore, sets out to answer these questions and examine the significance of women in pre-industrial European

Elise M. Dermineur is an associate professor of history at Umeå University and a Pro Futura Scientia Fellow at the Swedish Collegium for Advanced Study in Uppsala. Dermineur's publications include articles published in the *Journal of Social History*, *The Journal of Interdisciplinary History*, *Traverse Revue d'Histoire — Zeitschrift für Geschichte*, and *Social Sciences History*, among others. In 2017, she published *Gender and Politics in Eighteenth-Century Sweden*, a political biography of the Swedish queen Lovisa Ulrika (1720–1782).

Women and Credit in Pre-Industrial Europe, ed. by Elise M. Dermineur, EER 12 (Turnhout: Brepols, 2018), pp. 1–18.
BREPOLS PUBLISHERS 10.1484/M.EER-EB.5.115746

credit markets from 1400 to 1800. Thus, this book aims to provide empirical data and a comprehensive picture of pre-industrial European women's various roles and experiences in credit activities.

Debt, Credit, and Women in Pre-Industrial Europe

That women made economic contributions to their households in the management, care, and sale of livestock, farm products, and artisanal objects and in the production of textile items, is incontrovertible. Recent studies have emphasized the significance of women's labour throughout Europe.[1] Whether performing remunerated tasks or not, their contribution to the household and to their community was embedded in an economic system in which they were key economic agents. Similarly, inheritance patterns and dowry also gave women both access to a capital to manage and *de facto* a critical role in making them significant economic partners and agents.[2] Yet, the significance and extent of women's larger economic role has been neglected. 'The historical discussion of the economic role of women' notes Marjorie McIntosh, 'has often been somewhat superficial'.[3] Historians have often relegated women to live in the shadows of men, especially when it comes to financial exchange and credit. And yet, the role of women, not only as creditors but also as debtors, was significant, and informs us not only about the mechanisms of the local economy but also about patriarchy and gendered behaviour within the community. It is important to first focus on the recent developments regarding the study of pre-industrial credit in order to fully understand why we know so little about female actors in these markets.

[1] See among others Bennett, *Ale, Beer, and Brewsters*; McIntosh, *Working Women in English Society, 1300–1620*; Hanawalt, *Women and Work in Preindustrial Europe*; Howell, *Women, Production, and Patriarchy*; Simonton, *Female Agency in the Urban Economy*; Wiesner, *Working Women*; Ågren, *Making a Living, Making a Difference*; Whittle, 'Enterprising Widows and Active Wives'. See also the ongoing project Gender and Work 1550–1800 conducted by Maria Ågren at Uppsala University <http://gaw.hist.uu.se/what-is-gaw/research+project/>.

[2] Despite some legal restrictions, women could inherit from their parents' estate in certain parts of Europe, becoming thus a valuable partner in their household. Widows could also inherit from their deceased husbands and/or benefit from economic advantages such as usufruct of property. See especially Dermineur, 'Widows' Political Strategies in Traditional Communities'.

[3] McIntosh, *Autonomy and Community*, p. 175.

Recent Developments in the Analysis of Credit in Pre-Industrial Europe

Credit and debt have been at the heart of scholarly attention for some time now. Political historians have long underlined the vital role of public debt in the state-building process and in sustaining the military state.[4] High finance and its relation to trade have also attracted considerable attention.[5] More recently, however, historians have shed light on private transactions, small financial exchanges between peasants, artisans, small retailers, and petty bourgeois for whom credit was often a survival strategy and a frequent experience.[6] Craig Muldrew estimates that nearly 90 per cent of transactions were carried out on credit.[7] Several historians have contributed to a better understanding of private credit mechanisms, networks, intermediation, contracts, and economic functions in pre-industrial Europe.[8]

Recently, however, social and cultural historians have opened new research clusters with special reference to how and why capital and debt circulated between people. Laurence Fontaine, for example, following the path set by E. P. Thompson, has recently referred to a moral economy for the early modern period, showing the mechanisms of cooperation and solidarity at work in traditional communities when it came to credit and highlighting its social dimension. But, more importantly, she recognizes the vital importance of credit in early modern France, as she points to the emerging figure of the *Homo Creditus* in the seventeenth century, illuminating the fundamental significance of credit to economic practice and social relations throughout Europe — which was mutually formative in its impact — drawing attention to the multiplicity of circuits of credit at all levels of society. As Fontaine points out, microcredit is not a modern invention, and in pre-modern Europe it already helped people to subsist.[9] But it was certainly a *different* system of microcredit, based on interpersonal relations, reciprocity, solidarity, mutual trust, and

4 Dickson and Storrs, eds, *The Fiscal-Military State*; Stasavage, *States of Credit*; Tracy, *A Financial Revolution*.

5 Cassis, *Capitals of Capital*; Wennerlind, *Casualties of Credit*.

6 See for instance Fontaine, *L'économie morale*.

7 Muldrew, *The Economy of Obligation*.

8 It is impossible to produce an exhaustive list here. Among the most important works see for instance Hoffman, Postel-Vinay, and Rosenthal, *Priceless Markets*; Van Zanden, Zuijderduijn, and De Moor, 'Small Is Beautiful'.

9 Fontaine, *L'économie morale*, p. 156.

so on. Embedded in the pre-industrial society, credit had not only a key economic function but also, and perhaps more importantly, a social function.[10]

Similarly, Anglo-Saxon social historians, in particular British scholars, have taken the lead in pre-industrial credit and debt studies. Medieval and early modern British sources, in particular the abundant debt litigation, have engendered in turn a prolific literature.[11] It is unclear whether the abundance of British scholarship is due to a certain academic trend focusing on financial exchanges or if it is the result of the generous amount of available sources. One may suspect that Great Britain might have perhaps a greater 'culture of credit', to borrow a term coined by Craig Muldrew.[12] As a result, British scholars have recently focused their attention on the social dimension of credit.[13] Muldrew, for instance, underlines the importance of social credit, i.e. to possess a virtuous character and a reputation for honesty, in order to facilitate trust between parties in a world of asymmetric information. Following his path, a new generation of historians has focused on the social dimension of debt. One area, however, is still largely unexplored.

The Missing Chain: Women and Credit

William Chester suggests that 'pre-industrial forms and networks of credit usually provided a vital and important place for women'.[14] Yet, to date, not a great deal of attention has been devoted to the role of women in pre-industrial credit markets. Despite the number of studies existing on private credit and financial transactions, only a small amount of information and empirical data is available regarding women's participation in premodern credit markets, which makes comparisons and generalization almost impossible. Even though historians have emphasized that women's participation in financial exchanges existed, they have remained silent on its outreach and extent.[15] So far, we still know very little about this issue. British historians have once again taken the lead in studying the social aspect of lending

[10] See also Fontaine and others, eds, *Des Personnes Aux Institutions*.

[11] Schofield and Mayhew, *Credit and Debt in Medieval England*.

[12] Muldrew, *The Economy of Obligation*.

[13] Briggs, *Credit and Village*; Finn, *The Character of Credit*; Shepard, *Accounting for Oneself*.

[14] Jordan, *Women and Credit*, p. 125.

[15] Among the most important work, one can cite Jordan, *Women and Credit*; Lemire and others, *Women and Credit*; Laurence, Maltby, and Rutterford, eds, *Women and their Money*; Mulè, Guglielmotti, and Bertoni, *Dare credito alle donne*.

and have offered a modest constellation of relevant case studies, giving a scattered and incomplete picture.[16] Much work remains to be done. Certain features of the premodern society, in particular the patriarchal framework, makes the examination of women's role in financial exchanges challenging.

Women's economic activities were defined according to regional legal frameworks. Across medieval and early modern Europe, not only did these frameworks differ from one region to another but they also changed over time. In some parts of Europe, in England in particular, laws of coverture theoretically prevented married women taking an active role in trade; they could not contract or take part in legal dispute without their husband's participation.[17] This rigid system, however, was not without flaws. The equity courts, for instance, were willing to hear cases involving married women without a husband's participation.[18] Additionally, some gaps in the legal framework made it possible for a *feme sole* to trade and conduct business on her own behalf. Contrary to married women, single women and widows had greater legal possibilities. These women had the same legal rights as men to contract; participation in credit markets was thus possible, as Cathryn Spence has recently demonstrated.[19]

Similarly, Natalie Zemon Davis, Sarah Hanley, and Julie Hardwick, among others, have long pointed to an increasing restriction of women's legal possibilities that occurred in the sixteenth century.[20] 'Women suffered for their powerlessness' writes Zemon Davis, 'as changes in marriage laws restricted the freedom of wives even further, as female guilds dwindled, as the female role in middle-level commerce and farm direction contracted, and as the differential between male and female wages increased'.[21] This change was particularly visible in early modern France.

While the status of women undeniably changed with the implementation of legal discrimination against women after this patriarchal reaction in the sixteenth century, scholars have recently observed an interesting dichotomy. In theory, as

[16] See for instance Briggs, 'Empowered or Marginalized?'; Muldrew, '"A Mutual Assent of her Mind"?'; McIntosh, 'Women, Credit, and Family Relationships'; Spicksley, '"Fly with a Duck in thy Mouth"'. More recently, see Froide, *Silent Partners*.

[17] See for instance McIntosh, 'The Benefits and Drawbacks of Femme Sole Status'. See also Hardwick, *The Practice of Patriarchy*.

[18] McIntosh, 'Women, Credit, and Family Relationships'.

[19] Spence, *Women, Credit, and Debt*.

[20] See for instance Bennett, *Ale, Beer, and Brewsters*; Bennett, *History Matters*; Zemon Davis, *Society and Culture in Early Modern France*. Hanley, 'Engendering the State'; Hanley 'The Family, the State, and the Law'; Hardwick, *Family Business*.

[21] Zemon Davis, 'City, Women and Religious Change', p. 94.

Zemon Davis notes, in many regions of pre-industrial Europe, customs and legal canons often drastically limited female economic agency, preventing them from contracting and handling their assets freely. It was more difficult for women to access capital and property rights than it was for their male counterparts. Paradoxically, their assets became increasingly protected. In the case of bad management on the part of her husband, a woman could legally seek a separation of property, for example.[22] In practice, therefore, women circumvented legal rules and challenged patriarchal structures. In the period corresponding to the 'industrious revolution', married women even increased their participation in commercial exchange.[23] Women still owned and managed property in their own right; their economic participation remained extensive.

Despite legal constraints, therefore, women traded and took an active part in pre-industrial local markets. There is no doubt that they constituted an important chain in economic exchanges. But if one considers credit exchanges in particular, we are still fundamentally ignorant of the extent of women's capacity to lend *and* borrow, of gendered practices related to credit, of the conditions of women's access to credit, of the impact of female involvement in credit networks traditionally dominated by men, and of the effects of female participation in the economic life of their household and community.

Female Moneylenders and Investors. So far, female creditors have received the most attention.[24] Various types of female moneylenders have been identified. William Chester has noted that in German-speaking regions, female Jewish lenders were ubiquitous.[25] We can also find them here and there in various towns across Europe. In England, female landlords, shopkeepers, heiresses, among others, also took part in credit activities.[26] The contributions in this volume highlight the diversity of their experience.

Female lenders could be found at all levels of society. In England, a survey reveals that female investors made up between a fourth and a third of investors in the major companies, the Bank of England, and government debt.[27] Marital status,

[22] See Hardwick, 'Seeking Separations'.

[23] De Vries, *The Industrious Revolution*; Howell, *Commerce before Capitalism in Europe, 1300–1600.*

[24] See for instance Carlos and Neal, 'Women Investors in Early Capital Markets, 1720–1725'. Laurence, Maltby and Rutterford, eds, *Women and their Money, 1700–1950.*

[25] Jordan, *Women and Credit*, p. 21.

[26] Froide, *Silent Partners.*

[27] Froide, *Silent Partners*, p. 1.

once again, appears to be decisive in shaping female creditors' scope for action and lending possibilities — both legally and economically. Judith Spicksley, among others, has underlined the critical role of single women, especially heiresses.[28] According to her, about 73 per cent of single women's personal assets were tied up in lending.[29] In France, single women domestics were at the heart of capital redistribution.[30] Widows are often pictured as prominent moneylenders. Responsible for her own assets, with a retrieved full legal capacity over her patrimony, deprived of her husband's revenue, a widow often invested her capital in the credit market to secure her old age.[31] The data available concerning married women, on the other hand, tend to show a low participation in lending. But we may doubt that married women were not involved in one way or another in credit relations. The experience acquired as a single woman was certainly not useless as a married woman. Behind a married man, a married woman often pulled the strings backstage. This should not appear anomalous. After all, a married woman oversaw the managing of food and other household necessities, often carrying out shopping and trade on behalf of her household.[32]

Some restrictions, however, could apply to female moneylenders. As we have seen, legal restrictions did not prevent women from entering into credit relations. But it proved difficult for women to compete with men beyond the micro and local level. Many women often did not have enough capital to engage in large-scale trade and professional credit activities.

Female Borrowers. The attention devoted to female moneylenders has somehow eclipsed the significance of female borrowers, who have received little attention thus far. It is commonly assumed that female borrowers were not looking for capital to make substantial purchases such as land and public offices, or to pay guild fees or to establish a trade. On the contrary, it is usually understood that female borrowers were looking for funds to make ends meet, feed their children, and cope with all sorts of financial difficulties. If this picture might render a correct account of single women and widows, it is certainly less accurate for married women. Once again, these women appear rarely in the documents, overshadowed as they are by

[28] Spicksley, '"Fly with a Duck in thy Mouth"'; Spicksley, 'Women, "Usury" and Credit'.

[29] Spicksley, '"Fly with a Duck in thy Mouth"', p. 202.

[30] Fontaine, *L'economie morale*, p. 156. See also Dermineur, 'Single Women and the Rural Credit Market'.

[31] See especially Holderness, 'Widows in Pre-Industrial Society'; Dermineur. 'Widows' Political Strategies in Traditional Communities'.

[32] Shepard, 'Crediting Women in the Early Modern English Economy'.

their husbands. Elise M. Dermineur has recently demonstrated the pivotal role of married women in French rural credit markets in the eighteenth century. There, married women were increasingly associated with the deed as borrowers in order to reassure creditors, making these women, in turn, full joint partners at the household level.[33]

Intermediaries and guarantors. Pawn broking, second hand textile markets, peddling, for example, have often been described as areas in which female agents could be found in great numbers.[34] There, in small-scale markets, often at the limits of legality, women acted as creditors, borrowers, negotiators, guarantors, placing themselves at the core of the economic system. Recently, new scholarship has shed light on women's active role in credit brokering, serving as negotiators and intermediaries for others, especially for men. Maria Ågren demonstrates in this volume how Swedish women used their position at the heart of credit networks to help borrowers provide guarantees.

The activity of women in credit markets is a topic located at the crossroads of economic history and social history. It is fundamentally important to investigate the role of women in credit activities further as their role as investor, borrower, and intermediary is one of the missing links between those two fields. By looking at women's participation in credit markets, we not only do justice to social history but, more importantly, to economic history. Both social and economic historians have thus far neglected the consideration of gender as a category of analysis when examining pre-industrial financial exchanges. A bias that, we hope, is addressed in this book. To paraphrase Alexandra Shepard, we need to explore women's impact on the pre-industrial economy as much as the pre-industrial economy's impact on women.[35]

Methods of Analysis

In this volume, the authors place three key methodological perspectives in the foreground. First, the authors have considered gender as a category of historical analysis

[33] Dermineur, 'Les Femmes et Le Crédit Dans Les Communautés Rurales'; Dermineur, 'Female Peasants, Patriarchy, and the Credit Market'; Dermineur, 'Single Women and the Rural Credit Market'.

[34] McIntosh, 'Women, Credit, and Family Relationships'; Shepard, 'Minding their Own Business'; McIntosh, *Working Women in English Society*.

[35] Shepard, 'Crediting Women', p. 2.

in examining and interpreting their respective data. Often neglected by previous studies on pre-industrial credit markets, gender is at the core of this volume. Second, marital status is a key element when assessing the role and participation of women in credit markets. The three stages of a woman's life — singlehood, marriage, and widowhood — coupled with factors such as age and class, appear as critical elements for assessing the significance of women's financial exchanges. Obviously, the significance of marital status differs according to the period, the region, and the socio-professional class considered. It meant something different to be a peasant's widow in a remote village in Spain and an aristocrat's widow living in Stockholm. Adopting marital status as a category of analysis informs us not only on women's legal scope but also on the conditions of their access to wealth and capital, and their capabilities. Third, as already mentioned, beyond the significance of a woman's marital status, a dichotomy between legal rules and social practices existed. On the one hand, legal frameworks and regional customs often prevented women from contracting, doing business on their own, and managing their assets, thus denying them any economic agency. But on the other hand, historians have observed that women circumvented these legal restrictions with the tacit approval of their community. The pre-industrial market as an entity often succeeded in cracking the so-called patriarchal glass ceiling. The essays in this volume highlight and consider this tension between legal rules and social practices.

Finally, it is worth mentioning that certain periods of time seem to have been more advantageous for women to act as moneylenders or borrowers and to a larger extent as economic agents. One should not forget that credit activities are embedded in the local economy and subject to its social and economic environment.

The Sources

Uncovering medieval and early modern women's experiences often prove to be challenging because of the nature and conservation of the records. First, the documents often silenced the critical role of women in financial exchanges. Exclusively male scribes and male notaries frequently operated a gender bias in recording only the actions of men. They sometimes omitted to mention that husband and wife borrowed together for their joint household, recording only the man's name. And when appearing in the documents, women were often mentioned only by their first name and/or in relation to a man, their father or husband — the widow of the innkeeper, the wife of the miller, for example — making it difficult to identify these female agents. A few court litigations were, for example, never brought before the judge on the grounds that they involved a woman. Second, women were often involved in dealing with smaller loans than men. Scholars have labelled these exchanges as 'domestic' loans. Women frequently sold food products, homemade commodities, craft items, and livestock. They sold these products on tab with short deadlines. The transactions could be recorded in a private account book or could be just oral. In many instances, the sums involved did not make necessary to formally record the transaction. Most of these transactions therefore elude us completely. Finally, we are confronted with the scarcity of documents for certain periods and for certain regions. These gaps in the documents render comparison difficult and the assessment of female participation in credit markets incomplete. The picture we have is therefore imperfect. We are bound to work with only the visible tip of the iceberg, taking a chance at guessing what lies beneath the surface.

And yet, sources revealing female participation in financial exchanges do exist. In this volume, scholars have worked primarily with judicial records and notarial records. Notarial records provide critical information on institutionalized credit markets. In early modern France, Italy, and Spain, for example, notaries recorded deeds including a large proportion of loans. In their records, not only can we find women but we also note an increase throughout the pre-industrial period of their overall number not only as debtors but also as creditors. Litigation records, while focusing exclusively on conflicts and offering thus an incomplete picture of credit exchanges, are nonetheless a critical source. In judicial records, women also became more numerous as plaintiffs or defendants in debt related conflicts.[36] While these archival resources are the most common, others such as probate inventories, private account books, parish vestry registers, monastery account books, Jewish courts registers, pawn brokers books, etc. can also reveal women's credit activities. The essays in this volume reveal the diversity of sources historians can use to uncover women's experiences in credit markets.

Time and Space

This volume locates its case studies in a period particularly critical for the development of financial exchanges. First, between the Middle Ages up to the beginning of the nineteenth century, the world of financial exchange experienced several major changes and developments leading ultimately to the burgeoning of financial capitalism. In particular, the greater circulation of cash, the development and refinement of contracts, the improvement of the judicial system, all contributed to improving and democratizing loans and investments. From roughly 1400 to 1800, financial

[36] See Muldrew, '"A Mutual Assent of her Mind"?'.

tools became more elaborate and offered a large number of agents greater options for their investment and saving needs.

Second, this period is often described as a pivotal moment when the moral economy norms transformed and subsequently changed into a more individualistic form of exchange.[37] David Graeber suggested this with a concept he labelled 'everyday communism', in reference to the solidarity and norms of cooperation existing among peasants when it comes to the structure and organization of their traditional communities before financial capitalism, from the management of common lands to neighbourly and daily mutual assistance. Graeber points to the transition from 'everyday communism' to 'impersonal arithmetic', this latter model referring to the period after industrialization and the emergence of capitalism, a model based on inequality, oriented towards profit making and the de-personalization of exchange. While the situation varied across the various European regions, our approach is ultimately comparative and focused on this burgeoning period of change.

Finally, this period is also of significance for women. Several historians have argued that women benefitted from an economic golden age in the Middle Ages, therefore contradicting the rigid patriarchal framework of the time.[38] Women had economic prerogatives and scope in contributing to their household's quest for resources. This momentum seems to have stopped short with the development of a more general market economy at some point in the late seventeenth and early eighteenth century. Alice Clark points to the advent of 'capitalistic organization' to explain this change.[39] Judith Bennett, on the other hand, points to profitable female businesses — brewsters in her case — provoking the covetousness of men. Martha Howell, Barbara Hanawalt, and Merry Wiesner, among others, have noted the same phenomenon. Throughout Europe, women ceased to be competitive when production reached a greater scale than household production; women were, *de facto*, excluded from larger scale production.[40] The changes pertaining to the economy in the early modern period, especially the development of a market economy, undoubtedly affected women. Putting it simply, the transition between the Middle Ages and the early modern period, from a feudal economy to a market economy, from an economy of subsistence to the commercialization of surpluses,

[37] See especially Thompson, 'The Moral Economy'. See also Fassin, 'Les Économies Morales Revisitées'.

[38] See especially Bennett, *Ale, Beer, and Brewsters*; Clark, *Working Life of Women*.

[39] Clark, *Working Life of Women*, p. 196.

[40] Hanawalt, *The Wealth of Wives*; Howell, *Women, Production, and Patriarchy*; Wiesner, *Working Women*.

seems to have had a negative impact on women's economic opportunities and room for manoeuvre. In the eighteenth century, however, there were greater possibilities for women in the economic sphere, just before the advent of industrialization, rendering the picture more complex. We locate our cases in this period of transition and at the crossroads of all these changes.

The essays in this volume focus mainly on northern and western Europe. This editorial choice originates both from the constraint of sources available and the vitality of regional historiography in different parts of Europe. The reader may be surprised by the presence of many essays dealing with medieval and early modern England. At least two reasons justify this choice. First, British scholars have led the way regarding the examination of credit markets. Since the 1970s, British historians have established a considerable body of historiography on this question. Second, the excellent preservation of English medieval and early modern court records has allowed British scholars to be prolific. It is therefore logical to find them in good numbers in this book. Besides England, this volume covers a wide range of different regions. The south of Europe is represented with essays on Spain and Italy. Several essays focus on northern and central Europe such as Sweden, Germany, the Low Countries, and France. A balance has also been respected between urban and rural areas.

While focusing on female roles in credit activities, the essays span out from local informal networks and chains of credit to the world of high finance. The essays also cover a wide socio-professional spectrum, from elite women to female artisans, domestics, and peasant women. In doing so, this volume aims to highlight not only the variety of women's experience but also the significance, implications, and outcomes of women's participation in credit markets within their respective and various environments. Female creditors and borrowers' power and agency were expressed differently and found a different echo whether these women acted in small traditional communities or whether they took part in the world of capital markets.

While this book offers an overview of northern and western Europe female credit agencies and practices, the reader will not find much information regarding a few social and ethnic categories. Moneylending by ethnic minorities, in particular Jewish credit activities, does not appear in this volume. William Jordan has written extensively on this topic; the reader is especially invited to consult his work on this question.

Structure of the Book

This volume intends to shed light on two areas. The economic aspect is our prime concern. As indicated above, not many studies have given empirical data, including figures, on women's economic role in financial exchange. The proportion of female lenders and borrowers, the financial tools used, and the significance of their position in credit networks, are among our main concerns in this book. In this respect, this volume is ground-breaking. Second, we place special emphasis on the social dimension of credit. We highlight trust, empowerment, gendered behaviour, and emotions regarding indebtedness and credit management. This book tells the story of women's economic activities embedded in their society, their local communities, and their households. In many ways, it tells the story of patriarchy, authority, and power that differs from the traditional historiography. Through the lens of credit, the essays tell a history of everyday life.

While the regions studied and the time periods differ, the essays in this volume share common denominators; certain themes run through all of them. As many contributions show, the proportion of female borrowers and female moneylenders gradually increased across Europe from 1500 onwards, with more or less regularity and homogeneity. Throughout Europe, it is clear that urban and rural women not only took part in credit activities but also that their activities were of significance. Overall, throughout the period, women *had* access to the Market.

The spaces of credit and exchange, either formal or informal, conditioned women's freedom of action and often defined the extent of their credit activities and possibilities. Institutionalized credit was better suited to elite women. As borrowers, they had the means to secure their transaction and could, therefore, more easily identify available capital to borrow. As investors, they could rely on institutions to guarantee their patrimony and inheritance. They traded high returns for security. On the other hand, the lowest social groups relied heavily on informal markets and pawnbroking. Cash was often scarce for urban and rural workers or landless peasants. These populations owned only a small amount of possessions with which to secure their transactions.

This collection of essays is ultimately comparative; one of the most important contributions of this volume is to present a clearer picture of European women's credit activities through valuable data and a variety of regional cases. In order to highlight the diversity of women's credit experiences, we have preferred a chronological approach.

The first section of this book focuses on the medieval period. It highlights in particular the openness of credit markets to female agents. Richard Goddard explores the understudied, high-value transactions undertaken by women at English Staple Courts in the later Middle Ages. Goddard shows that, despite women representing a minority of investors, there appears to have been no particular injunction against women using this process of debt enrolment and recovery, albeit within a patriarchal society. Following this, Matthew Frank Stevens explores women's use of attorneys in English royal common courts in the fifteenth century, focusing especially on credit and debt litigation. His research shows that women were extensively involved in credit and debt litigation in late medieval England; they could easily resort to attorneys who gave them both the legal protection and social credit for their cases. In the next article, Teresa Phipps explores the role of women in urban credit networks in late medieval England, highlighting the links between commercial activity, legal action, and social manifestations of credit. In their capacity as traders, customers, and providers of various services, women had the capacity to extend credit and were also worthy of the credit of others. Lastly, Jaco Zuijderduijn investigates late medieval investment behaviour through life annuities in the Low Countries. He finds that women were prominent investors in life, joint, and survivor annuities, providing them with a secure income. But he also argues that this investment pattern might reveal a pattern of excluding women from inheriting real estate assets, compensating them with financial assets instead, resulting in their participation in financial markets.

The next articles focus on the early modern period. Ågren and Gayton deal with security and trust. Maria Ågren discusses women's role as intermediaries in early modern Sweden, with particular reference to their roles in providing security arrangements for borrowers, revealing a part of the informal economy for the most part still largely unexplored. Then, Juliet Gayton examines the participation of women in mortgage borrowing and lending in the rural credit market of seventeenth-century England, revealing that women were very active agents. In particular, women's copyhold of inheritance tenure provided married, widowed, and single women with rights to land, which enabled them to use it as security for a mortgage loan.

The articles by Shaw and Rosenhaft show how women needed the intercession and mediation of men in order to pursue their business endeavours persuasively. First, James E. Shaw considers the role of Italian women as creditors and investors across the late medieval and early modern periods, with particular focus on Venice. He shows that women played a key role in the 'financial revolution' of the early modern period, especially as the dowry system concentrated the ownership of liquid wealth in women's hands. He also argues that women asserted financial agency not only upon widowhood but also within marriage. In the following article, Eve Rosenhaft takes a biographical approach to women's experiences with credit relations, focusing on the ways in which a particular German merchant widow negotiated the demands of managing an inheritance encumbered by debt in the 1770s, in relation to male kin and advisers. Her article argues for closer attention to be paid to the ways in which the nexus of vernacular and financial languages of identity and affinity has changed over historical time, as changes in social structure and accompanying shifts in gender relations transformed the terms of economic subjectivity.

In the next three articles the authors show how women's participation in credit activities had some positive outcomes for them. Judith M. Spicksley highlights the role of English never-married women in credit transactions, thanks notably to inheritance from a father. Spicksley argues that the significant injection of capital had the potential to raise levels of economic activity as well as offer the women concerned a more independent lifestyle. In the next article Elise M. Dermineur also explores the social benefit offered to women through credit. She explores female participation and strategies in French local credit markets in the eighteenth century. Her article posits that women's participation in financial exchanges was of significance not only for their household and their communities, but that it also granted them social benefits in return, a form of empowerment. Margaret Hunt also highlights women's gains. Hunt examines the tension between 'status contracts' and 'money contracts' among women suing or being sued in the English Court of Exchequer in the first half of the eighteenth century. She shows how women valued their own work, whether or not it was done for pay. This also demonstrates the way the language of debt and credit and pay for work could be used instrumentally by women to enhance their bargaining power.

The final two articles focus on the increasing weight of indebtedness on households and particularly on women. Montserrat Carbonell-Esteller explores the small urban credit that developed in pawn institutions in Barcelona in the eighteenth century. Her article explores in particular the second half of the eighteenth century, a period in which women of different generations turned to this institution in order to survive. Following this, Francisco Cebreiro Ares explores the opportunities for women to gain access to credit and analyses their position in credit markets during the late-eighteenth century in Galicia. His research shows that demographic structures, inheritance regimes, male migration, and wages are the main factors in understanding the role of women in credit transactions at the end of the Old Regime. His article posits that the increasing proportion of women borrowers has a connection with the restructuring of the circuits of capital that took place after the Atlantic Wars of the 1780s and the demands for cash of the Treasury of the Spanish crown.

This collection of essays allows a critical comparison of credit markets, actors, instruments, networks, and gendered practices throughout Europe and throughout time.

In some respect, this volume is just a beginning, a first step towards greater aims. Much more needs to be done in order to uncover the full role of women in credit activities.

Works Cited

Secondary Studies

Ågren, Maria, ed., *Making a Living, Making a Difference: Gender and Work in Early Modern European Society* (Oxford: Oxford University Press, 2017)

Bennett, Judith M., *Ale, Beer, and Brewsters in England: Women's Work in a Changing World* (New York: Oxford University Press, 1999)

———, *History Matters: Patriarchy and the Challenge of Feminism* (Philadelphia: University of Pennsylvania Press, 2007)

Briggs, Chris, *Credit and Village: Society in Fourteenth-Century England* (Oxford: Oxford University Press, 2009)

———, 'Empowered or Marginalized? Rural Women and Credit in Later Thirteenth- and Fourteenth-Century England', *Continuity and Change*, 19.1 (2004), 13–43

Carlos, Ann M., and Larry Neal, 'Women Investors in Early Capital Markets, 1720–1725', *Financial History Review*, 11.2 (2004), 197–224

Cassis, Youssef, *Capitals of Capital: The Rise and Fall of International Financial Centres, 1780–2009* (Cambridge: Cambridge University Press, 2010)

Clark, Alice, *Working Life of Women in the Seventeenth Century* (Farnham: Routledge, 1992)

Dermineur, Elise M., 'Female Peasants, Patriarchy, and the Credit Market in Eighteenth-Century France', *Proceedings of the Western Society for French History*, 37 (2009), 61–84

———, 'Les Femmes et Le Crédit Dans Les Communautés Rurales Au 18e Siècle', *Traverse Revue d'Histoire — Zeitschrift Für Geschichte*, 2 (2014), 53–64

———, 'Single Women and the Rural Credit Market in Eighteenth-Century France', *Journal of Social History*, 48.1 (2014), 175–99

———, 'Widows' Political Strategies in Traditional Communities: Negotiating Marital Status and Authority in 18th c France', in *Gender and Political Culture, 1500–1800*, ed. by James Daybell and Svante Norrhem (Farnham: Routledge, 2016), pp. 123–39

De Vries, Jan, *The Industrious Revolution: Consumer Behavior and the Household Economy, 1650 to the Present* (Cambridge: Cambridge University Press, 2008)

Dickson, Peter George Muir, and Christopher Storrs, eds, *The Fiscal-Military State in Eighteenth-Century Europe: Essays in Honour of P. G. M. Dickson* (Burlington: Ashgate, 2009)

Fassin, Didier, 'Les Économies Morales Revisitées', *Annales: Histoire, Sciences Sociales*, 64.6 (2009), 1237–66

Finn, Margot C., *The Character of Credit: Personal Debt in English Culture, 1740–1914* (Cambridge: Cambridge University Press, 2007)

Fontaine, Laurence, *L'economie morale: pauvreté, crédit et confiance dans l'Europe préindustrielle* (Paris: Editions Gallimard, 2008)

Fontaine, Laurence, and others, eds, *Des Personnes Aux Institutions: Réseaux et Culture Du Crédit, Du xviie Au xxe Siècle En Europe* (Louvain: Bruylant Academia, 1997)

Froide, Amy M., *Silent Partners: Women as Public Investors during Britain's Financial Revolution, 1690–1750* (Oxford: Oxford University Press, 2016)

Hanawalt, Barbara A., *The Wealth of Wives: Women, Law, and Economy in Late Medieval London* (Oxford: Oxford University Press, 2007)

———, ed. *Women and Work in Preindustrial Europe* (Bloomington: Indiana University Press, 1986)

Hanley, Sarah, 'Engendering the State: Family Formation and State Building in Early Modern France', *French Historical Studies*, 16.1 (1989), 4–27

———, 'The Family, the State, and the Law in Seventeenth- and Eighteenth-Century France: The Political Ideology of Male Right versus an Early Theory of Natural Rights', *The Journal of Modern History*, 78.2 (2006), 289–332

Hardwick, Julie, *Family Business: Litigation and the Political Economies of Daily Life in Early Modern France* (Oxford: Oxford University Press, 2009)

———, *The Practice of Patriarchy: Gender and the Politics of Household Authority in Early Modern France* (State College: Pennsylvania State University Press, 1998)

———, 'Seeking Separations: Gender, Marriages, and Household Economies in Early Modern France', *French Historical Studies*, 21.1 (1998), 157–80

Hoffman, Philip T., Gilles Postel-Vinay, and Jean-Laurent Rosenthal, *Priceless Markets: The Political Economy of Credit in Paris, 1660–1870* (Chicago: University of Chicago Press, 2001)

Holderness, B. A., 'Widows in Pre-Industrial Society: An Essay upon their Economic Functions', in *Land, Kinship and Life-Cycle*, ed. by Richard M. Smith (Cambridge: Cambridge University Press, 1984), 423–42

Howell, Martha C., *Commerce before Capitalism in Europe, 1300–1600* (Cambridge: Cambridge University Press, 2010)

———, *Women, Production, and Patriarchy in Late Medieval Cities*, Women in Culture and Society (Chicago: University of Chicago Press, 1986)

Jordan, William Chester, *Women and Credit in Pre-Industrial and Developing Societies* (Philadelphia: University of Pennsylvania Press, 1993)

Laurence, Anne, Josephine Maltby, and Janette Rutterford, eds, *Women and their Money, 1700–1950: Essays on Women and Finance* (Farnham: Routledge, 2008)

Lemire, Beverly, Ruth Pearson, and Gail Grace Campbell, *Women and Credit: Researching the Past, Refiguring the Future* (London: Berg, 2001)

McIntosh, Majorie K., *Autonomy and Community: The Royal Manor of Havering, 1200–1500* (Cambridge: Cambridge University Press, 1986)

———, 'The Benefits and Drawbacks of Femme Sole Status in England, 1300–1630', *Journal of British Studies*, 44, no. 3 (2005), 410–38

———, 'Women, Credit, and Family Relationships in England, 1300–1620', *Journal of Family History*, 30.2 (2005), 143–63

———, *Working Women in English Society, 1300–1620* (Cambridge: Cambridge University Press, 2005)

Muldrew, Craig, *The Economy of Obligation: The Culture of Credit and Social Relations in Early Modern England* (London: Palgrave Macmillan, 1998)

——, '"A Mutual Assent of her Mind"? Women, Debt, Litigation and Contract in Early Modern England', *History Workshop Journal*, 55 (2003), 47–71

Mulè, Viviana, Paola Guglielmotti, and Laura Bertoni, *Dare credito alle donne: Presenze femminili nell'economia tra medioevo ed età moderna. Convegno Internazionale di Studi Asti, 8–9 Ottobre 2010* (Asti: Centro Studi 'Renato Bordone' Sul Lombardi, Sul Credito E La Banca, 2012)

Schofield, Phillip and Nick Mayhew, eds, *Credit and Debt in Medieval England, c. 1180-c. 1350* (Oxford: Oxbow Books, 2002)

Shepard, Alexandra, *Accounting for Oneself: Worth, Status, and the Social Order in Early Modern England* (Oxford: Oxford University Press, 2015)

——, 'Crediting Women in the Early Modern English Economy', *History Workshop Journal*, 79.1 (2015), 1–24

——, 'Minding their Own Business: Married Women and Credit in Early Eighteenth-Century London', *Transactions of the Royal Historical Society*, 25 (2015), 53–74.

Simonton, Deborah, *Female Agency in the Urban Economy: Gender in European Towns, 1640–1830* (New York: Routledge, 2013)

Spence, Cathryn, *Women, Credit, and Debt in Early Modern Scotland* (Manchester: Manchester University Press, 2016)

Spicksley, Judith M., '"Fly with a Duck in thy Mouth": Single Women as Sources of Credit in Seventeenth-Century England', *Social History*, 32.2 (2007), 187–207

——, 'Women, "Usury" and Credit in Early Modern England: The Case of the Maiden Investor', *Gender & History*, 27.2 (2015), 263–92

Stasavage, D., *States of Credit: Size, Power and the Development of European Polities* (Princeton: Princeton University Press, 2011)

Thompson, E. P., 'The Moral Economy of the English Crowd in the Eighteenth Century', *Past & Present*, 50 (1971), 76–136

Tracy, J. D., *A Financial Revolution in the Habsburg Netherlands:* Renten *and* Renteniers *in the County of Holland, 1515–1565* (Berkeley: University of California Press, 1985)

Van Zanden, Jan Luiten, Jaco Zuijderduijn, and Tine De Moor, 'Small Is Beautiful: The Efficiency of Credit Markets in the Late Medieval Holland', *European Review of Economic History*, 16.1 (2012), 3–22

Wennerlind, Carl, *Casualties of Credit: The English Financial Revolution, 1620–1720* (Cambridge, MA: Harvard University Press, 2011)

Whittle, Jane, 'Enterprising Widows and Active Wives: Women's Unpaid Work in the Household Economy of Early Modern England', *The History of the Family*, 19.3 (2014), 283–300

Wiesner, Merry E., *Working Women in Renaissance Germany* (New Brunswick: Rutgers University Press, 1986)

Zemon Davis, Natalie, 'City, Women and Religious Change', in *Society and Culture in Early Modern France* (Stanford: Stanford University Press, 1975), pp. 65–96

——, *Society and Culture in Early Modern France: Eight Essays* (Stanford: Stanford University Press, 1975)

High Finance: Women and Staple Credit in England, 1353–1532

Richard Goddard

Introduction: Women and Credit in Later Medieval England (and Beyond)

This article examines women as lenders and borrowers in high-value, generally wholesale and domestic commercial credit transactions in later medieval England. As is now well known, credit was widely available throughout later medieval society and was central to all medieval business. All trade depended upon credit — the deferred part-payment for goods sold or advances for future delivery of goods. The article therefore explores the level of female participation in high-value debt transactions and it considers the important question of the sources of capital for female lenders. It also investigates the role of women in the credit market in terms of credit worthiness and reputation and finally examines the impact of global forces, such as demographic crisis, bullion famine, and severe economic recession, upon the patterns of female lending and borrowing in later medieval England. In order to answer these questions, the article analyses the debts enrolled by women in English statute staple courts between 1353 and 1532.

Richard Goddard is associate professor of medieval history at the University of Nottingham. His books include *Lordship and Medieval Urbanisation: Coventry, 1043–1355* (Woodbridge, 2004); with John Langdon and Miriam Müller, eds, *Survival and Discord in Medieval Society: Essays in Honour of Christopher Dyer* (Turnhout, 2010); *Credit and Trade in Later Medieval England* (Basingstoke, 2016). He written extensively on the economic and social history of later medieval England in peer-reviewed academic journals.

Women and Credit in Pre-Industrial Europe, ed. by Elise M. Dermineur, EER 12 (Turnhout: Brepols, 2018), pp. 19–44.
BREPOLS PUBLISHERS
DOI 10.1484/M.EER-EB.5.115747

Credit in later medieval England was available from a wide variety of sources, but most commonly debt transactions were negotiated individually between merchants. The majority of credit transactions, especially those of lower value, were undertaken informally — perhaps transacted in the presence of witnesses or on the strength of a handshake — and thus only come to historians' attention when the debtors defaulted and the cases came to court. There were a large number of venues where cases of defaulted debt could be heard, including royal courts, such as Chancery or the Court of Common Pleas, and local courts such as borough and manorial courts or church courts, commonly for debt amounts of less than 40s.[1] For extra security, larger debt transactions were commonly enrolled at English statute staple courts. The statute staple was a royally-sanctioned debt registration system primarily for merchants which provided a system for the efficient recovery of defaulted debts between 1353 and 1532. Debts were registered in a number of mercantile courts, sited in towns, and especially ports, of commercial importance, such as Boston, Bristol, Exeter, Hull, Newcastle, Salisbury, and Westminster.[2] These are held by the National Archives under the class marks C 241 and C 152/65.[3] The workings of the system are best illustrated by an example. In 1364, Joan de Fosbury (or Forstbury) of Wiltshire, the widow of a merchant called John de Fosbury, came to the statute staple Court at Salisbury and enrolled an agreement there with Nicholas Pershutte, who described himself in the document as a 'merchant of Wiltshire'.[4] In this recognisance, which was a binding contract between the parties, Joan de Fosbury extended £200-worth of credit to Nicholas Pershutte 'for diverse merchandise'. The agreement stated that Pershutte was required to pay this money back just over a month later. This negotiated repayment period (thirty-six days) would give enough time for Pershutte to sell the goods he had acquired on credit in Wiltshire and repay Joan de Fosbury what he owed her. Joan, the creditor, retained a copy of the agreement and in this way Pershutte formally acknowledged his debt, thereby allowing the court to take appropriate action against him should he default.[5] Unfortunately Pershutte failed to repay the debt and widow de Fosbury sued him for the £200 in the Salisbury court. The documents, known as certificates, used in this study are certified extracts of the original credit agreement which were sent to

[1] Goddard, *Credit and Trade*, pp. 44–47.

[2] Goddard, *Credit and Trade*, pp. 4–5, 12.

[3] I would like to thank Hannah Ingram for generously allowing me access to her data on the TNA C152/65 certificates.

[4] The National Archives (hereafter TNA) C 241/147/118.

[5] Goddard, *Credit and Trade*, pp. 7–8.

Chancery to enable the sheriff to imprison Pershutte, impound his lands and goods, and deliver these to de Fosbury in order to repay the outstanding amount of the debt.[6] It is from these certificates, all the result of defaulted loan agreements passing through Chancery, that the debt evidence used in this article is gleaned. This process was relatively fast and provided the facilities by which England's trading community was able to borrow, often very large sums of money, relatively securely. Sums transacted in the staple courts at this period averaged at £85 and this credit was generally used to buy and sell merchandise within the English domestic economy. Some of this credit was used by English merchants redistributing imported goods throughout the kingdom.[7] For example, in 1367, two Florentine merchants, Roger Thomas and Thomas Blanchard, came to the staple court at Lincoln and sold £160-worth of goods to a partnership of a merchant, William Palmer of Caistor (Lincolnshire), and Agnes, the widow of William Fitz-Simon, also of Caistor, to be repaid twenty days later.[8] Although the certificates do not reveal such details, what is likely to have happened here is that the goods sold on credit by the Florentines were imports, brought in on Italian ships, and sold to the two Caistor merchants for redistribution within Lincolnshire. The business partnership of William Palmer and Agnes Fitz-Simon bought these imports on credit from the Florentines and then attempted to sell them, presumably in their home market of Caistor and its hinterland. Unfortunately, they failed to repay the Italians on time — perhaps because they were unsuccessful in selling all of the imported merchandise — and were consequently sued in the Lincoln court by the aliens, Thomas and Blanchard, only four days after the debt had fallen due. These two examples are wholly typical of the 9989 statute staple certificates from all of the English staple courts (excluding those from Yorkshire) submitted to Chancery between 1353 and 1532 in order to recover defaulted debts.[9] It is these certificates submitted to Chancery that comprise the principal evidence for this study. It is estimated that these certificates of defaulted debts represent about 20 per cent of all of the staple credit transacted in the later fourteenth and fifteenth centuries.[10] However, when recognisances and certificates are compared, there is no evidence to suggest that these defaulted debts

[6] Goddard, *Credit and Trade*, pp. 9–11.

[7] Goddard, *Credit and Trade*, pp. 85–95.

[8] TNA C 241/147/54.

[9] For Yorkshire, see, Kermode, 'Merchants, Overseas Trade and Urban Decline'; Kermode, 'Money and Credit in the Fifteenth Century'; Kermode, *Medieval Merchants*.

[10] Nightingale, 'Money and Credit', p. 63; Nightingale, 'Monetary Contraction and Mercantile Credit', p. 566; Goddard, *Credit and Trade*, pp. 15–16.

were in any way distinctive or materially different to those debts that were paid off on time. There is no evidence, for example, that women who used the staple system defaulted more often than men. Thus, the certificates provide the best and most comprehensive source for a penetrating analysis of English trade finance, and women's engagement with that market, in the later Middle Ages. One drawback of the certificate evidence is that we remain ignorant of interest charged on loans and sales credit at this time. As is well known, in the Middle Ages, usury, or the charging of interest on loans, was forbidden by Church law, making it impossible to know whether women negotiated different interest rates than men.[11]

Importantly in the context of women and credit, the statute staple courts operated a system of law known as *Lex Mercatoria*, or 'Law Merchant'. This was an internationally acknowledged body of customs used by merchants that recognized that those engaged in commerce were often itinerant and required speedy resolution of commercial disputes, particularly those involving broken debt and credit agreements. It recognized that merchandise could be perishable and needed to be delivered, often by the merchants themselves, to distant, often overseas, markets.[12] Unlike common law, this very practical system of dispute resolution seems not to have explicitly impeded or excluded women, married or otherwise, from presenting their debt plaints to staple courts.[13] Indeed Matthew Stevens argues that the rules of coverture were rarely enforced even in common law courts in 'economically-oriented' pleas of debt, detinue, and account, regardless of the attempts by borough customs to regulate female traders in towns.[14] Importantly therefore, women seem not to have been purposefully debarred from wholesale commercial pursuits, nor, as Teresa Phipps argues in this volume, were they denied access to the enforcement of debt laws, nor the collection of defaulted debts.[15] This apparent disinterest in gender by debt courts permits a clearer view of female commercial action.

Only a limited amount of research has been undertaken on medieval women's indebtedness. This has usually been studied in conjunction with women's varied roles within the urban economy. In the majority of the studies which focus on women's work, little attention is paid to women's specific role as debtors or

[11] Wood, *Medieval Economic Thought*, pp. 181–96.

[12] Goddard, *Credit and Trade*, p. 6; *Lex Mercatoria*, ed. by Basile and others , pp. 36–67.

[13] Briggs, 'Empowered or Marginalized?', pp. 13–43.

[14] Stevens, 'London's Married Women and Coverture in the Court of Common Pleas', p. 120; Stevens, 'London Women, the Courts and the "Golden Age"', pp. 67–88; for borough customs enforcing coverture in trading pleas, see, *Borough Customs*, ed. by Bateson, pp. 227–28.

[15] Teresa Phipps in this volume, pp. 73–94.

creditors. The records of debt are utilized to study women's commercial activities rather than exploring in detail the mechanisms of credit and debt transactions or women's status within these systems. These studies told the story of English women as the mistresses of their households, belaboured with maternal duties, yet still simultaneously capable of producing all manner of industrial goods or selling small items as hucksters, and still able to come home and brew enough ale to satisfy the consumption needs of an entire parish. A significant proportion of these working women appear to have been engaged in marginal occupations, with domestic service being a perennial characteristic of female employment.[16] In the course of their commercial activities, these women regularly lent and borrowed money and extended sales credit to customers or purchased goods on credit. When these types of low-level, commonly informal, commercial credit transactions went wrong, the disputes were settled in borough and manorial courts.[17] In these courts, women transacted debts less frequently than men. In Exeter's borough court for example, women comprised only a small proportion (approximately 10 per cent) of debt litigants. The amounts transacted, particularly by women acting on their own, were far lower, often less than half, than the mean value of men's debts.[18] Teresa Phipps found that whilst debt pleas involving women in the later fourteenth century were, on average, only slightly smaller in value (53d.) when compared to men's debts (68d.), women only counted for between 15 and 17 per cent of all debt litigation in the borough court of Nottingham, with a similar proportion of female debt litigants being present in Winchester (12–16 per cent) and with a lower participation rate in Chester (7 per cent) at the same time.[19] Chris Briggs similarly argued that women, both married and single, in rural communities had little direct access to credit and that this limited their commercial activities.[20]

However, the lower-value debt transactions pursued in borough courts — generally used to fund local retail commerce — were intrinsically different to the high-value credit transactions enrolled in staple courts. The mean debt amounts, for all litigants including both men and women, pleaded for in the borough courts

[16] *Inter alia*, Lacey, 'Women and Work in Fourteenth and Fifteenth-Century London', pp. 24–82; Kowaleski, 'Women's Work in a Market Town', pp. 145–64; Goldberg, *Women, Work and Life-Cycle in a Medieval Economy*.

[17] Phipps, 'Urban Women and Local Justice', p. 170.

[18] Kowaleski, 'Women's Work in a Market Town', pp. 149–51.

[19] Phipps, 'Gendered Justice?', p. 81; Phipps, 'Urban Women and Local Justice', pp. 136, 150.

[20] Briggs, 'Empowered or Marginalized?', pp. 13–43.

of Exeter, Colchester (Essex), Nottingham, Ramsey (Cambridgeshire) and Thornbury (Gloucestershire) ranged between 4s. and 11s. 7d. in the later Middle Ages.[21] As cited above, the mean value of debts registered at the English staple courts was £85 in the same period. Positioned between modest debt pleas brought to borough and manorial courts and the 'high finance' of the staple transactions was the Court of Common Pleas, studied by Matthew Stevens.[22] As in manorial and borough courts, debt pleas brought to this Westminster court were generally informal agreements (those unsupported by writs or recognisances). The proportion of married women litigants involved in these economically-orientated pleas of debt, detinue, and account was roughly 16 per cent in the Common Pleas and the average debt value for female litigants was £11 6s. 8d.[23] Whilst there are some passing similarities between the experiences of women using the staple courts for their debt transactions and those using borough or Common Pleas courts, a more analogous set of circumstances is seen in the records of credit agreements used in international or wholesale trade. Shennan Hutton's work on married women in Ghent in the mid-fourteenth century reveals that 24 per cent of the credit agreements listed in Ghent's aldermen's registers included at least one woman acting in her own name.[24] These transactions were used to fund trading ventures and as investment capital rather than being used for domestic purchases. As in the staple courts, Hutton argues that the aldermen did little to obstruct women, married or otherwise, in their commercial debt transactions, but rather enforced these debt contracts with what appears to have been relative even-handedness. In terms of debt amounts, women and men lent and borrowed small and medium-sized amounts in equal measure, but far fewer women transacted the largest sums. Many of these women came from the families of prominent business and political leaders of the city.[25] Wendy Childs's work on English mercantile credit used to purchase alien imports in the mid-fifteenth century (the debt amounts fell commonly between £2 and £200) demonstrates that married women, in partnership with their husbands, and particularly widows, extended only small sums to German merchants. This, when compared to the transactions of male merchants, marked these female

[21] Goddard, *Credit and Trade*, p. 149.

[22] Stevens, 'London's Married Women', p. 117.

[23] Stevens, 'London's Married Women', pp. 120, 130.

[24] Hutton, *Women and Economic Activities*, pp. 81–101.

[25] Hutton, *Women and Economic Activities*, pp. 82–90, 99; Hutton, 'Property, Family and Partnership', p. 116.

merchants out as peripheral or occasional dealers in foreign imports at that time.[26] These merchants did not use the staple system to enrol these debts but the international commercial context and size of these credit agreements are comparable to those brought before the staple courts and offer some scope for comparison. This article therefore seeks to broaden the study of women and debt by moving beyond the study of women and debt at the lowest level of the economy — in borough and manorial courts — to examine, for the first time, high-value debt transactions undertaken at English staple courts in the later Middle Ages.

Later Medieval Women and Staple Debt

In the broadest possible terms, it can be stated that 379 of the 9989 certificates studied here (3.79 per cent) between 1353 and 1532 feature women as active participants in the staple credit process either as lenders or borrowers. The vast majority of these agreements are likely to have been commercial in nature.[27] A similar proportion (2.6 per cent) is found in the recognisances enrolled at Coventry's statute merchant court.[28] Recognisances were the first part of the debt enrolment process and those from Coventry are rare survivals of all of the debt agreements enrolled at that court between 1392–1456 and 1521–1535, rather than just those certificates that were part of the defaulted debt recovery process which comprise the principal evidence used in this survey. The inclusion of the Coventry recognisances allows for a more exhaustive and precise picture of male and female lending and borrowing at this time to be drawn. The fact that the proportion of female users in both sets of records falls at about 3 per cent suggests that women were less frequent participants in wholesale, high-value debt transactions than they were in the lower-value, probably retail, credit disputes found in borough courts (7–17 per cent) or the Court of Common Pleas (*c.* 16 per cent). This is all the more compelling because borough or manorial courts which, as customary courts, adopted many principles of common law, the Law Merchant which operated in staple courts, as discussed above, did not seem to explicitly debar married women. Why did women participate only peripherally in English high-value trade finance in this period?

[26] Childs, '"To oure losse and hindraunce"', p. 85. This work deals only in passing with female debt.

[27] Goddard, *Credit and Trade*, pp. 21–28.

[28] *The Statute Merchant Roll of Coventry 1392–1416*, ed. by Beardwood (Dugdale Society Publications, 17, 1939); Coventry Record Office (hereafter CRO) BA/E/C/7/1–35.

The answers to this question tell us much about women's access to high finance, business opportunities, and capital within a patriarchal society.

The data from the staple certificates suggest that it was rare for women, other than widows, to transact staple debts by themselves. There is a small group of fourteen women who, unlike the majority of women using the staple, are not described in terms of their status as wife, widow, mother, or daughter who transacted credit deals on their own. Women such as Isabel de Claregge, who extended 92 marks to a Suffolk merchant named John Prycke in 1362; Joan Whaplode, who borrowed £20 from a London mercer in 1395, and Alice French of Oxford, who extended £40-worth of credit to a local customer, John Cheyne of Chenies (*Esnamstedecheyne*) in 1411.[29] These women could have been widows, although not described as such; they could have been single, as the 'single-woman' descriptor was not used in this context, or they could have been wives operating on their own. It is known, for instance, that Joan Whaplode's husband, John, was alive three years after Joan enrolled the debt agreement with the London mercer, Robert Sherwynd, at the Westminster staple.[30] This means that Joan was married at the time she transacted the deal. John is not cited at any point in the debt agreement. Even those who described themselves with reference to their living husbands could act alone, unlike, in theory at least, in those courts that utilized the conventions of common law. In 1518, Angela Johns enrolled a debt agreement at Westminster by which she lent £40 to a syndicate of three (one of whom was a woman) business people. Johns described herself in this certificate as 'wife of William Johns, mercer of London, recently wife of Thomas Burgogne'.[31] Despite being a newly remarried widow, she entered into this debt agreement without her new husband.

However, women who were not widows rarely acted alone. It was more common for women to act in partnership with men. Whole families could act together. In 1396, Henry Duraunt, citizen and barber of London, his wife Alice, and John, their son, transacted a deal together in which they borrowed £40 from a London tawer.[32] As discussed below, mothers (and occasionally stepmothers) lent and borrowed with their sons. In 1389, the 'merchant' Isabel Torinton of Bristol borrowed £300 from a Bristol merchant in partnership with her son, John, who was also described in the certificate as a 'merchant of Somerset'; in the mid-fifteenth

[29] TNA C 241/188/17; C 241/143/69; C 241/209/23.

[30] TNA C 143/427/12; C 146/435; John Whaplode died in 1400; see Corporation of London Record Office, CLA/007/EM/02/I/004; CLA/007/EM/04/002/259/291.

[31] TNA C 152/65/2/750.

[32] TNA C 241/188/47. A tawer is a person who prepares white leather.

century, Joan Langton extended credit in partnership with her son, John, to a partnership of two London merchants.[33] These children could not have been minors, so this suggests that these women played an important role in these ventures, possibly injecting capital into their businesses.

Table 1.1. Widows and wives in staple certificates with percentages (N = 313).
Source: TNA C 241 and C 152/65.

Descriptor	Debtors	Creditors	Total	Percentage of all female certificates (379)
Widow	86	107	193	50.9
Wife	66	54	120	31.7

Wives and widows comprise over 80 per cent of the female debts.[34] Those describing themselves as 'wife (*uxor*)' feature strongly amongst the female users of the statute staple, occurring in over one third of these certificates (see Table 1.1). In most of these cases, and unlike the Joan Whaplode and Angela Johns examples above, the transactions were enacted jointly with their husbands. For example, in 1406 John Cole, a wine merchant from London, and Juliana his wife received credit from a London grocer called Thomas Mayneld, and in 1360 John de Newborough, and his wife Joan, described in the certificate as 'merchants of Dorset', extended £100-worth of credit 'for divers merchandise' to a fellow Dorset merchant called William de Stupelton.[35] In these cases, as Table 1.1 shows, husbands and wives working together borrowed slightly more often than they lent. The fact that wives and husbands enrolling debts together — effectively creating a legally binding business partnership — were the second most common type of certificate involving women, supports the idea that medieval business was indeed a household-based affair, with all the opportunities for capital acquisition that marriage could bring. Indeed, it is likely that this underrepresents the proportion of women directly involved in high-value debt transactions at this time as wives may have been unnamed or silent partners in many of the remaining 9632 staple agreements that cited only men. Importantly in this regard, it was much more

[33] TNA C 241/143/69; C 241/190/27; C 241/248/6. Other examples include, C 241/249/42; C 241/156/7.

[34] The proportion of women using the English staple courts did change over time. This is discussed in more detail below.

[35] TNA C 241/204/29; C 241/145/84; for similar examples from the Coventry recognisances, see *The Statute Merchant Roll of Coventry*, ed. by Beardwood, pp. 8, 58.

common for women to work with their husbands than to become business partners with men to whom they were (apparently) unrelated. Alice Ive, of Tenterden in Kent, did extend credit with another local man to whom she does not appear to be related, John Petilysden of Rolvenden (4.5 km from Tenterden) in 1416, as did Cecilia Herberfield, who, with two other Oxford men, Roger Folkes and Robert atte Wood, extended 200 marks-worth of credit — possibly for goods supplied — to a Berkshire gentleman in 1441.[36] The Coventry recognisances tell a similar story. There were occasions when women, commonly the widows of important and wealthy local merchants, extended credit in partnership with other important Coventry merchants, as did Alice de Dodenhale.[37] As discussed below, it is likely that these widows possessed sufficient capital reserves to allow them to make a meaningful financial contribution when extending sales credit. But instances like these were relatively rare, suggesting that it was more conventional, within a patriarchal society like this one, to conduct business in partnership with a man with whom a woman had a spousal link.

The Quest for Capital: A Widow's Assets

Central to the discussion of women, credit, and trade is the question of access to capital. Managing, and particularly funding, a highly capitalized international trading venture, of the kind undertaken by Ghent's female merchants or those English women dealing in German imports required significant amounts of capital. However, Judith Bennett famously argued that women were disadvantaged and in a subordinate position in terms of capital acquisition. Single-women's limited access to capital in the later Middle Ages resulted in their virtual exclusion from the capital-intensive beer-brewing industry. Those who responded best to these new opportunities were those — generally men — who commanded the capital resources to invest in suitable premises, superior equipment, and waged labour. 'These expanding capital demands placed women at a severe disadvantage, a disadvantage that came to be seen most clearly among women who lacked ready access to the greater economic resources of men, that is single women and widows'.[38] Women's use

[36] TNA C 241/210/25; C 241/237/16. For other examples, see, C 241/202/58; C 241/190/72; C 241/275/280.

[37] *The Statute Merchant Roll of Coventry*, ed. by Beardwood, p. 53. Henry de Dodenhale was a heavy user of the statute staple system and mayor of Coventry. For Dodenhale's debts, see, TNA C 241/140/134; C 241/140/149; C 241/140/89; C 241/153/22.

[38] Bennett, *Ale, Beer, and Brewsters*, pp. 52–55, 88–92, 154, 150.

of, and participation in, the staple credit process needs therefore to be considered within this more demanding and onerous context of later medieval female merchants' access to capital.

Any comparison between male and female debt amounts is unrevealing for the simple reason that, as discussed above, it was less common for women to enter into staple debt agreements by themselves. Thus the mean debt amounts of certificates involving women (staple certificates: £91; Coventry recognisances: £87) are strikingly similar to the mean values of the sample as a whole (staple certificates: £85; Coventry recognisances: £69). The reason for this is that most debt transactions involving women, in common with those at the Court of Common Pleas studied by Stevens, were transacted jointly with men, often the woman's husband.[39] When women did enrol debt transactions singly, most commonly as widows, there is no evidence that the mean value of these debts (£85) differed greatly those of the sample as a whole (£85), nor were they substantially lower than when widows transacted debts in partnership with men (£98). By comparison, in Exeter's borough court, as in the staple, wives often appeared with their husbands in debt suits, with debt amounts being similar in scale to men's.[40] Exeter's borough court rolls recorded disputes over low-value debts (generally 14s. or less) that funded the city's local trade; the staple funded high-value wholesale domestic trade where the average debt value (£85) was over eighty times larger than those at recorded at Exeter. One conclusion that might be posited here is that as debt transactions increased in value, thus requiring larger injections of capital — such as those enrolled in the staple courts — the proportion of women participating in these commercial ventures fell — *c.* 3 per cent at the staple compared to 7–17 per cent found in borough courts and the *c.* 16 per cent female participation at the Court of Common Pleas. To put it another way, women were less active in 'high finance' — such as that represented by the staple — as this required control over significant resources or assets and possibly goes some way to explain the low *c.* 3 per cent participation rate of women in staple credit agreements.

Capital was available for women from a number of sources. An important source of capital was land. Using staple credit enabled users to convert a fixed asset like land into working capital. One woman who seems to have used her estates in this way was Coventry's Elizabeth de Clynton. In 1410 and 1414 she lent very large

[39] These exclude unrepresentatively large outliers in both sets of data. Goddard, *Credit and Trade*, p. 28; Stevens, 'London's Married Women', pp. 120, 130; Judith Bennett also argued that women gained access to capital through their husbands, see, Bennett, *Ale, Beer, and Brewsters*, pp. 88–92.

[40] Kowaleski, 'Women's Work in a Market Town', pp. 149–51.

sums (1000 marks and £400) to two different syndicates of Warwickshire businessmen.[41] Neither loan was repaid and she subsequently sued these syndicates through the courts. In the recognisance, she describes herself as 'Elizabeth, Lady of Clynton'.[42] John de Clinton (or Clynton), her third husband, held estates in Warwickshire (including the ancestral home of Maxstoke), Essex, Lincolnshire, Yorkshire and Norfolk (some of the Norfolk estates were held jointly with his wife).[43] He had died in 1389, leaving Elizabeth in control of a valuable body of landed assets. The assumption here is that she deployed some of these landed assets — thereby converting them into a more liquid configuration — in these transactions enrolled at Coventry's debt court.[44] As usual, the recognisances do not indicate what the money was to be used for, but it is not impossible that this was some form of venture capital. The certificates do not reveal Elizabeth de Clynton's motives or incentives, financial or otherwise, for being a party to these agreements. As stated above, we have no information about interest rates paid at this time and so any pecuniary benefits to her remain hidden from us. However, landed female creditors were not uncommon in the staple certificates sent to Chancery. Knights' widows, such as Lady Alice de Nevyle and Lady Joan Felton, lent to individuals using the staple.[45] However, it was more common for the wives of knights, such as the prolific Lady Alice Gyffard (with five certificates to five separate individuals, totalling £520), to transact debts jointly with their husbands.[46] Access to sufficient capital must therefore have played a key, self-selecting, role in financing high-value trade.

A second source of capital was dowries. Table 1.1 clearly demonstrates that widows, both singly and jointly with male business partners, were an important constituent of women's use of the staple. As is well known widows are more 'visible' than other women in medieval court records, not least because they were no longer

41 *The Statute Merchant Roll of Coventry*, ed. by Beardwood, pp. 60–61, 67.

42 *The Statute Merchant Roll of Coventry*, ed. by Beardwood , pp. 67–68; 70–71; TNA C 241/218/13.

43 *The Statute Merchant Roll of Coventry*, ed. by Beardwood , pp. 70–71; 'Inquisitions Post Mortem, Richard II, File 54', ed. by Dawes and others, pp. 249–263. *British History Online* <www.british-history.ac.uk/inquis-post-mortem/vol. 16/> [accessed 8 May 2016].

44 Postan, 'Credit in Medieval Trade', p. 248; Kermode, 'Money and Credit in the Fifteenth Century', p. 488.

45 TNA C 241/165/14; C 241/194/41.

46 TNA C 241/152/36; C 241/153/140; C 241/155/52; C 241/155/53; C 241/155/75; three other transactions she undertook alone, several years later, presumably as a widow, C 241/158/106; C 241/170/23; C 241/156/31.

hampered by the rules of coverture.[47] When discussing London widows, Barron shows that they were entitled, indeed expected, to continue or maintain their late husband's business, or indeed establish new business enterprises on their own. They had rights to occupy the family house, workplace, or shop, and a share in other lands and tenements belonging to the husband, and to a third (or half, depending on children) of the husband's goods and chattels. In mercantile households, where assets were often in the form of movable goods, this was an important source of capital. In London, these movable goods were the widow's to exploit as she wished. London widows were also given the opportunity to join the economic and social (but not political) life of guilds and merchant companies.[48] These factors may help to explain the fact that widows were the largest group of women to transact debt agreements individually using the staple. Just over half (55.8 per cent) of the widows who used the staple did so alone. Many, such as Joan Leverych (£40 in 1399) and Elizabeth Hawkins (200 marks in 1529) extended credit singly to merchants.[49] For example, Elizabeth Yarford, a London widow, gave £32 13s. 4d.-worth of credit in 1527 to a mercer and merchant of the Calais staple, John Pais, presumably, judging from the debtor's occupation, in some form of mercantile transaction.[50] However, the remaining (44.2 per cent) staple widows enrolled their debts with other men — sometimes their sons — perhaps in so doing supplying or increasing the amount of capital brought to the venture. For example, in two separate transactions in 1402 and 1407, the London widow, Joan Wight, extended a total of £36-worth of credit to a London tailor, Thomas Awdele (or Audley). In both transactions she acted in partnership with a London vintner called Alexander Sprot. Joan Wright's late husband, like the debtor, had been a tailor, suggesting perhaps a continuation of the family business.[51] In terms of the availability of specifically mercantile capital for staple widows, seventeen of these women's late husbands (8.8 per cent) were cited in the certificates as being members of important London livery companies: the Mercers, Haberdashers, Vintners, Drapers, Fishmongers, Grocers, and Leathersellers.[52] Their widows' use of the staple suggests that these men, all of whom would

[47] Barron, 'Introduction: The Widow's World in Later Medieval London', p. xiii.

[48] Barron, 'Introduction: The Widow's World in Later Medieval London', pp. xvii–xxii, xxviii.

[49] TNA C 241/192/79; C 241/281/133.

[50] TNA C 241/282/94.

[51] TNA C 241/198/77; C 241/202/58.

[52] See, *inter alia*, TNA C 241/182/71; C 241/212/9; C 241/272/15; C 241/186/81; C 241/209/63; C 241/212/13; C 241/266/43.

have been engaged in wholesale mercantile activities, not only bequeathed a viable business and the knowledge and connections that came with it, but also made over sufficient assets or movable goods to allow their widows to effectively continue their mercantile pursuits. Indeed, in general, those widows who contracted the largest debts were either widows of members of the gentry, such as Anne Tirell, widow of an esquire, who in partnership with another esquire, John Bowet, lent 800 marks in 1432, or the widows of merchants, such as Joan de Fosbury, cited above, whose husband, John, had been a Wiltshire merchant; or Agnes Spelly, who was the widow of a Bristol merchant called Ellis and who lent £200 to another Bristol merchant in 1391.[53] Thus the inheritance of viable assets must have played a decisive role in female participation in staple debt agreements. Indeed, access to capital and its use to fund trade at staple courts might have increased a woman's status and reputation and integrated her into powerful financial networks. This goes some way to explain the high proportion of widows engaged in staple high finance seen in Table 1.1.

Women as Guarantors? The Baroness and the Yeoman

In 1472, Simon Ludbrook, a London draper and Henry Ashbourne, another Londoner, extended £12-worth of credit to John Morteyne, a London tailor, and Katherine Morteyne, probably his mother.[54] This is likely to have been credit for raw materials, probably cloth to be used in the tailor's workshop — interestingly run by a mother and son partnership — rather than the more usual large-scale transaction for merchandise. It is tempting to ponder whether Katherine Morteyne was acting in this agreement as a respected and creditworthy guarantor for her inexperienced son or a relative who perhaps lacked a pristine credit record in the market place. If we read these join ventures between mothers and sons or widows and other business partners in this way, it slightly reorients our understanding of women and high finance in the late Middle Ages. Might certain women — creditworthy and reputable women with viable assets or capital — have been seen as more trustworthy and reliable than, at the

[53] TNA C 241/225/4; C 241/147/118; C 241/183/3. The gentry in this period regularly engaged in commercial activities, see, Goddard, *Credit and Trade*, pp. 24–28. Widows of gentry comprise 55.1 per cent (48 female certificates) of the female certificates; widows of merchants and associated wholesale traders, comprise 44.8 per cent (39 female certificates). However, accurate allocation of a late husband's status or occupation is only possible in 44.8 per cent (87 female certificates) of these certificates.

[54] TNA C 241/254/120. For a similar example, see, C 241/175/102.

very least, disreputable, men? Might they have been cited as partners in these transactions, not because they were actively involved in trade, but rather because they were providing security for less reputable or less experienced men? As is well known, credit relations in the face-to-face world of pre-industrial business were dependent upon social relations, trust, friendship, and networks, making a credit partnership with a reputable widow a powerful stratagem for furthering a trading career.[55] Within the staple evidence there are a number of occasions where a son is extended credit in partnership with his mother but then goes on to make deals on his own account. In 1389, Hugh Middleton, an esquire from Greenwich (Kent), borrowed £54 16s. from Londoner, Richard Blomvyle, a member of the Stockfishmongers' guild, probably here purchasing goods on credit for his household.[56] In this deal he was in partnership with a relation, probably his widowed mother, Elizabeth Middleton. Conjecturally the widow's creditworthy reputation, along with her (assumed) knowledge of her late husband's business, gave Hugh Middleton financial standing, placating the worries of the experienced London merchant and allowing the transaction to go ahead. Indeed, five months later, before the previous debt was due, Hugh Middleton and another esquire were extended credit (for £51 6s. 8d.) again by another London merchant, the grocer, Robert Chichele.[57] But this time, Hugh did not feel it necessary to include Elizabeth in the transaction. Might these events be read as an inexperienced or unknown debtor having found his feet in the market with his mother's help going on to transact business on his own? Other similar examples can be found in the staple evidence. In 1474, Thomas Robyns of the Fishmongers' Company of London was extended £12-worth of credit by another London Fishmonger.[58] Once again the certificate cites Alice Robyns, of Stratford le Bow (Middlesex), widow and again probably his mother, as the co-debtor. Four years later, Thomas Robyns was conducting business alone, his mother having supported his early forays into business.[59] As men could trade and make contracts on their own with no legal impediments, these connections between women and men might well indicate that wives and mothers were playing active roles in these transactions — as business partners, experienced advisors, or guarantors — rather than merely passively underwriting a debt with their reputation and resources. If reputable women, particularly those with viable

[55] Muldrew, *The Economy of Obligation*, p. 2; Howell, *Commerce Before Capitalism in Europe, 1300–1600*, p. 25.

[56] TNA C 241/189/31.

[57] TNA C 241/189/10.

[58] TNA C 241/258/117; for a similar example, see, C 241/270/12.

[59] TNA C 241/258/88.

assets, were considered a safe debt risk then other, non-familial examples should be locatable in the staple evidence. In 1465, an aptly-named yeoman from Hambleden (Buckinghamshire) called Robert Plough sought £44 16s. 1d.-worth of credit from a London mercer, Thomas Lymnor.[60] Yeomen were usually freehold peasant tenants or demesne farmers, often with extensive landholdings, so this would have constituted a very large and expensive transaction for him. In order to obtain this credit, the Buckinghamshire yeoman, who had probably never bought from the London mercer before, required extra security in order to more easily facilitate this transaction. However, Robert Plough had powerful friends. For this transaction he turned to Elizabeth Scrope (or Scroop), from Bolton (Yorkshire). Elizabeth was the widow of Henry, fourth Baron Scrope, a major Yorkshire landholder, soldier, and important royal servant and so she is likely to have exercised considerable influence.[61] We will never know how the yeoman and the baroness knew each other, probably meeting in Westminster where the debt was enrolled, but their partnership resulted in the credit being extended by the London mercer. Ultimately, the debt was not repaid on time and Robert Plough and Elizabeth Scrope were sued in the staple court. Therefore, there was always a risk associated with debt partnerships of this scale.

Seemingly, a woman's unshakable reputation could be used to smooth the way for a debt transaction even if the woman herself was dead. In 1528, George Tomson, citizen and barber of London, sought to borrow £100 from London mercer, Michael Dormer.[62] The certificate, rather unusually, sees him reeling off the names of his creditworthy relations in order to demonstrate that he was good for the debt. He points out that he is the stepbrother (although he describes him just as 'brother') and heir of William Magelyn, gentleman; both George Tomson and his stepbrother were sons and heirs of the now deceased widow, Margaret Tomson. He stresses his late, oft-married mother's social position, wealth, and status. The certificate describes her as the daughter and heiress of Thomas Upton, gentleman, now also deceased, then the wife of Richard Tomson, a Lincolnshire yeoman (George's father), now also deceased. Before her marriage to Tomson Margaret had been married to Thomas Magelyn, gentleman (William Magelyn's father), again also deceased. Whilst George may well have been fond of his mother and proud of her lineage, his emphasis on the fact that she had been the beneficiary of a number

[60] TNA C 241/254/19.

[61] P. W. Hammond, 'Scrope, John, Fifth Baron Scrope of Bolton (1437/8–1498)', *Oxford Dictionary of National Biography*, Oxford University Press, 2004 <www.oxforddnb.com/view/article/24961> [accessed 10 June 2016].

[62] TNA C 241/279/119.

of advantageous dowries, to which he now had access, allows him to suggest to the creditor that the resources required to repay the debt on time were readily available. As it happened, he failed to do so and was sued by Michael Dormer just four days after the debt was defaulted.

If, as suggested above, reputable women might be able to facilitate credit transactions then it might have been advantageous for merchants with poor credit histories to enter into business partnerships with trustworthy women of good repute. In 1363, the mercer John de Wisbech, of London, sought to borrow £40 from Adam Fraunceys, a wealthy, influential and powerful London mercer.[63] We are unaware of the circumstances of the transaction and the stipulations of the creditor, but John de Wisbech entered into it in partnership with his mother, Alice. It is possible that the experienced creditor, Fraunceys, was aware of Wisbech's credit record. Two years earlier, in 1361, Wisbech had failed to repay a £30 debt to a Suffolk clerk, thus possibly making Fraunceys more circumspect about extending credit to Wisbech this time without his mother being named in the certificate and acting as a guarantor.[64] Examples like these are not common and we do not know the details or circumstances of these transactions, but it is possible that in some cases women, and especially widows well provided with assets, enhanced debtors' social capital and reputation when negotiating credit agreements in staple courts.[65] Whilst female guarantors are difficult to identify with any certainty within the medieval data, it is an area worthy of further investigation.

'Golden Ages'? A Chronology of Women's Engagement with Staple Debt

The volume of staple debt evidence available allows some tentative conclusions to be drawn concerning the chronology of female participation in high-value debt transactions over the period 1353–1532. If the number of certificates sent to Chancery are divided decennially into (roughly) fifty-year blocks, then interesting patterns can be discerned. Figure 1.1 displays these data.

The patterns of borrowing and lending involving women outlined in Figure 1.1 suggest that the greatest number of women participated in staple credit transac-

[63] O'Conner, 'Finance, Diplomacy and Politics'.

[64] TNA C 241/143/83.

[65] Another possible example is James More; see TNA C 241/275/246; C 241/275/153.

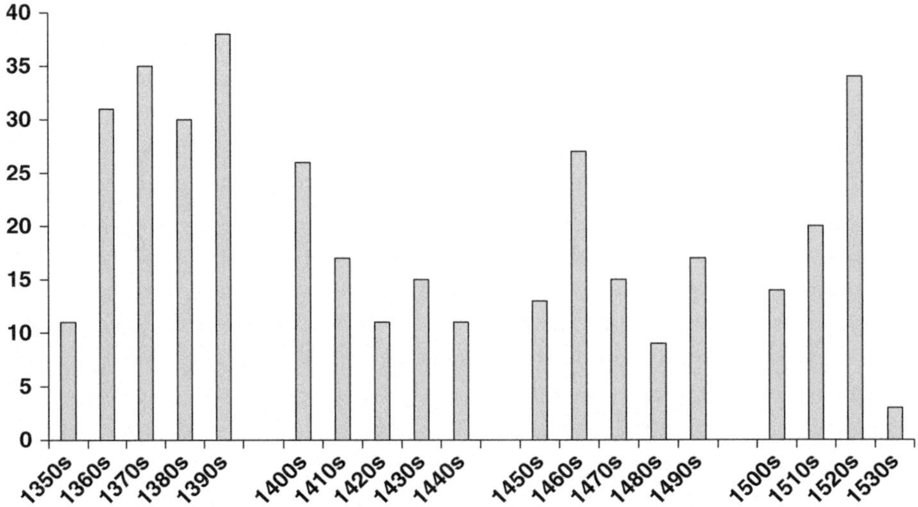

Figure 1.1. Decennial trends in staple debt registration involving women, 1353–1532 (N = 377). *Source:* TNA C 241 and C 152/65.

tions in the decades following the Black Death with particular growth in numbers of female certificates between the 1370s and the 1390s. The 1390s represent the high point of female participation in staple transactions with women contributing to thirty-eight certificates in that decade. One possible explanation for this apogee in female lending and borrowing using the staple is the so-called 'Golden Age' hypothesis, wherein, as a result of high mortality and depopulation resulting from repeated outbreaks of plague, economic opportunities for women may have increased.[66] This hypothesis has not always been greeted with enthusiasm and indeed, as discussed below, a simpler explanation for this late fourteenth-century peak in female debt traffic, and the patterns that follow it, can be advanced. The number of female certificates drop significantly in the next fifty-year period of the early fifteenth century with just over half the number of certificates involving women being sent to Chancery at that time. The real crisis in female certificates starts in the 1410s and continues until the end of the 1440s (see Figure 1.1). The number of female certificates in the next fifty-year period of the later fifteenth

[66] For a discussion of the 'Golden Age' hypothesis, see Barron, 'The "Golden Age" of Women in Medieval London', pp. 35–58; Hanawalt, 'Golden Ages for the History of Medieval English Women', pp. 1–24; Stevens, 'London Women, the Courts and the "Golden Age"', pp. 67–88.

century remains at a low ebb, but there is some evidence of a hesitant recovery. The 1460s represent a particular high point here with twenty-seven Chancery certificates involving women being enrolled in that decade. Some historians have argued that the rising population of the early sixteenth century might have reduced economic opportunities for women, as seen, for example, in increasingly restrictive craft regulations for women.[67] However, this period was one of growth in the number of female certificates being enrolled at staple courts in England. The number of female certificates rises continuously through the first three decades of the sixteenth century, with particular growth being shown in the 1520s with thirty-four female certificates, a number that almost recaptures the glories of the later fourteenth century.

This pattern of female staple debt enrolment follows, almost exactly, the trends exhibited by the complete set of nearly 10,000 surviving certificates. This pattern is represented in the decennial data described in Figure 1.2.

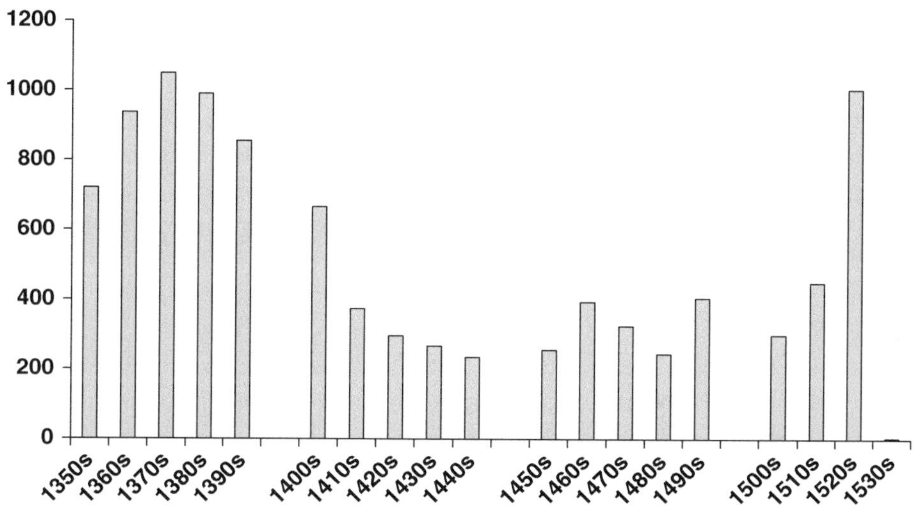

Figure 1.2. Decennial trends in staple debt registration, 1353–1532 (N = 9,841). *Source:* TNA C 241 and C 152/65.[68]

[67] Herlihy, *Opera Muliebria* , pp. 168, 190; Barron, 'The "Golden Age"', pp. 48–49; Barron, 'Introduction: The Widow's World in Later Medieval London", p. xxxiv.

[68] One hundred and forty-eight of the certificates do not have recoverable transactions dates. For a fuller discussion of these figures, see, Goddard, *Credit and Trade*, pp. 97–129.

A comparison of Figures 1.1 and 1.2 starkly reveals the minimal (*c.* 3 per cent) participation of women in staple debt agreements. From this comparison it can be seen that the general chronology of staple debt enrolment for men and women similarly peaks in the later fourteenth century, drops by more than half in the following fifty-year period, falls slightly in the later fifteenth century and starts its early sixteenth-century climb during the first thirty years of that century. This chronology fits well with our understanding of a confident post-plague business environment and economic resilience in the later fourteenth century,[69] followed by a severe recession in the early fifteenth century with particular economic problems being felt between the 1440s and 1470s.[70] The staple debt evidence places the gravest period of recession in the 1420s and 1430s, to be followed by what might be interpreted as a faltering recovery with large spikes in debt enrolments at staple courts in the late 1450s, early 1470s, and 1490s (albeit with each being followed by significant falls). The economic recovery of the following period seen in the debt evidence is similarly well attested in the historiography of the early sixteenth century. It was a period that marked the end of the agrarian crisis in England and the start of a recovery in both population and life expectancy in the kingdom.[71] Thus the most prosaic explanation of trends in female debt registration, in which golden ages play no part, is simply that, for the most part, female debt enrolment closely follows the chronology of economic growth and decline delineated throughout the sample as a whole. This is unsurprising as debt agreements involving women make up a very small part of this sample and, generally, when women became involved in staple debt registration, they tended to do so, as seen above, in partnership with men. What might this tell us about the gendering of women's economic involvement in high finance in the later Middle Ages? It does not seem to suggest a particularly gendered chronology. It could be argued that, despite the demographic collapse in the later fourteenth and fifteenth centuries, women did not fill the void but rather were subject to the same economic pressures of growth and decline experienced by male merchants in the economy as a whole.

[69] Bridbury, *Economic Growth*, pp. 25–27, 35–36; Hatcher, *Plague, Population and the English Economy, 1348–1530*, pp. 31–35; Britnell, *The Commercialisation of English Society, 1000–1500*, pp. 194–96.

[70] Britnell, *Britain and Ireland, 1050–1530*, pp. 327, 329, 330, 332; Goddard, *Credit and Trade*, pp. 109–119; Hatcher, 'The Great Slump', pp. 237–72.

[71] See, *inter alia*, Brown, 'Surviving the Mid-Fifteenth-Century Recession', pp. 209–31; Dyer, *Lords and Peasants in a Changing Society*, pp. 165–85; Hatcher and others, 'Monastic Mortality', pp. 667–87.

Conclusions: Beatrice Lavender and the 3 per cent Benchmark

Women represented only a minority of users of English staple debt — rarely more than 3 per cent — in the later Middle Ages. Yet there appears to have been no particular injunction against women using this process of debt enrolment and recovery, albeit within a pervasive patriarchal society. How should this low participation rate, lower than that of women suing for debt in borough courts or the Court of Common Pleas, be explained? The staple was predominantly used to fund English domestic wholesale trade and the marketing of imported goods within the kingdom. However, the capital requirements of investing, even in domestic trading ventures, required considerable resources in order to operate effectively within this competitive market. Women's low participation in high finance through the staple would seem to confirm that they were disadvantaged in terms of capital acquisition. At the same time, it is important to remember that this was also true for the majority of men. Most male English merchants were rarely involved in high finance on this scale. However, some women did become involved in lending and borrowing using the staple. The capital they employed could come from landed estates, but often women gained access to a husband's capital, commonly through marriage. Many of these women were the wives, widows, or daughters of important merchants, generally wealthy ruling members of mercantile urban oligarchies. One possible reading of the staple evidence suggests that some highly capitalized and creditworthy female debtors may have been employed as guarantors — rather than being actively engaged in wholesale trade — when entering into credit agreements with possibly profligate or inexperienced male business partners. This is difficult to establish with any certainty in the absence of further evidence, but it remains an unexpected and interesting perspective on women and debt in later medieval England.

One woman who used staple credit fairly regularly in the early sixteenth century, and who therefore might act as an exemplar, was Beatrice Lavender. Beatrice Lavender was a London widow, which perhaps hints where some of the venture capital for her business came from. She does not seem to have transacted debts in partnership with her husband before he died, and nothing has yet been discovered about him. She extended credit at least four times on merchandise to Londoners and members of the gentry of Kent and Suffolk. The amounts she extended were of medium value, ranging between £20 and £120. These certificates, of course, represent only those debts that were not repaid to her, so it likely that she transacted many other deals with customers about which we remain ignorant. Her busiest year was 1517 in which she lent a total of £120 in three separate transactions in March, July, and September of that year.[72] Two of her customers in that year were gentlemen from Kent and Suffolk and the third was a partnership of a brewer and a skinner of London. In one of these, for the largest amount (£60) Beatrice extended the credit in partnership with a London merchant, Thomas Barnewe.[73] It is conceivable that she used her capital and reputation to invest in Barnewe's trading venture. The way Beatrice's customers are described in the certificates allows some conjectural assessment to be made about her credit portfolio. It seems likely that the two gentlemen, John Grigby of Sevenoaks and Straumist Throkmerton of South Elmham (*Southelmham*), bought goods from Beatrice whilst in London — they lived relatively close to the capital — indeed she may have been a regular supplier of goods to these gentry households. One of the certificates specifically mentions, albeit in a formulaic way, that the credit was given 'for merchandise'.[74] Her other two customers in that year were (probably) members of two of the London livery companies — the Brewers and the Skinners. These men, Stephen Laurence and John Hatton, would have, in reality, been wholesale merchants dealing in malt and other products, including imported hops for beer in this period (for brewing) and furs and skins (as a skinner). These men failed to repay what they owed to Beatrice and she sued them relatively quickly — leaving no more than two months after these debts had defaulted — through the Westminster staple court. The speed at which merchants sued their defaulting customers speaks to the commercial requirement to recover outstanding debts as quickly as possible in the vigorous market of the early sixteenth century. She is found two years later extending £120 in one transaction to another Kent partnership, one of whom, William Wyllard of Leigh, is described in the certificate as a yeoman.[75] Finally, in 1523 Beatrice lent £60 to another London gentleman, Charles Kurvell, thereby returning once more to her familiar gentry customer base.[76] Assuming she had been extending credit successfully between these defaulted transactions recorded in the certificates, then she had had a respectable mercantile career for at least six years. It was women like Beatrice Lavender who satisfied a part — albeit a small part — of the ample demand for trade finance in England in the later Middle Ages.

[72] TNA C 131/102/8; C 152/65/2/83; C 152/65/2/15.

[73] TNA C 152/65/2/83.

[74] TNA C 152/65/2/83.

[75] TNA C 152/65/2/199.

[76] TNA C 241/277/33.

Works Cited

Manuscripts and Archival Sources

Deed Portfolios, Corporation of London Record Office, London, UK, CLA/007/EM/02/I/004 and CLA/007/EM/04/002/259/291

Statute Merchant Roll of Coventry, Coventry Record Office, Coventry, UK, BA/E/C/7/1–35

Statute Staple Certificates, The National Archives, Kew, UK, C 131, C 241/, C152/65

Primary Sources

Borough Customs, ed. by Mary Bateson, Selden Society Publications, II (London: Quaritch, 1906)

'Inquisitions Post Mortem, Richard II, File 54', in *Calendar of Inquisitions Post Mortem, Volume 16, Richard II*, ed. by M. C. B. Dawes, M. R. Devine, H. E. Jones, and M. J. Post (London, 1974)

Lex Mercatoria and Legal Pluralism: A Late Thirteenth-Century Treatise and its Afterlife, ed. by M. B. Basile and others (Cambridge: Ames Foundation, 1998)

The Statute Merchant Roll of Coventry 1392–1416, ed. by A. Beardwood (Dugdale Society Publications, 17, 1939)

Secondary Studies

Barron, Caroline M., 'The "Golden Age" of Women in Medieval London', *Reading Medieval Studies*, 15 (1989), 35–58

——,'Introduction: The Widow's World in Later Medieval London', in *Medieval London Widows, 1300–1500*, ed. by Caroline M. Barron and Anne F. Sutton (London: Hambledon Press, 1994), pp. xiii–xxxiv

Bennett, Judith M., *Ale, Beer, and Brewsters in England: Women's Work in a Changing World, 1300–1600* (Oxford: Oxford University Press, 1996)

Bridbury, A. R., *Economic Growth* (London: Allen and Unwin, 1962)

Briggs, Chris, 'Empowered or Marginalized? Rural Women and Credit in Later Thirteenth- and Fourteenth-Century England', *Continuity and Change*, 19 (2004), 13–43

Britnell, Richard, *Britain and Ireland, 1050–1530* (Oxford: Oxford University Press, 2004)

——, *The Commercialisation of English Society, 1000–1500* (Manchester: Manchester University Press, 1994)

Brown, A. T., 'Surviving the Mid-Fifteenth-Century Recession: Durham Cathedral Priory, 1400–1520', *Northern History*, 47 (2010), 209–31

Childs, Wendy, '"To oure losse and hindraunce": English Credit to Alien Merchants in the Mid-Fifteenth Century', in *Enterprise and Individuals in Fifteenth-Century England*, ed. by Jennifer Kermode (Stroud: Alan Sutton, 1991), pp. 68–98

Dyer, Christopher, *Lords and Peasants in a Changing Society: The Estates of the Bishopric of Worcester, 680–1540* (Cambridge: Cambridge University Press, 1980)

Goddard, Richard, *Credit and Trade in Later Medieval England, 1353–1532* (Basingstoke: Palgrave Macmillan, 2016)

Goldberg, P. J. P., *Women, Work and Life-Cycle in a Medieval Economy: Women and Work in York and Yorkshire* c. *1300–1520* (Oxford: Oxford University Press, 1992)

Hanawalt, B. A., 'Golden Ages for the History of Medieval English Women', in *Women in Medieval History and Historiography*, ed. by S. M. Stuard (Philadelphia: University of Pennsylvania Press, 1987), pp. 1–24

Hatcher, John, 'The Great Slump of the Mid-Fifteenth Century', in *Progress and Problems in Medieval England*, ed. by Richard Britnell and John Hatcher (Cambridge: Cambridge University Press, 1996), pp. 237–72

——, *Plague, Population and the English Economy, 1348–1530* (London: Macmillan, 1977)

Hatcher, John, A. J. Piper, and David Stone, 'Monastic Mortality: Durham Priory, 1395–1529', *Economic History Review*, 59 (2006), 667–87

Herlihy, D., *Opera Muliebria: Women and Work in Medieval Europe* (New York: Temple University Press, 1990)

Howell, M. C., *Commerce Before Capitalism in Europe, 1300–1600* (Cambridge: Cambridge University Press, 2010)

Hutton, Shennan, 'Property, Family and Partnership: Married Women and Legal Capability in Late Medieval Ghent', in *Married Women and the Law in Pre-Modern Northwest Europe*, ed. by Cordelia Beattie and Matthew Frank Stevens (Woodbridge: Boydell and Brewer, 2013), pp. 155–72

——, *Women and Economic Activities in Late Medieval Ghent* (Basingstoke: Palgrave MacMillan, 2011)

Kermode, Jennifer, *Medieval Merchants: York, Beverley and Hull in the Later Middle Ages* (Cambridge: Cambridge University Press, 1998)

——, 'Merchants, Overseas Trade and Urban Decline: York Beverley and Hull *c.* 1380–1500', *Northern History*, 23 (1987), 51–73

——, 'Money and Credit in the Fifteenth Century: Some Lessons from Yorkshire', *Business History Review*, 54 (1991), 475–501

Kowaleski, M., 'Women's Work in a Market Town: Exeter in the Late Fourteenth Century', in *Women and Work in Pre-Industrial Europe*, ed. by B. A. Hanawalt (Bloomington: Indiana University Press, 1986), pp. 145–64

Lacey, K., 'Women and Work in Fourteenth and Fifteenth-Century London', in *Women and Work in Pre-Industrial England*, ed. by L. Charles and L. Duffin (London: Croom Helm, 1985), pp. 24–82

Muldrew, Craig, *The Economy of Obligation: The Culture of Credit and Social Relations in Early Modern England* (Basingstoke: Palgrave MacMillan, 1998)

Nightingale, Pamela, 'Monetary Contraction and Mercantile Credit in Later Medieval England', *Economic History Review*, 43 (1990), 560–75

——, 'Money and Credit in the Economy of Late Medieval England', in *Medieval Money Matters*, ed. by D. Wood (Oxford: Oxbow, 2004), pp. 51–71

O'Conner, S. J., 'Finance, Diplomacy and Politics: Royal Service by Two London Merchants in the Reign of Edward III', *Historical Research*, 67 (1994), 18–39

Phipps, Teresa, 'Gendered Justice? Women, Law and Community in Fourteenth-Century Nottingham', *Transactions of the Thoroton Society*, 118 (2014), 64–85

——, 'Urban Women and Local Justice: Gender, Society and Litigation in Fourteenth Century England' (unpublished doctoral thesis, University of Nottingham, 2015)

Postan, M., 'Credit in Medieval Trade', *The Economic History Review*, 1 (1928), 234–61

Stevens, Matthew Frank, 'London Women, the Courts and the "Golden Age": A Quantitative Analysis of Female Litigants in the Fourteenth and Fifteenth Centuries', *The London Journal*, 37 (2012), 67–88

——, 'London's Married Women and Coverture in the Court of Common Pleas', in *Married Women and the Law in Pre-Modern Northwest Europe*, ed. by Cordelia Beattie and Matthew Frank Stevens (Woodbridge: Boydell and Brewer, 2013), pp. 115–31

Wood, Diana, *Medieval Economic Thought* (Cambridge: Cambridge University Press, 2002)

Women, Attorneys, and Credit in Late Medieval England*

Matthew Frank Stevens

Introduction

Three growing strands of the historiography of medieval women are brought together in this article. These regard women's knowledge and use of the courts, women's engagement with the credit market, and their use of attorneys. In recent years, quantitative research regarding the use of later medieval English courts has dispelled the old myth that women at law were mostly engaged in litigation over land.[1] That incorrect assumption had stemmed from the casual observation that a relatively high proportion of lawsuits for the possession of land involved female litigants. Emphasis has long been placed on the view that women were conduits through which male litigants might lay claims to land.[2] But, in later medieval English central and country courts, credit- and debt-related litigation often formed a substantial majority of the interpersonal litigation processed — for example,

* I would like to thank the editor, Elise M. Dermineur, and Charlie Rozier for their most helpful comments on earlier drafts of this material. All errors are, of course, my own.

[1] See Stevens, 'London's Married Women'.

[2] See, for example, Walker, 'Introduction'.

Matthew Frank Stevens (m.f.stevens@swansea.ac.uk), FRHistS, is a senior lecturer in medieval history at Swansea University and a fellow of the Royal Historical Society. He has wide ranging interests in the interrelationships between the economy, law, gender, and race in the medieval and early modern periods.

Women and Credit in Pre-Industrial Europe, ed. by Elise M. Dermineur, EER 12 (Turnhout: Brepols, 2018), pp. 45–72.
BREPOLS PUBLISHERS DOI 10.1484/M.EER-EB.5.115748

as much as 80 per cent of pleaded 'London-related' litigation, 1399–1500 (see below).[3] Likewise, in manor courts, peasant debt litigation was often the main form of interpersonal litigation.[4] Credit- and debt-related lawsuits were so much more numerous than lawsuits over land that, even though women were involved in a smaller proportion of debt lawsuits than land lawsuits, the largest number of lawsuits involving women were credit- and debt-related.

The dominance of credit- and debt-related pleas among women's litigation is amply demonstrated by the records of England's royal Court of Common Pleas. In the fifteenth century the Court of Common Pleas, which sat at Westminster, just west of London, was the principal national venue for civil litigation in the English realm. At any given time, there were four to nine thousand cases in progress at Common Pleas. This was several hundred times as many cases as the realm's second busiest central common law court, the Court of King's Bench, which heard a mixture of civil and criminal pleas.[5] Additionally, Chancery, which increasingly exercised jurisdiction in conscience (and eventually equity) towards the close of the Middle Ages, later to be associated with disadvantaged female petitioners in the early modern period, handled only a small volume of business in the fifteenth century, probably less than two hundred cases per year.[6] It is important to remember, however, that few lawsuits brought before any of these courts were pursued to the point of receiving a judgement before the courts. Like litigation today, medieval litigation was as likely intended to encourage an out-of-court settlement or simply to harry an adversary as it was to extract a final judgement. Considerably less than one fifth of lawsuits initiated at Common Pleas were ever answered by the defendant and disputed, or 'pleaded', before the justices. Pleading required both parties to appear, either on their own behalf, or by way of an appointed attorney. And only one fifth of pleaded cases resulted in a judgement by jury or other means, that is to say, less than 5 per cent of all lawsuits resulted in a judgement.[7]

[3] Table 2.1 below (5039 of 6321 cases); 69 per cent of cases brought by or against Londoners; Stevens, 'Londoners and the Court of Common Pleas', p. 241; 60 per cent (debt and detinue) of country court business, 1332–1413; Palmer, *The County Courts*, pp. 225–27 (Tables 8.1 and 8.2).

[4] Manor courts were highly variable, see Briggs, 'Manor Court Procedures'.

[5] Stevens, 'Londoners and the Court of Common Pleas', pp. 227–30; see also, Hastings, *The Court of Common Pleas*.

[6] McIntosh, *Working Women*, pp. 20–28; Haskett, 'The Medieval English Court of Chancery'.

[7] Stevens, 'Londoners and the Court of Common Pleas', pp. 227–29.

The Court of Common Pleas had four main sorts of jurisdiction: real actions, in land; personal actions, including actions of account, covenant, and debt over 40 shillings; mixed real/personal actions, including actions such as ejection from lands held for a term of years; and trespass, both against an individual and in breach of a statute of the realm, which jurisdiction was shared with King's Bench.[8] The 40 shilling minimum threshold for the value of disputes to be brought at Common Pleas indirectly excluded poorer artisans and traders, and all but the wealthiest of peasant cultivators. In general, litigants were most commonly described as practitioners of relatively affluent trades such as mercer, draper, or fishmonger, or as gentleman/gentlewoman, with clergy also forming a small but notable group of litigants.[9] Female litigants, with the exception of never-married adult women, were described in relation to their present or former husband, as 'wife of' or 'widow of'.[10]

Table 2.1 represents data collected as part of a substantial Centre for Metropolitan History, University of London project which calendared and published online fifteenth-century Court of Common Pleas cases involving London or Londoners that reached the stage of pleading before the royal justices. These 'London-related' cases were either laid in London, that is revolving around disputed events alleged to have taken place in London, or involved a litigant described as 'of London'. Among the 6321 London cases found from the sample years of 1399–1409, 1420–1429, 1445–1450, 1460–1468, 1480, and 1500 (all dates inclusive), 1083 cases, or 17 per cent, involved female litigants. And among the 1083 cases with one or more female litigants, 810, or 75 per cent, were cases of debt, detention of goods, or failure to render account of money managed on another's behalf (hereafter, 'credit- and debt-related' litigation). In contrast, this sample only yielded 41 cases disseisin, or dispossession of land, involving female litigants, although to this number we might add an unknown part of the 218 trespass cases, where accusations of forceful entry to property may have been used to prompt a court determination of lawful property possession.[11]

[8] Hastings, *The Court of Common Pleas*, p. 16.

[9] Stevens, 'Londoners and the Court of Common Pleas', pp. 241–43, esp. Table 12.6.

[10] See, Beattie, *Medieval Single Women*.

[11] Disseisin actions — alleging wrongful dispossession of lands, sources of revenues, or other rights — were increasingly shunned in favour of trespass actions — alleging a wrong by force of arms (e.g. housebreaking), misfeasance/deceit, or nonfeasance — which converted the tortuous real action into a potentially more efficient personal action. See, Sutherland, *The Assize of Novel Disseisin*. An approachable summary of Sutherland's work concerning the development cited here is Beckerman, 'Review: *The Assize of Novel Disseisin*'.

Table 2.1. London-related cases before the fifteenth-century Court of Common Pleas*. *Source: Court of Common Pleas: The National Archives CP40 1399–1500*, ed. by Mackman and Stevens. Years sampled, 1399–1409, 1420–1429, 1445–1450, 1460–1468, 1480 and 1500, all dates inclusive.

Writ type	**All cases**	**All cases with female litigants**	**Cases with a married female co-litigant****	**Cases with a not-married female litigant*****
Debt, detinue and account	5039	810	352	458
Trespass	1134	218	120	98
Disseisin	69	41	29	12
Other	79	14	10	4
Total	6321	1083	511	572

* For a breakdown of litigants by role (i.e. plaintiff/defendant) and marital status see Table 2.4 and associated discussion below.

** Married female litigants appeared as co-litigants with their husbands.

*** Not-married comprised never-married and widowed women.

The presence of so many female litigants before the court, in just less than one-in-six cases pleaded before royal justices, overwhelmingly in credit- and debt-related litigation, does more than just dispel the myth that women were mostly party to litigation over land. It prompts questions of women's knowledge of the law and means of accessing the courts. In the year 2000 Emma Hawkes broke ground on this topic with an important, if problematic, article attempting to assess 'women's knowledge of the common law' in late medieval England.[12] Hawkes herself fell into the trap of mistaking the high proportion of land lawsuits which involved women for an indication that women most frequently litigated over land, when, in fact women in royal courts most frequently litigated over debts, as discussed above. However, her work has done much to set an agenda for researching women's competence with the law, writing that 'a careful distinction should be made between legal activity and legal knowledge [...] Women were only rarely present in the courts, and yet their informed choices [...] suggest a sure understanding of the law.'[13] In the

[12] Hawkes, '"[S]he Will Protect and Defend"'.

[13] Hawkes, '"[S]he Will Protect and Defend"', p. 160.

context of this present article, choosing to appoint an attorney is understood as an 'informed choice'.

How confident women were of their ability to make use of the courts successfully would have had an important role to play in determining their willingness to act as creditors, in particular, and thus had an effect on community credit supply. Female and male children alike were under the legal guardianship of their father, closest adult male relative, or an appointed guardian while in their minority; this was interpreted as ending, in various contexts, between fourteen and twenty-one years of age.[14] Once adult, never-married women could extend or receive credit in their own name. However, like virtually all societies in medieval northern Europe, English law employed a form of gender guardianship, or 'coverture'.[15] Coverture held that, within marriage, man and woman were legally one entity, with the husband exercising exclusive control over their assets. In keeping with this, a 'husband could … [sue or] be sued for ante-nuptial debts' by way of claims made in right of a wife, normally citing his wife as a co-litigant.[16] If a wife should outlive her husband, as a widow, she subsequently enjoyed legal autonomy, and might again extend or receive credit in her own name.

Never-married and, especially, widowed women, were also legal co-creditors or co-debtors on behalf of deceased husbands, relatives, or associates who designated them as an executor of their will or who died intestate, which might lead to a woman's appointment as an administrator. About 53 per cent of wills enrolled in the London Husting Court before 1500 name a surviving wife who was to be a beneficiary of chattels or land, and a survey of sixteenth-century London wills found that 89 per cent of male testators named their wife as sole or joint executor.[17] Under common law, administrators or executors were obliged to settle a married man's debts, as owed to him or by him, from his assets moveable and immovable, reserving to his widow her reasonable dower.[18] Bequests, by will, were fulfilled from the residue of the deceased's assets, and widows could be held liable, with other heirs or assigns, for debts recorded by written instruments, which typically included a transmission-of-liability clause.[19] More than half of young widows remarried, often

[14] Philips, *Medieval Maidens*, pp. 32–34.

[15] Beattie and Stevens, 'Introduction', p. 7.

[16] Baker, *An Introduction*, pp. 483–85, 487 n. 52.

[17] Hanawalt, 'Remarriage as an Option', p. 146; Murray, 'Kinship and Friendship', p. 376.

[18] Protections against the despoliation of a widow's dower were malleable throughout the Middle Ages. Loengard, '*Rationabilis dos*', pp. 70–71.

[19] Brand, 'Aspects of the Law of Debt', p. 32.

still owed or owing debts from their first marriage, which were then pursued by or against such women together with a husband. Among the Court of Common Pleas lawsuits involving female litigants, as indicated in Table 2.1 above, in 60 per cent (212 of 352) of the debt-related cases in which the female litigant was a married co-plaintiff or co-defendant, she was litigating as an executor or administrator of a previous husband.

Women creditors and debtors came before the courts at various stages of their lives, as never-married, married, widowed, and remarried women, and in different capacities, as a not-married (that is, never-married or widowed) woman concerning arrangements of her own making, as a married co-litigant with a husband concerning ante-nuptial debts, or as an unmarried executor or administrator of a deceased party. For example, among the London-related lawsuits sampled from records of the Court of Common Pleas found to involve one or more female litigants (that is, 810 cases), about 43 per cent (352 of 810) of such cases feature a married co-litigant and 57 per cent (458 of 810) a not-married female litigant. And among these latter cases, with a not-married female litigant, roughly one third (156 of 458) feature a not-married co-litigant with a man, one third (129 of 158) feature a not-married woman litigating alone, and one third (179 of 458) feature a widow litigating alone.[20] A woman's legal knowledge and confidence in litigating must have varied widely relative to her life stage and the capacity in which she was acting at the time of litigation. The same could be said of male litigants, but the social and legal context within which female creditors interacted with the courts changed rapidly across the fourteenth and fifteenth centuries.

On the one hand, the fifteenth century saw a growing male consciousness of women's work, sexuality, and speech as charged issues, contributing to a 'tightening up' of the application of coverture across legal venues.[21] Before the Court of Common Pleas, the proportion of all lawsuits which involved female litigants fell from about 26 per cent in 1320–1329 to just 15 per cent in 1420–1429.[22] However, credit- and debt-related litigation remained a bastion of female participation, with the proportion of women's lawsuits before Common Pleas which were credit- and debt-related increasing over this same period, from 54 per cent to 60 per cent. The same trends are evident in the records of the London Sheriffs' Court, where a comparison of the years 1320 and 1461–1462 — the only years for which data are available — saw the

[20] Data drawn from Tables 2.1, 2.4, and 2.5. Some cases include a female plaintiff and defendant, fitting different categories.

[21] McIntosh, *Working Women*, p. 41; Stevens, 'London Women'.

[22] Stevens, 'London Women', p. 81.

proportion of cases in which women were litigants fall from 29 per cent to 19 per cent, while again the proportion of women's lawsuits which were credit- and debt-related grew from 53 per cent to 63 per cent.[23] Similar falls in the proportion of lawsuits involving female litigants in the decades approaching the turn of the fifteenth century have been identified in the manor and borough courts of Brigstock (Northamptonshire), Great Horwood (Buckinghamshire), Oakington and Sutton-In-The-Isle (Cambridgeshire), and Ruthin (Dyffryn Clwyd, Wales (later Denbighshire)).[24]

On the other hand, the precocious growth of the lawyering class, in the later fourteenth and especially the fifteen century, allowed men and women easily to find and to retain men learned in the law to represent them at court.[25] At the end of the thirteenth century, trained lawyers were considered to be of first-rate importance to the running of large and valuable estates, whether lay or ecclesiastical.[26] But such men, the most skilful of whom were trained in what would emerge by the early 1300s as the fledgling 'inns of court' between London and Westminster, were in relatively short supply and expensive, and many were kept on retainer by aristocrats and religious houses. By the fifteenth century, men educated in the law were available for hire in all corners of the realm, and relatively inexpensive, obviating the need to keep retained legal counsel. For example, Eric Ives, in his study of common lawyers, has described the tightly knit cadre of about 120 upper ranked lawyers who worked at Westminster *c.* 1500 as 'minute' compared to the rest of the profession.[27] The sample of 6321 London-related cases at Common Pleas represented in Table 2.1 includes about 1000 attorneys cited as representing either the plaintiff(s) or defendant(s) of those cases in 8664 of a possible 12,642 instances (that is, 68 per cent of the time), including 682 of a possible 865 instances in which a woman was represented by an attorney in credit- and debt-related litigation (that is 79 per cent of the time).[28] The proportion of pleaded cases in which an attorney was appointed, in any capacity, seems to have remained relatively static across the fifteenth century, but further research is needed. For men and women in positions of authority, such as abbots or prioresses, travelling to court to attend business on

[23] Stevens, 'London Women', p. 77.

[24] Stevens, 'London Women', p. 84.

[25] Brand, *The Origins of the English Legal Profession.*

[26] Ramsay, 'Retained Legal Counsel'.

[27] Ives, *The Common Lawyers*, p. 19.

[28] Overall, 6321 plaintiffs + 6321 defendants = 12,642 potential instances; Female litigants, see Table 2.4 below, 484 cases with a female plaintiff + 381 cases with a female defendant = 865 potential instances.

one's own behalf became associated with poverty, rather than the keen protection of one's legal interests.[29] While for the at-least-moderately affluent litigants who came before the Court of Common Pleas, which entertained pleas of no less than the notable sum of 40 shillings, the appointment of an attorney became an increasingly affordable option.[30]

The decline in women's capacity to directly access courts in late medieval England, coinciding with an increase in the availability of legal counsel which might represent women before those same courts, raises important questions. How often did women use legal representation before the fifteenth-century courts, at a time when their litigation came increasingly to focus on debt-related disputes? Did they do so more than men? The answers to these questions speak directly to the day-to-day considerations and lived experiences of fifteenth-century women, most, if not all, of whom would have extended or received credit at some stage of their lives.

To date, the only work to have engaged directly with these questions is Elizabeth Makowski's narrow study of six houses of Bridgettine nuns and their lawyers in England.[31] Bridgettine nuns were strictly enclosed and therefore, by rule, could not attend their own affairs at court, and were entirely reliant on legal representation. However Makowski's study is mainly contextual and focuses on an anecdotal range of select lawsuits, concluding little more than that some the nuns' lawyers were recruited from family and friends, and that 'lawyers laboured just as doggedly on their behalf as they did for their other clients'.[32] Beyond this, attention has been paid only to thirteenth- and early fourteenth-century medieval widows' use of attorneys, in seeking dower lands (see below).[33]

The remainder of this article draws on two record series of the Court of Common Pleas to investigate, quantitatively, the extent to which women's fifteenth-century credit- and debt-related litigation was mediated through legal representation, in order to answer, at least in part, the questions set out above. One record series employed is the 'plea rolls' of the Court of Common Pleas, specifically the sample of 6321 pleaded London-related cases, dating from 1399–1500, represented in Table 2.1 above. The other record series, investigated first, is the 'attorneys rolls', which have been

[29] Makowski, *English Nuns and the Law*, p. 3.

[30] On the permeation of lawyers through English society see Ives, *The Common Lawyers*, esp. pp. 7–22.

[31] Makowski, *English Nuns and the Law*.

[32] Makowski, *English Nuns and the Law*, pp. 46, 171; See also, Stevens, 'Review: Elizabeth Makowski'.

[33] Walker, 'Litigation as Personal Quest'; Walker, '"Litigant Agency"'.

preserved together with the plea rolls, sewn to the back of the plea rolls for safe keeping. These attorneys rolls record appointments of attorney, each by the plaintiff(s) or defendant(s) in a lawsuit laid before the Court of Common Pleas, with respect to that lawsuit only. If an individual, or group of individuals, was simultaneously party to several lawsuits, a separate appointment of attorney would be required with respect to each lawsuit, even should the same attorney be appointed in each instance. An attorney could be appointed by either party, at any stage of legal proceedings, but almost invariably prior to the stage of pleading, should the lawsuit proceed that far; only between 5 per cent and 20 per cent of litigation reached that pleading stage, increasing towards the end of the century, with the rest discontinued or settled out of court.[34] Like today, an attorney was a litigant's designated legal representative, but an attorney was not necessarily a trained or professional lawyer. It is impossible to know what proportion of persons appointed or acting as an attorney, in either the plea rolls or attorneys rolls, was trained in the law, but the frequent appearance of the same attorneys' names, often across dozens of unrelated lawsuits, strongly suggests that most attorneys in Common Pleas litigation were professional lawyers. For example, over 100 men acted as attorney in a dozen or more unrelated lawsuits, among those London-related cases represented in Table 2.1.[35] This suggests a substantial core of professional lawyers based at Westminster.[36]

An Overview from the Attorneys Rolls

A sample of appointments of attorney in the fifteenth century serves to illustrate the relative frequency with which women appointed attorneys. The legal year in medieval England, as observed by the king's central courts, was divided into four law terms, in each of which the central courts convened once. Each term followed a major feast day, namely Hilary term (St Hilary, 13 January), Easter term (moveable), Trinity term (moveable), and Michaelmas Term (St Michael, 29 September), at roughly quarterly intervals throughout the year; a recess was held between terms.[37] Lawsuits, once initiated — typically by way of an original writ (that is, a formal complaint demanding

[34] Stevens, 'Londoners and the Court of Common Pleas', pp. 227–29.

[35] *Court of Common Pleas: The National Archives, CP40*, ed. by Mackman and Stevens.

[36] See Brand, *The Origins of the English Legal Profession*.

[37] The duration of law terms varied considerably, relative to moveable feasts (e.g. Easter and Trinity Sunday) and volume of business, with Trinity and Michaelmas terms being longest. See Cheney, *A Handbook of Dates*, pp. 98–105.

justice in the king's name) — were first processed in the law term next following and usually adjourned from term to term until resolved.[38] Four plea rolls were produced annually to record the proceeding of the Court of Common Pleas, one reflecting each of the four law terms, to the back of each was appended an attorneys roll, itemizing appointments of attorney. Table 2.2 details sample data reflecting the first one hundred appointments of attorney — wholly or partially legible — on the Hillary term attorneys rolls of 1420, 1460, and 1500.

Women were proportionally no more or less involved with the appointing of attorneys than they would later be in seeing their cases through to the stage of pleading, despite the months or years of mesne process often required to secure the appearance of all litigants, or their representatives, before the justices. Across the three attorneys rolls samples, 17 per cent to 26 per cent of appointments of attorney were made by a woman acting either jointly with a man (usually as his wife) or alone. Further refined, 8 per cent or less of appoints of attorney were made by a woman acting alone, as either a never-married or widowed litigant. This is very similar to the roughly 17 per cent (1083 of 6321) of London-related pleaded cases indicated in Table 2.1 in which a woman was a litigant, and the 9 per cent (572 of 6321) of London-related cases in which a not-married woman litigated, either with or without representation by an attorney.

Parallels between appointment data and the records of pleaded cases are less apparent when, particularly for women, we look at the types of cases to which attorneys were appointed. Overall, credit- and debt-related litigation gave rise to 62 per cent of all appointments of attorney in 1420 and 1460, and 35 per cent of appointments in 1500, when debt was overtaken by disputes about land as the main case type to which attorneys were appointed. For men litigating alone, the appointing of attorneys to handle credit- and debt-related cases comprised more than 60 per cent of men's appointments in 1420 and 1460, falling to 40 per cent in 1500, when land disputes became more prominent. This is broadly reflective of the majority share of litigation pleaded before the fifteenth-century Court of Common Pleas that was credit- and debt-related, that is, as much as 80 per cent (5039 of 6321; Table 2.1) of pleaded cases. For women, in contrast, whether acting as a co-litigant with a man or as a litigant alone, only about a quarter of their appointments of attorney pertained to actions of credit or debt (11 of 47). Only for female co-litigants with men, in 1460, were appoints in debt litigation in the majority (4 of 7; Table 2.2). Overall, women acting alone or as co-litigants most often appointed attorneys to handle cases of disseisin (26 of 47 appointments).

[38] Hastings, *The Court of Common Pleas*, pp. 157–83.

Despite the relatively small number of appointments of attorney considered here, there is a discernable contrast between, on the one hand, the low numbers of appointments to represent women concerning credit- and debt-related litigation — just 11 such appointments versus 26 appointments concerning disseisin (Table 2.2) — and, on the other hand, the dominance of credit- and debt-related disputes among women's pleaded cases. Women appeared before the justices of Common Pleas in person, or by attorney, in nearly twenty times as many credit- and debt-related suits as actions pertaining to disseisin, that is, 810 versus 41 disputes, respectively. This contrast requires explanation.

These data of women's and men's appointments of attorney suggest two very tentative conclusions. First, women, and single women in particular, did not increase the frequency with which they appointed attorneys across the century, however more restrictive of women's activities the prevailing social framework may have become. Second, in contrast to male litigants, while most of women's lawsuits which would reach the stage of pleading were credit- and debt-related, that is 75 per cent (810 of 1083; Table 2.1) of their cases, women were more inclined to appoint attorneys to handle pleas concerning land, embodied by actions of disseisin, than to handle pleas concerning debt. There are several possible reasons why this was the case. Litigation over land may have been perceived as more complex, as witnessed by the precocious growth of a culture of employing conditional grants and intricate recoveries, or of higher value, as land represented a perpetual revenue stream.[39] Alternatively, widows, who were both regular litigants and dependent on the income of dower lands for survival, may have felt a greater imperative to seek legal counsel to attain those lands than to aid in the recovery of individual debts (see below), which by this period were usually secured by a bond, or written instrument.[40]

Details from the Plea Rolls

A closer look at the use of attorneys by litigants in cases at the stage of pleading — that is, the logical litigation mid-point between initiating a lawsuit and receiving a decision by jury, at which both parties were present in person or represented by an attorney and the lawsuit was distilled to a single yes/no 'issue' — shows that cases which involved one or more female litigants were more likely to also involve

[39] Baker, *An Introduction*, pp. 280–89.

[40] Walker, '"Litigant Agency"'.

Table 2.2. Sample, appointments of attorney, 1420, 1460, and 1500. *Source:* The National Archives, CP 40/636, 796 and 951 (attorneys rolls).

	No. of appointments (per cent of subtotal)			No. of male appointers acting alone (per cent of subtotal)			No. of male and female joint appointers			No. of female appointers acting alone			No. of appointers, gender illegible		
	1420	1460	1500	1420	1460	1500	1420	1460	1500	1420	1460	1500	1420	1460	1500
Debt, detinue and account	61 (62%)	48 (62%)	34 (35%)	56 (67%)	39 (64%)	29 (40%)	2	4	2	2	0	1	1	5	2
Trespass	26 (27%)	26 (33%)	5 (5%)	22 (27%)	18 (30%)	5 (7%)	2	3	0	2	2	0	–	3	–
Disseisin	11 (11%)	4 (5%)	59 (60%)	5 (6%)	4 (7%)	38 (53%)	3	0	15	3	0	5	–	–	–
Subtotal	98	78	98	83	61	72	7	7	18	7	2	6	1	8	2
Other/ illegible*	2	22	2	1	16	2	0	0	0	1	0	0	–	6	–
Total no.	100	100	100	84	77	74	7	7	18	8	2	6	1	14	2

* These are overwhelmingly illegible appointments.

appointed attorneys. In hard numbers, for both men and women, about 75 per cent to 80 per cent of their pleaded cases were credit- and debt-related cases of debt, detinue, or account (Table 2.1). Table 2.3 separates these credit- and debt-related cases into those with exclusively male litigants and those in which a female litigant was involved in some capacity. It does not differentiate dependent upon whether the female litigant acted as a plaintiff, as a defendant, or in both capacities within cases in each category. In all instances, plaintiffs were more likely to be represented by an attorney than defendants, suggesting that attorneys may have been considered an 'offensive tool' in litigation, perhaps associated with a need to employ an attorney to help secure from the king's chancery the correct royal writ, or formal written complaint, in order to initiate successful litigation.[41] Equally, plaintiffs, who were creditors, may have been better able to afford attorneys (see below).

Cases involving a female litigant were more likely to involve attorneys, appointed by plaintiffs or defendants, than those involving exclusively male litigants. But, while plaintiffs in cases involving a female litigant employed an attorney more than defendants, the difference between plaintiffs' and defendants' rates of appointment of attorney was considerably smaller in cases involving female litigants. In cases with exclusively male litigants, plaintiffs appointed an attorney 79 per cent of the time and defendants did so 55 per cent of the time, a difference of 24 per cent (Table 2.3). By comparison, in cases involving a female litigant acting in any capacity, plaintiffs appointed an attorney 82 per cent of the time and defendants did so 67 per cent of the time, a difference of only 15 per cent. And if cases involving only married female co-litigants acting with husbands in any capacity are isolated, plaintiffs appointed an attorney 83 per cent of the time and defendants did so 70 per cent, a difference of just 7 per cent (Table 2.4).

A detailed analysis of men's and women's use of attorneys by litigant role and marital status follows below (Tables 2.4 and 2.5). But it is worthwhile to consider first this general profile of appointments of attorney, wherein cases involving a woman more frequently involved an attorney, coupled with a higher relative use of attorneys by defendants. Much of the frequent use of attorneys in cases featuring a female litigant can be attributed to the complexity of such lawsuits. The majority of cases involving a female litigant were either those in which a never-married or widowed woman was a co-heir or co-executor of a will, or those in which a married female co-litigant and her husband sought or were pursued for monies owed to or by the wife from a time before her present marriage. For example, in 1461, Isabel, widow and executor of John Ryche, citizen and mercer of London, together with

[41] Baker, *An Introduction*, pp. 53–64.

two unrelated male co-executors, appointed high-profile attorney Thomas Torald (discussed below) to represent them in their lawsuit alleging that John Derham, citizen and mercer of London, owed them £86 13s. 4d., arising from two unpaid bonds of £43 6s. 8d. each, agreed between the late John Ryche and John Derham in 1459.[42] Derham represented himself, and refuted the bonds as forgeries. As indicated in Table 2.4, cases featuring married co-litigants were those in which both plaintiff and defendant were most likely to act through an attorney. Newly married couples frequently brought or answered such litigation. This suggests both that not-married female creditors sometimes may have lacked the requisite confidence, in either their own legal knowledge or in the fair treatment of female litigants before the court, necessary to initiate litigation, and that not-married female debtors may have been presumed unable to pay until marriage.[43] For example, in 1450 Roger Penyton and his wife Alice, widow and executor of Richard Brok of Hackney, Middlesex, appointed attorney Richard Levermore to represent them in their lawsuit alleging that John Gylle, citizen and tailor of London, owed them 10m. on a bond made between the late Richard and John at Hackney in 1438, twelve years earlier.[44] Roger and Alice claimed, via their attorney, that payment of the debt had been sought persistently (without litigation) before Richard's death, while Alice was a widow and after her marriage to Roger. John appointed high-profile attorney Thomas Torald to represent him in his defence that he had been given a written release from this debt by Richard back in 1440. The plaintiffs refuted the document as a forgery. Roger and Alice also brought an identical claim, again represented by Richard Levermore, against Roger Slak, citizen and Fishmonger of London, who appointed another high-profile lawyer, Robert Vaus (discussed below), to field precisely the same defence used by John Gylle.[45]

More complex still were lawsuits, not uncommon, in which a not-married or remarried female executor initiated or answered lawsuits pitted against other executors, following the death of both the original creditor and debtor.[46] In such cases

[42] The National Archives (hereafter TNA), CP 40/800, rot. 121.

[43] Such litigation following marriage suggests that not-married female debtors may have remained unmarried longer than their creditor counterparts. Stevens, 'London's Married Women', pp. 130–31.

[44] TNA, CP 40/759, rot. 115d.

[45] TNA, CP 40/759, rot. 305d.

[46] For example, TNA, CP 40/829, rot. 413 (remarried widow/executor and new husband versus male executors); TNA, CP 40/807, rot. 355 (remarried widow/executor and new husband versus a remarried widow/executor).

both plaintiffs and defendants invariably appointed an attorney. Lastly, all litigants in the lawsuits cited here lived within easy walking distance of Westminster, and so each presumably could have appeared on her or his own behalf. This strongly suggests that the decision to appoint an attorney must have been one of perceived need for his skills, rather than the convenience of his physical proximity to the court.

The disaggregation of men's and women's roles in lawsuits, their use of attorneys, and of female litigants by marital status, further emphasizes the strong correlation between marriage and representation by an attorney. Overall, women were more likely to be plaintiffs than defendants (484 pl. vs. 381 def.) in credit- and debt-related litigation, keeping in mind that some cases involved a female plaintiff and female defendant (Table 2.4). In addition, married female co-litigants were most likely, among female litigants, both to be plaintiffs and to be represented by an attorney, acting by attorney in 85 per cent of 229 cases as co-plaintiffs, and 72 per cent of 159 cases as co-defendants (Table 2.4, group A1).

Not-married women were more likely to be defendants than their married counterparts, especially when acting alone, as the only plaintiff or only defendant

Table 2.3. Litigants' use of attorneys, London-related pleaded cases of debt, detinue, and account, Court of Common Pleas, 1399–1500. *Source: Court of Common Pleas: The National Archives CP40 1399–1500*, ed. by Mackman and Stevens. Years sampled, 1399–1409, 1420–1429, 1445–1450, 1460–1468, 1480 and 1500, all dates inclusive.

	All cases		**Cases with male litigants only**		**Cases with a female litigant in any role**	
No. of cases in group	5039		4229		810	
	Plaintiff	Defendant	Plaintiff	Defendant	Plaintiff	Defendant
No. of cases, attorney appointed	4051	2869	3324	2276	665	539
Per cent of cases in group	80%	57%	79%	55%	82%	67%

Table 2.4. Women's use of attorneys, respective of marital status, London-related pleaded cases of debt, detinue, and account, Court Of Common Pleas, 1399–1500. *Source: Court of Common Pleas: The National Archives CP40 1399–1500*, ed. by Mackman and Stevens. Years sampled, 1399–1409, 1420–1429, 1445–1450, 1460–1468, 1480 and 1500, all dates inclusive.

Group	No. of cases	Plaintiffs' use of attorneys			Defendants' use of attorneys		
		Plaintiff, whatever gender, has attorney (per cent of 'No. of cases')	**No. of cases with female plaintiff**	**Cases with female plaintiff by attorney (per cent of 'No. of cases with female plaintiff')**	**Defendant, whatever gender, has attorney (per cent of 'No. of cases')**	**No of cases with female defendant**	**Cases with female defendant by attorney (per cent of 'No. of cases with female defendant')**
All cases with a female litigant (A1+A2)	810	665 (82%)	484	406 (84%)	547 (68%)	381	276 (72%)
A1 Cases with a married female co-litigant	352	292 (83%)	229	195 (85%)	247 (70%)	159	114 (72%)
A2 Cases with a not-married female litigant: acting with or without a male co-litigant	458	377 (82%)	255	211 (83%)	297 (65%)	222	162 (73%)
B Cases with a not-married female litigant, acting alone.(B is a subset of A2)	302	NA	153	121 (79%)	NA	155	107 (69%)

in a case (Table 2.4, groups A2 and B). In fact, not-married female litigants acting alone were the only group of women whose appearances before the court as defendants were as numerous as their appearances as plaintiffs (Table 2.4, group B). On the one hand, these independent female actors were notably less likely to appoint an attorney, as plaintiff or defendant, than married or not-married female co-litigants. On the other hand, they were still considerably more likely than men to employ an attorney, as defendants. As plaintiffs, both not-married women acting alone, and men, each appointed an attorney in 79 per cent of their cases. But, as defendants, not-married women acting alone appointed an attorney in 69 per cent of their cases, while men appointed an attorney just 55 per cent of their cases (Tables 2.3 and 2.4, group B). This makes not-married female litigants acting alone a 'middle group', between married female co-litigants and male litigants, in terms of the frequency with which they sought legal representation.

Understanding the decision of these not-married women acting alone to appoint, or not to appoint, an attorney is of particular importance. While litigant agency can never be established with certainty, these women are those most likely to have decided for themselves whether or not to employ an attorney. Two possible explanations present themselves for the middling frequency with which not-married women acting alone employed an attorney, especially as defendants. First there may have been a 'confidence gap' between male and female litigants. Not-married women acting alone may less often have felt they needed the assistance of an attorney than did their married counterparts who were engaged in complex litigation, and yet they may more often have felt they needed an attorney than male litigants. A probable 'confidence gap' can only be established by the data shown here if all else, beyond the complexity of cases, was more or less equal. The most obvious additional variables to consider are the value of debts sought and the wealth of the litigants. Regarding debt values, *prima facie* — all lawsuits concerning claims for 40s. or more — there is no obvious difference between the value of men's and women's lawsuits; the main factors determining debt values were debt type (typically, cash loan *c.* £5, sale of goods *c.* £10, or bond *c.* £20) and creditors' sensitivity to the state of the London economy.[47] Regarding the wealth of litigants, the second possible explanation for not-married lone female litigants' particular use of attorneys is that there was a wealth gap between not-married women and other groups of litigants. As suggested by Makowski, a lack of legal representation may be considered an indication of relative poverty.[48]

[47] Stevens, 'London Creditors', pp. 1083–1107, esp. 1089–93.

[48] Makowski, *English Nuns and the Law*, p. 3.

Neither of these explanations sits well with our knowledge of late medieval women. It is not unreasonable to suppose that, at least in part, the cause for any defendant to be less likely than a plaintiff to employ an attorney, in credit- and debt-related litigation, was 'relative poverty', defendants being alleged debtors. One must keep in mind the term 'relative poverty', as pre-modern people almost invariably acted simultaneously as both creditors and debtors, in complex webs of credit, although poverty nevertheless ensued when the balance of one's accounts tipped too far into arrears.[49] On this basis, we might well expect not-married female defendants appearing alone to be relatively poor, compared to married or male defendants. But, problematically, they employed attorneys in a significantly higher proportion of their cases than male defendants. The prospect of a 'confidence gap' between not-married women and men is more plausible, whether that took the form of less confidence in one's legal knowledge, or less confidence of fair treatment or success when acting alone in the masculine space of the court. But, is it realistic to expect not-married female defendants, that is, alleged debtors, to be so readily and more frequently able to afford an attorney when compared to men?

A closer look at these not-married female litigants in credit- and debt-related cases serves to resolve this point. These female litigants were either never-married women of legal majority, or widows. As indicated in Table 2.5, among cases featuring a not-married woman litigating alone as a plaintiff, or creditor, the female litigant was twice as often a never-married woman as a widow. Overall, these never-married creditor-plaintiffs acting alone were nearly as likely as male litigants (Table 2.3) to employ an attorney, while widow creditor-plaintiffs used attorneys considerably more, doing so as often as married co-plaintiffs — in 85 per cent of their cases. In contrast, in cases featuring a not-married woman litigating alone as a defendant, or debtor, the female debtor was nearly four times as often a widow as a never-married woman. As defendants, both groups of female debtor-defendants acting alone were equally likely to appoint an attorney, in 69 per cent of their cases — that is, less than married co-defendants (72 per cent of cases) and more than male defendants (55 per cent of cases; Tables 2.3 and 2.4).

These data reinforce the conclusion that creditor-plaintiffs were more likely to appoint attorneys than debtor-defendants, whatever their life stage. More importantly, they suggest that never-married women were substantially more likely to act as creditors than widows, and possibly more likely to feel the need to sue (Table 2.5). It seems that the never-married women litigating at Common Pleas were wealthier, or at least had considerably more credit-generating assets at their disposal, than did

[49] See, for example, Muldrew, *The Economy of Obligation*.

Table 2.5. Not-married female litigants acting alone, London-related pleaded cases of debt, detinue, and account, Court of Common Pleas, 1399–1500. *Source: Court of Common Pleas: The National Archives CP40 1399–1500*, ed. by Mackman and Stevens. Years sampled, 1399–1409, 1420–1429, 1445–1450, 1460–1468, 1480 and 1500, all dates inclusive.

	No. of cases	Never-married women		Widows	
		No. of cases, never-married women	Appeared by attorney (per cent of 'No. of cases, never-married women)	No. of cases, widows	Appeared by attorney (per cent of 'No. of cases, widows)
Plaintiff alone	153	100	76 (76%)	53	45 (85%)
Defendant alone	155	29	20 (69%)	126	87 (69%)

widows. This assessment is reinforced by Kate Staples's recent and extensive survey of inheriting daughters in medieval Londoners' wills. Here, she concluded that men more often bequeathed assets to women (daughters and widows) than to (lay)men, that daughters received more moveable wealth (such as cash) than sons, were seen as suitable heirs with business skills, and that their control of these assets (such as rental property) gave them genuine scope to manage and increase their net worth.[50] Cases before Common Pleas, in which newlyweds sought ante-nuptial debts owed to brides, suggest that never-married women tended to extend as credit larger sums of money than they borrowed.[51] Amy Froide has already established the significance of such 'women of independent means' in early modern England.[52] Likewise, recent case studies of women elsewhere in medieval Europe, such as Shennan Hutton's study of late medieval Ghent, have begun to call into question the emphasis historians tend to place on widows as moneylenders. Hutton found that 'single women investing their own property not only made far more loans than widows did, but their loans were also just as large'.[53] Widows, by comparison, might have

[50] Staples, *Daughters of London*, esp. pp. 71–109.

[51] Stevens, 'London's Married Women', p. 130.

[52] Froide, *Never Married*, pp. 117–53.

[53] Hutton, *Women and Economic Activities*, p. 90.

had additional financial commitments associated with their life stage, such as the rearing of children, conspicuous consumption to maintain their social standing, and the servicing of a former a husband's debts.

Having established the probable affluence of never-married women, the question remains: why did widows acting alone as creditor-plaintiffs appoint attorneys considerably more often than never-married women, despite presumably having less ready money and being less able to afford them? Likewise, one might question why an equal proportion of never-married and widowed female debtor-defendants acting alone appointed an attorney, despite widows, who comprised the lion's share of debtors, presumably being poorer and less able to afford the expense.[54] Again, the answer may lie in a 'confidence gap', as surely women at the life-stage of widow generally would have accrued more life-experience and legal competence. The explanation may be as simple as youthful (over)confidence versus mature consideration, as per William Shakespeare's refrain of a century later '...age is full of care [...]Youth is hot and bold, age is weak and cold; Youth is wild, age is tame'.[55] Widows may well have felt it best not to leave matters to chance, and so appointed an attorney if at all possible.

No comparable examination of never-married or widowed women's use of attorneys in credit- and debt-related litigation has been undertaken, but three studies of earlier medieval widows pursuing pleas of dower are somewhat instructive regarding widows' intense use of attorneys. Sue Sheridan Walker, in two articles, surveyed thirteenth- and early fourteenth-century widows' suits of dower before Common Pleas and elsewhere for what she termed 'litigant agency' and litigation as a 'personal quest'.[56] In these she affirmed that widows seeking dower were familiar with the legal processes involved in litigation, but nevertheless increased substantially the frequency with which they employed attorneys towards the mid fourteenth century, as the professionalism and complexity of legal proceedings increased.[57] Barbara Hanawalt has more recently undertaken a systematic survey of women's use of attorneys in actions of dower before the London courts, 1301–1405, and found that about 52 per cent of widows employed an attorney to represent them,

[54] Attorneys' fees were highly variable, ranging from a few shillings to several pounds, depending on the attorney's skill, and period and scope of employment. See Ramsay, 'Retained Legal Counsel'.

[55] Shakespeare, 'The Passionate Pilgrim', p. 1249.

[56] Walker, 'Litigation as Personal Quest'; Walker, '"Litigant Agency"'.

[57] Walker, '"Litigant Agency"', pp. 6–9.

while only about 32 per cent of the defendants they sued did so.[58] In fact, widows' use of attorneys rose across the period, and in Hanawalt's final sample, 1400–1405, some 75 per cent of widows employed attorneys, whereas just 19 per cent of the defendants they sued did so, with remarried widows calling upon attorneys more frequently than single widows.[59]

This extreme difference, highlighted by Hanawalt's research, between the high proportion of London widows who appointed attorneys and the low proportion of the predominantly male defendants they sued who did so, again suggests a 'confidence gap', here between male litigants and widows. This reasoning would posit that the use of attorneys by male debtor-defendants, in just 55 per cent of their credit- and debt-related litigation at Common Pleas (Table 2.3) — as opposed to 69 per cent of not-married female debtor-defendants acting alone (Table 2.5) — exhibits a great deal of (over)confidence in their legal skills. Moreover, at least some cases with all-male litigants were invariably complex cases involving executors or administrators of the type discussed above, making more remarkable still the low proportion of such cases in which male debtor-defendants appointed an attorney. But it may be that a combination of the two explanations already put forward may apply specifically to male debtor-defendants, that poorer male litigants less frequently employed attorneys, as did more confident litigants. While it strains what the source material can tell us, it is possible to envisage a gendered response to the challenges of litigation. On the one hand, widows, who comprised most lone female debtor-defendants, although comparatively poor, committed to appointing an attorney if they could at all afford to do so. On the other hand, male litigants, where poor debtor-defendants, were those who most willingly trusted in their own capacity to represent themselves in court. Such a gendered 'confidence gap' would make sense in light of our current understanding of the human psychology of risk taking, in which men are generally more likely to take risks, particularly with reference to what might be perceived as 'gambling'.[60]

Attorneys and Clients

Attorneys were an important tool in litigation, but how they were located and retained by male or female clients in the fifteenth century is as yet little explored.

[58] Hanawalt, *The Wealth of Wives*, pp. 98–99, 251 n. 16.

[59] Hanawalt, *The Wealth of Wives*, pp. 98–99, 251 n. 16.

[60] Harris, Jenkins, and Glaser, 'Gender Differences in Risk Assessment'.

Unfortunately the value of an appointed attorney to attaining a satisfactory outcome to litigation is hidden by the 95 per cent or more of lawsuits which were discontinued before reaching a judgement, presumably often settled out of court. As indicated above, the fifteenth century was a period in which the long-term retention of legal counsel by great families and institutions was largely replaced by the casual employment of lawyers, which were available to ordinary litigants in rapidly increasing numbers.[61] Two questions are particularly germane to the research presented here. First, did women have equal access to professional attorneys trained in the law? Second, did some attorneys specialize in serving, or discriminate against, female litigants?

First, regarding access to trained attorneys, there is no evidence to suggest that women had any less access to attorneys than did other litigants. It is evident from both the attorneys rolls and plea rolls that lawyers typically had close city, county, or regional affiliations. For example, the attorneys roll of Hilary term 1460 contains numerous clusters of appointments, such as seven appointments of attorney Richard Reynold, all to cases laid in Leicestershire, or six appointments of Henry Wheteley, all to cases laid in York or Yorkshire.[62] Where women's appointments of attorneys appear on the attorney's rolls they employed the same attorneys otherwise associated with cases laid in the same county as their own case, indicating that they did not have to go to extraordinary lengths, due to their gender, to locate legal counsel. For example, in 1420 Robert Tettebury was appointed in five London and Hertfordshire cases, in one of which he represented Alice Sphere as a co-litigant in a plea of debt.[63] The county lawyer, with a mixed client base and an interest in country affairs at large, was a well-known if sometimes maligned character in fifteenth-century England.[64] Walker has suggested that familial and community connections may well have encouraged widows, in particular, to make us of such county men in preference to 'top professionals'.[65]

The question of whether attorneys may have especially aided or discriminated against female litigants is considerably more difficult to answer. The most high-profile attorneys to appear before the Court of Common Pleas — those most often

[61] See Ramsay, 'Retained Legal Counsel'.

[62] TNA, CP 40/796, attorneys roll, rot. 1 & 1d.

[63] TNA, CP 40/636, attorneys roll, rot. 1d.

[64] This is as amply illustrated by the infamous murder of Devonshire lawyer Nicholas Radford by Sir Thomas Courtenay, son of the Earl of Devon, in 1455. Storey, *The End of the House of Lancaster*, pp. 167–70.

[65] Walker, '"Litigant Agency"', p. 14.

appointed — were London lawyers. The most frequently cited attorney from the sample of pleaded London-related cases examined here was Tomas Torald, who was recorded as attorney for either the plaintiff(s) or defendant(s) in a remarkable 468 of the 6321 cases sampled, with a long career spanning the 1440s–60s.[66] He represented a female client acting either alone or as a co-litigant in 41, or 9 per cent, of his cases; almost 90 per cent (36 of 41) of the cases Torald handled for his female clients were credit- and debt-related. The frequency with which he represented women is markedly lower than the roughly 17 per cent of cases before Common Pleas which involved female litigants, who were at least as likely as men to be represented by an attorney. The work of Torald is typical of that of other high-profile lawyers such as Robery Vaus (8 per cent of appearances representing women; 20 of 245), Thomas Adams (13 per cent; 25 of 188 appearances), or Robert Tettebury (12 per cent; 17 of 142 appearances) in showing a bias against female clients, but one which dissipates the less prominent the attorney. The modest gender bias in the client base of attorneys such as Thomas Adams, for example, may well be attributable to female litigants preferring county lawyers with whom they had a connection over such high-profile Westminster professionals, as Walker has suggested.[67] While it is plausible that a handful of the most high-profile Westminster lawyers may have turned away some female litigants, it could also be the case that some women, especially widows, might have been less able to afford their premium services.[68] And there is little evidence of such discrimination among the rank-and-file county attorneys of the realm.

Conclusions

Women were extensively involved in credit- and debt-related litigation in fifteenth-century England. Such litigation represented 70 to 80 per cent of all lawsuits for both married co-litigants and for not-married women or widows, whether litigating jointly or alone. All of these women made use of attorneys, with consistent frequency, across the fifteenth century. As a whole, a higher proportion of female litigants made use of attorneys than did men, particularly when acting as defendants. For married women, this was probably due to the complex nature of the

[66] *Court of Common Pleas: The National Archives CP40*, ed. by Mackman and Stevens. Years sampled, 1399–1409, 1420–1429, 1445–1450, 1460–1468, 1480 and 1500, all dates inclusive.

[67] *Court of Common Pleas: The National Archives CP40*, ed. by Mackman and Stevens.

[68] On attorneys' fees see Ramsay, 'Retained Legal Counsel'.

lawsuits they were involved in, by which married couples brought or answered claims regarding monies owed to or buy the women from before their current marriage. For not-married women, and especially the widows who most regularly acted alone as defendants, their greater reliance on attorneys than was shown by male litigants may well have sprung from a lack of confidence. This could have been either a lack of confidence in their legal abilities or in the rectitude of the court's legal machinery when interacting with female litigants. The tendency of the highest profile lawyers at Common Pleas to have a smaller share of female clients than would have been proportional to women's litigation through attorneys hints at some gender bias, possibly arising from misogyny or economic factors. But there is nothing to suggest that women were unable to appoint attorneys when they wished to do so. Indeed widows, a potentially vulnerable group within society, did so when acting alone as plaintiffs with greater frequency than anyone but married couples.

As discussed at the beginning of this article, female litigants appeared in English courts with decreasing frequency from the fourteenth to the fifteenth century, as society moved to conform more closely in practice to the theoretical limitations which common law and coverture placed on women.[69] However, for those women who had a case to bring, within those limitations, legal representation was consistently and readily available at the king's courts throughout the fifteenth century. While top lawyers may have been slightly less ready to welcome their business than that of male clients, appointments of attorney by widows amply demonstrate that where women felt they needed an attorney they had no difficulty in employing one. Ultimately, in a social environment that women likely would have found increasingly restrictive or repressive across the fifteenth century –we need think here, for example, of the rise of local fines for scolds and common gossips at this time — the availability of legal representation would have been key in providing women with the confidence to extend or to take credit.[70] Knowing that they would be able to access and to interact with the courts effectively via an attorney if they did not feel confident to do so on their own, as plaintiffs or defendants, would have assisted women to stand firm against the rising tide of misogyny, and to remain fully integrated in late medieval English credit networks. Moreover, the positive implications for women of being able to readily employ an attorney, as and when needed, extend not only to the credit- and debt-related litigation considered here, but to all forms of legal action.

[69] See Stevens, 'London Women'.

[70] Jones and Zell, 'Bad Conversation?'; David Underdown, 'The Taming of the Scold'; Well, 'Politics and Gender'.

Works Cited

Manuscripts and Archival Sources

The National Archives, CP 40/555–954 (plea rolls)
The National Archives, CP 40/636, 796, and 951 (attorneys rolls)

Primary Sources

Court of Common Pleas: The National Archives, CP40 1399–1500, ed. by Jonathan Mackman and Matthew Frank Stevens (London: British History Online, 2010), <http://www.british-history.ac.uk/no-series/common-pleas/1399-1500> [accessed 20 March 2017]

Shakespeare, William, 'The Passionate Pilgrim' in *The Complete Works of Shakespeare* (Ware: Wadsworth, 1996)

Secondary Studies

Baker, John Hamilton, *An Introduction to English Legal History*, 4th edn (London: Butterworths, 2002)

Beattie, Cordelia, *Medieval Single Women: The Politics of Social Classification in Late Medieval England* (Oxford: Oxford University Press, 2007)

Beattie, Cordelia, and Matthew Frank Stevens, 'Introduction: Uncovering Married Women', in *Married Women and the Law in Premodern Northwest Europe*, ed. by Cordelia Beattie and Matthew Frank Stevens (Woodbridge: Boydell, 2013), pp. 1–10

Beckerman, John S., 'Review: *The Assize of Novel Disseisin*. By Donald W. Southerland', *The Yale Law Journal*, 83 (1974), 634–36

Brand, Paul, 'Aspects of the Law of Debt, 1189–1307', *Credit and Debt in Medieval England, c. 1180–c. 1350*, in Phillipp R. Schofield and Nicholas J. Mayhew (Oxford: Oxbow, 2002), pp. 19–41

——, *The Origins of the English Legal Profession* (Oxford: Oxford University Press, 1992)

Briggs, Chris, 'Manor Court Procedures, Debt Litigation Levels, and Rural Credit Provision in England, c. 1290–c. 1380', *Law and History Review*, 24 (2006), 519–58

Cheney, Christopher Robert, ed., *A Handbook of Dates for Students of British History*, rev. by Michael Jones (Cambridge: Cambridge University Press, 2000)

Froide, Amy M., *Never Married: Singlewomen in Early Modern England* (Oxford: Oxford University Press, 2005)

Hanawalt, Barbara Ann, 'Remarriage as an Option for Urban and Rural Widows in Late Medieval England', in *Wife and Widow in Medieval England*, ed. by Sue Sheridan Walker (Ann Arbor: University of Michigan Press, 1993), pp. 141–64

———, *The Wealth of Wives: Women, Law, and Economy in Late Medieval London* (Oxford: Oxford University Press, 2007)

Harris, Christine R., Michael Jenkins, and Dale Glaser, 'Gender Differences in Risk Assessment: Why Do Women Take Fewer Risks than Men?', *Judgement and Decision Making*, 1 (2006), 48–63

Haskett, Timothy Shaw, 'The Medieval English Court of Chancery', *Law and History Review*, 14 (1996), 245–313

Hastings, Margaret, *The Court of Common Pleas in the 15th Century: A Study of Legal Administration and Procedure* (Ithaca: Cornell University Press, 1947)

Hawkes, Emma, '"[S]he Will Protect and Defend her Rights Boldly by Law and Reason…": Women's Knowledge of Common Law and Equity Courts in Late-Medieval England', in *Medieval Women and the Law*, ed. by Noël James Menuge (Woodbridge: Boydell, 2000), pp. 145–62

Hutton, Shennan, *Women and Economic Activities in Late Medieval Ghent* (Basingstoke: Palgrave Macmillan, 2011)

Ives, Eric William, *The Common Lawyers of Pre-Reformation England: Thomas Kebell, a Case Study* (Cambridge: Cambridge University Press, 1983)

Jones, Karen, and Michael Zell, 'Bad Conversation? Gender and Social Control in a Kentish Borough, c. 1450–c. 1570', *Continuity and Change*, 13 (1998), 11–31

Loengard, Janet Senderowitz, 'Rationabilis dos: Magna Carta and the Widow's "Fair Share" in the Earlier Thirteenth Century', in *Wife and Widow in Medieval England*, ed. by Sue Sheridan Walker (Ann Arbor: University of Michigan Press, 1993), pp. 59–80

Makowski, Elizabeth M., *English Nuns and the Law in the Middle Ages: Cloistered Nuns and their Lawyers, 1293–1540* (Woodbridge: Boydell, 2011)

McIntosh, Marjorie Keniston, *Working Women in English Society, 1300–1620* (Cambridge: Cambridge University Press, 2005)

Muldrew, Craig, *The Economy of Obligation: The Culture of Credit and Social Relations in Early Modern England* (Basingstoke: Macmillan, 1998)

Murray, Jacqueline, 'Kinship and Friendship: The Perception of Family by Clergy and Laity in Late Medieval London', *Albion*, 20 (1988), 365–85

Palmer, Robert, *The County Courts of Medieval England, 1150–1350* (Princeton: Princeton University Press, 1982)

Phillips, Kim Marie, *Medieval Maidens: Young Women and Gender in England, 1270–1540* (Manchester: Manchester University Press, 2003)

Ramsay, Nigel, 'Retained Legal Counsel, *c.* 1275–*c.* 1475', *Transactions of the Royal Historical Society*, 35 (1985), 95–112

Staples, Kate Kelsey, *Daughters of London: Inheriting Opportunity in the Late Middle Ages* (Leiden: Brill, 2011)

Stevens, Matthew Frank, 'London Creditors and the Fifteenth-Century Depression', *The Economic History Review*, 69 (2016), 1083–1107

———, 'London Women, the Courts and the "Golden Age": A Quantitative Analysis of Female Litigants in the Fourteenth and Fifteenth Centuries', *The London Journal*, 37 (2010), 67–88

———, 'Londoners and the Court of Common Pleas in the Fifteenth Century', in *London and Beyond: Essays in Honour of Derek Keene*, ed. by Matthew Davies and James A. Galloway (London: [publisher], 2012), pp. 225–45

———, 'London's Married Women, Debt Litigation and Coverture in the Court of Common Pleas', in *Married Women and the Law in Premodern Northwest Europe*, ed. by Cordelia Beattie and Matthew Frank Stevens (Woodbridge: Boydell, 2013), pp. 115–31

———, 'Review: Elizabeth Makowski, *English Nuns and the Law in the Middle Ages: Cloistered Nuns and their Lawyers, 1293–1540*', *Speculum*, 89 (2014), 799–801

Storey, Robin Lindsay, *The End of the House of Lancaster* (London: Barrie and Rockliffe, 1966)

Sutherland, Donald W., *The Assize of Novel Disseisin* (Oxford: The Clarendon Press, 1973)

Underdown, David, 'The Taming of the Scold: The Enforcement of Patriarchal Authority in Early Modern England', in *Order and Disorder in Early Modern England*, ed. by Anthony Fletcher and John Stevenson (Cambridge: Cambridge University Press, 1985), pp. 116–36

Walker, Sue Sheridan, 'Introduction', in *Wife and Widow in Medieval England*, ed. by Sue Sheridan Walker (Ann Arbor: University of Michigan Press, 1993), pp. 1–16

———, '"Litigant Agency" in Dower Pleas in The Royal Common Law Courts in Thirteenth- and Early Fourteenth-Century England', *The Journal of Legal History*, 24 (2003), 1–22

———, 'Litigation as Personal Quest: Suing for Dower in the Royal Courts: 1272–1350', *Wife and Widow in Medieval England*, ed. by Sue Sheridan Walker (Ann Arbor: University of Michigan Press, 1993), pp. 81–108

Well, Rachel Judith, 'Politics and Gender in Crisis in David Underdown's "The Taming of the Scold"', *History Compass*, 11 (2013), 381–88

Creditworthy Women and Town Courts in Late Medieval England

Teresa Phipps

Introduction: Credit, Courts, and Urban Society

The urban courts of late medieval England served as early forms of small claims courts, hearing the commercial complaints of town residents and attempting to resolve their disputes at low cost and with minimal disruption to everyday life. These courts grew as their respective towns developed, reflecting the key commercial and marketing functions of urban communities, where day-to-day trade rested on transactions based on credit. This article uses court records to examine the role of women in credit transactions in fourteenth-century England, drawing specifically on records from Nottingham, Chester, and Winchester to illustrate various important aspects of women's roles in credit networks. The court rolls indicate the extent and nature of women's involvement in these networks — what they bought and sold, from/to whom, at what value, and how these deals played out in the urban economy and in court. This in turn has implications for how we understand the gendered nature of credit, both financial and social. Finally, we must consider how these everyday commercial issues intersected with the construction and understanding of women's legal status within their local courts. By allowing access to the workings of credit relationships at the most ordinary level, the court rolls reveal the intertwining of commercial credit, the marital partnership, personal and

Teresa Phipps is a research assistant in the Department of History at Swansea University on the AHRC-funded project 'Women Negotiating the Boundaries of Justice: Britain and Ireland *c.* 1100-*c.* 1750'. She completed her PhD at the University of Nottingham in 2015 where she studied women's involvement in local justice in late medieval English towns.

Women and Credit in Pre-Industrial Europe, ed. by Elise M. Dermineur, EER 12 (Turnhout: Brepols, 2018), pp. 73–94.
BREPOLS PUBLISHERS DOI 10.1484/M.EER-EB.5.115749

household reputation, and the ways in which litigation was used to enforce and lay claim to these multifaceted forms of credit.

The evidence here arises from the fourteenth-century records of three English towns: Nottingham, Chester, and Winchester. These were towns of middling size and status, each the centre of local trade with influence over their hinterlands as well as being centres of local administration and law. Each town had a population of between 3000–6000 before the Black Death of 1348, and all three ranked outside the top twenty wealthiest towns in England.[1] The towns' local courts met regularly to hear the complaints of residents arising from trade, the breakdown of interpersonal relationships, and disputes over property. Winchester was the ancient capital of England, and though its status had declined by the later medieval period as crown administration moved to Westminster, the legacy of its royal ties remained strong, the town itself being held directly from the king.[2] Its court was named the 'court of the city of Winchester', recorded at the top of the rolls documenting the business of local justice. Chester also had a unique administrative role as the centre of the county palatine held by the Earl of Chester. It was home to the palatine's exchequer, law courts, and officials, leading it to be termed a 'mini-Westminster'.[3] However, the city itself had significant independence from the county, with local government and justice overseen by the mayor and sheriffs.[4] Civil litigation that did not involve disputes over land was mainly heard in the Pentice Court, from which the evidence for this article is drawn.[5] Finally, Nottingham was perhaps the most 'ordinary' of the three towns, a county town and home to a royal castle, but without any special or unique status. It can instead be understood as a more typical provincial borough, where local residents brought their complaints about one another to the borough court, run by the two bailiffs and termed the 'court of the town of Nottingham'.

The courts had jurisdiction over the more minor disputes of local residents, and though they had much in common, each followed its own customs and practices in administering and recording local justice. The common law clearly exerted consid-

[1] On urban populations, rankings, and the urban hierarchy see Dyer, 'Ranking Lists', pp. 747–70. On Nottingham's population see Foulds, 'The Medieval Town', p. 56; for Chester see Laughton, *Life in a Late Medieval City*, pp. 11–12; for Winchester see Keene, *Survey of Medieval Winchester*, I, pp. 366–67.

[2] On medieval Winchester and its status see Keene, *Survey of Medieval Winchester*, I, p. 7.

[3] Laughton, *Life in a Late Medieval City*, p. 11.

[4] On the county palatine see Clayton, *The Administration of the County Palatine of Chester 1442–1485*, pp. 31, 59.

[5] So-called because it was held in the wooden extension — a pentice — that abutted St Peter's Church at the centre of the city.

erable influence over these customary courts, with legal practice and record-keeping formulae often reflecting the traditions of the central courts. By comparing women's legal actions arising from credit transactions across different towns and their courts, this study offers an overview of women's crediting activities across English towns, as well as identifying important ways in which this varied from place to place. Women's role in the premodern economy, as revealed by local court records, has been the focus of various studies over the past few decades. While earlier studies focussed on women's work and their economic role in towns, more recently historians have begun to address women's legal status in economic litigation, thereby revealing the link between commercial activity and legal action under various jurisdictions.[6] The aim here is to continue to develop this analysis, by examining and comparing women's roles in credit transactions and relating this both to their legal status and to the notions of creditworthiness that underpinned the social and commercial functions of urban life.

Tracing Credit and Debt in Town Courts

Credit and debt were ubiquitous features of the medieval economy.[7] Goods and services were exchanged with the agreement that payment would be made at a later date, and money was also loaned between individuals. Debts heard in local courts ranged from a few pence owed for ale, bread, or milk, to sums of several shillings owed for wholesale purchases of food or cloth, or unpaid wages sought by servants from their masters. The pleas therefore cover the whole spectrum of urban life and economic activity, including that which involved women.[8] Buying on credit did not represent a lack of capital or an act of financial risk-taking in the same way that it might do today. Individuals and households were involved in multiple credit networks whereby they owed money to, and were themselves owed by, their

[6] Kowaleski, 'Women's Work in a Market Town', pp. 145–64; Hanawalt, *The Wealth of Wives*; Stevens, 'London Women, the Courts and the "Golden Age"', pp. 67–88; Stevens, 'London's Married Women', pp. 115–32; Spence, *Women, Credit and Debt in Early Modern Scotland*; Spence, '"For His Interest"?', pp. 173–90.

[7] Nightingale, 'Money and Credit in the Economy of Late Medieval England', pp. 51–71; Kowaleski, *Local Markets and Regional Trade in Medieval Exeter*, p. 349.

[8] For this reason, court rolls have previously been used to study women's working lives in various towns. For example Kowaleski, 'Women's Work in a Market Town', pp. 145–64; Lacey, 'Women and Work in Fourteenth and Fifteenth Century London', pp. 24–82 and Hutton, 'Women in Fourteenth Century Shrewsbury', pp. 83–99.

neighbours, relatives, and business contacts.[9] Debt was not, therefore, a symptom of financial crisis or mismanagement (though of course in some instances it may have been), but rather a general indicator of commercial activity. Indeed, a larger number and range of debts could in fact represent broader commercial activity and even prosperity, as indebtedness reflected an individual's trading connections. Chris Briggs has argued that being in debt, particularly in times of prosperity, was evidence of full participation in commerce.[10] Even when non-payment of a debt led to court action, this did not necessarily mean that the relationship between creditor and debtor had completely broken down, and many people continued to trade with those whom they had previously sued for debt. Debts were frequently acknowledged in court, indicating that court action could serve as a normal, final stage in some credit transactions.

Pleas of debt and detinue therefore dominated the business of many town courts.[11] For example, the Nottingham court rolls for the year 1394–1395, which survive in particularly good condition, include at least 142 separate debt and detinue pleas heard over the course of the year, of a total of at least 201 suits brought that year.[12] Debt pleas also regularly referred to loans of money, usually described as an amount owed or borrowed, or sometimes 'for his purse'.[13] Pleas of detinue, meanwhile, concerned goods that had been withheld or not delivered on time. The vast majority of debts pursued in local courts were under 40s. in value, and were simply agreed orally at the point of exchange. There was no obligation to record credit under 40s. in writing, though some pleas referenced other tools such as tally sticks.[14]

[9] Howell, *Commerce Before Capitalism*, p. 25.

[10] Briggs, *Credit and Village Society*, p. 152.

[11] Harding argued that trade was the basic reason for the existence of town courts. Harding, *The Law Courts of Medieval England*, p. 43.

[12] Nottinghamshire Archives (hereafter NA) CA 1294. Only pleas with details concerning the subject of the dispute have been counted here, making this a minimum number for overall debt pleas in the year. These pleas represent those which were followed through in court following initial registration of the complaint in the list of new pleas that features at the end of each session's court roll, and thus can be considered as those pleas which were actually heard in court. The majority of the other suits were trespass pleas (forty-eight), with eleven suits concerning broken covenants, usually relating to commercial agreements or service.

[13] NA CA 1294 rot. 20. Plea brought by William Thrompton against Robert Hayward concerning 10d. loaned.

[14] Schofield, 'Introduction' in Schofield and Mayhew, eds, *Credit and Debt in Medieval England*, p. 5; Brand, 'Aspects of the Law of Debt, 1189–1307', pp. 23–24. From the early 1290s, a royal writ was required to litigate for debts over 40s., but these writs were not available outside

Litigation thus offered an alternative means of registering a debt in writing within the official records of the town. When debtors acknowledged their debts, this was also entered into the town's court rolls, serving as official documentation of the transaction, without the effort and expense of formally registering a debt. This makes court records an essential source for the study of urban credit networks, though they only report obligations that were not met.[15] A further innumerable amount of credit transactions were never recorded, probably accounting for a significant portion of the medieval credit market. The records of debt litigation in town courts are not therefore representative of the whole credit market, but illustrative of the extent and nature of the credit transactions and networks within the local community.

The court rolls are brief and formulaic, recording only the most important facts of each plea — the identities of the litigants, the nature of the plea, usually the value of the debt and sometimes what the payment was for. Nevertheless, they offer an invaluable insight into both the personal and commercial aspects of medieval urban trade and the agency of individuals within multiple local networks. For many of the individuals found in these records, those below the level of the urban oligarchy or mercantile elite and particularly women, this may be the only surviving evidence of their lives and interactions. Yet these records do not just reveal credit in the financial sense. Martha Howell has highlighted the personal nature of credit relationships, whereby trust and knowledge of a person's social credit was intrinsic to the functioning of these arrangements.[16] Common knowledge about the status of others was central to what Craig Muldrew has termed the 'culture of credit', the 'public means of social communication and circulating judgement about the value of other members of communities'.[17] The value of individuals may have pertained to their economic status — their actual financial capacity to repay the debt owed, for example — but this was also tied to their reputation as a person who could be trusted to fulfil their part of a deal. It was no good being wealthy but not trustworthy. Purchases made on credit can thus be understood as evidence of the buyer's (debtor's) creditworthiness, while selling goods on credit demonstrated

royal courts, meaning that in theory these local courts were limited to debts under 40s., although it is apparent that this rule was not always adhered to in town courts. Some pleas concerning debts over 40s. can be found across various courts. A tally stick was a piece of wood marked with notches to indicate payment made or owed, and then cut in half with one half kept by each party.

[15] Brand, 'Aspects of the Law of Debt, 1189–1307', p. 23.

[16] Howell, *Commerce Before Capitalism*, p. 25.

[17] Muldrew, *The Economy of Obligation*, p. 2.

connections and integration within the urban commercial community, which allowed creditors to make judgements about the creditworthiness of others, as well as their own ability to accept delayed payment or offer loans. Women's involvement in credit networks and transactions therefore indicates both their financial status and their level of integration within the local commercial community, facilitated by trust and public knowledge.

It is important at this stage to set out some of the issues involved in identifying women and their status in town court records. While we find numerous women in the records of litigation, usually identified by their personal name, it can be difficult to classify their identity further, particularly by marital status. We know that those women named alongside their husband as 'his wife' were married, but many other women were recorded by their full name only, and were rarely labelled widows or single women, or according to other descriptors of marital status.[18] While we might assume that these lone women were indeed not married, it is problematic to order women according to these marital categories without further evidence. Some women were occasionally termed widows, but this appears so infrequently in the fourteenth-century records that it is likely to reflect the somewhat incidental choice of scribes to record the status of particular women, or the significance of their widowed status in relation to a particular plea, rather than a more systematic means of classifying women by marital status. The implication of this for the study of women and credit is that, while married women can usually be identified, it is not possible to systematically assess or compare the actions of never married women and widows. The actions of women in debt litigation — as creditors and debtors — will be considered in turn to understand the nature of women's role in credit transactions from both perspectives.

Women as Creditors

The court rolls provide probably the only evidence of female crediting activity in this period at this lower, everyday scale, identifying women's use of their local court to pursue debts owed to them.[19] These women sold goods or services not for immediate payment, but instead trusting that the purchaser would pay at the agreed date. The proportion of pleas that featured female litigants varied from place to

[18] '*uxor eius*'. On the classification of single women, see Beattie, *Medieval Single Women*, pp. 124–43.

[19] For women's involvement in credit networks at a higher scale, see Goddard, this volume.

place and over time, as displayed in Table 3.1 below. They were most active in Nottingham, indicating a more prominent economic role, or greater propensity and ability to use the court to settle credit disputes compared to elsewhere. The table separates the proportion of women known to be married (by appearing in court with their husbands), and it is this presence or lack of married women that helps to account for some of the disparity in female debt litigants across the different towns. These patterns will be examined in more detail later. Overall the statistics indicate that women accounted for a minority of those who extended credit and then brought pleas to court, though these were not such low numbers that they should be ignored or dismissed as insignificant.

Table 3.1. Female creditors in Nottingham, Chester, and Winchester courts.[20]

NOTTINGHAM			CHESTER			WINCHESTER		
Year	**All female creditors (%)**	**Married female creditors (%)**	**Year**	**All female creditors (%)**	**Married female creditors (%)**	**Year**	**All female creditors (%)**	**Married female creditors (%)**
1323–1324	8	3	1317–1318	12	4	1299–1300	8	1
1375–1376	14	5	1378	3	0	1365–1366	11	0
1394–1395	13	7	1395	8	0	1385–1386	8	1

Beyond these statistics, we can understand more about the nature of women's crediting activity through the details recorded in relation to individual complaints. At Chester in 1317, Margery de Wolful complained that Thomas de Sondone detained one mark (13s. 4d.) from her. Thomas came to court and acknowledged the debt, so the court ordered that Margery be repaid and Thomas was fined an unspecified amount (probably a few pence).[21] In the same year, Alice, widow of John Hammes, complained that Matilda le Spenser owed her 3d. for milk that she had sold to her. Matilda acknowledged the debt and was ordered to repay the 3d.

[20] Source: NA CA 1258b, CA 1279, CA 1294; Cheshire Archives and Local Studies (hereafter CALS) ZSR 21, ZSR 81–85, ZSR 109–112; Hampshire Record Office (hereafter HRO) W/D1/3, W/D1/13, W/D1/37.

[21] CALS ZSR 21 rot. 8d.

plus 2d. damages to Alice.[22] Even a low value debt such as this was worth bringing to court in order to secure repayment. At Nottingham in April 1376, Magota Waturleder complained that Matthew de Skydby owed her a debt of 13d. for water. We can assume, from her surname and the nature of the debt, that Magota's work was in the provision of water in the town. In this case, an inquest jury was summoned to decide on the case. These juries did not deliberate on the arguments from both sides, but instead simply reported on the 'facts' of the case. They were comprised of local men who, through their local knowledge and connections, would be expected to know whether Matthew did indeed owe the debt to Magota. However, we have no details of how they came to their decision, simply the recording of either a guilty verdict or a statement that the plaintiff had brought a false complaint. In this instance, the jury reported that Matthew did not in fact owe the money so Magota was fined 3d. for bringing an unjust suit.[23] The Winchester rolls from 1365 record successful suits brought by Amya Uppam and Agnes Kembestre, who recovered debts of 4s. 6d. and 8s. 8d. from Philip Benstede and Andrew Frere respectively.[24] In 1386, Alice Broun complained that Robert Bonne, a butcher, owed her 22d. for service. While Robert did not initially respond to the complaint in court, he later acknowledged the debt, but at the lower sum of 12d.[25] Alice was working for Robert, perhaps in domestic service, and when he did not pay her as agreed she took him to court. In this instance, working in service for payment at a later date can itself be interpreted as an extension of credit.

Some women sought debts of more substantial sums. In 1385, Alice Mercer secured repayment of a debt of 30s. 7d. owed to her by Agatha Spycer (also called a merchant in other pleas).[26] These two women were clearly engaged in commerce of significant value, indicated by the large sum exchanged and corroborated by their surnames and descriptions as merchants. Alice had sufficient capital that she could afford to extend significant credit, and though the agreement eventually resulted in legal action, she must have trusted in Agatha's ability and fidelity to repay the debt when expected. The bonds of trust that underpinned credit agreements meant that debt litigation was not purely an economic action. Smail has highlighted the

[22] CALS ZSR 21 rot. 4. None of the court rolls record whether these damages were ever actually paid, we simply have to assume that they were.

[23] NA CA 1276 rot. 16.

[24] HRO W/D1/13/ rot. 3d, rot. 9.

[25] HRO W/D1/13 rot. 6.

[26] HRO W/D1/37 rot. 3d. Agatha Spycer was called *mercatori* in a complaint made by John Wyneslowe de London, merchant. HRO W/D1/37 rot. 8d.

nature of debt litigation as a moral and social sanction, arguing that litigants in late medieval Marseille used the courts to punish individuals with whom they had fallen out.[27] While this may have been true of some pleas, Smail's depiction of debt litigation as an expression of hatred is somewhat at odds with that of English town courts, where debt litigation was an ordinary feature of commercial relationships, attested to by the high volume of pleas and litigants and representing commerce at all levels and all sections of society. Whether arranging for deferred payment of a few pence or of 30s., women of all statuses and occupations were part of an economic system that relied on these transactions, based on community knowledge and a certain level of trust that the debtor or purchaser would deliver on their part of the arrangement. The existence of the borough court offered an option for enforcement if this trust was broken.

Married women were also involved in the extension of credit, though the extent to which they featured in the resulting litigation varied across different towns. The reconstruction of women's crediting is therefore mediated by the ability of women of different statuses to access justice in their respective local courts. Under English Common Law, the principle of coverture set out that married women had no independent legal identity. Instead, they were 'covered' under the guardianship of their husband, meaning that wives were not, in theory, able to take legal action concerning issues of goods, money and property.[28] This culture of coverture underpinned all of women's legal action, though the complete legal invisibility of women has been shown to have been something of a legal fiction.[29] Court records allow us to access the 'lived reality' of real women's legal status, revealing some considerable scope for married women to represent themselves and their interests via their local courts.[30] However, it is noteworthy that married women's roles in commercial litigation differed from one town to another, demonstrating considerable variation in the way in which local courts understood the legal role of married women in agreeing and enforcing credit transactions. In Nottingham, married couples used the court to enforce credit arrangements made either by wives or by couples jointly, with the records of these pleas suggesting that wives played a significant role in the

[27] Smail, *The Consumption of Justice*, p. 139.

[28] On coverture and the status of wives see *Henry de Bracton*, ed. by Thorne (known as 'Bracton'), vol. 2, p. 31, vol. 4, p. 335. On the interpretation of coverture under Common Law see Butler, 'Discourse on the Nature of Coverture', pp. 24–44. For other jurisdictions, see chapters by Beattie, Stevens, and Spence in Beattie and Stevens, eds, *Married Women and the Law*.

[29] Stretton, 'Coverture and Unity of Persons in Blackstone's Commentaries', pp. 112, 115.

[30] Butler, 'Medieval Singlewomen in Law and Practice', p. 60.

course of litigation. However, the records from Winchester and Chester rarely feature these joint suits, suggesting that custom here devised this legal and commercial role to husbands. At Chester, six couples brought debt pleas to the Pentice Court in 1317–1318, but none have been recovered for the later stages of the century. At Winchester in 1299, only one couple featured in litigation as creditors, none in 1365–1366, and again only one in 1385–1386. This varying access to justice therefore determines what we can recover about the role of married women in credit networks and the urban economy more broadly, whether or not it had a real impact on their everyday ability to extend and access credit.

Where couples did litigate together, these actions reveal the crediting actions of spouses and provide an insight into the nature of the marital partnership. This may have arisen through wives acting as representatives or agents of their husbands, or may in fact have represented a more widespread ability of wives to enter into transactions based on everyday household and business purchases.[31] However, when debts were not repaid, wives could not bring their complaints to court alone. Though we might dismiss this joint litigation as evidence of the restrictions of coverture, and of husbands' effective accountability for their wives' commercial actions, we can in fact use these pleas as a means to examine wives' crediting activities and the range of credit transactions that they were parties to. At Nottingham in June 1395, Robert Glade and his wife Joan complained that Robert Cowper owed them 20d. for a tun (a large barrel usually used to hold wine). While Cowper initially denied the debt, he later acknowledged it and deposited the money in court, plus damages of 3d.[32] In December 1363, William of Skegby and his wife Petronella complained that William Daniell owed them 10s., which William had lent to him 'by Petronella', and should have been repaid at Michaelmas that year. Though William Daniell denied the claim, the jury said that he did owe the money and he was also ordered to pay 6d. damages and a 3d. fine to the court.[33] It was in fact Petronella who initiated the claim two months earlier, shortly after William Daniell had first defaulted on the repayment.[34] In this first entry, she was simply called Petronella of Skegby, with no mention of her marital status, though subsequent entries feature William

[31] On wives acting making purchases as their husbands' agents see Beattie, 'Married Women, Contracts and Coverture'. Under common law, it seems that husbands were required to give consent for their wives' purchases made under coverture. McIntosh has noted that wives could be named as their husbands' representatives in credit transactions. McIntosh, 'Women, Credit, and Family Relationships in England, 1300–1620', pp. 151–52.

[32] NA CA 1294 rot. 20, 22.

[33] NA CA 1273 rot. 4; '*per Petronella*'.

[34] NA CA 1273 rot. 1.

and Petronella together. It may have been that Petronella attempted to bring the suit on her own, but due to coverture, she was required to continue her plea jointly with her husband. These joint pleas were relatively common in Nottingham, and in some years married women litigating with their husbands accounted for over 50 per cent of all female debt litigants.[35] While the liability of husbands for debts contracted by their wives has been acknowledged elsewhere, this more proactive role which saw couples acting jointly as plaintiffs in debt complaints extends the scope for married women's legal action in relation to their crediting activities.[36]

On some occasions, men brought complaints that specifically cited the key role of their wives in credit transactions. At Nottingham's court in 1336, William le Spicer complained that William Casteleyn owed him a debt of 2s. He claimed that Alice, his wife, had lent the money to William Casteleyn and he had not repaid the debt when it was due three months later.[37] The jury ordered that William Casteleyn should recover the 2s. plus 8d. in damages. Clearly Alice had the agency and ability to agree the loan of 2s. to William Casteleyn, though she was not directly involved in the plea. We know that spouses could bring these complaints together, but on this occasion they chose not to do so, demonstrating flexibility in the intersections of wives' commercial and legal actions, which may have been down to decisions made by husband and wife over who should plead in a particular suit. This example, and others like it, indicates that some married women could exercise agency within credit networks, despite their theoretically 'covered' status.

The involvement of Nottingham wives in debt pleas was not typical, however. At Chester in 1317, William le Blund and his wife Margery successfully sued Henry de Doncaster and his wife Elena for 3s. 8d. owed for half a bushel of malt wheat, plus damages of 2s. Henry and Elena were ordered to repay the debt and damages, as well as fine of 6d. to the court.[38] A handful of other couples acted in similar pleas. But over time, as Table 3.1 shows, Chester couples disappeared from the court records in these commercial pleas, suggesting a shift in the way that married women were able to access justice when it came to resolving commercial disputes based upon credit. While there is no additional evidence to suggest that married women withdrew from the local economy, it is likely that their husbands simply

[35] In 1323–1324, only four couples were involved in debt litigation in Nottingham; this rose to twenty-three in 1375–1376 (43 per cent) and twenty-four in 1394–1395 (56 per cent). NA CA 1258b, CA 1279, CA 1294.

[36] Beattie, 'Married Women, Contracts and Coverture', p. 146.

[37] NA CA 1262 rot. 6d, 9d.

[38] CALS ZSR 21 rot. 1.

complained alone when disputes arose. Similarly, the Winchester data features no wives as creditors in joint debt pleas, and only two in detinue pleas across the whole sample. These contrasts thus reveal the specific way in which local courts interpreted married women's legal status as creditors in these commercial disputes.

Women as Debtors

It may be tempting to view complaints of debt as examples of failed commercial agreements, and thus female debtors as miscreants who evaded the rules of trade. Yet evidence of women's debts reveals more about their creditworthiness and trust in their ability to fulfil credit arrangements. When compared to Table 3.1, Table 3.2 reveals that women were slightly more likely to feature in court as debtors than as creditors, though not to the extent that we should characterize women's involvement in credit networks as only being that of those who owed money to others. Furthermore, women's indebtedness represents their integration into local commercial networks and the trust of their creditors, so these figures in fact indicate women's propensity to engage in trade networks. At Chester and Winchester, there was a notable fall in the proportion of female debtors. As noted earlier, married women came to be excluded from debt litigation as plaintiffs (creditors), and this was replicated by their absence as defendants (debtors) too.

Table 3.2. Female debtors in Nottingham, Chester, and Winchester courts.

NOTTINGHAM			CHESTER			WINCHESTER		
Year	**All female debtors (%)**	**Married female debtors (%)**	**Year**	**All female debtors (%)**	**Married female debtors (%)**	**Year**	**All female debtors (%)**	**Married female debtors (%)**
1323–1324	12	3	1317–1318	14	5	1299–1300	13	5
1375–1376	15	5	1378	10	1	1365–1366	16	1
1394–1395	13	7	1395	5	1	1385–1386	12	2

Some women owed significant sums to their creditors. We know that at least some of these were widows, appearing to have significant commercial independence and responsibility, probably through their continuing of their husbands' businesses. Four of the thirteen female debtors in Chester's Pentice Court in

1317–1318 were described as widows, though this does not necessarily mean that others were not. In 1317, Lucy Waterfal, widow, acknowledged a debt of £6 14s. 8d. owed to John de Thornham.[39] In the same year Alice, the widow of John Jamube, faced William le Rous in a suit concerning 54s. that she had failed to pay him. The debt had been recorded using a tally stick, which William brought to court to prove his claim, leading Alice to acknowledge the debt. She probably had little choice once the tally was produced.[40] It was relatively rare for women to be specifically recorded as widows, so the fact that it was noted in these instances further suggests a link to the commercial activities of their late husbands. These may have been debts accrued by the men, though there is no explicit reference to this in the records. Alternatively, the debts may have been accrued by the women themselves through their continuing of their husbands' businesses after their death. Either way, these women were significant figures within Chester's local credit network. Chris Briggs has suggested that debtors were 'sued not because they were in dire economic straits [...] but because it made sense to them to wait until the last possible moment before meeting their obligations'.[41] The fact that the two widows cited here acknowledged their debts once the pleas had been brought to the court, rather than contesting them, certainly suggests that this may well have been the case.

Elsewhere, other lone 'single' women were also the subject of numerous debt pleas. At Nottingham in November 1395, Matilda Rotur claimed that she had loaned 31d. to Joan, the widow of Richard Samon, which should have been paid at Michaelmas 1394, but nothing had been paid over a year later. Joan acknowledged the debt and repaid it along with 5d. in damages.[42] Later in the year the two women were back in court: this time Joan sought a debt of 4s. from Matilda, though the jury reported that she only owed 3s.[43] Perhaps Joan was pushing her luck trying to recover more than she was owed, or the oral nature of the credit agreement meant that she misremembered the actual sum agreed, or perhaps the jury got it wrong. These two women may have been in regular business with one another, with other

[39] CALS ZSR 27 rot. 5. It is not clear why such a large sum was able to be recovered through the Pentice court, as debts over 40s. typically fell outside the jurisdiction of town courts. It may have been that Chester's status as the centre of the palatinate allowed the court to hear larger debts. Brand, 'Aspects of the Law of Debt, 1189–1307', p. 23.

[40] CALS ZSR 31 rot. 3. The existence of the tally may have been why the parties were able to use their local court to settle this higher value debt.

[41] Briggs, *Credit and Village Society*, p. 152.

[42] NA CA 1295 rot. 4.

[43] NA CA 1295 rot. 7d.

arrangements being fulfilled satisfactorily and on time. We should not assume that the business of the individuals found in the court was characterized only by missed payments and broken agreements.

Some married women were named as debtors alongside their husbands, though again the extent of this varied between towns, as Table 3.2 shows. Some Chester couples featured as defendants during the earlier fourteenth century, indicating the significant role of wives in credit agreements, despite their marital status, which in theory should have limited their agency and ability to transact debts and agree contracts. At Chester in March 1318, John Cook complained about money he was owed for mutton by William de Forneby and his wife Christina. John Cook had sold the mutton to Christina, a merchant, on the understanding that she would pay him for it at the agreed date. Christina acknowledged the debt in court.[44] In a similar suit, William and Alice de Ellehale, also called merchants, were brought to court by William le Rous, who alleged that they owed him 42s. that he had lent to Alice.[45] William le Rous died before the dispute could be resolved, but the case serves to demonstrate the significant credit extended to Alice, indicative of her social and financial status and initial trust that she would pay back the debt. In both instances the court rolls provide evidence of wives in credit agreements of significant value, acting independently of their husbands until the agreement resulted in legal action, responding to allegations concerning the debts owed, though they could not be sued independently because of their marital status. It is rare to find such detail concerning who transacted a debt in these records, so it may be that extra attention was paid in these instances precisely because of the issues of coverture that arose from these pleas, warranting the specific arrangements of the debts to be set out so clearly.[46] After the early fourteenth century, married women all but disappear from the Chester court rolls. In the 1395 records, only one married couple featured in a debt plea when Robert de Germyn, a chaplain, sued John Shodeskin and Elena his wife for a debt of 40s.[47] This marks an apparent change to their legal status in these pleas in line with a stricter interpretation of coverture, whereby men would have represented their wives' commercial transactions and been held accountable for their debts.

[44] CALS ZSR 21 rot. 8. She was called '*mercatrici*'.

[45] CALS ZSR 21 rot. 9. They were called '*mercatores*' and individually '*mercator*' and '*mercatrici*'.

[46] Cathryn Spence has noted how it is possible to ascertain which half of the marital partnership was responsible for contracting a debt in early modern Scottish burgh court records. Spence, 'For his Interest', p. 182.

[47] CALS ZSR 108 rot. 1.

At Winchester, married women featured only in a handful of pleas concerning the detention of goods. Richard le Canevaser complained in November 1299 that Robert and Alice Strut detained (withheld) a hood, and it is evident that the presence of both Robert and Alice was required as Alice was essoined (the practice of entering an excuse for not attending court) separately, indicating that the two spouses were individually required to come to court or to follow the correct procedure if not able to attend.[48] Other couples featured in similar complaints of detinue later in the period. Here there was a distinction between complaints seeking repayment of money and those concerning withheld goods, with wives seemingly playing no legal role in the former due to coverture.

In contrast, numerous couples featured as debtors in Nottingham's court across the period. The rolls sometimes recorded individual responsibility for the transaction in which the debt was accrued, though at other times they simply listed the names of spouses as joint debtors. In March 1365, Roger Base complained that William de Preston and his wife Agnes owed him 2s. for bread that Agnes had bought from him, plus 10d. damages. The couple denied the debt, though the overall outcome of the plea is unknown.[49] Here we see Agnes's (alleged) central role in the transaction, agreeing credit on this purchase of an everyday necessity, which may have permitted her independent action under the so-called 'law of necessaries', though this still theoretically required consent of the husband.[50] Other pleas suggest joint accountability for debt. In June 1372, John Averay complained that John and Margery Coke owed him 26d.; a few years later the same couple were accused of owing 12d. to William Etwell, as well as other complaints concerning unspecified amounts, suggesting the couple's repeated trade as marital partners.[51] In 1375, Matthew Skegby sued Alice and John Sutton, claiming that they owed him 10s. for garlic and onions, the substantial sum indicating wholesale trade.[52] In the same year, Richard Dandeson complained that Richard Candler and his wife Agnes owed him 32d. for candles, which they refused to pay. Though the couple initially denied the claim, they later came to an agreement and Richard and Agnes paid a fine to the court, suggesting they acknowledged the debt.[53] These examples not only suggest the joint role of various couples in agreeing, disputing and

[48] HRO W/D1/3 rot. 3.

[49] NA CA 1274 rot. 7.

[50] Beattie, 'Married Women, Contracts and Coverture', pp. 134–36, 154.

[51] NA CA 1280a.

[52] NA CA 1279 rot. 12.

[53] NA CA 1279 rot. 11.

eventually fulfilling credit agreements, but also depict the nature of their commercial activities.

In some instances, husbands were held individually accountable for debts accrued by their wives. We know that this was customary in some towns, such as Ipswich, where husbands were to answer for the debts of their wives accrued before marriage.[54] Matthew Stevens has also argued that wives' involvement in debt litigation arose from their debts accrued while single, which their husbands became responsible for upon marriage.[55] This may have explained some of wives' litigation in Nottingham, though the records are not explicit in referencing pre-marital debts, and the evidence of couples jointly pursuing debts certainly demonstrates that this was not the only explanation for wives' debt litigation. In October 1366, Margaret le Forster complained that Richard Candeler owed her 2s. 6d. for a portable lead vat (probably used in brewing). She claimed that Agnes, Richard's wife, had bought the pot from Margaret, and the payment had been outstanding since April that year.[56] This was an exchange between the two women, but while it was Agnes who had bought the vat on credit, it was her husband whom Margaret decided to sue in court. However, the fact that the same couple were later sued together, demonstrates once again a degree of flexibility in the way the marital partnership was represented at law, in this case probably being determined by the creditor in their choice of who to name in their complaint, rather than necessarily being indicative of a pre-marital debt. The same men who came to court together with their wives also litigated alone in other cases, drawing a distinction between different debts and demonstrating that those which drew wives into court alongside their husbands arose from transactions in which the women had played an active role.

For married women, ties of family and household were central to both the practical and social construction of credit within urban society. In towns like Nottingham, where joint litigation was common, creditors would have known that if they agreed a sale with a married women and this led to litigation, the couple could be called upon to represent their credit arrangements together. Muldrew has highlighted the importance of household credit, whereby the honesty and fidelity of all household members contributed to the reputation of that household.[57] This would have been part of the assessment involved in making the initial credit agreement. As central figures to the management of the household, it should not be surpris-

[54] Usages and Customs of Ipswich, cap. 56, in Richardson, ed., *The Annalls of Ipswche*, p. 35.

[55] Stevens, 'London's Married Women', pp. 118–19, 129.

[56] NA CA 1276a rot. 2.

[57] Muldrew, *The Economy of Obligation*, p. 158.

ing that wives were involved in these agreements and named in litigation alongside their husbands. The fact that this was common practice in some towns refutes the assertion that, while wives may have acted as their husbands' agents, when legal action occurred only he would be named as the debtor.[58] They were both expected to come to court, and separate essoins were sometimes recorded when one or both spouses did not appear.

The presence of wives in debt litigation, as both creditors and debtors, extends our understanding of the economic and legal agency of married women beyond the custom of *femme sole* that existed in some English towns, granting married women 'sole' status and legal responsibility for their separate business endeavours.[59] There is no evidence of the *femme sole* custom existing in Nottingham, though the role of wives in debt pleas as discussed here demonstrates an alternative means by which wives' ties of credit and debt were managed through the local court. As Tim Stretton has argued, wives acted independently in many aspects of day-to-day life, earning money, buying and selling goods, and accepting gifts.[60] However, when it came to engaging in legal disputes arising from these activities, different courts interpreted the limits of coverture and the capabilities of wives in litigation in unique ways.

Many women (and men) appeared in court as both creditors and debtors, reminding us again that litigation could simply be a function of local credit ties, rather than a crisis-point in trading relations. One such woman was Joan Brailsford from Nottingham. In 1394–1395, she brought a suit against Richard Brasse in order to recover 3s. 11d. loaned to him, as well as 7 ½d. for ale.[61] Here we see credit not just in the form of deferred payment, but also as a cash loan, demonstrating that she had enough capital to lend cash to others. Perhaps Richard Brasse was someone with whom she traded regularly, allowing for a relationship of trust to build up leading to the loaning of money. Joan also used the court in an attempt to recover a large debt of £4 from John and Richard, sons of William de Etwall; she claimed the money was owed for bronze pots that they had bought from her. This time Joan was fined by the court for bringing an unjust suit.[62] She was also the subject

[58] McIntosh, *Working Women in English Society, 1300–1620*, p. 95.

[59] On *femme sole* women see McIntosh, 'The Benefits and Drawbacks'.

[60] Stretton, 'The Legal Identity of Married Women', p. 313.

[61] NA CA 1294 rot. 21, rot. 23.

[62] NA CA 1294 rot. 8, rot. 9, rot. 10. These pots may have been used for brewing. Again, this was a higher value debt than was theoretically permitted in the borough court.

of the complaints of others, including 4s. owed to John Russell for spices.[63] Joan was therefore an active member of the town's commercial community and regular user of the court to pursue and settle various debts. Her frequent legal action was apparently not detrimental to her commercial activities, as her numerous appearances demonstrate a wide range of business contacts who may not have chosen to trade with her if she had a poor reputation. Other women and men also appeared frequently over the course of several years in a range of debt pleas, further demonstrating that this litigation was part of the regular course of doing business in the urban community, rather than indicative of failed business deals.

A final, albeit brief, observation concerns the value of women's crediting activities. The potential to measure this is limited by both the condition of the court rolls and the brevity of the details recorded therein, though the Nottingham records offer some scope for this analysis. The average value of known credit transactions in the year 1394–1395 was approximately 68d., or 5s. 6d. The average for women's credit transactions was approximately 53d., or 4s. 5d.[64] Women were therefore involved in transactions of, on average, lower value than the whole urban population, though this was not substantially lower. Married women, through the household economy, were tied to credit transactions of higher value than their single neighbours. The average value of their credit transactions was approximately 6s., largely in line with the whole town's average, and higher than the average transaction of 3s. 9d. in which lone women (single women/widows) featured, though the sample size is small. The more notable difference in women's crediting activities is in the overall proportion of women who litigated for debt across the various courts, where they never accounted for more than 17 per cent of all debt litigants at court, as the Tables displayed earlier in this article reveal.

Conclusion: Creditworthy Women, Custom, and Coverture

The court records demonstrate the integration of numerous women within local credit networks, either through independent trade, as agents or representatives of their husbands, or as their partners. They contain a wealth of detail on the crediting activities of urban women of various statuses and in a range of commercial activities, of which only a handful have been discussed here. Statistical analysis suggests

[63] NA CA 1294 rot. 4.

[64] NA CA 1294. This calculation is based on the total of 142 pleas where the value of the debt was recorded, but discounts one exceptionally high debt of £4 claimed by Joan Brailsford for bronze pots.

that women played a marginal role in local credit networks, and accounted for a minority of litigants. But this was not to the extent that we should consider women to have been exceptional litigants or to not have been creditworthy at all. Qualitative analysis of individual agreements and disputes demonstrates that women were not simply household managers or marginal, petty traders; their legal action spanned a wide range of transactions, from everyday provisioning to wholesaling and higher value mercantile trade. Rather than representing fractured or contentious trading agreements, women's roles in debt litigation are demonstrative of their general integration into local credit networks, arising from their wide-ranging economic activities.

Credit was not simply a financial issue, and these records also offer an insight into the intersecting social and fiscal construction and assessment of credit and its legal ramifications. As traders, customers and providers of various services, women had the capacity to extend credit and were also worthy of the credit of others, as a result of judgements and knowledge about their own status, based upon trust and local community knowledge. These towns were relatively small in terms of population and physical size, making the common knowledge of individual and household status and fidelity a central determinant to economic activity and prosperity.

The court records represent women's crediting activities at the lowest level, accessed through the filters of legal custom and the limits imposed upon women under coverture. The comparison of different towns and local jurisdictions has revealed important differences in the legal action that women could take in relation to credit arrangements in their local courts, despite their similarities and common jurisdiction. While some towns, such as Nottingham, allowed women of all marital statuses considerable scope to represent their credit transactions under local law, others, such as Winchester and Chester, allowed little room for married women to manage their credit relationships via their local court. Coverture was locally constructed and understood, meaning that the real extent to which we can access the crediting activities of all women — including those who were married — is thus determined by the legal customs of different towns.

Works Cited

Manuscript and Archival Sources

Nottinghamshire Archives

CA 1258b
CA 1262
CA 1273
CA 1274
CA 1276
CA 1276a
CA 1279
CA 1280a
CA 1294
CA 1295

Hampshire Record Office

W/D1/3
W/D1/13
W/D1/37

Cheshire Archives and Local Studies

ZSR 21
ZSR 27
ZSR 31
ZSR 81–85
ZSR 109–12

Primary Sources

Henry de Bracton: De legibus et consuetudinibus Angliae, ed. by Samuel E. Thorne (Cambridge, MA: Harvard University Press, 1968–1977), 4 vols

Richardson, William H., ed., *The Annalls of Ipswche: the lawes customes and governmt of the same, collected out of ye records books and writings of that towne by Nathll Bacon serving as recorder and town clark in that towne. Anno. Dom. 1654* (Ipswich: S. H. Cowell, 1884)

Secondary Studies

Beattie, Cordelia, 'Married Women, Contracts and Coverture in Late Medieval England', in *Married Women and the Law in Premodern Northwest Europe*, ed. by Cordelia Beattie and Matthew Frank Stevens (Woodbridge: Boydell and Brewer, 2013), pp. 133–54

——, *Medieval Single Women: The Politics of Social Classification in Late Medieval England* (Oxford: Oxford University Press, 2007)

Beattie, Cordelia, and Matthew Frank Stevens, eds, *Married Women and the Law in Premodern Northwest Europe* (Woodbridge: Boydell and Brewer, 2013)

Brand, Paul, 'Aspects of the Law of Debt, 1189–1307', in *Credit and Debt in Medieval England c. 1180–c. 1350*, ed. by Phillipp Schofield and Nicholas Mayhew (Oxford: Oxbow, 2002), pp. 19–41

Briggs, Chris, *Credit and Village Society in Fourteenth-Century England* (Oxford: Oxford University Press, 2008)

Butler, Sara M., 'Discourse on the Nature of Coverture in the Later Medieval Courtroom', in *Married Women and the Law: Coverture in England and the Common Law World*, ed. by Tim Stretton and Krista Kesselring (Montreal: McGill-Queen's University Press, 2013), pp. 24–44

——, *Divorce in Medieval England: From One to Two Persons in Law* (Abingdon: Routledge, 2013)

——, 'Medieval Singlewomen in Law and Practice', in *The Place of the Social Margins, 1350–1750*, ed. by Andrew Spicer and Jane L. Stevens Crawshaw (Abingdon: Routledge, 2016), pp. 59–78

Clayton, Dorothy J., *The Administration of the County Palatine of Chester 1442–1485*, Chetham Society 3:35 (Manchester: Manchester University Press, 1990)

Dyer, Alan, 'Ranking Lists of English Medieval Towns', in *The Cambridge Urban History of Britain, vol. 1 600–1540*, ed. by David M. Palliser (Cambridge: Cambridge University Press, 2000), pp. 747–70

Foulds, Trevor, 'The Medieval Town', in *A Centenary History of Nottingham*, ed. by John Beckett (Manchester: Phillimore & Co., 1997), pp. 56–71

Hanawalt, Barbara, *The Wealth of Wives: Women, Law, and Economy in Late Medieval London* (Oxford: Oxford University Press, 2007)

Harding, Alan, *The Law Courts of Medieval England* (London: Allen and Unwin, 1973)

Howell, Martha, *Commerce Before Capitalism in Europe, 1300–1600* (Cambridge: Cambridge University Press, 2010)

Hutton, Diane, 'Women in Fourteenth Century Shrewsbury', in *Women and Work in Pre-Industrial England* , ed. by Lindsey Charles and Lorna Duffin (London: Croom Helm, 1985), pp. 83–99

Keene, Derek, *Survey of Medieval Winchester* (Oxford: Clarendon Press, 1985), 2 vols

Kowaleski, Maryanne, *Local Markets and Regional Trade in Medieval Exeter* (Cambridge: Cambridge University Press, 1995)

——, 'Women's Work in a Market Town: Exeter in the Late Fourteenth Century', in *Women and Work in Preindustrial Europe*, ed. by Barbara Hanawalt (Bloomington: Indiana University Press, 1986), pp. 145–64

Lacey, Kay E., 'Women and Work in Fourteenth- and Fifteenth-Century London', in *Women and Work in Pre-Industrial England*, ed. by Lyndsey Charles and Lorna Duffin (London: Croom Helm, 1985), pp. 24–82

Laughton, Jane, *Life in a Late Medieval City: Chester 1275–1520* (Oxford: Windgather Press, 2008)

McIntosh, Marjorie Keniston, 'The Benefits and Drawbacks of Femme Sole Status in England, 1300–1630', *Journal of British Studies*, 44 (2005), 410–38

———, 'Women, Credit, and Family Relationships in England, 1300–1620', *Journal of Family History*, 30 (2005), 143–63

———, *Working Women in English Society, 1300–1620* (Cambridge: Cambridge University Press, 2005)

Muldrew, Craig, *The Economy of Obligation: The Culture of Credit and Social Relations in Early Modern England* (Basingstoke: Palgrave, 1998)

Nightingale, Pamela, 'Money and Credit in the Economy of Late Medieval England', in *Medieval Money Matters*, ed. by Diana Wood (Oxford: Oxbow, 2004), pp. 51–71

Schofield, Phillipp, and Nicholas Mayhew, eds, *Credit and Debt in Medieval England c. 1180–c. 1350* (Oxford: Oxbow, 2002)

Smail, Daniel Lord, *The Consumption of Justice: Emotions, Publicity and Legal Culture in Marseille, 1264–1423* (Ithaca: Cornell University Press, 2003)

Spence, Cathryn, '"For his Interest"? Women, Debt and Coverture in Early Modern Scotland', in *Married Women and the Law in Premodern Northwest Europe*, ed. by Cordelia Beattie and Matthew Frank Stevens (Woodbridge: Boydell and Brewer, 2013), pp. 173–90

———, *Women, Credit and Debt in Early Modern Scotland* (Manchester: Manchester University Press, 2016)

Stevens, Matthew Frank, 'London's Married Women, Debt Litigation and Coverture in the Court of Common Pleas' in *Married Women and the Law in Premodern Northwest Europe*, ed. by Cordelia Beattie and Matthew Frank Stevens (Woodbridge: Boydell and Brewer, 2013), pp. 115–32

———, 'London Women, the Courts and the "Golden Age": A Quantitative Analysis of Female Litigants in the Fourteenth and Fifteenth Centuries', *The London Journal*, 37 (2012), 67–88

Stretton, Tim, 'Coverture and Unity of Persons in Blackstone's Commentaries', in *Blackstone and his Commentaries: Biography, Law, History*, ed. by Wilfred Prest (Oxford: Hart, 2009), pp. 111–27

———, 'The Legal Identity of Married Women in England and Europe 1500–1700', in *Europa und seine Regionen: 2000 Jahre Rechstgeschichte,* ed. by Andreas Bauer and Karl H. L. Welker (Köln: Böhlau Verlag, 2007), pp. 309–21

The Ages of Women and Men: Life Cycles, Family, and Investment in the Fifteenth-Century Low Countries

Jaco Zuijderduijn*

Introduction

In the later Middle Ages, the human life cycle was often visualized as 'the ages of man': representations of the various stages individuals would go through during their lifetimes.[1] These included such stages as youth, young adulthood, maturity and, at the very end, old age. Artists did not fail to point out how these stages would each present opportunities and challenges, and they painted a particularly bleak picture of old age. Late medieval representation of the elderly is not unlike how present-day economic literature regards old age, identifying it as one of the life-cycle 'squeezes': periods during which a household's resources are at risk. Labour productivity decreases during old age, creating a so-called 'retirement squeeze'. This difficult period in the life cycle is preceded by others, such as the 'early adulthood squeeze' brought on by marrying, setting up a household, having children, and caring for them.[2]

* I am grateful for comments received at 'Women and Credit in Pre-industrial Europe. An International Symposium', and to Meta Henneke for her valuable feedback on this article.

[1] Burrow, *The Ages of Man*.

[2] Another difficult period is the 'middle adulthood squeeze', which is caused by adolescent children who require expensive education. However, since most late medieval families did not spend much on their children's education, this period probably did not present them with any serious problems (Di Matteo, 'Wealth Accumulation', p. 300).

Jaco Zuijderduijn (cornelis.zuijderduijn@ekh.lu.se) is senior lecturer, Department of Economic History, School of Economics and Management, Lund University.

Women and Credit in Pre-Industrial Europe, ed. by Elise M. Dermineur, EER 12 (Turnhout: Brepols, 2018), pp. 95–120.
BREPOLS PUBLISHERS DOI 10.1484/M.EER-EB.5.115750

Recent literature has suggested that people in the later Middle Ages used financial instruments to deal with the 'early adulthood squeeze' and 'retirement squeeze'.[3] Financial markets, it is argued, allowed newly-weds to borrow to set up a household, and they also provided individuals with opportunities to invest their savings and to disinvest when they were faced with large expenses, either at marriage or during old age. But even though broad participation in financial markets has been established for the later Middle Ages,[4] we are still not very well informed about how individuals used financial instruments in the course of their lives. Did they actively make use of financial markets, by saving in times of plenty, and using up savings in more difficult times, such as during the aforementioned 'squeezes'? Or did individuals' investment behaviour not follow a clear pattern? Our lack of knowledge of the age at purchase of financial instruments is without doubt a major problem standing in the way of a better understanding of market participation throughout the life cycle: we know the names, residences, and sometimes even occupation or social status of thousands of investors in various financial instruments, but generally not their age. As a result, we are still largely in the dark about the actual link between the life cycle and financial markets.

We know equally little about how men and women made use of financial markets throughout the life cycle. Male and female life cycles differed in certain respects, with men marrying slightly later and being more likely to remarry when widowed, and women marrying younger, less likely to remarry, and therefore being more likely to end up widowed. Male and female property ownership also differed: in the Low Countries women received a dowry when they married and one way to put this capital to use may have been to invest in financial markets. The receipt of a dowry provided women with an investment opportunity,[5] whereas the likelihood of ending up as a widow presented them with a considerable risk. Did this encourage women to make use of the opportunities financial markets offered for making investments? The fact that medieval women were prominent investors, for instance in annuities issued by towns in the Low Countries, seems to suggest so: in

[3] De Moor, 'Girl Power'; Bouman, 'From Hardship to Benefit'; Pfister, 'The Proto-Industrial Household'. A study of the more recent past is Lilja and Backlund, 'To Navigate'.

[4] Zuijderduijn and De Moor, 'Spending'; Zuijderduijn and De Moor, 'Preferences'.

[5] In marriage the husband decided over the community property: the property the spouses brought to the marriage, such as the dowry, and the property accumulated during the marriage (Schmidt, *Overleven*, 59). To protect the lineage, wealthy townsmen could in theory negotiate a marriage contract prescribing that the dowry would not end up in the male line (Brand, *Over macht*, 321); in practice most couples appear to have been able to manage their assets without too many restriction though (Howell, *The Marriage Exchange*, 199).

some instances they were the recipients of more than half of the annuities issued by town governments, such as in the north-eastern town of Zutphen.[6] If this is indeed a pattern, was this related to characteristics of the female life cycle,[7] such as women being recipients of dowries at marriage and being more likely than men to end up in widowhood? Or was it due to women being more passive and conservative than men, and aiming mostly to secure their own well-being and that of their children, as has also been suggested?[8] In this respect widows in particular are believed to have favoured specific financial instruments such as life annuities, which yielded relatively high returns and provided them with a secure income during the remainder of their lives.

In this article we use a new dataset to explore late medieval investment behaviour, focusing on the gender and age of annuitants of life annuities. We will pay particular attention to two types of annuities: those contracted on one life, and those contracted on two lives. These financial instruments still exist today and are known as 'single life annuities' and 'joint and survivor annuities'. Today's retirees can choose either one — just as their medieval predecessors could. The pros and cons of investing in 'joint' life annuities have been summarized as follows:

> By protecting women who outlive their husbands from the loss of pension income, joint and survivor annuities can improve economic outcomes for elderly widows. But joint and survivor annuities also reduce retirement income and consumption levels when both spouses are alive.[9]

Investing in a joint and survivor annuity to secure a certain income is relatively expensive; a single life annuity is less expensive, but does not offer security to the surviving spouse. The same differences apply to late medieval life annuities.

In the later Middle Ages, life annuities were usually contracted between one or two annuitants on the one hand, and an institution on the other.[10] Towns in particular often issued life annuities in an attempt to attract money; as a result

[6] Van Schaïk, 'The Sale of Annuities', p. 113. Elsewhere their participation was less spectacular, but still substantial, see the figures mentioned in Hanus, *Tussen stad en eigen gewin*, p. 70.

[7] Hanus, *Tussen stad en eigen gewin*, p. 72.

[8] Jordan, *Women and Credit*; McIntosh, *Working Women*. For contemporary economies, see Hinz, McCarthy, and Turner, 'Are Women Conservative Investors?'.

[9] Johnson, Uccello, and Goldwyn, 'Single Life vs. Joint and Survivor Pension Payout Options'.

[10] For valuable comparisons see Froide, *Silent Partners*.

they had to pay annuities until the annuitants passed away. One of these cities was Haarlem, to the west of Amsterdam. In the late fifteenth century Haarlem sold single life annuities, which could be obtained by paying a principal; in return Haarlem was under obligation to pay out an annuity until the annuitant passed away. The yield was usually 12.5 per cent per annum, which was quite high compared to other investment opportunities.[11] Haarlem also offered joint and survivor annuities, the yield of which was usually 10 per cent; in return Haarlem had to make payments until the surviving annuitant passed away. After the passing away of the annuitant the heirs usually were entitled to one more payment; after that payments stopped. Haarlem did not repay the principal. Prospective investors thus had to decide on which type of annuity to invest in, and also who the annuitant would be; it was not necessary for the investor to be the annuitant, as annuities could also be bought for third parties. Parents often decided to put annuities on their children, aunts and uncles made nieces and nephews recipients of life annuities.

A dataset of 431 life annuities issued by the city of Haarlem in 1482–1491 is used to explore how these financial instruments were connected to male and female life cycles and family life. The data concern investors from Haarlem, but also from numerous other cities in the northern Low Countries; most came from the ranks of the elite and the middling groups of urban society. Our data are quite unusual in giving ages at purchase of annuitants, and therefore allow us to investigate how investment was linked to the life cycle. The data also provide insight in the (family) relationships of 'joint and survivor' annuitants. Combining these data allows a profile to be established of the life-cycle position of annuitants, as well as the family relationships underlying joint and survivor annuities.

Sample

In this paper we use the data of 431 life annuities issued by the town of Haarlem in 1482–1491. The data were compiled by Geertruida de Moor, based on the accounts of the treasurers of Haarlem (*tresoriersrekeningen*) who were responsible for annuity payments.[12] Fortunately they also recorded the age at purchase of the annuitants — something that was hardly ever done in the later Middle Ages. Why the treasurers of Haarlem decided to record age at purchase is unknown, but the reason is easy to guess: many late medieval cities created a substantial public debt, including life annuities that had to be paid out until annuitants passed away. Recording the age

[11] Zuijderduijn, 'Spending'.

[12] De Moor, 'De tussen 1482/1483 en 1490/1491 bij de stad Haarlem afgesloten lijfrenten'.

at purchase may have allowed the treasurers to make projections of when urban public debt would decline due to the deaths of annuitants. Also, it may have helped them to prevent fraud, for instance when the heirs of an already deceased annuitant continued to claim payments.[13] However, in spite of these potential advantages, few other city governments appear to have recorded the ages of annuitants.

Towns in the Low Countries created substantial public debts by issuing annuities.[14] Haarlem raised 72,121 guilders by selling life annuities between 1482 and 1491[15] and on top of this, the city also raised 55,479 guilders by selling redeemable annuities;[16] in these years, Haarlem's net revenues were less than 20,000 guilders per annum on average.[17] The city depended largely on financial markets to be able to pay taxes and other financial contributions to the ruler Maximilian of Habsburg (Regent 1482–1493; Regent 1506–1515), who was almost constantly pressed for cash that he needed in order to pay for his military ventures.[18] Most of the money Haarlem raised by selling annuities went to the ruler; only a small proportion was spent on public works.[19]

Of the life annuity sales, Haarlem raised 49,983 guilders (69 per cent) by selling life annuities to inhabitants of the northern Low Countries, and the remaining 22,138 guilders (31 per cent) by sales to inhabitants of Flanders and Brabant. Our sample concerns the life annuities sold in the northern Low Countries,[20] totalling 431; of these eighty-five were sold to inhabitants of Haarlem, 315 to those of other

[13] Zuijderduijn, 'Foreign Investment', gives an example of the city of Leiden acquiring an *attestatie de vita* before paying an annuity to an elderly annuitant.

[14] Zuijderduijn, *Medieval Capital Markets*, Chapter 3 and the literature cited there.

[15] Van Loenen reports life annuities worth 72,121 guilders sold in 1482–1483 and 1490–1491; De Moor reports life annuities worth 49,983 guilders. The discrepancy is probably due to De Moor not reporting annuities sold in Brabant and Flanders (Van Loenen, 'De rente-last', p. 131; De Moor, 'De tussen 1482/1483 en 1490/1491 bij de stad Haarlem afgesloten lijfrenten').

[16] Redeemable annuities were bought for a lump sum, and yielded the investor an annual return (the annuity). Redeemable annuities were paid out until the principal was returned to the investor, the investor's heirs, or anyone else that managed to acquire the annuity, for instance by buying it. As long as these financial instruments were not redeemed, annuities could easily continue to exist for more than a century.

[17] Van Loenen, 'De rente-last', p. 131.

[18] Zuijderduijn, 'De schuldvraag', pp. 29–30.

[19] Zuijderduijn, 'Het lichaam', p. 118.

[20] For unknown reasons, De Moor only included annuity buyers from Holland, Zeeland and Utrecht, and excluded those from Flanders and Brabant. The latter are therefore not included in the dataset.

cities in the county of Holland, and another thirty-one to people living outside of Holland, in the provinces of Utrecht and Zeeland. Of the funds thus raised, 18.2 per cent came from Haarlem, 76.0 per cent from cities elsewhere in Holland, and 5.8 per cent from cities outside of Holland. Through annuity sales, the city government of Haarlem thus managed to attract funding from inside Haarlem, but also outside.

Between 1482 and 1491, Haarlem issued 132 single life annuities and 299 joint and survivor annuities (see Table 4.1). Investors in single life annuities ran a considerable risk of the annuity being terminated before the investment was earned back (due to the untimely death of the sole annuitant). These annuities therefore yielded the greatest returns: average interest rates can be calculated at approximately 12.2 per cent per annum. On average, annuitants would have had to live for eight years to break even on their investment. For investors in joint and survivor annuities the risk of both annuitants dying before the investment was earned back was lower, which is reflected in the average interest rate of approximately 9.9 per cent per annum; for these financial instruments, the break-even point was reached when the surviving annuitant lived for ten years.[21]

Before we discuss the social profile of the annuitants, it is important to point out that the majority of life annuities were offered for sale in the market; Haarlem sent representatives to cities, where they were to contact local brokers and get in touch with potential annuity buyers.[22] Only occasionally did cities force the wealthiest of their own citizens to invest in annuities; Haarlem could only wrest such 'forced loans' from the inhabitants of Haarlem itself, however, and since the vast majority of the annuities in our sample were marketed outside of Haarlem, we may safely assume they were contracted by individuals who were not being pressured, but looking to invest in financial instruments befitting their needs.

Before we proceed to our analysis, it is important to get an idea of the social background of the investors. Life annuities cost about 100 guilders on average (Table 4.1), about one to two year's wages for a skilled worker. Life annuities therefore were an option for people who either had sufficient savings, or had received a sizable inheritance.[23] The precise social background of the vast majority of the

[21] Inflation rates at the time were modest at slightly over 1.0 per cent; whether annuitants took inflation into account when they purchased an annuity is unknown.

[22] See the discussion in: Zuijderduijn, 'Foreign Investment' and Feenstra and Muller, 'Wie wil wachten op het zoet?'.

[23] Evidence for saving by late medieval middling groups in Dordrecht and other cities in Holland is presented in Zuijderduijn and van Oosten, 'Breaking the Piggy Bank'. Evidence of people from middling and lowering groups holding financial instruments is presented in Zuijderduijn and De Moor, 'Preferences of the Poor'.

Table 4.1. Haarlem life annuities issued in the northern Low Countries, 1482–1491. *Source:* De Moor, 'De tussen 1482/1483 en 1490/1491 bij de stad Haarlem afgesloten lijfrenten'.

	One life	Two lives	All
All	132	299	431
Haarlem	14	71	85
Holland excl. Haarlem	101	214	315
Outside Holland	17	14	31
Yield: mean/ median (in guilders)	12.2/ 12.5	9.9/ 10	
Price: mean/ median (in guilders)	107.1/ 96	119.8/ 100	

728 annuitants in our sample is unknown. We know some came from the ranks of the elites,[24] such as one lord and 18 ladies (*joffers*), who are also likely to have been noble persons. Another forty-two annuitants could call themselves master (*meester*), which suggests they had studied at a university.[25] On the other hand we also encounter a few persons who were certainly from middling groups, such as a tailor,[26] a barber,[27] a painter,[28] and a cooper.[29] Another social group we can distinguish is the clergy: among the annuitants there were seventy-seven religious men and eighteen religious women (13 per cent of all annuitants). Among the males, we encounter three monks and seventy-four priests; among the women nine nuns and nine beguines.[30] Clergymen seem to have preferred single life annuities over joint and survivor annuities, which were proportionally much more popular among clergywomen (Table 4.2). In the literature, life annuities have been portrayed as

24 Recent literature on urban elites investing in public debt includes Baguet, 'Social Change'; De Vijlder and Limberger, 'Public or Private Interests?'; Stasavage, *States of Credit*.

25 E.g. Albrecht Dirksz. from Amsterdam and Pieter Bartholomeus van Wassenaar from Leiden, who had studied medicine, and Wouter Egbertsz. from Dordrecht, who had studied theology.

26 Roelof Roelofsz. from Dordrecht and Govert Jansz. and Martijn Jansz. from Dordrecht.

27 Thomas Jansz from Dordrecht.

28 Simon Jansz from Dordrecht.

29 Willem Gerritsz. from Dordrecht.

30 The monk and nuns lived in Mariënbron in the region Dordrecht, Koningsveld and St. Agnes in the region The Hague, St. Michielsklooster, St. Catharijneklooster, and Porta Coeli Heemstede in the Haarlem region, Leeuwenhorst and Rijnsburg in the Leiden region.

an ideal way to provide for family members entering into a religious community and therefore requiring a fixed annual income (something called *zuster-* or *kloosterprovene*).[31] Although ages at purchase for religious persons were relatively high — thirty-eight years for clergymen and thirty-seven for clergywomen — average ages at purchase for monks and nuns were lower and in line with the idea they received life annuities from relatives to help them provide for life as clergy.[32] Of the clergymen and clergywomen who contracted joint and survivor annuities, 44 per cent did so with relatives, while there are no indications of relatives being involved in 56 per cent of the cases. What seems a straightforward alternative — contracting a joint and survivor annuity with a fellow religious person — was only implemented in six contracts.[33] Religious persons' investment in annuities has also been explained by their lack of access to some other investment opportunities: in the Low Countries the clergy and secular clergy, such as canons regular and beguines, were usually barred from investing in land, and were therefore forced to turn to financial instruments.[34] Indeed, authorities often put restrictions on the alienation of landed property to the clergy, making it impossible for religious women and men to invest in real estate.[35]

Ages at Purchase

For the vast majority of the annuitants, it is difficult to say much about their social status: we have to make do with names and family relationships, age at purchase, and principal sums. Yet these data do provide the possibility of studying the relationship between the life cycle and family conditions on the one hand and

[31] Bakker, *Bedelorden*, pp. 131–32; De Moor, *Verborgen en geborgen*, p. 487; Schilder, *Amsterdamse kloosters*, p. 91; Dokkum and Dijkhof, *Oude Dordtse lijfrenten,* p. 57; Stoop, *Schrijven in commissie*, p. 66. De Moor points out that life annuities were sometimes purchased in anticipation of children entering into religious communities (De Moor, *Verborgen en geborgen,* p. 93).

[32] The mean age of three monks at purchase was thirty-one (with a range of 30–33) and that of nine nuns was 29.8 (with a range of 16–50); quite a few of the latter were in their early twenties, which was a common age for professing (Zuijderduijn, 'Living la Vita').

[33] Including the sisters Elizabeth and Baarte Vranckendr. (both beguines) and Elizabeth and Janneken Aarmsdr. (both beguines).

[34] Callewier, *De papen van Brugge*, pp. 250–51. Regarding financial instruments, the clergy also faced restrictions with respect to mortgages on land; annuities issued by cities such as Haarlem (which were not secured on land) may therefore have been their instrument of choice.

[35] Zuijderduijn, *Medieval Capital Markets*, pp. 59–62.

Table 4.2. Religious persons as annuitants. *Source:* De Moor, 'De tussen 1482/1483 en 1490/1491 bij de stad Haarlem afgesloten lijfrenten'.

	One life	**Two lives**
Religious persons		
Males	34	43
Females	3	15
All annuitants		
Males	79	253
Females	51	345

participation in financial markets on the other. Our sample provides data on the age at purchase of 730 annuitants (132 in single life annuities, 598 in joint and survivor annuities). The average age of the annuitants was 29.3 years; single life annuitants were slightly older at 31.1 years, and joint and survivor annuitants slightly younger at 28.9 (Table 4.3). Among single life annuitants males were older on average, while among joint and survivor annuitants females were older; even though the differences are not big, they may be connected to gendered investment patterns.

Gendered patterns also become clear when we look at the age distribution of single life annuitants and joint and survivor annuitants (Figures 4.1 and 4.2). Among the single life annuitants men outnumbered women (59 per cent to 41 per cent) and they were in the majority in every age category. Males aged 30–50 were particularly keen investors: 53.8 per cent of all male annuitants were in this age category. Among the joint and survivor annuitants the patterns is reversed: females outnumbered males (57 per cent to 43 per cent) and women were in the majority in every age category. Our sample thus suggests that two-life annuities were preferred by/for women, and one-life annuities by/for men. Even though it is difficult to explain this pattern, it may be useful to point out that Haarlem's single life annuities were apparently not often used to provide a bride with a dowry — which was the practice elsewhere in late medieval Europe, for example in Italy.[36] Here family members used single life annuities to provide newly-wed wives with a dowry; by doing so, the marriage gift contributed to the new household, and it was also protected against mismanagement or even misappropriation by the husband. Since the latter could not alienate the annuity, the financial instrument was sure to

[36] Kirshner and Pezzolo report on this practice in Italy (Kirshner, *Marriage, Dowry, and Citizenship*, p. 85; Pezzolo, 'Bonds and Government Debt', p. 150).

be there when the husband passed away and the wife became a widow. The absence of a peak in Figure 4.1 at women's average age at first marriage (which was around twenty-five)[37] suggests that even though families in the late medieval Low Countries had similar concerns with respect to securing marriage portions,[38] this did not often bring them to use a single life annuity as a dowry.

Table 4.3. Ages of annuitants. *Source:* De Moor, 'De tussen 1482/1483 en 1490/1491 bij de stad Haarlem afgesloten lijfrenten'.

	One life	**Two lives**	**All**
N	128	583	711
Mean age	31.1	28.9	29.3
Median age	32	29	30
Males			
N	77	251	328
Mean age	32.4	28.0	29.2
Median age	33.5	28	31
Females			
N	51	332	383
Mean age	29.1	29.7	29.6
Median age	29	30	30

Out of 730 individuals in the dataset, the gender could not be determined in 2 cases, and the age at purchase could not be determined in 17 cases. The table is therefore based on ages at purchase of 711 annuitants.

Children did not feature much as single life annuitants (6.1 per cent of all single life annuitants), but they were more prominent as joint and survivor annuitants (17.3 per cent of all joint and survivor annuitants). Boys were slightly in the majority among the single-life annuitants (53 per cent of the annuitants aged up to twenty), and girls among the joint-and-survivor annuitants (55 per cent of the annuitants aged up to twenty; Figures 4.1 and 4.2). The low number of single life annuities

[37] Late medieval ages at first marriage are difficult to obtain. Data coming from Leiden, to the south of Haarlem, suggest an average of c. 22 years reported by a small group of married individuals in 1540–1541. In Amsterdam in the 1580s and 1590s the average age at first marriage was c. 23.5–25 years (De Moor, 'Girl Power', pp. 16–17).

[38] Zuijderduijn, 'Grave Concerns'.

purchased on behalf of children provides further clues with respect to investment behaviour. From a strictly economic point of view, purchasing a single life annuity for a child could well have been most profitable. Once children had survived the first couple of years, their life expectancy was quite high, and taking out a single life annuity for them would have been relatively profitable — this high profitability was due to Haarlem not adjusting yields to take account of the age at purchase.[39] The high profitability of investing in various life annuities is demonstrated in the appendix: a single life annuity on a child was likely to bring a return that was at least 25 per cent more compared to alternative uses of life annuities, and to raise the return per annum by at least 2.5 percentage points. Figure 4.3 gives the expected return on single life annuities per age at purchase: an investor taking out a single life annuity for a child aged less than one could expect a return of 9.1 per cent. The line increases to a maximum of 9.3 per cent at an age at purchase of five, and then declines. Yields drop below 8 per cent at the age of thirty, and below 6 per cent at the age of forty-seven. After an age at purchase of sixty-seven, losses rather than

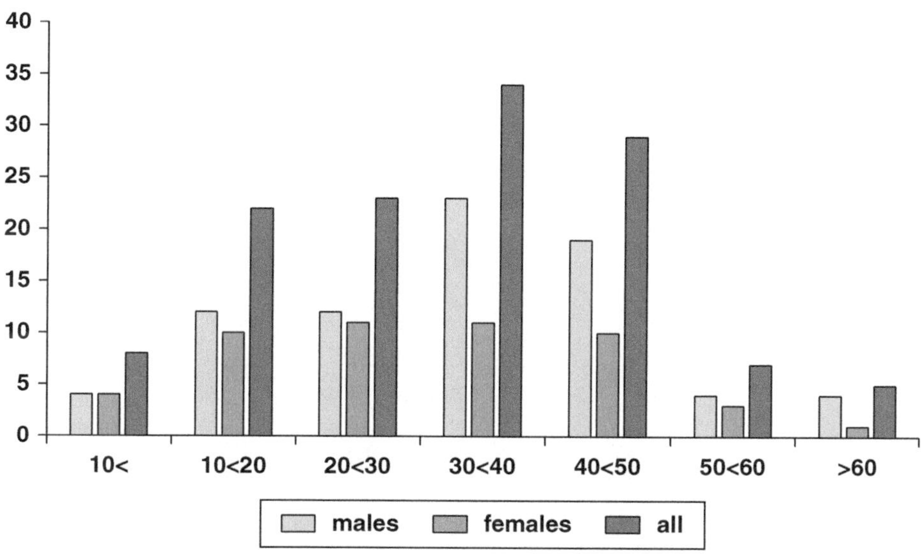

Figure 4.1. Single life annuities: age at purchase. *Source:* De Moor, 'De tussen 1482/1483 en 1490/1491 bij de stad Haarlem afgesloten lijfrenten'.

[39] A regression analysis of interest rate as a function of age showed a very low correlation of r^2 0.01: age only explains 1 per cent of variation in the interest rates on Haarlem's single life annuities.

profits were to be expected because the average annuitant did not live long enough to reach the break-even point; the yield at an age at purchase of sixty-eight was -0.2 per cent. Figure 4.3 also gives the number of annuitants per age category: the most profitable age categories — children and teenagers — were underrepresented.

Whereas children hardly ever appear as single life annuitants, no fewer than 117 children were joint and survivor annuitants. Based on this, should we conclude that many investors were driven by considerations other than maximizing profit? To answer this question we should begin by asking whether investors *did* not try to maximize their profits, or *could* not maximize their profits. To begin with the latter: Haarlem did allow the investing public to purchase annuities for children, selling a modest number of single life annuities to annuitants aged 0–9 (6 per cent of all single life annuities); six of these were at interest rates of 12.5 per cent, one was at 11.8 per cent and another one at 10.0 per cent.[40] Apparently the

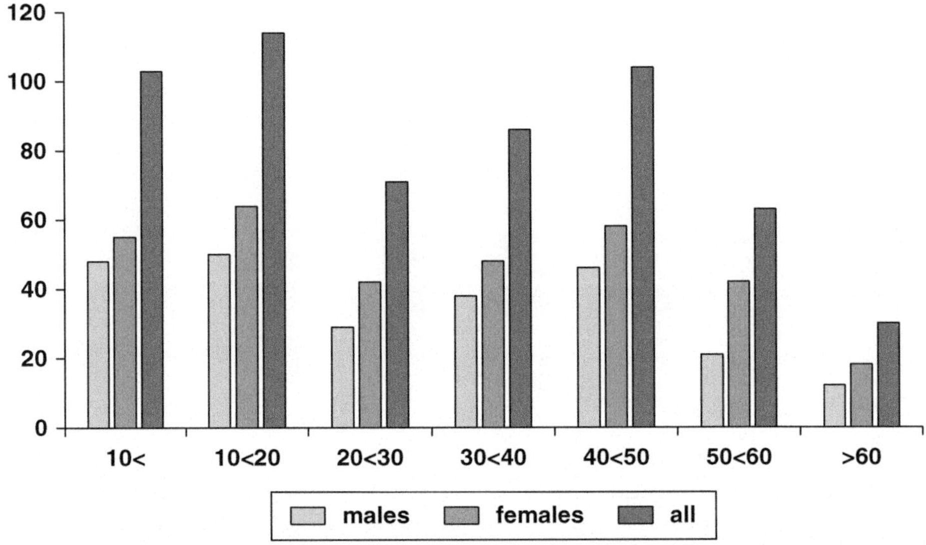

Figure 4.2. Joint and survivor annuities: age at purchase. *Source:* De Moor, 'De tussen 1482/1483 en 1490/1491 bij de stad Haarlem afgesloten lijfrenten'.

[40] Haze Jacob Walichsdr. (age four, yield 12.5 per cent), Margriet Claas Jansdr (age eight, yield 12.5 per cent), Agnes Claas Jansdr (age six, yield 12.5 per cent), Pieter Willemsdr. (age five, yield 12.5 per cent), Katrien Jansdr. (age nine, yield 12.5 per cent), Adriaen Everts. Lappen (age six, yield 10 per cent), Joost Adriaan Jacobsz. (age five, yield 11.8 per cent), Daniël Gerolfsz. Van Vorselaar (age five, yield 12.5 per cent).

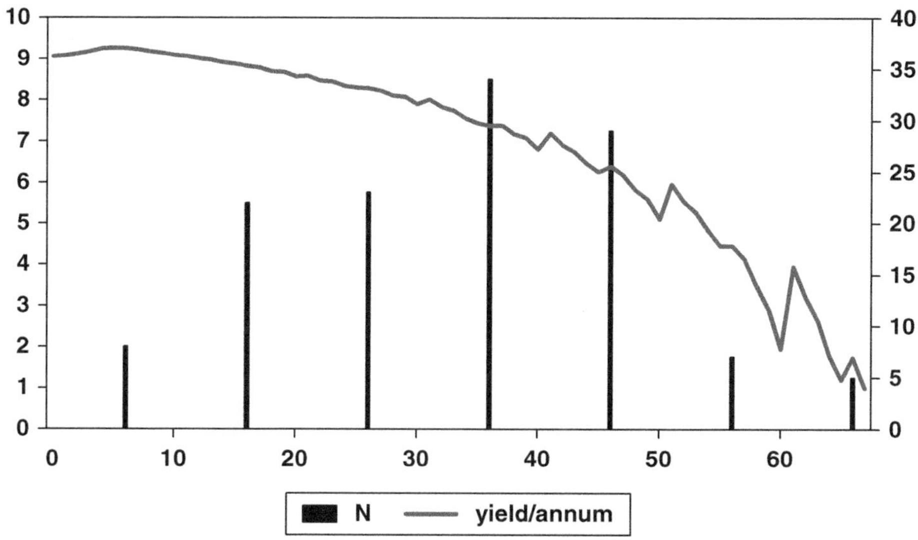

Figure 4.3. Single life annuities: annuitants per age category and yield/annum. *Sources*: life expectancies taken from Herlihy's calculations of age-specific life expectancy for Pistoia in 1427 (Herlihy, *Medieval and Renaissance Pistoia*, pp. 283–86); De Moor, 'De tussen 1482/1483 en 1490/1491 bij de stad Haarlem afgesloten lijfrenten'.

Left axis: yield/annum in %

Right axis: N of annuitants per 10-year age category (0<10, 10<20, etc.).

city did not fervently oppose selling single life annuities to children, it just was not very successful in doing so: a contemporary report states how, when Haarlem tried to sell single life annuities in 1471, prospective investors refused to invest in single life annuities, demanding joint and survivor annuities instead.[41] This suggests that the investing public's preferences may have been behind the overrepresentation of children in joint and survivor annuities: at purchase, 117 of these financial instruments contained an annuitant aged 0–9 (39 per cent of all joint and survivor annuities). It has been suggested that parents refrained from investing in child single life annuities because they feared their children would demand the annuity once they reached adulthood.[42] This was not the case in Haarlem though: here,

[41] '*because some demanded to purchase* [joint or survivor annuities]' (*mar om datter eenige waren die niet coipen en wilden dan om twee liven*) (Van Loenen, 'De rente-last', p. 8, my italics).

[42] Hanus suggests this was a likely scenario (Hanus, *Tussen stad en eigen gewin*, p. 76).

investors could stipulate in the contract that they themselves would receive the annuity they purchased for a child, and their spouse after they had passed away, followed by the child only after both parents had passed away. Numerous contracts issued by Haarlem contain this stipulation, so it would have been perfectly possible for parents and other adults to profit from a financial instrument that 'speculated' on a child's longevity.[43] In addition a single life annuity on a child provided a fixed income in the event the parent(s) passed away; for children this amounted to an insurance against orphanhood. All of this does not explain why investors preferred joint and survivor annuities over single life annuities. Perhaps we should consider another characteristic of late medieval society that could have influenced investment behaviour: the fear of untimely death.[44] If investors *believed* children ran an equally great (or greater) risk of dying as adults, they may have *perceived* single life annuities contracted on children as too risky, and may have preferred joint or survivor annuities that insured both adult and child of a lifelong income. To be sure, our best data on late medieval demography indicates that children's life expectancy was considerably higher than that of adults, so investing in single-life annuities on children would usually have been beneficial for adults and children. However in a time when demographic data were unavailable, contemporaries may have perceived the risk of a child dying prematurely as too high, causing low demand for single life annuities on children.

Returning to Figures 4.1 and 4.2, the proportion of single life annuitants over fifty was low — understandable considering annuitants' slim chances of reaching the break-even point. The oldest single life annuitant was Claas Pietersz., whose age at purchase was seventy; his chances of profiting were quite low (see Figure 4.3) but perhaps Claas was in good health and confident that he would live for many more years? Another possibility is that Claas lacked relatives to assign as co-annuitants, and therefore decided to invest in a single-life annuity. Altogether only 9.4 per cent of all single life annuitants and 16.3 per cent of all joint and survivor annuitants were over fifty. The two oldest in the latter category were the eighty-year-old widow Lobburch Simonsdr., who took out a contract with her fourty-four-year-old daughter Geertruid Jan Florisdr., and the eighty-year-old Katrien Pietersdr., who took out an annuity contract together with thirty-nine-year-old Joriden Harmansz. de Smid.

[43] Van Loenen, 'De rente-last', 4. Van Loenen gives the example of a joint and survivor annuity on Anthonis Bladelijn aged eighteen, and Margriet van Diepenbroeck, aged fourteen, to be collected by Pieter Bladelijn (Van Loenen, 'De rente-last', pp. 12, 13–16).

[44] The fear of untimely death is mentioned in Herlihy, *The Black Death*, pp. 80–81. It should be distinguished from the risk of untimely death, as mentioned in Imhof, *Lebenserwartungen*, p. 38.

Such investments were perhaps still not very prudent — a single life annuity on the younger annuitant would have had a higher yield — but including a much younger annuitant did at least reduce the risk of losing the entire investment because of the death of the surviving annuitant.

Finally, in the literature widows have been identified as prominent investors in life annuities. Since wives often outlived their husbands, they were likely to inherit, and at some point face the question of what do with the estate.[45] One option was to invest in a life annuity, which yielded a relatively high lifelong return. Indeed some historians have noticed that widows could be quite prominent participants in late medieval financial markets;[46] it has been suggested this was also because widows had the freedom to invest, whereas wives were usually subject to their husbands.[47] In addition, elderly widows are likely to have faced the question of how to secure an income in the face of reduced labour capacities; investing savings in an annuity was one way to secure an income.[48] Our dataset does not contain many widows, however: only eight, who contracted eleven joint and survivor annuities (and not one single life annuity). Their average age was 55.6, and that of their fellow annuitants 21.4; in ten cases their fellow annuitants were their children.[49] We should also point out that these widows had joint contracts with nine females and only two males.[50] Contrary to what has been observed elsewhere,[51] the widows in our sample also did not invest high sums, purchasing life annuities worth 8.6 guilders on average (the average of joint and survivor annuities involving parent-child pairings was 11.2 guilders, see Table 4.5). Only two widows invested more than 11.2 guilders: Geertruide Foppendr. from Leiden, together with her daughter Barbare, bought an annuity worth 12 guilders, and Margriet Hendriksdr., also from Leiden, together with her daughter Reinse, purchased an annuity worth 15 guilders.

[45] Schmidt, *Overleven*.

[46] Hanus, *Tussen stad en eigen gewin*, pp. 72, 76. Others such as Van der Heijden found a much lower share of widows (Van der Heijden, *Geldschieters van de stad*, p. 164).

[47] Van der Heijden, *Geldschieters van de stad*, pp. 161–62.

[48] Reduced labour capacities of the elderly are discussed in: Zuijderduijn, 'Wie waren oud'. The advantages and disadvantages of investing in annuities as a means of old age provisioning are discussed in: Zuijderduijn, 'Pap en brood'; Zuijderduijn, 'Good fresh air'.

[49] Only the relationship between Geertruida Frederiks Weinen, the sixty-five-year old widow of Jan Roemer, and six-year-old Dirkje Jan Claasdr. Ruysch is unknown.

[50] It is difficult to explain this bias: it does not seem to have been the result of the inheritance system benefiting sons over daughters, and women trying to compensate daughters for this: sons and daughters inherited equally (Phillips, *Well-Being*, p. 107).

[51] Tracy, *A Financial Revolution*, pp. 154–56; Hanus, *Tussen stad en eigen gewin*, pp. 72, 76.

Gender and Life Cycles

Joint and survivor annuities can tell us something about how financial markets were used in family life. Who were the people who paired up in a joint and survivor annuity contract? Our sample contains 299 joint and survivor annuities: the city accounts explicitly mention family relations in 142 contracts and we were able to deduce family relations in another sixty-two, mainly by comparing surnames. Of course, this is not a watertight method, so these deduced family relations are recorded separately. Table 4.4 shows that 8.8 per cent of the joint and survivor annuities were purchased by couples, a rather low proportion that seems to indicate that investing in an annuity was not the only means available to secure the livelihood of the surviving spouse. Rather, surviving spouses appear to have relied on the community property, which they would usually continue control until they also passed away.[52] Furthermore 29.0 per cent of the joint-and-survivor annuities were contracted on a parent and a child, 25.3 per cent on siblings, and 5.7 per cent among other family members. This means that more than two thirds of the joint and survivor annuities were a 'family affair'.[53]

Couples invested in joint and survivor annuities at an average age of 43.2 (Table 4.5): their actions must be regarded as an attempt to secure an income during old age and to provide for the longer-living partner. The average age of the elder spouse was 48.0, and that of the younger spouse 38.0. Couples invested in an annuity worth 17.8 guilders per annum on average: they received the equivalent of more than seventy days' wages of a skilled labourer,[54] or about three months' wages. Such an amount could make a crucial difference during old age, and especially during widowhood. In the parent-child category the average age was lower (28.5): the older annuitant was 43.0 on average, the younger one 11.2. The value of the annuities was also relatively low at 8 to 12 guilders, equivalent to forty-four to forty-eight days' wages. This does not come as a big surprise, since one might assume children usually did not contribute savings to the principal; couples probably had more scope for investing in larger annuities. Moving on to the next category, the average age of the siblings contracting joint and survivor annuities was 22.5; the older annuitants were 26.1 on average, the younger 19.1. In the 'other family' category the average was 27.1; the older annuitants were 39.1 on average, the younger 14.2.

[52] Howell, *The Marriage Exchange*, p. 211.

[53] Hanus arrived at similar figures for Bois-le-Duc (Hanus, *Tussen stad en eigen gewin*, p. 76).

[54] De Vries and van der Woude, *The First Modern Economy*, pp. 610–11.

It appears that this category mostly consisted of aunts and uncles paired with nieces and nephews.

Most joint and survivor annuities were shared by males and females (50.7 per cent), another 16.5 per cent involved two males, and 32.8 per cent involved two females. Males were older on average when the annuitants were a couple (this reflects the fact that husbands tended to be older than wives) but also when the annuitants were siblings (Table 4.5). Females were older on average when the annuitants were parent and child, and in the case of other family relations, or when the connection was unknown. When we take a closer look at the parent-child pairings (Table 4.6), it appears that females were in the majority as parents (66.3 per cent) and children (58.1 per cent). So when joint and survivor annuities were purchased, mothers were more likely to be an annuitant than fathers, and daughters more likely than sons. We should not go so far as to see this as indicating female preference, though, as it is usually impossible to determine whether these investments were contracted at the initiative of the mother or of other family members. A joint-and-survivor annuity on a mother and daughter could have been purchased at the initiative of the mother, and reflect her preferences; it could also have been purchased at the initiative of the father or another relative.[55]

What it may reflect, though, is the logic of intergenerational transfers in the late Middle Ages: in Holland there was a partible inheritance system where both men and women inherited. To prevent the inheritance process from breaking up the family property and producing small, uneconomic units, brothers would usually buy out their sisters' share in land, houses and business inventories, and compensate them with money or annuities. More junior family members, such as nieces, could also inherit, and they may have been compensated in a similar way. Winding up an estate could thus result in providing such heirs as women, nieces, and also male junior family members with money rather than other assets. Since keeping cash at home was potentially dangerous and also unprofitable, investing it in an annuity may have been a straightforward thing to do.[56] The effect was many women showing behaviour we would nowadays think of as 'modern': they emerged as prominent investors in financial markets. This amounts to a paradox of women's participation in financial markets, which can point to both females' weak position with respect to males, who prevented them from holding real estate, and at the

55 Van Loenen, 'De rente-last', pp. 12–16.

56 In cases where the estate lacked ready cash, it was impossible to invest in such life annuities as Haarlem offered for sale. However, there was always the possibility of compensating heirs with annuities secured on family land.

same time to their empowerment as investors. Women being pushed into financial investments is also in accordance with the large number of pairings of mothers and daughters in joint and survivor annuities: in the event that two generations of females inherited, it may have made sense to combine their funds in a joint and survivor annuity. Such inheritance practices may furthermore help explain the large number of female annuitants in the sample aged between thirty and forty: at this age they were most likely to lose their surviving parent and inherit.

Finally, there is an interesting pattern in the 'unknown' category: here the average age of the first annuitants was high in pairings of males with males (38.4) and females with females (44.2), while that of the second annuitant was rather low (13.2 and 15.3 respectively). This suggests the existence of contracts involving adults and non-related children (or at least the Haarlem city government was unaware of a family relationship). Table 4.7 provides a closer look at the 'unknown' category, and confirms the predominance of the large age-gap — and also in pairings of males and females (which is not picked up in Table 4.6). In 83.7 per cent of the cases the gap was larger than ten years, and in 67.4 per cent of the cases it was larger than 20 years. So in the absence of family relationships, many joint and survivor annuities were contracted by people from different generations. Perhaps the most straightforward explanation for this is godparenthood, which was very common in the late Middle Ages, and created strong relations between non-relatives[57] — and may have led to children and godparents entering into financial contracts.[58]

Table 4.4. Family relations in joint and survivor annuities. *Source:* De Moor, 'De tussen 1482/1483 en 1490/1491 bij de stad Haarlem afgesloten lijfrenten'.

	Certain	Deduced	Total
Couple	26	–	26 (8.8%)
Parent–child	81	5	86 (29.0%)
Siblings	19	56	75 (25.3%)
Other family	3	14	17 (5.7%)
Unknown	–	93	93 (31.3%)

[57] Alfani and Gourdon, 'Spiritual Kinship', p. 15.

[58] One reason for this construction may have been godparents acting as guardians of orphans, and being responsible for estate management. One way to take care of an inheritance may have been to invest the orphan's inheritance in a joint-and-survivor annuity. In Holland in the course of the later Middle Ages a civic institution called *weeskamer* emerged, that monitored such estate management (Zuijderduijn, 'Grave Concerns', p. 346 n. 13).

Table 4.5. Joint and survivor annuities: gender composition. *Source:* De Moor, 'De tussen 1482/1483 en 1490/1491 bij de stad Haarlem afgesloten lijfrenten'.

	m–f			m–m			f–f		
	Av. age male	Av. age female	Av. value	Av. age male1	Av. age male 2	Av. value	Av. age fem 1	Av. age fem 2	Av. value
Couple	45.0 (26)	41.3 (24)	17.8 (26)	–	–	–	–	–	–
Parent–child	23.4 (36)	28.3 (35)	11.8 (37)	50.3 (12)	11.2 (13)	12.7 (14)	43.1 (33)	16.4 (28)	10.0 (35)
Siblings	22.4 (25)	16.2 (25)	13.9 (25)	25.3 (14)	20.2 (14)	8.1 (15)	32.3 (21)	22.1 (22)	10.8 (22)
Other family	25.8 (14)	32.6 (14)	7.8 (14)	–	–	–	22.3 (3)	6.7 (3)	9.3 (3)
Unknown	31.8 (39)	35.1 (42)	13.1 (42)	38.4 (18)	13.2 (18)	10.1 (18)	44.2 (33)	15.3 (31)	9.5 (33)
Total	29.8 (130)	30.8 (140)	13.2 (144)	37.5 (44)	11.0 (46)	10.2 (47)	40.29 (90)	17.1 (84)	10.0 (93)

Table 4.6. Joint and survivor annuities: parent–child pairings. *Source:* De Moor, 'De tussen 1482/1483 en 1490/1491 bij de stad Haarlem afgesloten lijfrenten'.

	Male parent	Female parent	Total
Male child	14	22	36
Female child	15	35	50
Total	29	57	–

Table 4.7. Age gap for the 'unknown' category. *Source:* De Moor, 'De tussen 1482/1483 en 1490/1491 bij de stad Haarlem afgesloten lijfrenten'.

	0–9	10–19	20+	Total
m–f	8	6	24	38
m–m	3	5	10	18
f–f	3	3	24	30
Total	14	14	58	

Conclusion

The life annuities Haarlem sold between 1482 and 1491 to elites and middling groups in various cities in the northern Low Countries provide new insights into the late medieval investing public because they include the age at purchase of annuitants. From an economic point of view, purchasing single life annuities for children would have been most profitable. But even though Haarlem allowed investors to take out single life annuities for children, only a few people decided to do so. Investors might have perceived the risk of untimely death as too high to justify purchasing annuities for children, or they might have given more weight to incentives other than just profit. In this respect, recent studies have claimed financial instruments could be used not only for financial gain, but also to deal with specific moments during the family life cycle. The single life annuity might for instance have been useful in providing women with a dowry. Our analysis does not contain many single life annuities on women at the average age at first marriage, though. Another use of financial instruments might have been by widows looking to reinvest inherited wealth in a single life annuity to secure their livelihood during old age. However, the number of widows in our sample is very low. In fact women did not feature prominently among single life annuitants: most single life annuitants were men in their thirties and forties. Women were in the majority among joint and survivor annuitants though. Since these financial instruments had two annuitants, the risk of losing the investment due to death was less compared to single life annuities, but so were the returns. In this respect most women in our sample held less risky financial instruments than men, who were more likely to invest in single life annuities. Whether this finding tells us all that much about female preferences remains difficult to tell, since we are generally unaware of the decision-making process leading to the investment. The fact that women formed the majority of investors in Haarlem's life annuities could be a reflection of either female investment behaviour, or of male decision-making on behalf of women.

Our dataset also allows for an analysis of pairings of joint and survivor annuitants. The majority of these concerned two family members teaming up. Where annuitants were parent and child, there was an overrepresentation of mothers and daughters. We speculate that this female presence may be due to the 'paradox' of female participation in financial markets: in partible inheritance systems, male heirs may have tried to prevent the splintering of land, houses, and business inventories, by making sure these assets did not go to sisters, nieces, and other junior family members. As compensation the latter received either financial instruments or cash (which was likely to be invested in financial instruments as well). Such inheritance practices may have reduced women's property ownership, and may have driven them into financial markets. This could help explain the large number of women of all ages among Haarlem's annuitants, as well as the large number of pairings of mothers and daughters and the large number of female annuitants in the sample aged between thirty and forty.

On the other hand we should not exclude the possibility that women took the initiative to invest in financial instruments: life annuities yielded high returns and may have been an attractive way to secure an income during old age. Most of Haarlem's annuitants received an annuity equivalent to several months' wages for an unskilled worker, and clearly this could make a crucial difference during old age. The majority of these financial instruments were contracted by adults, presumably after they had amassed the necessary savings or inherited wealth. By investing in a life annuity, they assured the annuitant(s) of an additional income. In terms of insurance, joint and survivor annuities may have been particularly attractive since they could be used to secure two generations: the older annuitant received a steady lifelong income, which could also be used to support the younger annuitant. The younger annuitant was assured of an income in the event the older annuitant passed away. Since such an income could be of crucial important for the well-being of orphans, increasing their ability to remain above subsistence level, and perhaps also to acquire a skill during adolescence, for younger annuitants joint and survivor annuities may have amounted to an insurance against impoverishment in the event of a parent passing away.

To summarize, our analysis did not yield clear-cut links between life-cycle events such as first marriage or widowhood and investing in a life annuity. Such an investment nevertheless provided family members with financial security, regardless of the life-cycle stage: single life and joint and survivor annuities provided annuitants with a lifelong income, and offered protection against the 'retirement squeeze' during old age. In addition, we suggested inheritance patterns may have driven women to invest in financial markets, and this may help explain why women constituted the majority of Haarlem's joint and survivor annuitants.

Works Cited

Manuscripts

Loenen, Jacques C. van, 'De rente-last van Haarlem in de vijftiende eeuw' (manuscript available at City Archives Haarlem, n.d.)

Secondary Studies

Alfani, Guido, and Vincent Gourdon, 'Spiritual Kinship and Godparenthood: An Introduction', in *Spiritual Kinship in Europe, 1500–1900*, ed. by Guido Alfani and Vincent Gourdon (Basingstoke: Palgrave, 2012), pp. 1–43

Baguet, Jelten, 'Social Change and Markets for Urban Credit. Political Elites as Investors in Urban Annuities in Sixteenth Century Ghent', *Financial History Review*, 23 (2016), 347–67

Bakker, Folkert Jan, *Bedelorden en begijnen in de stad Groningen tot 1594* (Assen: Van Gorcum, 1988)

Bouman, Annemarie, Tine De Moor, and Jaco Zuijderduijn, 'From Hardship to Benefit: A Critical Review of the Nuclear Hardship Hypothesis in Relation to the Emergence of the European Marriage Pattern', *CGEH working paper*, 28 (2012)

Brand, Hanno A., *Over macht en overwicht: stedelijke elites in Leiden (1420–1510)* (Louvain: Garant, 1996)

Burrow, John Anthony, *The Ages of Man: A Study in Medieval Writing and Thought* (Oxford: Clarendon Press, 2011)

Callewier, Hendrik, *De papen van Brugge: de seculiere clerus in een middeleeuwse wereldstad* (Louvain: Universitaire Pers Leuven, 2014)

Di Matteo, Livio, 'Wealth Accumulation and the Life-Cycle in Economic History: Implications of Alternative Approaches to Data', *Explorations in Economic History*, 35 (1997), 296–324

Dokkum, Herman W., and Eef C. Dijkhof, 'Oude Dordtse lijfrenten', in *Oude Dordtse lijfrenten: Stedelijke financiering in de vijftiende eeuw*, ed. by L. M. Verloren van Themaat, Herman W. Dokkum, Eef C. Dijkhof, J. T. Roggen, and N. Sanderson (Amsterdam: Verloren, 1983), pp. 37–88

Feenstra, Alberto, and Sabine Muller, 'Wie wil wachten op het zoet? De laatste adem van Amsterdamse kopers van Groningse lijfrenten, 1660–1760', *Historisch jaarboek Groningen* (2016), 46–65

Froide, Amy M., *Silent Partners: Women as Public Investors During Britain's Financial Revolution, 1690–1750* (Oxford: Oxford University Press, 2016)

Hanus, Jord, *Tussen stad en eigen gewin: Stadsfinanciën, renteniers en kredietmarkten in 's-Hertogenbosch (begin zestiende eeuw)* (Amsterdam: Aksant, 2007)

Heijden, Manon van der, *Geldschieters van de stad: Financiële relaties tussen stad, burger en overheden 1550–1650* (Amsterdam: Bert Bakker, 2006)

Herlihy, David, *The Black Death and the Transformation of the West* (Cambridge, MA: Harvard University Press, 1997)

——, *Medieval and Renaissance Pistoia: The Social History of an Italian Town, 1200–1430* (New Haven: Yale University Press, 1967)

Hinz, Richard P., David D. McCarthy, and John A. Turner, 'Are Women Conservative Investors? Gender Differences in Participant-directed Pension Investments', in *Positioning Pensions for the Twenty-First Century*, ed. by Michael S. Gordon, Olivia S. Mitchell, and Marc M. Twinney (Philadelphia: University of Pennsylvania Press, 1997), pp. 91–103

Howell, Martha C., *The Marriage Exchange: Property, Marriage and Gender in Cities of the Low Countries, 1300–1550* (Chicago: Chicago University Press, 1998)

Imhof, Arthur E., *Lebenserwartungen in Deutchland vom 17. bis 19. Jahrhundert* (Weinheim: Wiley VCH, 1990)

Johnson, Richard W., Cori E. Uccello, and Joshua H. Goldwyn, 'Single Life vs. Joint and Survivor Pension Payout Options: How do Married Retirees Decide?' *Final Report to the Society of Actuaries and the Actuarial Foundation* (2003) <https://www.soa.org/research/research-projects/pension/research-single-life-vs-joint-and-survivor-pension-payout-options-how-do-married-retirees-choose.aspx>

Jordan, William Chester, *Women and Credit in Pre-Industrial and Developing Societies* (Philadelphia: University of Pennsylvania Press, 1993)

Kirshner, Julius, *Marriage, Dowry, and Citizenship in Late Medieval and Renaissance Italy* (Toronto: University of Toronto Press, 2015)

Lilja, Kristina, and Dan Backlund, 'To Navigate the Family Economy over a Lifetime: Life-Cycle Squeezes in Pre-industrial Swedish Towns', *European Review of Economic History*, 17 (2013), 171–89

McIntosh, Marjorie K., *Working Women in English Society, 1300–1620* (Cambridge: Cambridge University Press, 2005)

Moor, Geertruida de, 'De tussen 1482/1483 en 1490/1491 bij de stad Haarlem afgesloten lijfrenten', *Ons voorgeslacht*, 49 (1994), 85–104

———, *Verborgen en geborgen: Het Cisterciënzerinnenklooster Leeuwenhorst in de Noordwijkse regio (1261–1574)* (Hilversum: Verloren, 1994)

Moor, Tine de, and Jan Luiten van Zanden, 'Girl Power: The European Marriage Pattern (EMP) and Labour Markets in the North Sea Region in the Late Medieval and Early Modern Period', *The Economic History Review*, 63 (2010), 1–33

Pezzolo, Luciano, 'Bonds and Government Debt in Italian City-States, 1250–1650', in *The Origins of Value: The Financial Innovations that Created Modern Capital Markets*, ed. by William N. Goetzmann and K. Geert Rouwenhorst (Oxford: Oxford University Press, 2005), pp. 145–64

Pfister, Ulrich, 'The Protoindustrial Household Economy: Toward a Formal Analysis', *Journal of Family History*, 17(2) (1992), 201–32

Phillips, Derek, *Well-Being in Amsterdam's Golden Age* (Amsterdam: Amsterdam University Press, 2008)

Schaïk, Rémi van, 'The Sale of Annuities and Financial Politics in a Town in the Eastern Netherlands. Zutphen, 1400–1600', in *Urban Public Debts: Urban Government and the Market for Annuities in Western Europe (14th–18th Centuries)*, ed. by Marc Boone and Paul J. J. G. Janssens (Turnhout: Brepols, 2003) pp. 109–26

Schilder, Marian, *Amsterdamse kloosters in de middeleeuwen* (Amsterdam: Vossiuspers AUP, 1997)

Schmidt, Ariadne, *Overleven na de dood: Weduwen in Leiden in de Gouden Eeuw* (Amsterdam: Samenwerkende uitgeverijen Prometheus/Bert Bakker, 2001)

Stasavage, David, *States of Credit: Size, Power and the Development of European Polities* (Princeton: Princeton University Press, 2011)

Stoop, Patricia, *Schrijven in commissie: De zusters uit het Brusselse klooster Jericho en de preken van hun biechtvaders (ca. 1456–1510)* (Hilversum: Verloren, 2013)

Tracy, James D., *A Financial Revolution in the Habsburg Netherlands:* Renten *and* Renteniers *in the County of Holland, 1515–1565* (Berkeley: University of California Press, 1985)

Vijlder, Nicolas de, and Michael Limberger, 'Public or Private Interests? The Investment Behaviour of Public Officials in Antwerp during the Early Modern Period', *Financial History Review*, 21 (2014), 301–26

Vries, Jan de, and Ad van der Woude, *The First Modern Economy: Success, Failure and Perseverance of the Dutch Economy, 1500–1815* (Cambridge: Cambridge University Press, 1997)

Zuijderduijn, Jaco, 'De schuldvraag. Monetaire politiek, publieke schuld en wanbetaling in Holland, ca. 1466–1489', *Low Countries Journal of Social and Economic History — Tijdschrift voor Sociale en Economische Geschiedenis*, 9 (2012), 27–46

———, 'Foreign Investment: Interregional Public Debt in the Northern Low Countries, 15th–16th Centuries', *Working paper* (2013) <https://lu.academia.edu/JacoZuijderduijn>

———, '"Good, Fresh Air and an Expert Medical Service": Old Age Pensioners in Leiden's St. Hiëronymusdal Retirement Home, Sixteenth Century', *The History of the Family*, 21 (2016), 195–213

———, 'Grave Concerns: Entailment and Intergenerational Agency in Amsterdam, 1600–1800', *The History of the Family*, 16 (2011), 343–53

———, 'Het lichaam van het dorp: Publieke schuld op het Hollandse platteland rond 1500', *Low Countries Journal of Social and Economic History — Tijdschrift voor Sociale en Economische Geschiedenis*, 5 (2008), 107–32

———, 'Living la Vita Apostolica: Life Expectancy and Mortality of Nuns in Late-Medieval Holland', *CGEH working papers*, 44 (2013)

———, *Medieval Capital Markets: Markets for Renten, State Formation and Private Investment in Holland (1300–1550)* (Leiden: Brill Academic Publishers, 2009)

———, 'Pap en brood tijdens de oude dag. Gepensioneerden in Amsterdam, c. 1500', *Low Countries Journal for Social and Economic History — Tijdschrift voor Sociale en Economische Geschiedenis*, 12 (2015), 23–50

———, 'Wie waren oud in de Gouden eeuw?' *Jaarboek de zeventiende eeuw* (2017), 23–40

Zuijderduijn, Jaco, and Tine De Moor, 'Preferences of the Poor: Market Participation and Asset Management in Sixteenth-Century Holland', *European Review of Economic History*, 17 (2013), 233–49

———, 'Spending, Saving or Investing? Risk Management in Sixteenth-century Dutch Households', *The Economic History Review*, 66 (2013), 38–56

Zuijderduijn, Jaco, and Roos van Oosten, 'Breaking the Piggy Bank: What Can Historical and Archaeological Sources Tell us about Late-medieval Saving Behaviour?', *CGEH working papers*, 65 (2015)

Appendix

The table gives six scenarios for investing 200 guilders in life annuities. Investors deciding to purchase a single life annuity on a child would receive an annuity of 25 guilders. Assuming life expectancy at birth was approximately twenty-five years, the investors could expect to earn 25 × 25 = 625 guilders on average. Since the principal of 200 guilders would not be recovered, the net yield would be 425 guilders in twenty-five years, or a nominal yield of 8.5 per cent per annum.[59] Another scenario would have been to invest the 200 guilders in a single life annuity on an adult. Assuming the life expectancy of the average adult, from the time of making the investment, was a further 15 years, the expected return would be 15 × 25 = 375 guilders on average. The net yield would be 175 guilders over 15 years, or 5.9 per cent per annum.[60] The four other scenarios for investing in life annuities do not exceed a 6.0 per cent return per annum either: clearly the highest return was to be had for single life annuities on children.

	Expected return (guilders)	**Yield per annum**
Single life annuity of 200 guilders on child	625	8.5%
Single life annuity of 200 guilders on adult	375	5.8%
Single life annuity of 100 guilders on parent, and single life annuity of 100 guilders on child	500	6.0%
Joint and survivor annuity of 200 guilders on two children	500	6.0%
Joint and survivor annuity of 200 guilders on two adults	375	5.8%
Joint and survivor annuity of 200 guilders on parent and child	500	6.0%

[59] 425/25 = 17 guilders per annum; 17/200 guilders = 8.5 per cent.

[60] 175/15 = 11.7 guilders per annum; 11.7/200 guilders = 5.9 per cent.

Scenarios 200 Guilder Investments in Annuities

Assumptions: interest for single life annuity is 12.5 per cent, for joint and survivor annuity 10.0 per cent; life expectancy for child is twenty-five years, for adult fifteen years. Life expectancies based on Herlihy, *Medieval and Renaissance Pistoia*, pp. 283–86. Evidence of life expectancies in fifteenth-century Holland probably being as high as in Italy: Zuijderduijn, 'Living la Vida Apostolica'.

We used nominal interest rates since this was probably closest to late medieval practice: annuities were paid out in hard cash to the annuitant, and we are unaware of annuitants reinvesting these sums. However, if we were to use a compound interest-rate scenario and assume late medieval investors reinvested their annual returns immediately at a 12.5 per cent yield, we end up with an end result of 6171 guilders — a yield of 173 per cent per annum over the thirty-five-year period.

Providing Security for Others: Swedish Women in Early Modern Credit Networks

Maria Ågren

By availing themselves of the possibility of borrowing from others, people can immediately get access to things for which they would otherwise have to wait. Consequently, credit is closely linked to the dimension of time for those who resort to borrowing. For lenders, by contrast, security is the key factor: to have some sort of guarantee that the debtor will honour his or her promise and repay when a certain period of time has elapsed. The meaning of credit arrangements thus differs depending on whether they are seen from the point of view of the creditor or the debtor. Of course, debtors and creditors may sometimes have a common interest in rolling over the debt instead of paying off the principal, but this generally presupposes that the creditor is confident that the debtor will be able to continue paying. Thus, the creditor has to trust the debtor and the trust is often based on some form security. In this article, 'trust' is defined as the belief that the debtor will eventually pay, while 'security' is understood to be social and legal arrangements that inspire such trust.

In modern society, a mortgage is a good example of how security is created: it is a legal arrangement securing the creditor's claim through the debtor's real

Maria Ågren is professor of history at Uppsala University. Her work focuses on the intersection of economic, social, legal, and gender history. Her dissertation (1992) deals with indebtedness, its legal framework and social consequences in early modern rural society. She is the author of e.g., *Domestic Secrets: Women and Property in Sweden, 1600–1857* (UNC Press 2009) and *The State as Master: Gender, State Formation and Commercialisation in Urban Sweden, 1650–1780* (MUP 2017). She is the leader of the Gender and Work research project and the GaW infrastructure project, as well as the editor of the project publication *Making a Living, Making a Difference: Gender and Work in Early Modern European Society* (OUP 2017).

Women and Credit in Pre-Industrial Europe, ed. by Elise M. Dermineur, EER 12 (Turnhout: Brepols, 2018), pp. 121–142.
BREPOLS PUBLISHERS DOI 10.1484/M.EER-EB.5.115751

property. In such a system, the creditor does not have to trust the debtor's person; it suffices to trust the legal system's capacity to monitor the use of mortgages. Similar arrangements existed in early modern society too. It was, however, also common to secure debts in other ways, for instance through the debtor's movable property or good name. Even more interesting, debts could be secured by the property or good name of people *other than the debtor*. A person who was not, by any account, creditworthy might still obtain credit through other people, often but not necessarily his/her family and friends. Security was created in several ways. The interplay of various forms of security arrangements, and women's roles in these arrangements, are at the core of this article.

More precisely, I will discuss three different ways of providing security for others and how women took part in and were affected by such arrangements. The first type of arrangement was to stand in for others: to lend others movable property that they could in turn use as collateral, or to allow others to 'borrow' one's general reputation as an upright and creditworthy person. The second type of arrangement was to act as guarantor or, in early modern parlance, to stand surety or (in Swedish) to provide *caution*. This was a formalized and legally binding promise to pay someone else's debt, should he or she fail to do so. The third type of arrangement was to allow a family member to use one's lands as collateral, through a mortgage or in other and less formal ways.

The analysis of these three types of arrangement will show that early modern credit relations were based on a plethora of interlocking legal and social mechanisms designed to create security and involving more people than just debtor and creditor. Some of these mechanisms were highly formalized and can easily be spotted in the historical sources, whereas others were informal and difficult to trace in the archives. If we do not make the attempt to understand how formal and informal mechanisms were interlinked, we will underestimate the dynamics of early modern credit and its role in long-term socio-economic development.

It is, however, a misleading but common assumption that credit always presupposes trust. Credit can also be coerced. This was often the case in early modern society, not least in the state sector. Therefore, the plethora of interlocking mechanisms included face-to-face trust, security-creating institutions *and* relations of power. The literature on credit tends to play down the importance of coercion, but coercion is an obvious theme in the history of states, credit, and gender.

The geographic focus of the study is Sweden. It is important to notice that unlike countries such as France, Italy, and the Netherlands, Sweden did not have a notary system proper and, consequently, there are no notarial archives. How could such a system work? In France, notaries confirmed legal transactions between private parties and preserved evidence thereof. Notaries also acted as brokers, channelling information and putting people into contact with each other.[1] By contrast, in Sweden (which at this point in time included Finland) many legal transactions were confirmed and made public in primary level courts. Transfer of land to a person outside the seller's kin group was the most formalized type of transaction; the medieval law laid down that such transactions be duly announced at the local court. In the course of the early modern period, the demand for publicity through courts was extended to other types of transaction. At the beginning of the eighteenth century, courts started keeping more systematic registers of land transactions and uncontested credit secured with real estate.[2] Contested credit, i.e., credit transactions that was subject to litigation, had of course been handled in court already in the Middle Ages.[3] Thus, Swedish courts fulfilled some of the functions that notaries had in many other European countries. Swedish courts did not, however, act as brokers of credit, in the way French notaries did. Such brokerage was usually carried out by private persons, as we shall see later in this article.

In the absence of notarial records, medieval and early modern Swedish credit arrangements must be mapped in other ways. Court records are a valuable albeit time-consuming option. Before 1730, only contested credit surfaces in the court material and there is no guarantee that all contested credit is captured. The evidence is often anecdotal and the degree of detail varying. An early systematic study of court litigation in a mid-eighteenth-century Swedish region showed that in the mining court 33 per cent of the case load consisted of debt cases whereas in the first instance rural court between 4 and 9 per cent of the case load consisted of debt.[4] After 1730, the courts' special registers (Sw. *inteckningsprotokoll*) list uncontested credit for which real property was used as security. There is of course reason to believe that these registers only make visible the tip of an iceberg of credit.

However, the eighteenth century was also the time when probate inventories became legally required and more widely used. For some groups of people (notably widows and widowers), probate inventories were used even before 1700.[5] Gradually covering an ever-larger share of the population, the Swedish probate inventories

[1] See e.g. Dermineur, 'Trust, Norms of Cooperation', p. 502.

[2] Ågren, *Jord och gäld*, p. 48.

[3] Franzén, *Sturetidens monetära system*.

[4] Ågren, 'Att lösa ekonomiska tvister', pp. 495–97.

[5] In 1667, a statutory law prescribed that widows and widowers had to set up a probate inventory before they remarried. Fagerlund, *Handel och vandel*, p. 103. In the nobility, probate inventories seem to have been used more widely. See Riksarkivet Marieberg, collection Adliga bouppteckningar.

include assets, credit, and debt. A study of probate inventories from one south-Swedish town suggests that women's share of all recorded debt was 18 per cent in the period 1674–1715. Analysis of the court records from the same town suggests that their share of all debt cases was some 13 per cent. Most of these women were widows.[6] A study of court records from a rural area in the period 1645 to 1725 also shows that both women and men were involved in conflicts about payment (many of which probably concerned debt), but men more often than women.[7] Thus, there is no doubt that women were involved in credit relations, but the source material is generally too sparse and fragmentary to allow us to measure the actual extent of their engagement.

In this study, I make use of a wide variety of sources: incidental information gleaned from cases presented at urban courts of first instance (mainly from the small town of Örebro in central Sweden); credit law and land law; state-level documents pertaining to legislation and customs administration; probate inventories; and data from the Gender and Work database.[8] The time-frame is approximately mid-seventeenth to mid-eighteenth century. As will be explained in some detail later on, these one hundred years were formative for Swedish private and public credit, both of which were subject to political and legislative interest as well as experimentation. My purpose is not to quantify large empirical datasets — and the sources do not lend themselves to that sort of analysis — but to use various types of evidence, both anecdotal and more systematic, to draw a tentative map of how issues of financial security were handled over time and how distinctions such as private/public and formal/informal threaten to make women's involvement in credit networks less visible.

Lending Security to Others: Movable Property and General Creditworthiness

Credit was ubiquitous in early modern society.[9] Both women and men were engaged in providing, brokering, negotiating, and receiving credit. Moreover, not only were heads of households involved in these networks but also servants: servants acted as creditors (waiting for their wages to be paid), debtors, and facilitators.[10]

[6] Fagerlund, *Handel och vandel*, pp. 105, 111, 113. Similar results have been found by Dermineur. See her article in this volume.

[7] Andersson, *Tingets kvinnor och män*, p. 279. See also pp. 74 f.

[8] For the primary sources, see Works Cited.

[9] See e.g. Muldrew, *The Economy of Obligation*.

[10] Spence, *Women, Credit, and Debt*.

While unmarried women (meaning single women and widows) were conspicuous among those who lent their capital to others in England,[11] it was primarily wives and widows who extended credit in the Swedish context. A recent study based primarily on court records showed that 80 per cent of women who were active in the credit market were either married or widowed.[12] Another recent study based on petitions showed that 86 per cent of all women who petitioned in their roles as creditors were either currently married or widowed. In both studies, single women rarely appeared in the credit market,[13] even if there were exceptions. For instance, a young servant girl was apprehended and brought to court because she had pawned a piece of clothing so as to obtain cash and buy something to eat. The clothing belonged to her master which was why the case ended up in court.[14]

The difference between Sweden and England is not surprising; as Amy Erickson has pointed out, an important characteristic of early modern England was the relatively strong legal capacity vested in single women and widows and the weak legal capacity of married women.[15] In Sweden, by contrast, it was the 'ever-married' women who could act in markets with authority.[16] Widows had approximately the same legal capacity as men (just as in England), and while married women were formally under marital guardianship, in practice they were clearly very involved in all forms of trade.[17] Wives and widows often attended Swedish early modern courts to repay the household's creditors and claim payment from their husbands' debtors.[18] Thus, Swedish single women were worse off in terms of legal capacity than English single women over the age of twenty-one, while Swedish wives were better off than English wives. The credit market bears witness to these differences.[19]

The notion that women were particularly suitable for renegotiating debt to obtain better terms was obviously widespread in Europe, and it was based on the belief that, for instance, landlords and bakers would be more compassionate

[11] Spicksley, '"Fly with a Duck in thy Mouth"'.

[12] Ågren, *Making a Living, Making a Difference*, Chapter 3.

[13] Israelsson, 'For I willingly acknowledge the debt', Table 2. See also Fagerlund, *Handel och vandel*, p. 113.

[14] Gender and Work (GaW) Database, case 961.

[15] Erickson, 'Coverture and Capitalism', p. 3.

[16] A term borrowed from Amy Froide. See Froide, 'Marital Status as a Category of Analysis'.

[17] Lindström and others, 'Mistress or Maid'.

[18] GaW Database, cases 8970, 11066, 9602, 10651, 3902, 4854, 4722, 6441.

[19] For comparison see Froide, *Silent Partners*. See also the articles by Spicksley and Hunt in this volume.

to women appealing to them for respite.[20] Access to a discourse of vulnerability could be one possible reason for women's involvement in the credit market, but it was not the only one. Many women obviously had access to many forms of capital. Some knew where credit could be found and were able to act as brokers. Others were particularly knowledgeable about values and could assist creditors in assessing pawned objects. Still others were simply regarded as creditworthy, for reasons that are sometimes hard to pinpoint, but it gave them special opportunities in the credit market.

It is in this light that we should read the following court case which concerns a woman who was asked to raise credit for someone else. In 1655, Nils Larsson in Örebro asked a married woman by the name of Kerstin to raise three *daler* for him.[21] Kerstin was asked to borrow money from an unnamed third person, pass it on to Nils, and keep a silver spoon of his until he had repaid her. Why the creditor would accept this arrangement is somewhat unclear: Kerstin was the one who could use the spoon and conceivably sell it if the loan was not paid back, and who, therefore, derived some material benefit from the arrangement. The creditor appears to have had none. How are we to understand this case? Why did Nils not go directly to the creditor and offer his spoon as collateral for the loan he needed? The case is too brief to tell with certainty, but it is possible that Kerstin was regarded as a more hardworking and upright person than Nils.[22] It is also possible that Nils was a stranger in town; we simply do not know. What we do know is that the creditor agreed to lend Kerstin money without a pawn as security whereas Nils foresaw or imagined he would be treated differently. Kerstin rented out her creditworthiness to Nils and got to retain the spoon for a period of time in return. In this way, she in fact provided security for him. Without her, he would not have been able to get the money immediately and might not have been able to get it at all.

As this case illustrates, people who lacked creditworthiness themselves could nevertheless obtain small loans if they hid their involvement behind other people. In so doing, the former profited from the latter's better reputation, social connections, and economic resources. Apparently, men could hide themselves behind women but the opposite was also true. For instance, Sisilia, a married woman, borrowed a silver bowl from Nils Olofsson Bergman in 1698. Then, without Nils's knowledge, she used it as collateral for a loan of 100 *daler* and ended up in court.[23]

[20] Hunt, *Women in Eighteenth-Century Europe*, p. 199.

[21] Uppsala, Landsarkivet, Örebro Kämnärsrätt, A 1 vol. 7, 2 May 1655.

[22] Cf. Hardwick, *Family Business*, pp. 164, 168.

[23] Uppsala, Landsarkivet, Örebro Kämnärsrätt, A 1 vol. 7, October 1698.

The stand-ins (in these examples Kerstin and Nils Olofsson Bergman) would probably profit from the arrangements, even if it is sometimes hard to see exactly how. These practices created chains of credit that could be very complex. The debtor did not have a direct relationship with the creditor at the farthest end of the chain; instead, one or several intermediaries separated them. Such arrangements can be found in modern society too, for instance when parents borrow money from a bank to allow a child, who is not sufficiently creditworthy, to buy something the child needs and cannot wait to have. The important point is that there was no face-to-face trust, nor any formal institutions to make up for the lack of such trust. Nevertheless, credit could be extended and obtained.

Such convoluted credit arrangements were sometimes crucial to people's survival. Unfortunately, they can be difficult to find in the historical records and to investigate in a systematic fashion. It is unlikely that transactions such as the one between Nils Larsson and Kerstin or between Sisilia and Nils Olofsson Bergman were based on written contracts and, even if there were contracts, it is unlikely that the parties would fall upon the idea of having them registered at court. This probably means that the parties' respective rights and duties were vaguely defined. Paradoxically, vaguely defined contract conditions can sometimes offer opportunities to the historian as the likelihood increases that parties will end up in court, making the arrangements visible. In 1692 for instance, Isak Brant borrowed a silver item from Marja Swensdotter, who explicitly consented to it being re-pawned to a certain Jacob Jonson. When she wanted to have her property back, it turned out however that Jacob had extended more credit for it than she thought it was worth. Presumably, this made it hard for her to redeem her property.[24] Marja's role seems to have been different from that of Kerstin since she had lent a concrete object rather her own creditworthiness as security. Offering Marja's silver as a pledge, Isak could obtain credit from Jacob, but while Marja's initial reason for allowing him to use her property in this way may have been a genuine willingness to help, their relationship obviously soured later on.

Many other cases illustrate the system of providing security to others by allowing them to hide themselves behind one's good reputation or pledge property that was not theirs. Clearly, these informal arrangements involved risk. For instance, a soldier tried to drown himself in desperation because, as he later claimed (in 1690), a ring he had borrowed from a woman had been stolen from him. His intention had been to use the ring as a pawn in order to get cash to purchase some clothes.

[24] Uppsala, Landsarkivet, Örebro Rådhusrätt och magistrat, court record, 5 December 1692.

Presumably, he had promised to give the ring back to her as soon as possible and he claimed to be devastated at the prospect of not being able to do so.[25] Both the soldier and the woman seem to have been strangers in town. Those who lacked property and were unable to provide security for their loans nevertheless tried to access the credit market by borrowing security from others.

Although people knew it could be risky to stand in for less creditworthy people or to lend out property to others to use as collateral, it was probably not easy to say no to such requests. A court case from mid-eighteenth-century Örebro illustrates how emotional pressure could be brought to bear on the person who had something to lend. According to the testimony of Greta Lotta Richter, married to customs inspector Hans Wigart, Catarina Lenbom had come to the Wigart house when Richter was still confined to bed, having given birth to a child that subsequently died. Catarina had implored Greta Lotta to lend her a gilt silver bowl which she, Catarina, needed to be able to pay off a debt. Greta Lotta gave in, but when her husband found out that the silver bowl was missing, he took the case to court.[26] In court, Catarina argued that the Wigart couple had destroyed her good name and reputation. The bowl was returned to its owners and the case was solved amicably, but Lenbom later went bankrupt. Clearly, she had been in a very difficult situation when she asked Greta Lotta to help her. Greta Lotta, in her turn, was put under hard emotional pressure.

Both women and men appeared in these cases as providers of security in the form of pawnable objects (typically silver) or as stand-ins or brokers of credit. But they could also play other roles. For instance, a shoemaker wanted to borrow a sum of money in 1757, using some of his own silver artefacts as collateral. He turned to a local burgher who, apparently, did not have access to ready cash. In his turn and for unclear reasons, the burgher commissioned Anna Maja Tholin, the widow of a shipmaster, to pawn the shoemaker's silver items for him. Anna Maja later claimed to have raised the money from Mr von Aken, pharmacist and one of the leading men in town in the 1750s.[27] Anna Maja was probably chosen for this task because she had a reputation for being able to correctly assess the value of pawned objects. This was a special skill, and not necessarily one every burgher possessed. There was even a special title for women who did this sort of work: pawn-woman

[25] Uppsala, Landsarkivet, Örebro Rådhusrätt och magistrat, court record, 5 May 1690.

[26] Uppsala, Landsarkivet, Örebro Accisrätt, vol. A no. 1, 380 (3 October 1746?). See also GaW Database, case 11147.

[27] Uppsala, Landsarkivet, Örebro Kämnärsrätt, A 1 no 14. 1757.

(Sw. *pantekvinna*).[28] Other studies have shown that male creditors sometimes used women intermediaries to assess the correct value of pawned objects.[29] The shoemaker must have believed that von Aken would rather do business with the burgher than with him, and the burgher may have believed that von Aken would trust Anna Maja's assessment of the value more than his. Both the burgher and Anna Maja were essential as intermediaries and facilitators. Clearly, security and trustworthiness were key issues in this complicated case.

People shared the experience of lending security to others: clothing, silver items, or jewellery that could be used as collateral for loans, or one's good name. Such forms of security were available to a larger segment of the population than was the case with the other major form of collateral, real estate. It was a simple, everyday way of assisting one's relatives, neighbours and friends.[30] However, it was also a form of assistance that could easily lead to thwarted hopes and frustration. Objects travelled down chains of credit in ways that made them difficult to retrieve for the owners. The debtor could find him or herself indebted both to the person who had lent the object and to the person who had provided the cash. Therefore, while essential and indispensable to everyone, such credit practices were also a potential source of discontent and dispute.

Chains of credit did not only arise as a result of practices such as hiding behind more creditworthy people. Even when the debtor was perfectly able to provide security for him- or herself, the pawned objects could subsequently be passed on to third parties, creating larger networks of interdependence. For instance, a Stockholm furrier and his wife pawned some valuable clothing to a lieutenant and in return obtained a loan of 120 *daler*. When they wanted to redeem their pawn in 1748, the lieutenant was unable to produce it. He had, it transpired, used the clothing to raise cash from a (to us) anonymous person. In a similar way, a golden ring travelled as pawn from one person to another in the 1690s. First pledged by the wife of a lower state servant to another wife, the ring was then deposited in the local church as security for an 18 *daler* loan. The ring was then redeemed by another state servant who in his turn transferred it to the mayor of Örebro.[31]

Since these arrangements were never systematically registered, the main way we can learn of their existence is by reading the court records closely. It is the credit

[28] Fagerlund, *Handel och vandel*, p. 116.

[29] Korda, *Labors Lost*, pp. 45f, 54–92; Hardwick, *Family Business*, p. 156.

[30] For other examples. see Uppsala, Landsarkivet, Örebro Rådhusrätt och magistrat, court record, 24 March 1690; Örebro Kämnärsrätt, November, December 1684.

[31] GaW Database, cases 5267, 8411.

arrangements that went wrong that turn up in court records and so, we cannot use this information to quantify how common it was to lend security to others in these informal ways. What these cases do show, however, is that collateral of some kind, whether material or symbolic, was of paramount importance even in small-scale credit transactions and that people found ways — although sometimes risky and precarious — of providing such security.

Were there any connections between this micro-level of credit and the larger and more formalized macro-level on which early modern companies and states acted? How did creditors ensure the security of their loans when actors and institutions unknown to each other interacted in more complex credit relationships? British scholarship has shown that macro- and micro-levels were directly connected and became increasingly integrated in the early modern period. Women's investment of capital in commercial and state enterprises played a central role in this process.[32] Both women and men bought stocks, shares, and bonds, as for instance their inventories and wills show, and in this way they both strengthened the early modern state and became dependent on it. Credit integrated society, as John Brewer has argued.[33] There is new research for early nineteenth-century Sweden suggesting that here too women and men invested in state bonds,[34] but we know less about these connections for the early modern period and little about their integrative function. In the following section, more formalized credit will be in focus, credit that was extended by individual people or larger credit institutions. The focus will be on how credit connections linked people in local societies, how borrowers provided security, and what role women could play in these contexts.

Old and New Ways of Providing Security

Early modern state formation had a decisive impact on credit markets. Across Europe, ambitious and aggressive states sought to expand their military capacity and for this, they needed financial resources. As cash was often hard to come by, states had to devise methods that encouraged owners of capital to lend their money on shorter or longer terms. The voluminous literature on state formation describes in detail how different states chose different methods; England was famous for its

[32] Laurence, Maltby, and Rutterford, *Women and their Money*.

[33] Brewer, *Sinews of Power*, pp. 182–90. See also Tilly, *Coercion, Capital*, who also stresses the link between state formation, war-making, and access to credit.

[34] See for instance, Winton, 'Kvinnliga investerare'.

early and successful creation of a national debt, whereas France was infamous for the pervasive role of venality, that is, the sale of state offices.

People who were believed unable or unwilling to repay their private loans could have their good name tarnished, as Catarina Lenbom's case bears witness to, and the same was true of states. The French and Spanish states had problems raising credit after they had defaulted on a large scale in the sixteenth century.[35] In Sweden too, there was awareness at the highest level of state that creditors had to feel safe if the credit market was to flourish. The patchiness with which the national legal code treated credit was perceived to be a problem. Dating back to 1350, the legal code said very little about the recovery of debt and how the relationship between debtor and creditor was to be balanced. While it was clearly misleading to claim, as some seventeenth-century lawyers did, that people in the Middle Ages did not resort to credit but always paid up front, it is true that the medieval legal regulation of credit was insufficient and did cause conflicts in the seventeenth century.[36]

After years of legal and political debate, where the interest of providing incentives to creditors was weighed against the need to protect debtors, a new credit law saw the light. It is telling that when King Charles XI commented on the new rules in 1684, he said that 'if any damage is to ensue from this [new legislation], then it is better that he suffers, who has an obligation to another man, than he, who in good faith lent of his own'. His words suggest that hereafter it was the interests of creditors that the law should heed, rather than those of debtors.[37]

State formation thus brought about an intensified interest in credit law and some strategically important reforms were carried out to improve the situation of creditors. Issues of security became crucial. The background was both that the state needed to improve its own creditworthiness and that a well-functioning credit market was increasingly seen as a vital part of a well-functioning society. But the interest was not restricted to reform of credit law; it also involved a commitment to improving access to credit and making better use of existing capital. For instance, Salomon von Otter, the administrative head of the navy in the 1690s, acquired permission from the king to use accumulated capital to set up a small loans bank in the port town of Karlskrona. According to von Otter's autobiography, it was impossible at this time to deposit large amounts of capital against interest in the recently established Bank of Sweden (set up in 1668, twenty-six years before the

[35] Ertman, *Birth of the Leviathan*, p. 98.

[36] Ågren, *Domestic Secrets*, Chapter 3.

[37] Ågren, *Domestic Secrets*, Chapter 3, esp. p. 74. For an analysis of the credit legislation as a whole, see Ågren, *Jord och gäld*, pp. 40–62.

Bank of England). In order to make the capital 'fertile', von Otter's bank lent it out at interest, provided that the borrower could post security in the form of 'silver, gold, jewellery, copper, tin' but not at this time in the form of 'house or manor'.[38]

The early years of the Bank of Sweden were fraught with problems.[39] Still, the bank did extend credit and people did avail themselves of this possibility. Even if most customers belonged to the nobility, the bank was not at all unwilling to give small loans to people of less elevated status. The first loan was for instance given to a clergyman who borrowed 50 *daler* silver, with a silver jug as security. The bank also extended loans as small as 3 *daler* silver and, on one occasion, the board of directors explicitly stated that it was 'necessary not to say no to poor people who need credit'.[40] In the 1690s, the bank established short-lived branch offices in Falun, Gothenburg and Örebro, probably because these places were commercial hubs for the Swedish iron industry. A detailed analysis of the bank's customers remains to be carried out but it is clear that both men and women were among its customers.[41] The fact that pawns were used to provide security for the Bank of Sweden (as well as for von Otter's bank) shows how even comparatively large institutions had to securitize loans in ways not dissimilar to the one used in small-scale credit networks.

For it was not only that people pawned their own property to get bank loans. Just as in small-scale credit networks, security could be borrowed from others in the form of movable property, and people also used others as intermediaries, largely for their 'good name.' In Örebro, city councilor Petter Nalleen wanted to borrow 300 copper *daler* from the Bank of Sweden in the 1690s. Since Nalleen apparently lacked resources that could be used as security, he had asked his friend customs official Anders Månsson Lind to borrow the money on his behalf, which he did with his own property as collateral. It is not clear what this property consisted of. However, we know from previous research that state servants such as customs officials and postmasters were often very active in the credit market because they had access to both networks of information and state capital.[42] Therefore, it is not surprising that Anders Månsson Lind played the role of stand-in for Nalleen.[43] The reason why

[38] Salomon von Otter, 'Landshöfdingen Bar: Salomon von Otters lefwernes beskrifning', pp. 126–27.

[39] See also Murphy, *The Origins of English Financial Markets*.

[40] Brisman, 'Den Palmstruchska banken', p. 157.

[41] On the early history of the Bank of Sweden, see Brisman, 'Den Palmstruchska banken', pp. 151-60, 168, 203–210.

[42] Droste, 'The Terms of Royal Service'; Ågren, *The State as Master*.

[43] Uppsala, Landsarkivet, Örebro Kämnärsrätt, A 1 vol. 7, February 1698.

he took the case to court seems to have been that he wanted it to be publicly known that he and Petter Nalleen had made this arrangement. The public announcement strongly suggests that the bank's local representatives knew who the real debtor was but did not mind having the customs official act as an intermediary.

These examples show that even a large state institution like the bank adapted to the practices of small-scale urban credit markets. Security for loans were demanded, but the bank accepted security in the form of small, portable objects — that were probably easy to steal and therefore suboptimal — or property that did not in fact belong to the debtor but to someone in their social network. Pawning and standing in for others were practices used both in transactions between people and in transactions between people and institutions. In many ways, the bank's early procedures for extending credit were shaky (later on, they started to require real property as security for loans), but they tapped into customary ways of providing security for oneself or for others.[44]

Another example of how state institutions adapted to small-scale credit arrangements is the use of guarantors. A guarantor was a person who promised to pay instead of the debtor, should the latter default on his debts. Guarantors were used in many contexts but in spite of this, guarantorship was poorly regulated in law. For instance, when a man applied for burgher rights in a city or town, he had to have guarantors who certified that he was a reliable and honorable person. Guarantors were also used to raise credit. Bodil, a married woman from Gävle, acted as guarantor for her sister Karin in the 1530s. Her sister had purchased textiles and other goods from a Stockholm merchant, to the value of 500 *marks*. Some decades later, Margrete Kocks acted as guarantor for her brother, also in Stockholm. When her brother's creditor demanded that she stand by her promise, Margrete's two guardians took action to annul the promise.[45]

The use of guarantors was picked up and widely used in the burgeoning state administration. Thus, employees of the state who were in charge of state money — typically bailiffs and customs officials but others as well — had to have one or several guarantors who provided security for them. If the bailiff failed to deliver the taxes he was in charge of, then his guarantors would have to step in and pay instead. This meant that, effectively, the state servants were considered to be temporary debtors of the state while they were responsible for the state's money.

[44] The exact extent to which women borrowed money from the bank has not been established but we do know that women were among the bank's customers. See ongoing work by Christopher Pihl, Uppsala University.

[45] GaW Database, cases 9389, 10195.

Without guarantors, the state would refuse to employ the man in question. Guarantors' securities were commonly called *caution* in Sweden and were given in writing. Both women and men can be found among those who provided *caution* for state employees, even if men were more common. For instance, when Hindrich von Schwaitz took up the position as customs inspector for the inland customs and excise at Blockhusudden, Stockholm, in July 1693, he had three guarantors, one of whom was Anna Stiernhöök. Similarly, when Anders Sahlin was given responsibility for the inland customs at Brattfors in 1694, he had five guarantors, one of whom was Ingrid Jönsdotter.[46] Many of the women appearing as providers of security were widows. It is probable that, originally, it was the couple who had provided the security but after the death of the husband, the widow was the one who appeared at court and in the historical records.

The state checked whether or not those who provided security for its employees were acceptable: local courts had to affirm that these people had sufficient wealth to guarantee the state incomes for which the state servant would become responsible. Before Sven Schening was accepted as customs official in Örebro (in the 1690s), he had to have his guarantors Lars Schening and Nicolaus Jönter vetted and approved by the court. The mayor of Örebro, Magnus Callander, affirmed that Jönter had the necessary assets to be a guarantor, but was unable to say anything certain about Lars Schening as he did not live in town but in another part of the country. Callander did, however, report that according to rumour, Lars Schening was well-off.[47] Once again, we see how the mechanisms for providing security for creditors tapped into traditional and informal methods of spreading information about creditworthiness. In this case, the state did not trust Sven Schening but it had little option but to trust the mayor and his sources of information.

In the 1690s and the early 1700s, the Swedish state was particularly preoccupied with whether the customs officials had *cautionister* who could be trusted. Year after year, long lists of guarantors were drawn up, and many officials were ordered to find new guarantors who could provide better security.[48] For instance, Hindrich von Schwaitz was ordered to get himself a new guarantor instead of Anna Stiernhöök (in 1695) who was apparently not thought to be wealthy enough. This

[46] Stockholm, Riksarkivet, Marieberg. Överdirektörens vid småtullarna och accisen arkiv, E 1, Kautioner. Vol. 6, pp. 77f, 153 f.

[47] Stockholm, Riksarkivet, Marieberg. Överdirektörens vid småtullarna och accisen arkiv, E 1, Kautioner. Vol. 6, pp. 203 f.

[48] Stockholm, Krigsarkivet. Kammarkollegium, Tull- och licentkontoret, F 1 vol. 9, 'Cautioners Beskaffenhet för Efterskrivna Tull-licent och Accis Betjänte' (1689). Similar inventories of *cautioner* were made every year until 1711.

was not an easy task, especially since the incomes from Blockhusudden, where von Schwaitz worked, were assessed in 1689 at 60,000 silver *daler*.[49] These were also war years and guarantors were not exactly queuing up to provide security. In the words of another seventeenth-century customs official, his friends were unwilling to provide security since 'they have been hard hit through promises they have given previously for bailiffs [...] and other servants of the crown'. The official said that he was ashamed to ask anyone for *caution* because they might think that he did not have the confidence of the crown.[50] There are examples of guarantors whose property was seized by the state and who had to seek compensation from the state servant.[51] In 1695, a government body (*Kammarkollegium*) demanded that all customs officials pledge their own property, and that their wives sign the pledge along with their husbands. In Arboga, for instance, Arvid Elfving and his wife Sara Johansdotter Arbman pledged their whole property: both movable and immovable property, both property they currently had and property they might acquire in the future.[52] These were very hard conditions indeed, and they show how coercion could be a significant component in credit relations. They also show women's involvement.

The demand for spouses to provide security together was a consequence of the perceived need to give creditors stronger legal rights. It was also consistent with how the state tended to make little of married women's rights to separate property in the late seventeenth century. Since the Middle Ages, a married woman's inherited landed property had automatically been defined as her separate property. It was 'automatic' in the sense that the protection was there even if there was no pre-nuptial agreement or other form of contract. This rule was not born out of a medieval awareness of women's precarious situation and a wish to strengthen their individual property rights; instead, it was an expression of the importance Swedish law attached to protecting lineage property and making sure that such property did not easily leave the kin group. But as a side effect, married women's rights to their inherited property were in fact relatively secure. Such property was part of the marital economy and the head of household — usually the husband — did manage it. He did not, however, have the right to sell such property unless certain conditions were fulfilled. Among these conditions, the most important one was the requirement that the wife and her

49 Krigsarkivet. Kammarkollegium, Tull- och licentkontoret, F 1 vol. 9.

50 Smith, *Studier i svensk tulladministration*, II, p. 127.

51 Uppsala, Landsarkivet, Örebro Rådhusrätt och magistrat, court records, 22 September and 20 October 1656, pp. 211, 218.

52 Riksarkivet, Marieberg. Överdirektörens vid småtullarna och accisen arkiv, E 1, Kautioner. Vol. 7.

relatives give prior consent to the sale. Without such consent, the husband could not proceed to sell her land. Consequently, if he used his wife's land as security for his loans, this was a poor form of security from the creditor's point of view. The wife and her relatives always had the right to veto such sales.[53]

In a society where people must have lent each other security all the time, and where family networks were ubiquitous, the rules pertaining to married women's inherited landed property could be seen as an anomaly. Would not a spouse and her relatives be among the first people to turn to if one needed someone to provide security for a loan? The use of guarantors certainly suggests that this was the case. It is possible that in many cases the wife and her kinsmen did not use their veto right but readily gave their consent to using land as collateral, or even to its eventual sale. This is not something we can investigate in a systematic manner since neither agreement nor refusal to a sale normally left a paper-trail in the archives. We do however find examples of consequences that could ensue, both when consent was given and when it was withheld. Wills and probate inventories occasionally include meticulous information on property that had been amicably transferred from wife to husband. The fact that people kept track of such transfers shows that the idea of keeping spouses' property separate and the need to protect the wife's interests, should this separation be impossible to uphold, were no empty letters of the law. Legal disputes also bear witness to the importance attached to married women's separate property.[54]

Seen from the point of view of real estate law, rather than credit law and credit practice, the kin veto was not an anomaly at all. Before the 1720s, Swedish real estate law gave kinsmen a far-reaching right of first refusal whenever a piece of land was offered for sale to someone outside the kin group.[55] The right of first refusal was a well-established legal principle,[56] and the right of kinsmen to veto the sale of 'their' land by a man who had married into the lineage was simply a special case of a generally accepted principle.

With the increasing concerns in the late seventeenth century about the allegedly inadequate legal protection of creditors, the kin veto came to be seen as an obstacle to credit. How could a creditor know whether a particular piece of land belonged

[53] Theoretically, there was also the option of using the spouses' common property as security for loans. Whether the wife's part of such property could be used or not was however a bone of contention. Ågren, *Domestic Secrets*.

[54] Ågren, *Domestic Secrets*, pp. 100–39.

[55] GaW Database, case 9526.

[56] Kinsmen's right of first refusal was called *bördsrätt* and was not abolished until the mid-nineteenth century. See Winberg, *Grenverket*.

to the wife or to the husband? The creditor would observe what lands the man, who wanted to borrow money, had in his possession and assume that they could all be regarded as security. The creditor would then be very unpleasantly surprised if the man failed to repay and the land proved impossible to seize as the wife and her kinsmen refused to allow it. Regardless of whether or not this was a wide-spread problem in practice, this was the kind of situation legislators liked to put forward when arguing that the kin veto had to be abolished.

And in the end they won the argument. In the new national legal code promulgated in 1734, the kin veto was no longer there. The husband still had to have his wife's (but not her relatives') consent if he wanted to sell her inherited lands, and the code mentioned that the judge could have a private conversation with the wife if he feared that the husband had used coercion to obtain her consent. Nevertheless, the legal protection of married women's rights to separate property was from now on re-structured with a view to improving the security of creditors. In effect, it made it easier for husbands to borrow security from their wives.[57] The law was now less interested in protecting the debtors — in line with the principle formulated by King Charles XI — and, although possibly involuntarily, it also took away rights previously vested in married women and their kinsmen.

Simultaneously with the abolition of the kin veto, new legal technologies were developed with a view to keeping track of debts and, more precisely, of the order in which creditors were to be compensated. An early example of this was the way in which those who extended credit to ironmasters could have his or her claim registered at court so as to have a preferential right.[58] The method of registering claims was gradually adopted outside the iron-producing sector as well. In the seventeenth-century urban economy, for example, we find many cases of ordinary people going to the local court to have their claims recorded. Thus, the wife of the vicar in Wallersta had her claim on Anders Olofsson's widow for 28.5 copper *daler* recorded in the magistracy court of Örebro in the 1690s. Others who recorded their claims in the same court were Eric Swensson who had extended a loan of 60 copper *daler* to Anna Pärsdotter, and Petter Rosendahl who had bought a promissory note of 60 copper *daler*, money that had originally been extended by Jeremias Skiutz to Beata Seenquist.[59] As mentioned above, Anders Månsson Lind also made his three-partite credit arrangement public.

[57] Ågren, *Domestic Secrets*.

[58] This type of arrangement was known at the time as *förlag*, a meaning the word does not have today when *förlag* means publishing house. See Munktell, *Bergsmans- och bruksförlag*.

[59] GaW Database, cases 7241, 7261, 8421.

The method later (from 1730) became known as *inteckning*, literally 'inscription', that is, in the court record. Only real estate could be subject to *inteckning*, which was a form of mortgage. The debt was secured with collateral, however, the collateral was not transferred to the creditor but remained in the hands of the owner. Just as in the iron industry, creditors whose claims were secured through *inteckning* would have a preferential right to compensation, should the debtor default.[60] The Bank of Sweden tried to secure its claims on debtors' property by using this method. Before the loan was granted, careful investigations of the value of the collateral were carried out. Many burgher families in Örebro raised capital with their urban properties as security in the 1750s, 1760s and 1770s.[61] In the same way, farmers in southern Dalecarlia raised capital with their farms as security.[62]

The point of mortgage-like arrangements like the ones just described was precisely to create security for creditors. It was expected that, in contrast to methods such as pawning of movable or immovable property, the new arrangements would allow for more flexibility. Creditors would, it was hoped, have complete security for their lent-out capital without having to take over the time-consuming management of the property. Creditors would not have to fear that the collateral was being sold behind the creditor's back. In practice, it did not always work in this way. In 1768, for instance, representatives of the Bank of Sweden complained that courts did not always make sure that the bank's interests were well protected. Despite the fact that the bank did have land as security for many of its loans, owners/debtors were apparently able to sell the land in question to others. In connection with this complaint, the Royal Court of Appeals in Stockholm issued a clarifying statement in 1776, to the effect that all mortgages be noted in the ordinary court records, so that owners/debtors were prevented from using the same piece of property as collateral for several loans.[63]

Conclusion

Credit markets do not work without mechanisms for providing security. Such mechanisms do not, however, have to take the formalized and impersonal form

[60] Ågren, *Jord och gäld*, pp. 47–50.

[61] Uppsala, Landsarkivet, Örebro rådhusrätt och magistrat, bouppteckningar och arvskiften [probate inventories], vols 9 (1756–1760), 11 (1767–1771), 12 (1772–1777).

[62] Ågren, *Jord och gäld*, p. 123.

[63] Ågren, *Jord och gäld*, p. 49.

that we associate with modern societies. Early modern credit markets developed mechanisms of their own to provide security for creditors. People with small means could borrow security from others in the form of movable property, such as silver items. They could also hide themselves behind others, whose reputation was better than their own and who could therefore act as stand-ins. In these ways, people who lacked economic and social capital could nevertheless get access to credit that may have been essential to their survival. For larger economic commitments, there were other methods. People acted as guarantors for each other, for instance when they wanted to obtain state offices or become members of urban communities. Credit arrangements could be publicly declared in local societies, and information about credit and debt was spread by brokers and by word of mouth.

To provide security for others, one had to have resources: economic resources, social connections, knowledge, authority, and a good name. Obviously, a considerable number of women had such resources, as their active involvement in credit markets shows. They stood in for others who were less creditworthy, they lent their good names to others, they protested when their good names were questioned, they acted as guarantors and, if their kinsmen approved, they could use their inherited property to improve their husbands' creditworthiness. They also borrowed and lent, assessed the values of pawned objects and acted as facilitators. But not all women had such resources and not all women could provide security. While it is impossible to say with any degree of certainty whether it was only middling and elite women who carried out these tasks, it is likely (judging both by previous research and by the evidence presented here) that most women active in credit markets were married or widowed. Marital status had a decisive impact upon Swedish women's economic agency.

It is possible that predictability was improved during this period. One indication is the fixing of nominal legal interest at between 5 and 6 per cent in 1687.[64] Of course, interest rates had existed before and interest rates could be manipulated after 1687.[65] Other indications of increased predictability are the incremental changes in credit law that enhanced the position of creditors. The use of mortgages to protect claims secured by real estate is a good example. Still, a larger-scale credit institution like the Bank of Sweden long relied on what would seem to be old-fashioned methods for providing security. Initially, the bank lent out its capital against

[64] Ågren, *Jord och gäld*, pp. 42–47.

[65] Around 1800, interest rates were higher; Ågren, *Jord och gäld*, p. 120. See also ongoing work on the early days of the Bank of Sweden by Patrik Winton, Peter Ericsson, and Christopher Pihl, Uppsala University.

pawned objects. In the eighteenth century, the bank still had problems with insufficient protection of its claims.

Transparency and publicity were seen as crucial for the creation of trust in the credit market. Ideally, everyone should easily be able to find information about the creditworthiness of others. Everyone should also be able to find out the extent to which property was encumbered by claims from creditors with preferential rights. Evidence could be found in the court records. Publicity was, however, a sensitive issue. Social groups who were highly dependent on credit, like the nobility, were opposed to the public flaunting of their economic situation precisely because it might undermine their good names.[66] While not a noblewoman, this was also the kind of concern Catarina Lenbom voiced when the Wigart couple undermined her reputation by taking their dispute about a pawned object to court. Regardless of whether we look at credit practices on the level of local communities or at the systemic level of credit law, there was a tension between the quest for transparency on the one hand and the need for loans and protection of reputation on the other hand.

With the growth of early modern states, significant changes took place in credit markets, and Sweden was no exception. In order to improve the conditions of creditors, the traditional ways of protecting married women's inherited property were curtailed. Henceforth, it was easier for husbands to squander or sell their spouses' inherited land. More importantly, husbands could use such property as a source of security when they acted in the credit market. The state also made formal promises of security (*caution*) compulsory for state servants who handled money. These demands created strong bonds between the state, its employees and their guarantors, among whom women were also to be found. The bonds were stronger but also, if the state servant failed to deliver the taxes on time, potentially very destructive for the guarantors. Whether we consider the customs official wives who had to sign pledges with their husbands or the woman who was persuaded to lend a silver bowl behind her husband's back, social pressure and coercion were part of many early modern credit relations. Both women and men were affected by these coercive structures. The implication is that 'trust' is an insufficient theoretical concept when analysing early modern credit. People did not just extend credit because they trusted the other party or the institutional framework. Sometimes, they extended credit even though they lacked trust, simply because they had to.

[66] Ågren, *Jord och gäld*, p. 50.

Works Cited

Manuscripts

Stockholm, Riksarkivet Marieberg, Överdirektörens vid småtullarna och accisen arkiv, Kautioner

Stockholm, Krigsarkivet. Kammarkollegium, Tull- och licentkontoret

Uppsala, Landsarkivet, Örebro Accisrätt

Uppsala, Landsarkivet, Örebro Kämnärsrätt

Uppsala, Landsarkivet, Örebro Rådhusrätt och magistrat, Court records

Uppsala, Landsarkivet, Örebro Rådhusrätt och magistrat, Probate inventories

Primary Sources

Gender and Work Database, <http://gaw.hist.uu.se>

Salomon von Otter, 'Landshöfdingen Bar: Salomon von Otters lefwernes beskrifning'. Published in *Det swenska biblioteket*, utgifwit af Carl Christoffer Gjörwell. Stockholm 1–6, 1757–61, Del 3 (Stockholm: Nyström & Stolpe, 1759)

Secondary Studies

Ågren, Maria, 'Att lösa ekonomiska tvister — domstolarnas främsta sysselsättning på 1700-talet?', *Historisk Tidskrift*, 108 (1988), 481–511

———, *Domestic Secrets: Women and Property in Sweden, 1600–1857* (Chapel Hill: UNC Press, 2009)

———, *Jord och gäld: Social skiktning och rättslig konflikt i södra Dalarna ca 1650–1850* (Uppsala: Uppsala University, 1992)

———, ed., *Making a Living, Making a Difference: Gender and Work in Early Modern European Society* (New York: Oxford University Press, 2017)

———, *The State as Master: Gender, State Formation and Commercialisation in Urban Sweden, 1650–1780* (Manchester; Manchester University Press, 2017)

Andersson, Gudrun, *Tingets kvinnor och män: Genus som norm och strategi under 1600- och 1700-tal* (Uppsala: Uppsala University, 1998)

Brewer, John, *The Sinews of Power: War, Money and the English State, 1688–1783* (London: Unwin Hyman, 1989)

Brisman, Sven, 'Den Palmstruchska banken och Riksens ständers bank under den karolinska tiden', in *Sveriges riksbank 1668–1918: Bankens tillkomst och verksamhet* (Stockholm: Norstedts, 1918), pp. 81–230

Dermineur, Elise, 'Trust, Norms of Cooperation, and the Rural Credit Market in Eighteenth-Century France', *Journal of Interdisciplinary History*, 45.5 (2015), 485–506

Droste, Heiko, 'The Terms of Royal Service: Post Servants' Finances, c. 1700', in *Connecting the Baltic Area: The Swedish Postal System in the Seventeenth Century*, ed. by Heiko Drotse (Huddinge; Södertörns högskola, 2011), pp. 123–74

Erickson, Amy L., 'Coverture and Capitalism', *History Workshop Journal* 59 (2005), 1–16

Ertman, Thomas, *Birth of the Leviathan: Building States and Regimes in Medieval and Early Modern Europe* (Cambridge: Cambridge University Press, 1997)

Fagerlund, Solveig, *Handel och vandel: Vardagslivets sociala struktur ur ett kvinnoperspektiv. Helsingborg ca 1680–1709* (Lund: Lund University, 2002)

Franzén, Bo, *Sturetidens monetära system: Pant eller penningar som information i köpstaden Arboga* (Stockholm: Stockholm University, 1998)

Froide, Amy, 'Marital Status as a Category of Analysis', in *Singlewomen in the European Past, 1250–1800*, ed. by Amy Froide (Philadelphia: University of Pennsylvania Press, 1999)

———, *Silent Partners: Women as Public Investors during Britain's Financial Revolution, 1690–1750* (Oxford: Oxford University Press, 2016)

Hardwick, Julie, *Family Business: Litigation and the Political Economies of Daily Life in Early Modern France* (Oxford: Oxford University Press, 2009)

Hunt, Margaret R., *Women in Eighteenth-Century Europe* (New York: Pearson Longman, 2009)

Israelsson, Jezzica, '"For I willingly acknowledge the debt, and have never denied to pay it": Widows, Wives and Single Women as Creditors and Debtors in 18th-Century Uppsala' (Unpublished paper presented at the Urban History conference in Helsinki 2016)

Laurence, Anne, Josephine Maltby, and Janette Rutterford, eds, *Women and their Money 1700–1950: Essays on Women and Finance* (London: Routledge, 2009)

Lindström, Jonas, and others, '"Mistress or Maid": The Structure of Women's Work in Sweden, 1550–1800', *Continuity and Change* 32.2 (2017), 225–52

Korda, Natasha, *Labors Lost: Women's Work and the Early Modern English Stage* (Philadelphia: University of Pennsylvania Press, 2011)

Muldrew, Craig, *The Economy of Obligation: The Culture of Credit and Social Relations in Early Modern England* (Basingstoke: Macmillan, 1998)

Munktell, Henrik, *Bergsmans- och bruksförlag intill 1748 års förlagsförordning* (Uppsala: Uppsala universitets årsskrift, 1934)

Murphy, Anne L., *The Origins of English Financial Markets: Investment and Speculation before the South Sea Bubble* (Cambridge: Cambridge University Press, 2009)

Smith, William, *Studier i svensk tulladministration, II: Tulltjänsten i landsorten på Kristinas tid* (Stockholm: Sveriges allmänna tulltjänstemannaförenings skriftserie, 1955)

Spence, Catherine, *Women, Credit, and Debt in Early Modern Scotland* (Manchester: Manchester University Press, 2016)

Spicksley, Judith M., '"Fly with a Duck in thy Mouth": Single Women as Sources of Credit in Seventeenth-Century England', *Social History* 32 (2007), 187–207

Tilly, Charles, *Coercion, Capital, and European States, AD 990–1990* (Oxford: Blackwell, 1990)

Winberg, Christer, *Grenverket: Studier rörande jord, släktskapssystem och ståndsprivilegier*. Rättshistoriskt bibliotek, vol. 38 (Stockholm: Institutet för rättshistoriska studier, 1985)

Winton, Patrik, 'Kvinnliga investerare i den svenska statsskulden 1800–1808', in *Allt på ett bräde: Stat, ekonomi och bondeoffer*, ed. by Peter Ericsson, and others (Uppsala: Uppsala universitet, 2013), pp. 117–28

Women's Participation in Rural Copyhold Mortgages in Seventeenth-Century England

Juliet Gayton

In October 1606, the manorial court of Meonstoke in Hampshire recorded that a copyholder Bridgit Nicholl, wife of Owen, having been alone and secretly examined by the estate steward, willingly and without compulsion, and with the consent of her husband, surrendered up a close (i.e., an enclosed piece of land) called Shawford containing ten acres. The land was surrendered to Edward Eyles of the nearby village of Exton. However, a condition was placed on the surrender, whereby if she, or her husband, should pay to Edward the sum of £30 a year later, then the surrender would be void. In undertaking this surrender, Bridgit became the first recorded mortgage borrower in Meonstoke — and she was female.[1]

This surrender was significant for a number of reasons. Firstly it demonstrates the use of land as security to obtain credit only a few years after changes to the English laws of usury had made it easier to do so. Secondly, historiography has suggested that most married women could not own land at this time, and yet this land was clearly held by Bridgit, and she could use it as collateral for a loan. Thirdly, the agreement was made and recorded at a lord's manor court because Brigit held her

[1] Winchester, Winchester College Archives (WC) Court Book (CB) 23047, p. 92.

Juliet Gayton is an independent researcher with a focus upon rural history in seventeenth-century England, in particular land tenure and land transfer, including temporary transfers for sub-tenure and mortgages.

Women and Credit in Pre-Industrial Europe, ed. by Elise M. Dermineur, EER 12 (Turnhout: Brepols, 2018), pp. 143–172.
BREPOLS PUBLISHERS DOI 10.1484/M.EER-EB.5.115752

land by 'copyhold of inheritance' tenure which was very widespread at that time, but which no longer exists. The court roll records therefore provide a rich, quasi land registry, documentary source of copyholder mortgage agreements which has rarely been tapped before. This article will use manorial data collected from Meonstoke and Crawley, two rural villages in the southern English county of Hampshire. However, the results should be applicable to copyholders of inheritance in the rest of England.

The context of Bridgit's action was that credit using inter-personal lending reached something of a zenith in seventeenth-century England. The reform of the usury laws in the late sixteenth century created a new freedom to charge a certain amount of interest on loans, which had not been legally possible before, so that a flowering of borrowing and investment resulted after 1598.[2] However, formal financial institutional lending only emerged after the founding of the Bank of England in 1694 in what has been termed the Financial Revolution; therefore, most activity in the credit market of this century was via person to person arrangements. Holderness, Spicksley, and Muldrew identified the different types of credit options available to borrowers and lenders during the century, while Froide has detailed the many new opportunities that arose after it.[3] Before the 1690s, the main instruments included formal bills, bonds, and mortgages, or informal pawns, trade and sales credits, overdue rents and wages. After 1694 the formal options expanded exponentially to include stock and share options in the Bank of England in companies such as the East India and South Sea, city corporations, and state and charity lotteries.[4]

This research focusses on the pre-Financial Revolution period wherein bonds, bills, and mortgages were the only formal credit instruments, and of these mortgages were agreed in large number between freeholders. However, there was another land tenure of copyhold and Tawney commented that copyholder mortgages were a popular option as the manor court records provided an open and public record of the agreement (as distinct from the individual and often hidden deeds between freeholders).[5] Moreover, they were less costly because there were no legal charges in either drawing them up or seeking redress for unpaid monies as there were with

[2] 'Usury Acts 13 Eliz. 1 C8 and 31 Eliz.1 C18' (1571 & 1598). These initially permitted interest up to 10 per cent.

[3] Holderness, 'Credit in English Rural Society'; Spicksley, "Fly with a Duck in thy Mouth"; Spicksley, 'Usury Legislation, Cash and Credit'; Muldrew, *The Economy of Obligation*; Froide, *Never Married*; Froide, *Silent Partners*.

[4] Froide, *Silent Partners*, p. 3.

[5] Tawney, 'The Rise of the Gentry', p. 20.

most bills and bonds. Despite this, most previous authors studying credit have only given copyholder mortgages a passing mention, and have focussed on probate records for their documentary sources, in which very few mortgages were found. Muldrew, for example, found that a mere four out of 1352 probate accounts from Hampshire contained a mortgage.[6] The role of the copyholder mortgage in the seventeenth-century credit market is therefore due for re-examination, particularly in relation to female participation.[7]

Holderness concluded that 'moneylending was a fully developed feature of relatively remote rural areas by the mid seventeenth century if not earlier'.[8] In this context the article will explore the nature and extent of women's participation in both borrowing and lending mortgages in rural England in the long seventeenth century (1600–1735). Specifically, it will examine the borrowing practices of female copyholders, and the lending patterns of women who provided mortgage loans to both male and female copyholders. The two groups of borrowers and lenders were different, and the issues affecting them were not the same, so this article will address them in turn.

Female Borrowers: Access to Land

The mortgage was a credit instrument in which land was used as collateral, so access to, and rights of, landholding was an essential prerequisite.[9] Traditional historiography has suggested that English women had almost no access to land in the early modern period, unless it was freehold or they were single or widows, because the common law rule of coverture regarded a married woman as one entity with her husband. She therefore had no separate possessions, unless specifically identified in a pre-marriage contract.[10] Erickson has examined how coverture operated in reality, and found that women's perceptions of their possessions and their legal

[6] Muldrew, *The Economy of Obligation*, p. 105 Table 4.1.

[7] Copyholder mortgages for all genders are examined in Gayton, 'Mortgages Raised'. Some copyhold/tenant right mortgages were found in French and Hoyle, 'The Land Market of a Pennine Manor'.

[8] Holderness, 'Credit in English Rural Society', p. 106.

[9] The term 'land' will be used throughout to include all real estate, whether it was only land, or a dwelling or a combination of both.

[10] In fact her husband only gained a life interest and afterwards it would return to the widow or her heirs.

entitlement were not necessarily the same thing.[11] So a day-to-day reality and pragmatism gave many women effective ownership, while the fiction of coverture was preserved. Hence in the opening example of Brigit Nicholl, the court record refers to her acting 'with permission of her husband', so that couverture was nominally complied with.

During the period between about 1400 and 1840 the three most common forms of land tenure in England were freehold, leasehold, and copyhold. Of these, copyhold was the most widespread in many rural areas. It was referred to as a 'customary tenure' because the landholders were tenants of the lord of the manor, and their rights to hold their property were 'according to the custom of the manor' — which customs were set out for each manor. They paid a sub-market rate of rent to the lord plus fines and heriots for any changes such as death and inheritance, or sale and purchase of holdings. A tenant's entitlements were enshrined in a copy of the relevant court roll entry, hence the term 'copyhold'.

Within this tenure system, single and widowed women could be tenants in their own right. They could inherit by custom or a will; they could purchase, sublease the land, or use it as collateral for a mortgage loan.[12] Married women could also become copyholders, and enjoy similar rights to land, provided that their husbands were involved to comply with coverture. The way in which this worked varied in the manors studied according to the preferred policy of the lord. The Bishop of Winchester (who owned Crawley) was the most conservative and required newly married female tenants to surrender their land to their husbands in court. Thereafter they came to court with their husbands. Later in the seventeenth century this relaxed, and it became common in Crawley for marriage settlements to be enacted in the manorial court to provide a joint ownership, which was probably a way of circumventing coverture restrictions. Couples then attended court jointly. Winchester College (who owned Meonstoke) were less stringent lords. Married women were not required to surrender their property to their husbands, but if they came to court then their husbands merely accompanied them. In both cases the woman was then privately pre-examined '*sola and secret*', as in the case of Bridgit Nichol, to check for coercion. Finally, married women in all manors who did not have land in their own right, could, if widowed, enjoy their former husband's premises during

[11] Erickson, 'Possession', p. 379.

[12] 'Custom' of inheritance usually identified the next heir as a son or, in the absence of sons, a daughter. All the Hampshire manors of study had inheritance to the youngest child or 'Borough English'.

their widowhood, provided that they did not remarry.[13] If they wished to obtain a mortgage loan they usually brought the heir-in-waiting with them. The embargo on remarriage will emerge later as an important factor for some widows as it meant that they had to find a way to support themselves and their children without the resources of a new husband.

Mechanisms of Mortgage Borrowing

All the procedures for agreeing a mortgage loan by a copyholder had to take place in the manor court as the matter was considered to be a form of temporary transfer of rights and entitlement, and only to be enacted with the lord's agreement. The mechanism was the conditional surrender as illustrated by Bridgit Nicholl. By the seventeenth century the borrowing tenant usually kept and used their property during the term of the mortgage. It was not passed to the lender. If problems arose then the matter was brought to the manor court; if they failed to pay it was technically forfeit to the lender, but this rarely happened. The lords were fairly lenient for a while if repayment was delayed.[14]

So when copyholder mortgages became popular with the tenantry after the final amendments to the Usury statute in 1598, all these conditional surrenders were recorded and successful repayment ('satisfaction') was usually recorded too. Indeed, the Bishop of Winchester's estates had so very many to record that from 1598 he established a series of mortgage registers solely for that purpose.[15] The importance of these records cannot be overemphasized as they contain a record of *all* mortgages at the point of agreement. Many historians have had to rely on probate or litigation records for information, and these only exist for those mortgages which appear in an inventory or probate account or ended in dispute. They therefore provide only a partial picture with a snapshot of a credit history. Furthermore the litigation results have tended to give an undue impression that mortgages were chiefly used for crisis financing and desperate debt.

Unfortunately the survival of manorial records has been notoriously fragmented and patchy, but in the cases where a good long set of records does exist, they provide a remarkably full picture of land transfer behaviour. The research results presented here have been drawn from the extensive estate records of the Bishop of

13 A right sometimes called 'freebench'.

14 In the national background was the development of the equity of redemption which may have encouraged customary lords to more leniency.

15 Winchester, Hampshire Record Office (HRO) 11M59/C7/1 et seq.

Winchester, and Winchester College.[16] Both estates possess centuries of almost unbroken records. The mortgage records are therefore as complete as is possible for the time.

The Scale and Nature of Women's Mortgage Borrowing

Earlier research carried out by this author examined the whole copyhold tenantry and profiled all their land transfer activities during the second half of the seventeenth century in eight different manors in the chalk downlands of Hampshire.[17] The linear profiling and landholding reconstruction produced far more detailed information about the tenants than is usually available from a cursory charting of land sales or mortgage loans. This was invaluable background to mortgage borrowing activity, which could thus be placed in the context of what went before, and what happened to the land afterwards. Informed estimates could then be made as to why the tenants were borrowing.

Table 6.1 shows the profile of female tenants in the two manors. These were the women who had the ability and potential to borrow mortgages, because they had the appropriate landholding rights. The pattern within each manor was very similar throughout the century, so the average (mean) figures here are representative.[18]

Overall the villages had a remarkably uniform rate of total female tenant copyholders of about 24 per cent. Widows and married women who held land in their own right formed about 95 per cent of these female tenants in both manors.[19] There were few spinster tenants, and this may have been because the status was usually transitory. They had guardians whilst under twenty-two years of age, and mostly did not remain as spinsters for long after reaching their majority. The main difference between the manors can be seen with married women who held jointly

[16] Principal court roll series in: Winchester, HRO Bish 11M59/E1/125/3 to /143/1 and 11M59/C7/1/1/1–59, WC CBs 23047–58.

[17] Gayton, 'Tenants, Tenures and Transfers'.

[18] The Table and most of this article uses the term 'spinster' as this is how the manorial source documents described them. It would be incorrect to describe them as 'never-married' because they had not died, and may have married after their mortgage activity. The term 'single' would technically have to include widows too.

[19] As previously explained, Meonstoke married women technically had to take their husbands with them to court, but I have recorded them as holding in their 'own right' as they effectively did so.

Table 6.1. The mean profile of female copyhold tenants at any one time (seventeenth century). *Source:* Manorial court records augmented by taxation and probate records.

Female status		**Widowed**		**Spinster**	**Married**		**Mean total female**	**Mean manor total tenants**	**Mean % temale tenants**
		own right	*widowhood*		*own right*	*joint*			
Meonstoke	*Av No*	3	4	1	4	3	15.	63	*23.8*
	%	*20.0*	*26.7*	*6.7*	*26.7*	*20.0*			
Crawley	*Av No*	2	1	0	2	4	9	37	*24.3*
	%	*22.2*	*11.1*	*0*	*22.2*	*44.4*			
Total mean	*Av No*	5	5	1	6	7	24	100	*24*
	%	*20.8*	*20.8*	*4.2*	*25.0*	*29.2*			

with their husbands. There were more in Crawley, which reflects the Bishop's policy, mentioned earlier, of requiring single women to surrender to their husbands upon marriage, and the use of the pre-marriage settlement to create a joint ownership.

Turning specifically to mortgage activity, Table 6.2 shows how many different tenants actually borrowed using their land for a mortgage and how many mortgages they used.

Table 6.2. Numbers of different borrowers and mortgages showing gender division in Meonstoke and Crawley 1600–1735. *Source:* Manorial court rolls for Meonstoke and Crawley.

		No. of borrowers	% of gender	% of tenants*	No. of mortgages	% of gender	Mean no. mortgages per borrower
Female	**Widow**	6	*29*	*42*	13	*34*	2.2
	Spinster	3	*14*	*4*	8	*21*	2.7
	Married	12	*57*	*54*	17	*45*	1.4
Total female		21	*17*	*24*	38	*9*	1.8
Total male		103	*83*	*76*	369	*91*	3.8
Total all		124			407		

* Summary figures from bottom line of Table 6.1.

Although the sample size for women is small, the pattern shows that more than half of the female borrowers were married women, but this was in proportion to their greater presence as tenants. Widow borrowers were lower in number than their tenant proportion and spinsters higher. The married borrowers only borrowed once or twice; widows on average twice and spinsters a mean of almost three times, although the spinster sample is skewed by much borrowing by one person, Honor Collins of Meonstoke. In terms of total female compared with male, rather fewer women borrowed than their mean presence in the manor, and they only raised half as many mortgages each as the males. So the women were active, but not quite so active as the men.

The pattern through time of the volume of new mortgages agreed during the long seventeenth century, divided by gender, is shown in Figure 6.1 for Meonstoke.[20]

[20] Meonstoke had by far the larger number of tenants and mortgage borrowers so is the better sample size.

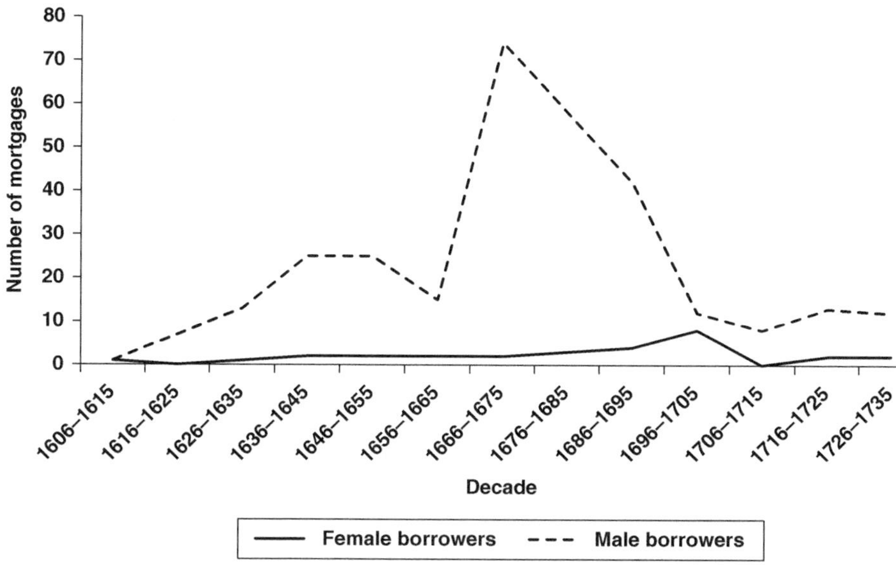

Figure 6.1. Volume of mortgages borrowed in Meonstoke by decade 1600–1735.

Female borrowing can be seen to have been continuous but very flat, apart from a small peak in the later 1690s. It does not show the high peaks and troughs of the male trends, which dipped during the Civil War and Commonwealth (1642–1660) and then peaked after the Restoration of the monarchy in the 1670s. Rather, it is one of continuous low level sustained activity, and does not appear to be responding to the same forces as those of the men. This may be a reflection of the reasons for borrowing explored later in this article. Both female and male mortgage activity declined noticeably in the early eighteenth century and this probably reflects the significant increase and diversification in credit instruments at that time. Borrowers then had far more options, and Froide has concluded that 'women were won over from land' (as an investment) during the Financial Revolution.[21] Although her comment related to lenders rather than borrowers, it seems possible that borrowers were diverted in the same way.

Some features of female borrowing were very similar to those of males: for example the length of term for repayment of a loan. Only 10 per cent of mortgages were for more than three years and only 5 per cent for less than one year. The length preferred was one, two or three years. So mortgages were being used for relatively short-term borrowing by both genders. Interest rates were similar and were capped

[21] Froide, *Silent Partners*, p. 119.

by Statute. The Acts of 1571–1598 set 10 per cent, which in 1624 was reduced to 8 per cent. By 1651 it was 6 per cent, and in 1713 it was reduced to 5 per cent. The pattern of the actual interest rates charged for the Meonstoke and Crawley mortgages adheres to these and did not differ by gender. The type of land and the size of acreage used as security for a mortgage also did not differ between males and females. Slightly more than half the mortgages used land only as collateral; 18 per cent used a dwelling only, and the remainder offered a dwelling and land.

There were small differences in the amount of principal raised in individual mortgages and these are summarized in Table 6.3. It shows that 55 per cent of all mortgages raised by both women and men were for less than £100; 79 per cent female and 83 per cent male were for under £200. It was only in amounts over £400 that women borrowers were absent, and there were very few (2 per cent) amongst the men. So the pattern of female borrowing was not significantly different from male in terms of the amount borrowed, and that £200 to £300 was the usual upper limit. It appears that the lenders probably set this limit, as any borrower who needed more than about £200 took out separate parallel mortgages using other parts of their landholding to acquire a higher total sum.[22]

Table 6.3. Amounts borrowed in each new mortgage, Meonstoke and Crawley 1600–1735. *Source:* Manorial mortgage records as before.

Amount borrowed	**Male***		**Female**				
	No.	*%*	*Wid*	*Spin*	*Mar*	*Total*	*%*
£500+	4	*1*					
£400–<£500	4	*1*					
£300–<£400	13	*3*			2	2	*5*
£200–<£300	43	*12*	4		2	6	*16*
£100–<£200	103	*28*	3	3	3	9	*24*
£50–<£100	83	*22*	2	3	4	9	*23.5*
£1–<£50	119	*33*	4	2	6	12	*31.5*
Totals	366		13	8	17	38	

* Three male mortgage amounts were not available for Meonstoke.

[22] No women took out multiple mortgages at the same time so this was a difference with male borrowers.

Muldrew discovered that credit relationships occurred 'all over the social scale', and the finding accords with those of Froide.[23] To test this, the occupations and social standing of all the mortgage borrowers were examined and were indeed variable, although most tenants fell into the middling levels of society. It was not, however, easy to carry out an analysis of the women separately as they were usually just described as 'widow' or 'spinster' in the records. Their relative wealth was probably indicated by the size of their land holding, which was in turn the basis for their borrowing. One woman held only half a cottage, whereas others held up to 100 acres, and there was no particular pattern or grouping by size.

Reasons for Mortgage Borrowing

The reasons why a person wanted to borrow with a mortgage are often unknown. The records of agreements, probates or litigation, usually just show the details of the contractual pair and the terms of repayment. There is little to suggest why the borrower may have needed credit. However, such information is important to an understanding of the nature of the credit market, if it can be discovered. The traditional view of mortgages has often been that they were primarily used in a crisis, but such a view was often formed when the only available documentary source was litigation.[24]

The mortgage analysis presented in this article had the advantage of the availability of results from an earlier background study of the copyholdings and tenants for the period 1645–1705.[25] This research used the manorial records to database all tenant land transfer activities, of which mortgages formed a part. Each copyholding was followed through the sixty-year period to see when changes occurred. These included events such as deaths and inheritance; sale and purchase; licences to sublet or rebuild; marriage settlements, and the conditional surrenders of mortgage. Parish registers then augmented the information about baptisms, marriages, and burials, and where wills were left, the probate records were used to find kin relationships and any legacies and debt at the time of death. Landholding and tenant profiles were then constructed and provided clues about what was happening in the tenant's life before, during, and after they were using mortgages. The

23 Muldrew, *The Economy of Obligation*, p. 97. Froide, *Silent Partners*, p. 64.

24 For example: Tawney, *The Agrarian Problem*.

25 Gayton, 'Tenants, Tenures and Transfers'.

profiles could then be used to make a reasoned estimate of why the copyholders may have needed credit at any particular time. Both male and female tenants featured in these results. The method is not without its inaccuracies, but the sixty-year profile of all tenants did provide a clear picture of the background to their mortgage activity in a way which is not normally available when studying merely lists of mortgage loans or probate and litigation records.

Five categories of motivation for borrowing were then identified.[26] They were to facilitate and help to fund a copyholder's need to:

- purchase a new property, or refurbishment or building costs of an existing one.
- save longer-term, or investment in business or commercial activity
- pay for marriage portions, marriage settlements, or upkeep of children
- distribute legacies and pay off inherited debt after someone had died
- cope with financial difficulties (often of an unspecified kind).

A sixth category of 'Not Known (NK)' contained those where an estimate could not be made of the motivation, and chiefly consisted of tenants who borrowed at the very beginning or end of the study period, and whose profile was therefore truncated. (So it was not known what may have led up to, or what happened after, the mortgage borrowing.) It is important to note that no evidence was found that the NK category would have differed in its distribution of motivation if further details of those copyholders could have been found. It was the timing of their mortgages which affected whether they were NK, and the timing showed no correlation between categories and date.

Table 6.4 summarizes these apparent reasons for each mortgage borrowed, divided by the gender of the borrower, and for women by their marital status. The results for females should be used with caution, as the sample sizes in individual categories are very small.

Overall, the table reveals a significantly different pattern between the reasons for female and male borrowing, apart from the purpose of purchasing property which was around 14 percent for both, and the category of financial difficulties which affected both around the level of 25 per cent. It is perhaps not surprising that a mean of 57 per cent of female borrowing (including 73 per cent for widows) was heavily focussed on family-related activity such as marriage or child support

[26] A fuller exploration of the ways these reasons were arrived at is given in Gayton, 'Mortgages Raised'.

Table 6.4. Estimated reasons for mortgage borrowing, Meonstoke and Crawley 1645–1705*. *Source:* Manorial records and tenant holding reconstructions as before.

Borrower	**Reasons**	**Purchase refurb or building**	**Business invest or savings**	**Marriage and/or children**	**Inherited legacies or debts**	**Financial difficulties**	**Not known (NK)**	**Total mortgages**
Female:								
Widow	*No.*	2	1	4	4			11
	%	*18%*	*9%*	*36.5%*	*36.5%*			
Spinster	*No.*	1		1	3	2		7
	%	*14%*		*14%*	*43%*	*29%*		
Married	*No.*	1			4	4	1	10
	%	*10%*			*40%*	*40%*	*10%*	
Total female		4	1	5	11	6	1	28
		14%	*4%*	*18%*	*39%*	*21%*	*4%*	
Total male	*No.*	42	77	11	35	73	62	300
	%	*14%*	*25.5%*	*4%*	*12%*	*24%*	*20.5%*	
Total all	*No.*	46	78	16	46	79	63	328
	%	*14%*	*24%*	*5%*	*14%*	*24%*	*19%*	

* Ten female and sixty-nine male mortgages in Table 6.2 fell outside the 1645–1705 period used here.

and dealing with legacies to children. By comparison, 16 per cent of male motivation was involved in these two categories, and the majority of that was for the payment of inherited debt after the decease of a parent. Only one woman, Mary Horner, who had to manage her husband's drapery business while a widow, borrowed for support to a business compared with between one quarter and one third of mortgages by men.

Some specific examples of female borrowing by category will serve to illustrate how the reasons were assessed. In the first category — to purchase or refurbish — this motive was assigned if the court rolls showed that a copyholder had just purchased a property before borrowing, or had requested a licence to build or refurbish a dwelling. Mary Bensteed was widowed in 1695 and inherited 'the north end of a mansion house with two rooms and a little garden at an annual rent of 12 pence', which her husband Henry had purchased in 1663.[27] Coincidentally, the occupier of the other half of the house also died in 1695 and so Mary decided to purchase it from the heir. The whole house and orchard were then united in one ownership by 1697. The price of a cottage in Meonstoke at that time was between £20 and £40, and so this purchase is thought to be why Mary immediately borrowed £20 in a mortgage over a three-year term at 5 per cent interest.[28] She offered the whole house as security to Daniel Budd, a yeoman of neighbouring Exton, but after only a year she paid back the loan.

A few borrowers were assessed to have been borrowing to support the bringing up of children and providing marriage portions, but were chiefly widows. This is not surprising, because when a male copyholder died, his widow was not allowed to remarry unless she forfeited the property, so most did not seek a new marriage to help to pay for the upkeep of young children. They had to rely on legacies, which may not have been sufficient either for the payment of grants named in the husband's will, or for the upkeep of children before reaching their age of majority. An example was provided by Margaret Wayte of Crawley who inherited a house and forty-four acres from her father, when she was a child. In 1662 she married a Richard Carter and baptized a daughter and a son, but within ten years she was a widow with two young children. By 1679, the daughter would have been a teenager growing to a marriageable age and in 1679 Margaret used all her Crawley land as security for a mortgage loan of £80 at 6 per cent interest for three years.[29] After that mortgage she agreed a

[27] Winchester, WC CB 23056 p. 138.

[28] Winchester, WC CB 23057 p. 6.

[29] Winchester, HRO Bish 11M59/E1/125/142/1 p. 48d.

second loan for £100 at 4 per cent for 2 years in 1684. At this point her daughter married a William Matthew, a carpenter, and her portion was £100 — which matches the amount of her mother's mortgage. Finally when Margaret's son came of age she surrendered the copyholding to him on condition that he paid her an annual annuity of £4 per annum. These transactions indicate that Margaret's purpose was to provide dower for her daughter and then to set up her son with the land, whilst still providing for herself in older age. All are family-related reasons.

The need to pay legacies and inherited debt was the largest category, at around 40 per cent, for all types of women but second lowest for men. Widows were often charged with distributing legacies — which the estate might not have funds to cover, so they needed to borrow; and/or they were charged with bringing up young children as above, whereas men were rarely involved in this way. Honor Collins, a spinster, inherited copyholdings in Meonstoke in 1651 when she was only two years old, and once she arrived at her majority in 1671, she spent many years and four or five mortgages trying to pay off the associated encumbrances and building up a dower. Elizabeth Sparshott inherited her husband John's land in Meonstoke after he had made a series of imprudent loans to a John Collins which were never repaid. John Sparshott had therefore left his wife with troubled financial debts and between 1694 and 1697 she obtained a short series of mortgages for £260 for three years at 5 per cent interest. The later mortgages were probably roll-overs to pay off the previous, as the level of debt had been considerable. Elizabeth then died in 1699 so her son Thomas inherited the debt and had to continue borrowing.

Finally the category of 'financial difficulties' affected both women and men, but married women in particular and no widows. In a sense, widows struggling to pay legacies as above, were experiencing 'financial difficulties', but the reason for their difficulties could be identified. The general category of financial difficulties here includes those for whom a clear purpose covered by the other previous categories was not found, but who had financial troubles. Married women were particularly involved in this category and were those who held the land jointly with their husbands and so became responsible with them when things went wrong. A typical example was provided by Joan Forder who married Lomer Shallett in 1693. As part of the marriage settlement, Lomer surrendered his Meonstoke copyhold land of 100 acres to himself and Joan, so that they then held it equally and jointly. All went well at first and they baptized six children between 1694 and 1704. However some disaster occurred, around the turn of the century, because the Winchester Dean and Chapter's copyhold register dated 1701 for Exton (a neighbouring parish where the Shalletts actually lived) refers to the lord's offer of a discount for a fine 'in consideration of the poor shattered circumstances of the tenant'.[30] Such circumstances must have run deep, as in 1705 they jointly borrowed a mortgage for £300 from Edward Hatch, a malster, for three years at 5 per cent using thirty-seven of their Meonstoke acres as security.[31] The amount was never repaid and was recorded as still outstanding in the Meonstoke court records for 1724 when their son Edmund came to claim the property as heir. A seemingly very attractive settlement when Joan married Lomer, had descended into severe financial difficulties.

This section has revealed the motivation for borrowing for many of the copyholders during the second half of the seventeenth century. The focus by women on family-related issues is a significant, if not unexpected, finding. Within that focus, widows borrowed to support children and legacy payments as they would lose their land if they remarried, and so needed to provide for their families themselves. Married and unmarried women were also involved with legacy payments if they inherited from a parent, but also some joint ownerships fell into general financial difficulties if some unexpected issue arose. Even so, there was little sign of desperation and crisis, as was suggested by previous research mentioned above. Perhaps the mortgage was not the best instrument for crisis management, as it was longer term and not immediate.

Female Mortgage Lenders: Access to Capital

The lenders or providers of mortgages to the copyholders were always named in the manorial documents, but the extent to which further information was provided varied. A proportion of them lived in one of the manors studied, in which case background profile information was available. However, for those living outside the research manors, probate records were the main source of information about lenders.

The question of access to capital is key to any investigation of lending. Spicksley examined sources of funds available to single women and found three clear trends during the seventeenth century.[32] The first was an increasing tendency for fathers to leave money, rather than moveable goods, to their daughters.[33] The second was that daughters became able to access their capital before marriage; and thirdly there

30 Winchester, HRO D&C DC/J10/3/2 p. 86.

31 Winchester, WC CB 23057 p. 56.

32 Spicksley, "Fly with a Duck in thy Mouth", p. 199.

33 See also Jaco Zuijderduijn, 'The Ages of Women and Men', this volume.

was a tendency for fathers with available money to give some to their daughters during their lifetime. These all meant that single women had more money at an earlier age, and in the absence of much employment opportunity, they needed to invest it in order to protect their capital and raise income. Their overall lending pattern therefore increased as the seventeenth century progressed. Others, such as Dermineur, researching in the eighteenth century have found that women working in domestic service could receive large legacy payments for either or both of arrears of wages or gifts, which then gave them funds to lend.[34] In this study, it was found that the source of funds for single women and widows was usually from an inheritance after the death of their parent, husband, or close kin. Only one married woman offered a loan for a mortgage, and this was Mary Budd, wife of Edward, who lent £15 at 5 per cent to Thomas West for one year in 1716.[35] There is no information about the source of her funds, or an indication of why other married women did not lend although couverture usually meant that they did not have access to their own funds.

Another issue was why women with money to lend and invest may have chosen a mortgage to do so, rather than any other credit instrument. Whereas the borrowers may have used a mortgage because land was the main possession that they had to offer as security, lenders had perhaps more choice. However as indicated in the introduction, this choice was very limited throughout most of the seventeenth century, particularly for larger sums of money. Froide found that women were investing in both bonds and mortgages after 1660 rather than sales or trade-related credit, and that in Southampton (a port city in Hampshire not far from Meonstoke and Crawley), bonds and mortgages were definitely preferred.[36] She also noted that single women appeared to prefer credit instruments where formal written records of the transactions were made. This finding accords well with Tawney's view, mentioned earlier, that copyholder mortgages were particularly attractive to potential lenders as the manor court carefully recorded the agreements without the need for payment for legal services and could deal with any failures to pay without further expenses of suing. In a context of the absence of formal notaries or equivalent in English rural areas at this time, the manorial court system must have seemed a particularly secure way of lending.

Froide, writing about the later period of the Financial Revolution, then found that investment opportunities 'increased exponentially' after the mid-1690s, and

[34] Dermineur, 'Single Women and the Rural Credit Market in Eighteenth-Century France'.

[35] Winchester, WC CB 23057 p. 117d.

[36] Froide, *Never Married*, pp. 132–34.

that women embraced the full range of them and moved away from land-related investments like mortgages.[37] However, the purpose of the lending could affect which instrument was selected. Women were not risk averse and participated in lotteries and share ventures, but if their primary objective was regular income to support their older age or for regular family support, then bonds or government stock were considered more secure and could provide longer term annuities.[38] The short-term copyholder mortgages would then have appealed less to older and widowed investors in particular.

Dimensions of Lending

The proportion of female to male lending in Table 6.5 is shown as just over 17 per cent of all mortgages and nearly 26 per cent of individual lenders. This difference was because on average women made one loan, whereas men made two. The proportion of female lenders is higher at 26 per cent than for women borrowers (17 per cent in Table 6.2 above).

Table 6.5. Women as the proportion of mortgage lending and lenders 1600–1735.
Source: Manorial records as before.

	Number of mortgages lent by:			**Number of individual lenders**			**Mean no. mortgages lent per lender**	
Manor	*Female*	*Male*	*% Female*	*Female*	*Male*	*% Female*	*Female*	*Male*
Meonstoke	57	277	*17.1*	46	126	*26.7*	1.2	2.2
Crawley	13	60	*17.8*	7	28	*20.0*	1.9	2.1
Totals	70	337	*17.2*	53	154	*25.6*	1.3	2.2

Table 6.6 then expands these figures further to show the marital status of females and the numbers of mortgages lent. Unmarried women formed the largest group of lenders at 55 per cent with widows at 38 per cent. Then 85 per cent of all female loans were made with a one-off mortgage; whereas only 57 per cent of male lenders lent once. The pattern suggests that women were using mortgage lending for short-term one-off purposes, whereas some of the men were indulging in

[37] Froide, *Silent Partners*, p. 11.

[38] Froide, *Silent Partners*.

longer-term regular lending. Far fewer women offered more than four mortgages, and those that did were widows like Abigail Rothwell, whose story follows later. Like many of the widow borrowers, she had to provide for young children after her husband's early death and it could take up to twenty years for them to reach their majority. There was no evidence that any women lent in series in order to procure a pension. However, the sample size is very small and there is no information about other loans which the women may have offered in other villages outside the study manors. As mentioned earlier, the mortgage was probably not the credit instrument for an annuity.

Table 6.6. The number of mortgages lent by an individual, according to gender and status. *Source:* manorial records as before.

	All	**Male**		**Female**		**Status of female lenders**			
No. morts lent		*No.*	*%*	*No.*	*%*	*Widows*	*Spinsters*	*Married*	*NK*
7+	7	7	*5*						
6	6	5	*3*	1	*2*	1			
5	8	7	*5*	1	*2*	1			
4	10	9	*6*	1	*2*		1		
3	12	12	*8*	0	*0*				
2	31	26	*17*	5	*9*	1	4		
1	133	88	*57*	45	*85*	17	24	1	3
Tot. lenders	207	154		53		20	29	1	3
						38%	55%	2%	6%

Spicksley's findings, quoted above, found that single female lending increased during the seventeenth century. To see whether this pattern was similar in Hampshire, Figure 6.2 shows lending to Meonstoke copyholders divided by gender, and marital status for the women, during the long seventeenth century.

The graph shows a slow start to the century, and that women did not have much activity during the sub-peak in male activity during the 1630s. After the dip during the English Civil War and Commonwealth (1642–1660) noted previously for Figure 6.1, the male lending peaked quickly, and both widows and unmarried women's lending increased significantly. The overall level for females then remained higher during the second half of the century, which mirrors Spicksley's findings. Widows had peaks and troughs against the spinsters' smoother curve. (As much of the capital came from legacies, a correlation was run between

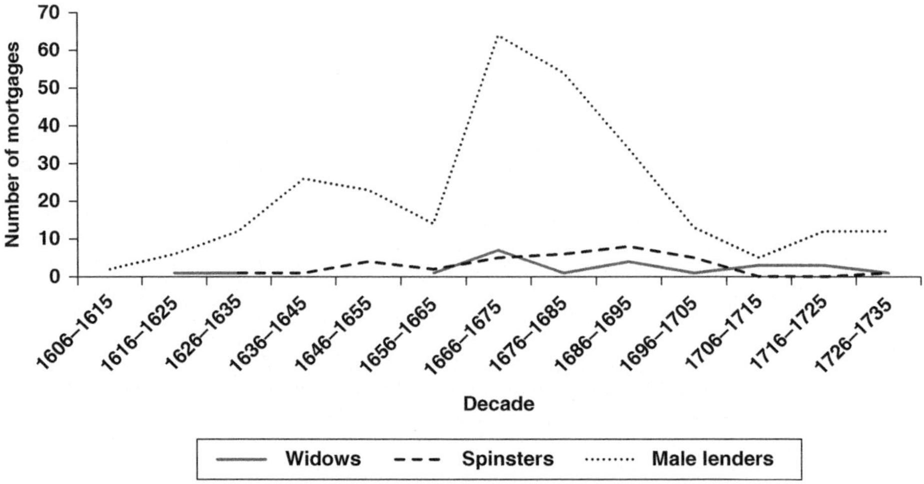

Figure 6.2. Female and male mortgage lending; Meonstoke 1606–1735.

burials and female lending as the two might be expected to link, but they did not.) All lenders then showed a remarkable decline in the very early eighteenth century, which was probably due to the diversification of investment opportunity during the Financial Revolution.

Both Spicksley and Froide found that the range of amount of single women's lending was very wide; from a few pounds to more than a thousand.[39] To examine this, Table 6.7 summarizes male and female lending by plotting the highest amount that was lent in any one mortgage.[40] It shows that the range was indeed wide, but that half the lending was for less than £100. About 30 per cent of both genders lent under £50, and a further 22 per cent between £50 and £100. However, nearly 36 per cent of female lenders lent between £100 and £200 whereas only 21 per cent of males did so. The situation reversed for the category between £200 & £300, and more men lent even higher amounts, although only 10 per cent of men lent more than £300 (cf. 4 per cent of women). It would seem that for women the normal limit was about £200, and for men £300. It is not clear whether this was because women had less money to offer or whether they were less willing to accept more risk.

[39] Spicksley, "Fly with a Duck in thy Mouth", p. 191, Froide. *Never Married*, p. 132.

[40] In other words, if a lender provided funds several times, then the highest of those that they offered.

Table 6.7. Maximum amounts lent in a mortgage, divided by gender. *Source:* Manorial court records as before.

Amount	**Male***		**Female**	
	No.	%	*No.*	%
£500+	4	*2.6*		
£400+	3	*2.0*	1	*1.9*
£300 +	10	*6.6*	1	*1.9*
£200+	27	*17.8*	4	*7.5*
£100 +	32	*21.1*	19	*35.8*
£50–£99	32	*21.1*	12	*22.6*
<£50	44	*29.0*	16	*30.2*
	152		53	

* Figures for two of the men not clear, so omitted.

The social status of early modern women is difficult to determine as most had no official occupation. However, because most lenders' capital came from legacies, the status of their benefactor could be used to imply that of the receiving woman. Table 6.8 summarizes the occupation groups of the benefactors.

Table 6.8. The status of the provider of capital for female lenders. *Source:* Manorial court records as before and probate records.

Heirs of:		**Gents**	**Merchants**	**Farmers**	**Artisans**	**Total***
Widows	No.	2	3	14	1	20
	%	10%	15%	70%	5%	
Spinsters	No.	0	9	17	1	27
	%		33%	63%	4%	
Total female		2	12	31	2	47
		4.3%	25.5%	66.0%	4.3%	

* Source not clear for six lenders

The results show that two thirds of female lenders, whether widows or spinsters, were beneficiaries of farmers — mainly yeomen or husbandmen. The dominance of this agricultural group is interesting as it has sometimes been thought that lenders were chiefly based in towns. However, southern England at this time was a wealthy farming area with agrarian capitalism developing rapidly, so the legacies probably reflect this. The other third of spinsters were beneficiaries of merchants living in local towns, but widows were divided between merchants and minor gentry. (Where known, these merchants were drapers or glovers and some also held office as mayor or alderman.) There were two beneficiaries from artisans: a shoemaker and a tanner. Again, Muldrew's finding that credit relationships occurred 'all over the social scale' seems to have been confirmed here.[41] However, although there were some quite poor borrowers, the female lenders here were focussed overwhelmingly in the middling section of society; a result also found by Froide.[42]

In addition to status and occupation, the location of lenders in relation to the manor of the borrowers was investigated to determine whether the activity was chiefly local or had a wider basis. It was also relevant to assess whether the lending pattern was one of urban to rural with lenders mainly based in towns and cities, or whether it occurred within the rural community. Table 6.9 plots the results, and includes Winchester city as a separate category because that is where the lords and stewards lived.[43]

The overall pattern which emerges for Table 6.9 is mostly similar for males and females, although one clear difference within the female split is that three times as many unmarried women than widows lived in a local town or in Winchester. They were the category of daughters of merchants shown in Table 6.8. Otherwise, around half of all lenders lived either in the same village as their borrower or in adjoining villages. A further mean of 14 per cent lived in other rural villages in Hampshire but at a distance from that of the borrower. Very few were located in local towns, and none in Hampshire cities save for a mean of 12.5 per cent in Winchester. A tiny proportion lived in London and they were all sons and daughters of the manors. So this shows a very localized rural credit market with no evidence of an urban/rural pattern.

The reasons why women lent were difficult to quantify as all those whose histories could be traced had received an inheritance and legacy and appeared, therefore, to be wishing to make this capital work for them. The subsequent marriage of spinsters or younger daughters after lending suggests that the development of a good marriage portion was a frequent objective. Similarly, the need to pay deferred legacies to underage children when they later reached twenty-one years of age seems to have been a

[41] Muldrew, *The Economy of Obligation*, p. 97.

[42] Froide, *Silent Partners*, p. 63.

[43] Hampshire has two large port cities of Southampton and Portsmouth in addition to Winchester.

Table 6.9. The location of lenders in relation to the manor of their borrowers: 1600–1735. *Source:* Manorial court records and probate records as before.

	Lender location							
	Same village	*Neighbouring village*	*Local town*	*Winchester city*	*Village in county*	*London*	*NK*	*Total*
Widows	5	8		3	3	1	2	22
	23%	*36%*		*13.5%*	*13.5%*	*5%*	*9%*	
Spinsters	9	7	2	7	1	1	3	30
	30%	*23%*	*7%*	*23%*	*3%*	*3%*	*10%*	
Female totals*	15	15	2	10	4	2	5	53 *
	28%	*28%*	*4%*	*19%*	*8%*	*4%*	*9%*	
Male	25	48	11	16	26	3	25	154
	16%	*31%*	*7%*	*11%*	*17%*	*2%*	*16%*	
All	40	63	13	26	30	5	30	207
	19%	*30%*	*6%*	*12.5%*	*14.5%*	*2.5%*	*14.5%*	

* The one married lender, Mary Budd, was not assigned a row in the main chart as she the only person in her category. However, she lived in the same village as her borrower so she has been added into the row of Female totals under the column for 'same village'.

motive for many widows. One thing is fairly clear. The objective in lending was not to obtain the land. On the rare occasion that the land came to the lender because of the death of the borrower and failure by the heirs to pay in a timely fashion, then the land was sold to raise the capital to pay off the loan. The mortgage was not being used as a device to grab land; it was entirely as an investment.

Lenders and Borrowers Linked

Having examined the borrowers and lenders separately, there remains the question of how they were introduced to each other. There were no official intermediaries such as the Continental Notaires in England at this time, and although professional money lenders existed in towns, and lawyers were certainly involved in a variety of credit-related contractual work, they were not involved with these copyholder mortgages. The reason is because the manorial court acted as recorder and overseer of these loans, so that other agents were not needed. The matter of introduction was therefore left to more informal local networks of intermediaries such as village officials, neighbours or distant relatives as is illustrated by the case of Abigail Rothwell which follows. However, it seems likely that the lord's steward may sometimes have advised as he would know the personal circumstances of his borrowing tenants at least, and probably some of the background of the lenders. In fact, many of the mortgages were not agreed in the actual manorial court, but in what was described as 'an extra' court, involving the relevant parties appearing before the steward in Winchester. The loan agreement was then merely recorded retrospectively in the court rolls of the next formal court.

Risk assessment would have been important in deciding from whom to borrow or to whom to lend. Muldrew found that, during the seventeenth century in particular, trust was essential in developing credit relations.[44] An additional analysis was therefore carried out using this study data to see what relationship, if any, existed between borrower and lender. The proportion who were close kin was small overall at 10 per cent, although it was higher for women at 17 per cent. Another 9 per cent of both men and women shared a surname and may have been distantly related, and 50 per cent of women and 35 per cent of men then seem to have borrowed from lenders with known close ties to the village of the borrower. This left only 24 per cent of women and 46 per cent of men lending/borrowing between people with no known ties. It is possible that this result is because the women were researched

44 Muldrew, *The Economy of Obligation*.

in more detail here than was possible in the larger study, and thus more ties were discovered. Alternatively it shows that women more often lent to closer kin or those with village ties than did men. The pattern does suggest that risk assessment was heavily dependent on local knowledge, which is not surprising in an era before computerized credit ratings or bank account records. Two lender case studies will illustrate how the introductions and risk assessment may have occurred.

Lender Case Studies

Elizabeth and Dulcibella Searle, two spinster sisters, jointly lent £100 at 5 per cent interest over a term of three years in 1676 to Thomas Wyatt of Meonstoke who provided security in the form of two large closes of land totalling eighteen acres. They were daughters of Matthew Searle and were in their early twenties in 1675 when their father — describing himself as a yeoman farmer — died leaving them a legacy of £45 each.[45] It seems probable that the majority of the £100 lent by the sisters came from these legacies.

The borrower Thomas Wyatt needed a mortgage to pay legacies in his own father's will, and would have been seeking suitable lenders. It transpires that both he and the Searle girls were born in the early 1650s in Meonstoke, and must therefore have known each other from childhood, so no outside introduction would have been necessary. By 1676 all three of them had recently lost their fathers, and both fathers had been respected members of the Meonstoke community, so presumably trust would have been established by reputation and personal knowledge too. Thomas repaid the mortgage at the end of term and did not then renew with the Searle girls who both married in the following year. This mortgage therefore appears to have been lent in order to increase the girls' marriage portions, and to help a known friend and neighbour who had legacies to pay.

Abigail Rothwell, widow, of Warnford (near Meonstoke) lent £260 in 1686 to John Godwin of Crawley at 5 per cent interest over six years. He offered a house and cottage and thirty-three acres of land as security.[46] Abigail lived some twenty miles from Crawley, and had no obvious connections with it, or the Godwin family. She would therefore have fallen into the category of 'no known ties' to the borrower, were it not for the discovery of the will of her husband who had died the year before the mortgage agreement.

[45] Winchester, HRO will 1675P/30.

[46] Winchester, HRO Bish 11M59/E1/129/2 p. 14d.

The probate records of Abigail's husband John Rothwell, a yeoman farmer, show that he specifically left the sum of £300 to his wife 'in full satisfaction of her jointure made to me before our marriage'.[47] So this was the source of her capital. The date of their marriage is not known, but they baptized a son, John, in March 1686 — which was posthumously; so an assumption must be that Abigail was comparatively young and would need to invest funds for herself and her growing son over the next twenty-one years or so. Hence her ability to use almost £300 in a mortgage loan to gain interest, and the offering of a particularly long term of six years.

An English will often named 'overseers' who would help the executor and ensure that the wishes of the testator were carried out. John Rothwell appointed two overseers — one of whom was a William Godwin of Seavington, who was a friend and wealthy farmer living near Warnford. However, he had also been born in Crawley, and was either the uncle or cousin of John Godwin. He was thus in an excellent position to know both the financial circumstances of Abigail after the execution of John Rothwell's will, and also the situation of his cousin John Godwin. The personal connections between the Rothwells and the Godwins are thus revealed, and no doubt William Godwin acted as intermediary.

Conclusion

This study has examined a section of the seventeenth-century rural credit market not revealed in previous research. It has been shown that copyhold of inheritance tenure, which was widespread at that time, could provide married, widowed, and single women with rights to land which enabled them to use it as security for a mortgage loan. At any one time, up to one quarter of the copyhold tenantry were female and so they had this potential to use mortgages to access credit. The way in which they did so involved conditional surrenders of their land in the manorial court, and these court records, provided they have survived, are a source of unrivalled details of *all* mortgages agreed, rather than the partial picture derived from probate or litigation. They were also cheaper to effect than the legal mortgage agreements used by freeholders and were regarded as more reliable and attractive for lenders.

Widows, unmarried, and married women all borrowed regularly throughout the century. The amount of credit raised in a loan usually varied between £10 and about £200, and the land offered as collateral ranged from half a house to a

[47] Winchester, HRO will 1685A/081.

hundred acres. The agreed term for repayment was often three years, so that this type of mortgage was of most use to those wanting short to medium term capital. Compared with male borrowers, the most significant difference in pattern was found in the apparent reasons for acquiring a mortgage. Women's needs were focussed on family matters such as child support and marriage, and the distribution of legacies, while men borrowed more to purchase and support business activities. The default rate on all loans was low, and there was little evidence of the use of mortgages as a credit instrument when in crisis.

Female lenders were an unrelated group who had access to funds. Restricted effectively to widows and unmarried women, they had chiefly acquired their capital by inheritance, and two-sthirds of their benefactors were farmers, rather than urban-based merchants or aristocracy. Their pattern of lending was low during the first half of the century but then rose after 1660. This fits well with the findings of Spicksley and Holderness that female access to capital increased in the second half of the century and made women important contributors in the credit market. However, after the 1690s the opportunities for using many other types of credit instrument led to a decline in lending for mortgages which accords with the findings of Froide.

Both borrowers and lenders were overwhelmingly from the middle stratum in rural society. The way in which the two groups were introduced and linked did not require the services of lawyers or professional moneylenders as all recording and oversight was provided by the manorial court. The lord's stewards may have helped, but otherwise most borrowers and lenders lived within five miles of each other and local networks of contact would have been used to assess risk and build trust, as Muldrew also found. Widows in particular borrowed and lent very locally, whereas more lending unmarried women lived in nearby towns. Comparatively few loans were agreed between close kin, who would presumably normally have used informal arrangements rather than the formal mortgage contract.

Overall the main objective of both the female borrower and lender was to support family-related needs and derive income and investment. This was effected by inter-personal mortgage loans at a time when other formal financial institutional facilities had not yet been developed. Women copyholders participated fully in the credit market in this way, as did female lenders. A window has been provided into the world of the copyholder mortgage, which, despite its widespread use in England, has until now been largely unstudied.

Works Cited

Manuscript and Archival Sources

Winchester, Hampshire Record Office, 11M59/C7/1 et seq.

Winchester, Hampshire Record Office, 11M59/E1/125/3 to /143/1 and 11M59/C7/1/1/1–59

Winchester, Hampshire Record Office, 11M59/E1/129/2 p. 14d

Winchester, Hampshire Record Office, 11M59/E1/125/42/1

Winchester, Hampshire Record Office, DC/J10/3/2

Winchester, Hampshire Record Office, 1685A/081 Will & Inventory of John Rothwell

Winchester, Hampshire Record Office, 1675P/30 Will & Inventory of Matthew Searle

Winchester, Winchester College Archives, Court Book 23047–58

Winchester, Winchester College Archives, Court Book 23056 Admission of Mary Binsteed

Primary Sources

'Usury Acts 13 Eliz. 1 C8 and 31 Eliz.1 C18' (1571 and 1598)

Secondary Studies

Dermineur, Elise M., 'Single Women and the Rural Credit Market in Eighteenth-Century France', *Journal of Social History*,48.1 (2014), 175–99

Erickson, Amy Louise, 'Possession — and the Other One-Tenth of the Law; Assessing Women's Ownership and Economic Roles in Early Modern England', *Women's History Review*, 16 (2007), 369–85

French, H. R., and R. W. Hoyle, 'The Land Market of a Pennine Manor: Slaidburn, 1650–1780', *Continuity & Change*, 14 (1999), 349–83

Froide, A. M., *Never Married: Singlewomen in Early Modern England* (Oxford: Oxford University Press, 2005)

———, *Silent Partners: Women as Public Investors During Britain's Financial Revolution 1690–1750* (Oxford: Oxford University Press, 2016)

Gayton, Juliet D., 'Mortgages Raised by Rural English Copyhold Tenants 1605–1735', in *Land and Credit: Mortgages in the Medieval and Early Modern Countryside*, ed. by Christopher Briggs and Jaco Zuijderduijn (Switzerland: Palgrave Macmillan, 2018), pp. 47–80.

———, 'Tenants, Tenures and Transfers: The Landholding Experience of Rural Customary Tenants in Some Hampshire Downland Manors, 1645 to 1705.' (PhD Dissertation, Exeter University, 2013). <https://ore.exeter.ac.uk/repository/handle/10871/13990>

Holderness, B. A., 'Credit in English Rural Society before the Nineteenth Century, with Special Reference to the Period 1650–1720', *Agric. Hist. Rev.*, 24 (1976), 97–109

Muldrew, Craig, *The Economy of Obligation: The Culture of Credit and Social Relations in Early Modern England* (London: Palgrave, 1998)

Spicksley, Judith M., '"Fly with a Duck in thy Mouth": Single Women as Sources of Credit in Seventeenth-Century England', *Social History*, 32 (2007), 187–207

———, 'Usury Legislation, Cash and Credit: The Development of the Female Investor in the Late Tudor and Stuart Periods', *Economic History Review*, 61 (2008), 277–301

Tawney, R. H., *The Agrarian Problem in the Sixteenth Century*. 1967 reprint edn (New York: Harper & Row, 1912)

———, 'The Rise of the Gentry: 1558–1640', *Economic History Review*, 11 (1941), 1–38

Women, Credit, and Dowry in Early Modern Italy

James E. Shaw

Introduction

In recent years the new history of capitalism has shifted attention away from production and wage labour to emphasize the role of financialization. In this, special attention has been given to the role of money, understood in the broad sense of a social technology of credit.[1] Historians have highlighted the emergence of new institutions, practices, and attitudes regarding money, profit, and exchange relations during the early modern period, which constituted a 'financial revolution'.[2] Obtaining social status through 'having a living' rather than 'getting one', women's investment played an important role in circulating capital within the broader

1 Ingham, *The Nature of Money*.

2 Sklansky, 'The Elusive Sovereign'.

Dr James E. Shaw, Senior Lecturer in History at University of Sheffield, is a historian of early modern Italy, focusing on the relationship of legal structures (laws, practices, institutions) to the daily practices of economic life. His first book, *The Justice of Venice: Authorities and Liberties in the Urban Economy, 1550–1700* (Oxford University Press, 2006) examined how ordinary people experienced market justice in early modern society. His second book, *Making and Marketing Medicines in Renaissance Florence* (Rodopi, 2011) co-authored with Professor Evelyn Welch, used the accounts of a renaissance apothecary to challenge existing understandings of renaissance pharmacy and the retail market. His current project *Debt in Venice*, examines fraud and usury cases from early modern Venice to reveal a world of secret dealings and manipulation, and the ways that economic relations were tightly embedded in social networks.

Women and Credit in Pre-Industrial Europe, ed. by Elise M. Dermineur, EER 12 (Turnhout: Brepols, 2018), pp. 173–202.
BREPOLS PUBLISHERS DOI 10.1484/M.EER-EB.5.115753

economy.[3] Much of this scholarship has focused on England. Amy Erickson has argued that the specific condition of women under English law facilitated their activities as investors: for example, unmarried women could take decisions about investments without needing the approval of male guardians.[4] Similarly, Judith Spicksley has made the case for the prominent role of single women as investors in England.[5] Although the financial agency of married women in England appears much more limited, due to the rules of coverture (see discussion elsewhere in this volume), there were ways around these restrictions in practice.[6] Nevertheless, the exceptionality of England seems questionable when considered in comparative perspective.[7]

This article considers the case of Italian women and their role as creditors across the late medieval and early modern periods, with particular attention given to Venice. The first section outlines the dowry system and the restrictions and protections that this placed on women's capital. Women possessed clear legal rights to separate property, but in practice they often exercised these through a process of negotiation with kin. Despite the restrictions of the usury laws, the commercial and financial institutions of Italian city-states offered many possibilities for women to invest money for profit. The second section considers the relative attraction of these opportunities for legitimate investment alongside informal moneylending, highlighting the profits and potential risks in each case. The third section uses a case study from early modern Venice to reveal how dowry litigation can reveal women's financial agency even within the context of marriage.

Women and Capital

The roman law tradition that was diffused throughout Italy clearly recognized married women's legal personhood. There were important local variations in implementation: in Florence, statutes tend to place limits on wives' control of property, and women required a male representative in court;[8] in Venice, state laws and

[3] Shepard, 'Crediting Women', pp. 5–6. See also Hartigan-O'Connor, 'Gender's Value in the History of Capitalism'.

[4] Erickson, 'Coverture and Capitalism'.

[5] Spicksley, 'Women, "Usury" and Credit in Early Modern England'; Spicksley, '"Fly with a Duck in thy Mouth"'. See also Spicksley, this volume.

[6] Erickson, 'Coverture and Capitalism', p. 5; Fontaine, 'Il posto delle donne', p. 516.

[7] See for example the essays in Sperling and Wray, eds, *Across the Religious Divide*.

[8] Kuehn, 'Daughters, Mothers, Wives, and Widows', p. 105; Kuehn, '"Cum Consensu Mundualdi"'.

institutions played a particularly active role in defending women's property rights.[9] Nevertheless, the general principle was that husbands and wives were separate persons who were not obligated for each other's debts — instead, liability extended along the lines of the male lineage.[10] Even during marriage, women often maintained separate finances to their husbands, and this was particularly the case if they had received separate bequests from former husbands, mothers or other kin — such wealth was considered separate from their dowries and not subject to a husband's control.[11] In Italy, married women were legally constituted as 'passing guests' in their husband's household, rather than full members.[12] A woman could not expect to inherit from her husband — by default the husband's estate would pass to any children and then to other male kin. Formally speaking, wives were not joint partners in a family unit, but were legally separate from their husbands' affairs.

The concept of women having separate property and legal personhood within marriage was expressed primarily through the laws of dowry.[13] These were established in the late medieval period: in 1143 in Genoa, for example, the widow lost her traditional right to one third of the couple's estate; instead she could now ask only for return of her dowry, a precisely quantified sum that was independent of her husband's fortunes.[14] The dowry was regarded as a form of open-ended credit: although it was given to the groom to manage during the course of the marriage, the wife retained a residual claim on her husband's estate. She (or her heirs) could demand that the dowry be repaid in the event of the dissolution of the marriage due to annulment, the separation of the couple, the death of either partner, or if the husband were verging on insolvency.[15] Often governments put extensive legal protections in place to ensure that women could assert these claims. For example, in Venice, dowries had to be registered at a government office, and the groom and

[9] Chojnacki, 'Getting Back the Dowry'. See also Bellavitis, 'Women, Family, and Property in Sixteenth-Century Venice'; Brizio, 'In the Shadow of the Campo', pp. 122–23; Sperling, 'Marriage, Kinship, and Property in Portuguese Testaments (1649–1650)', p. 164.

[10] Kuehn, 'Debt and Bankruptcy in Florence', p. 359.

[11] Chojnacka, *Working Women of Early Modern Venice*, p. 32; McGough, 'Women, Private Property, and the Limitations of State Authority', p. 38.

[12] Klapisch-Zuber, 'The "Cruel Mother"', p. 118.

[13] Sperling and Wray, 'Introduction', pp. 6–7.

[14] Bezzina, *Artigiani a Genova*, p. 139.

[15] Kirshner, 'Wives' Claims against Insolvent Husbands in Late Medieval Italy'; Fontaine, 'Women's Economic Spheres and Credit in Pre-Industrial Europe', p. 19.

his kin were expected to guarantee the return of the dowry by posting their own immovable property as collateral.[16] In Italy, the wife was the number one creditor of her husband, her rights protected by law and state institutions, but her claim on his estate was limited to her dowry, rather than her being joint partner in the household.

The general process of dowry inflation taking place across the period had important consequences for the role of women in finance. Dowries became more significant not only due to their greater size, but also because they increasingly consisted of mobile, liquid wealth in the form of cash, material goods, and financial instruments.[17] By contrast, male inheritance increasingly consisted of real estate holdings, whose use was often restricted by the use of *fideicommissa* (entails) designed to keep patrimonies intact.[18] Women's property was therefore particularly significant as a key source of liquid assets that conditioned families' marital and business strategies. In Renaissance Florence, the memoirs of Gregorio Dati make clear how his business opportunities were tied to his control of dowry assets through successive marriages.[19] For the parents of elite brides, putting the dowry together could require significant investment activity. In Florence, for example, the state dowry fund encouraged families to start saving for dowries when their daughters were still young, channelling this capital into government debt.[20] Judith Spicksley has shown how single women in England were frequently active in moneylending, usually for the purpose of augmenting their marriage portion.[21] In Italy, women's dowries were larger, and savings were usually started earlier by fathers on behalf of their daughters, with control of the funds subsequently passing to husbands on marriage. Women's capital played a key role in Italian society, but it was typically managed by men on their behalf.

16 Bellavitis, 'Women, Family, and Property in Sixteenth-Century Venice' pp. 176–77; Lanaro, 'La restituzione della dote', p. 766; Chojnacki, 'Patrician Women in Early Renaissance Venice'; Chojnacki, *Women and Men in Renaissance Venice*, pp. 128–29; Ambrosini, 'Penombre femminili', p. 307; Ferraro, *Marriage Wars in Late Renaissance Venice*, pp. 136, 146.

17 Bellavitis, 'Women, Family, and Property in Sixteenth-Century Venice'; Lanaro and Varanini, 'Funzioni economiche della dote', p. 94.

18 Lanaro and Varanini, 'Fidecommesso, doti, famiglia'. For comparison, see Zuijderduijn, this volume, pp. 111–12.

19 Brucker, *The Society of Renaissance Florence*, pp. 29–31.

20 Kirshner and Molho, 'The Dowry Fund and the Marriage Market in Early Quattrocento Florence'; Molho, *Marriage Alliance in Late Medieval Florence*.

21 Spicksley, 'Women, "Usury" and Credit in Early Modern England', pp. 265, 268–69, 271, 274–75.

Women's financial agency was closely bound up with the life cycle, and was conditioned by their family relations.[22] Women generally only came to exercise direct control over their assets on widowhood, a situation which was particularly likely for elite families, where husbands tended to be older than wives. Nevertheless, women often found that the exercise of their legal rights was constrained by social obligations. Alessandra Sambo's study of the Tiepolo family in seventeenth-century Venice shows how the legal rights of women might be overridden in practice. In 1637, Donata Tiepolo formally donated all her dotal property to her husband, but a week later she registered a 'secret protest' as proof that she had not done so voluntarily, a precautionary measure which enabled her to successfully contest the donation after his death.[23] Similarly, for a widow, actually exercising the right to reclaim her dowry might involve her in bitter struggles with her husband's kin and even her own children.[24] To incentivize widows to make the 'right' choice, a husband might use his will to provide for his widow, and to appoint her as guardian of the children, but on condition that she did not reclaim her dowry.[25] As a result of such arrangements, many widows chose not to reclaim their dowries (and therefore not to remarry), instead administering their children's financial assets on their behalf.[26] How dowry rights functioned in practice was a matter for negotiation, across both sides of the family and across generations.[27]

Another way in which Italian women expressed financial agency was through their wills.[28] Through wills, women might abrogate the ordinary rules of succession, as in the case of Lippa, a Sienese widow of the late fourteenth century, who willed her house to her daughter and then down the female line of succession to her great-granddaughter.[29] Women had considerable testamentary freedom to decide between the competing claims of their children from different marriages, their natal

[22] Zuijderduijn, this volume, pp. 95–97.

[23] Sambo, 'Strategie d'immortalità', pp. 570–74. On the 'secret protest' see 'Strategie d'immortalità', pp. 578–81, and Shaw, 'The Informal Economy of Credit'.

[24] Chabot, 'Lineage Strategies and the Control of Widows in Renaissance Florence'; Klapisch-Zuber, 'The "Cruel Mother"'; Kuehn, 'Daughters, Mothers, Wives, and Widows', p. 110.

[25] Kuehn, 'Daughters, Mothers, Wives, and Widows', p. 111.

[26] Kuehn, 'Daughters, Mothers, Wives, and Widows', p. 109; Cecchini, 'A World of Small Objects', p. 43.

[27] Chojnacki, *Women and Men in Renaissance Venice*, pp. 130, 142; Queller and Madden, 'Father of the Bride', p. 707; Cox, 'The Single Self', pp. 526–28.

[28] Chojnacki, 'Patrician Women in Early Renaissance Venice', pp. 183–85.

[29] Brizio, 'In the Shadow of the Campo', p. 125.

and marital kin, and other social connections.[30] The bequests made by women to their daughters contributed significantly to the dowry inflation of the late medieval period.[31] Alternatively, women might find a valuable source of institutional support outside the family by making bequests to monastic and charitable institutions, and by appointing these institutions as their executors.[32] Cattarina Conti, who litigated with her husband over control of her dowry, found refuge in the Venetian house of the *Convertite*. Through a subsequent bequest of 8000 ducats, she gave the institution a vested interest in ensuring that her will was executed.[33] Such institutions could also provide a refuge for those without kin, as at the hospital of Santa Maria Nuova in Florence, where widows could invest sums to obtain residency rights as well as modest pensions to support them for the rest of their lives.[34] Testamentary agency was exercised by married women as well as by widows. In Venice, husbands were not allowed to be present when married women drew up their wills, in order to prevent undue influence.[35] Women's relative freedom as testators can be contrasted to the case of men, who were legally obliged to meet the claims of male heirs and also to make provision for their daughters; they had to be able to meet the dotal claims of their wives and those of their male kin; and their freedom of action was further limited by fideiussory controls on landed property.

Although women's financial agency became manifest on widowhood, women could also exercise a degree of informal control over their assets within marriage.[36] In Venice, similar proportions of widows, married women, and spinsters had dealings with notaries across the period 1565–1625.[37] Married women had the faculty of making their will independently of their husband, and they could administer any separate nondotal property they had received through bequests or gifts.[38] In addition, married women might exercise informal influence over their dotal assets even

[30] Lanaro and Varanini, 'Funzioni economiche della dote', pp. 99–102.

[31] Queller and Madden, 'Father of the Bride', pp. 695–97.

[32] Cavallo, *Charity and Power in Early Modern Italy*; McGough, 'Women, Private Property, and the Limitations of State Authority'; Carbonell-Esteller, this volume, p. 317.

[33] McGough, 'Women, Private Property, and the Limitations of State Authority', pp. 41–43.

[34] Chabot, 'Widowhood and Poverty in Late Medieval Florence', p. 300.

[35] McGough, "Women, Private Property, and the Limitations of State Authority', pp. 37–38; Sambo 'Strategie d'immortalità', p. 576.

[36] Petti Balbi, 'Forme di credito femminile', p. 23.

[37] Chojnacka, *Working Women of Early Modern Venice*, pp. 41–42.

[38] Kirshner, *Marriage, Dowry, and Citizenship*, pp. 83–85.

within marriage.[39] In fifteenth-century Florence, the wife of Tommaso Dati sold a piece of land to a widow despite its being technically under her husband's control.[40] Again, this would depend on the state of relations within the family. Chojnacki argues that a married woman's residual right to reclaim the dowry gave her husband, his kin, and any children of the relationship an incentive to treat her well, in the hope that she would choose not to exercise those rights in the future.[41]

Although the default legal position was that Italian wives had rights to separate property, this did not preclude marriage from functioning as a form of partnership. Indeed, couples could exploit the privileged legal status of the dowry as a means of limiting their liability for debts.[42] For this reason, in thirteenth-century Pavia, creditors often insisted that wives assume liability along with their husbands, acting as guarantors of the debt, and similar practices can be found in seventeenth-century France.[43] In effect this meant that wives might be involved in transactions as partners along with their husbands, at least at the level of giving their formal assent.[44] In similar fashion, mothers often helped their male children to raise capital by guaranteeing their debts.

Although these sorts of guarantees might imply a merely passive role, in which women assumed liability through a sense of familial obligation, there are also cases showing a more direct sense of active partnership, as for example when wives also acted as agents for their husbands when the latter were away on commercial or other business.[45] Christine de Pisan wrote that because husbands were often away, their 'wives should be wise and sound administrators and manage their affairs well [...] They should have all the responsibility of the administration and know how to make use of their revenues and possessions'.[46] In late medieval Genoa, wives often represented their husbands in commercial dealings,[47] and the sorts of practical business skills that might be developed by patrician women are exemplified

[39] Chojnacka, *Working Women of Early Modern Venice*, p. 29.

[40] Kuehn, 'Daughters, Mothers, Wives, and Widows', p. 107.

[41] Chojnacki, *Women and Men in Renaissance Venice*, pp. 128–29; Ambrosini, 'Penombre femminili', p. 307; Bellavitis, 'Dare credito', p. 265.

[42] Bellavitis, 'Dare credito', p. 265; Erickson, 'Possession', p. 371.

[43] Bertoni, 'Investire per la famiglia', pp. 55–57; Fontaine, 'Il posto delle donne', p. 516.

[44] Fontaine, *The Moral Economy*, pp. 131, 135–36.

[45] Petti Balbi, 'Forme di credito femminile', pp. 20–23.

[46] Christine de Pisan, *The Treasure of the City of Ladies*, p. 130, quoted in Laurence, Maltby, and Rutterford, eds, *Women and their Money, 1700–1950*, p. 11.

[47] Bezzina, *Artigiani a Genova*, pp. 92, 95.

by the case of Ginevra Lomellini, who (according to Boccaccio) could 'read, write and cast up accounts better than as if she were a merchant'.[48] In Prato, Margherita Datini worked in close partnership with her husband, the merchant Francesco, acting as his agent when he was away on business, negotiating with debtors, learning to write, and to keep financial records.[49] This sense of partnership was particularly strong among mercantile and artisan households, where wives could gain practical experience in managing the business along with their husbands, often continuing the activity as widows after their deaths. Among artisan families, in fact, it was typical for husbands to name their wives as their executors and heirs, recognizing them as partners in the household despite the theoretical separation of property rights.

Women as Investors

Women's key role as creditors should be understood as a result of the gender structures of the economy — significant amounts of liquid capital were concentrated in the hands of women, but they played a marginal role in direct management of businesses. Denied socially respectable alternatives in the productive economy, women were generally obliged to invest capital in ventures organized by men. Women's prescribed role was to manage the household assets, including consumption, savings, and investment — family honour required the seclusion of women from public life: as Leon Battista Alberti noted, 'it would hardly win us respect if our wife busied herself among the men in the marketplace, out in the public eye'.[50] For women, a key marker of social status was not having to work for a living — this marked the divide between the working classes and the 'better sort', which included not just the nobility but also women of middling status.[51] Although many working class women worked in craft production, they were generally confined to the lower levels of the economy, typically working from home in putting-out systems of spinning, weaving, knitting, and lace-making that became prevalent in the early

[48] Boccaccio, *Decameron*, trans. J. M. Rigg, II, 9. See Petti Balbi, 'Forme di credito femminile', p. 15; Vitullo, 'Femininity in the Marketplace'.

[49] Crabb, 'Gaining Honor as Husband's Deputy'; Crabb, '"If I could write"'.

[50] Alberti, *The Family in Renaissance Florence*, p. 20, quoted in Matchette, 'Women, Objects, and Exchange in Early Modern Florence', p. 245.

[51] Ambrosini, 'Penombre femminili', p. 309, Chojnacka, *Working Women of Early Modern Venice*, p. 47.

modern period. Lacking any guild protection or representation, women's labour was cheap and easily exploited by male-controlled merchant capital.[52]

Despite the theoretical restrictions of the usury laws, which remained in force across the period, there were many legitimate channels in which women could invest for profit. This was a strongly financialized and mercantile society in which specific types of investment were recognized as legitimate by governments, lawyers, and by the church. These included for example equity investment in business partnerships (where the interest was justified in terms of the risk), mortgages and annuities on collateral of real estate (where the interest was presented as 'rent'), and government bonds (where the interest could be justified in terms of a gift in return for patriotic duty, and to cover the opportunity cost of investment). In the sixteenth century it also became possible to invest in charitable loan-banks called *Monti di Pietà*, which were able to raise capital more easily by paying interest to depositors.[53] The development of such systems over time has been described as a 'savings revolution',[54] and the growing supply of capital was reflected in the decline of interest rates across the period, falling to around 5–6 per cent in the seventeenth century and subsequently to 3–4 per cent in the eighteenth century.[55]

Before these sorts of credit instruments became widely accessible, significant numbers of women were able to invest in business ventures through *commenda* contracts.[56] These were an effective way of facilitating the flow of capital into entrepreneurial activity, developed in the commercial republics of medieval Italy and probably following models used in the wider Mediterranean.[57] These enabled women to become passive investors in medium-term business ventures, investing capital but leaving the active management of the business to a male business

[52] Allerston, 'An Undisciplined Activity?'; Della Valentina, 'The Silk Industry in Venice'; Caracausi, 'Beaten Children and Women's Work in Early Modern Italy'; Goldthwaite, *The Economy of Renaissance Florence* pp. 324, 338, 372.

[53] Goldthwaite, *The Economy of Renaissance Florence*, p. 472. See also Carbonell-Esteller, this volume, pp. 303–04.

[54] Carter and Goldthwaite, *Orpheus in the Marketplace*, p. 355; Vaquero Piñeiro, 'I censi consegnativi', p. 91; Muldrew, 'From Credit to Savings?', p. 394.

[55] Pezzolo, 'L'economia', p. 423; Munro, 'Usury, Calvinism, and Credit in Protestant England', pp. 17–18; Homer and Sylla, *A History of Interest Rates*, p. 140; Corazzol, *Livelli stipulati*, p. 30.

[56] Angelos, 'Women in Genoese commenda Contracts, 1155–1216'.

[57] González de Lara, 'The Secret of Venetian Success'; Koehler, 'Islamic Finance as a Progenitor of Venture Capital'; Greif, 'Contract Enforceability and Economic Institutions in Early Trade'.

partner (often a relative). In early thirteenth-century Genoa, women constituted over 20 per cent of investors in such contracts.[58] Similarly, in Pavia in 1292, Tisina Isimbardi invested money in a merchant venture, for a 50/50 share of the profit and the loss.[59] In Messina in 1473, two noblewomen invested capital in the form of precious fabrics in a commercial venture to Catalonia made by Giovanni Pitti.[60] There are even examples from thirteenth-century Venice of married women investing capital separately from their husbands.[61]

In similar fashion, women might also invest in the craft industries, retail trades, and service sector. In fifteenth-century Rome for example, women were prominent in investing capital and also acting as managers of inns and taverns,[62] and similar cases exist in Naples and Aversa.[63] Often such investments were made by widows wishing to carry on their husbands' business. An example is Caterina Pirogallo in early seventeenth-century Milan, who took legal action to get control of the estate of her husband, a bookseller and publisher. Subsequently she formed a partnership with her husband's former business associate in order to run the business, which included four shops.[64] Although Caterina had probably picked up practical knowledge through working with her husband, it is typical of such cases that she found it necessary to work with a male partner. When a woman obtained restitution of her dowry in the form of the former husband's shop, she typically got men to manage this in practice.[65]

There were often high returns associated with such investments, but also additional risks — ventures might fail, and women might be liable for the company's debts. Furthermore, women's position as mostly passive investors meant that they might be exploited by the men directly involved in administration. In mid-fifteenth-century Venice, Isabetta Pessato was convinced to shift her investments from the government debt into a drapery business, where she obtained a return of 18 per cent. However, Isabetta's businesses partners cheated her by concealing the

[58] Petti Balbi, 'Forme di credito femminile', p. 16; Bezzina, *Artigiani a Genova*, p. 95.

[59] Bertoni, 'Investire per la famiglia', p. 65.

[60] Figliulo, 'Lo spazio economico dei mercanti messinesi', p. 766. See also Mulé, 'Note sulla presenza femminili', p. 173.

[61] González de Lara, 'The Secret of Venetian Success', pp. 254, 274.

[62] Ait, 'Donne in affari', pp. 61–70.

[63] Colesanti and Fragnoli, 'Operatrici economiche', pp. 67–68.

[64] Fregulia, 'Stories Worth Telling', pp. 125–26, and for similar cases, pp. 128–29.

[65] Fregulia, 'Widows, Legal Rights, and the Mercantile Economy of Early Modern Milan', p. 235.

true extent of the profits, and it was only after many years that her son was able to obtain what was due through litigation.[66] Unless they could scrutinize the accounts for themselves, women were vulnerable to being cheated by their business partners and agents.

Although women continued to participate in these more risky forms of investment into the early modern period, many women preferred safer alternatives.[67] One of these was the public debt. In late medieval Italy, republican governments in particular began to raise money for war through forced loans, whereby citizens were obliged to contribute to the public purse according to their means, but were subsequently compensated with interest.[68] In Venice this system was established as early as 1207, with the funded debt or *Monte Vecchio* paying 5 per cent interest to creditors by the 1260s.[69] Women were often prominent among such investors, given the importance of their dowries: in fourteenth-century Genoa, for example, women made up from around one half to two-thirds of all investors.[70] By investing their dowries in the public debt, Genoese women could earn legitimate interest at around 8 per cent on long-term loans and do their patriotic duty at the same time.[71] Such investments were not entirely free of risk: governments might suspend interest payments during wartime, and at such times the price of bonds on the secondary market could plummet.[72] In 1509 Girolamo Priuli described the losses of those Venetians who depended on their income from the public debt, highlighting the plight of widows and also of many 'poor maidens and virgins' whose dowries were invested there.[73] By the mid-sixteenth century, governments moved away from the forced loan system, finding that they could raise money more easily by offering competitive rates to investors. Rather than obliging citizens to buy bonds, the Venetian government increasingly raised money by selling fixed-term or life annuities to citizens who voluntarily made deposits at the Mint.[74] This is unlikely to have made much difference to the gender balance of investors: in the Low

[66] Mueller, *The Venetian Money Market*, p. 537.

[67] Kamenaga-Anzai, 'Attitudes towards Public Debt in Medieval Genoa', p. 259.

[68] Mueller, *The Venetian Money Market*, pp. 454–58.

[69] Munro, 'The Medieval Origins of the Financial Revolution', pp. 515–16; Mueller, *The Venetian Money Market*, p. 459.

[70] Petti Balbi, 'Forme di credito femminile', p. 18.

[71] Kamenaga-Anzai, 'Attitudes towards Public Debt in Medieval Genoa', p. 247.

[72] Mueller, *The Venetian Money Market*, pp. 461–63, 472.

[73] Lizzul, 'The Utility of Wealth in the Era of the Public Debt 1300–1500', p. 284.

[74] Pezzolo, *L'oro dello Stato*, p. 175; Pezzolo, 'L'economia', pp. 418–20.

Countries, where city governments raised money via annuities rather than forced loans, women were also prominent investors in the public debt.[75]

Another favoured means of investing wealth at a profit were *censi* contracts, which appeared in the fifteenth century, and became widespread from the 1530s.[76] Their popularity increased following their approval by a series of papal bulls, such as that of Nicholas V in 1452, which limited the interest rate to 10 per cent,[77] and that of Pius V in 1569, which limited the interest rate to 7 per cent.[78] Such contracts effectively allowed creditors to purchase the rental income on property as a kind of annuity. Although the rent might be paid in produce or cash, by the late sixteenth century such contracts were generally purely financial instruments. In fifteenth-century Sciacca, the widow Flora was involved in numerous contracts of this sort.[79] In the 1530s, women of the Roman aristocracy were typically able to obtain around 10 per cent per annum interest on such contracts.[80] Like government bonds, *censi* were instruments for long-term investment, although the returns were relatively modest. They were open-ended contracts in which the creditor could not demand the return of the capital, and therefore attractive to investors seeking a perpetual or lifetime income stream.[81] Although relatively secure in many ways, such contracts were not entirely risk-free: creditors might struggle to obtain payment in the event of default, or if the property in question passed to another owner, potentially resulting in costly litigation.[82]

The legitimacy of *censi* made them a popular means of investment by religious institutions, including many convents. A survey of 1642 in Naples showed that convents drew the majority of their income from investments consisting largely of *censi*, a pattern also found in other regions of Italy.[83] In 1724 the convent of San Vincenzo in Lodi loaned over 5700 lire to the Miccoli brothers in the form of a *censo* contract. In this case the bulk of the capital actually consisted of the dowry

[75] Zuijderduijn, this volume, pp. 111–12.

[76] Vaquero Piñeiro, 'I censi consegnativi', pp. 61–64, 69; Colombo and Dotti, *Oikonomia urbana*, p. 33.

[77] Munro, 'The Medieval Origins of the Financial Revolution', p. 524.

[78] Corazzol, *Livelli stipulati*, p. 31; Carter and Goldthwaite, *Orpheus in the Marketplace*, p. 164.

[79] Mulé, 'Note sulla presenza femminili', pp. 171–72.

[80] Vaquero Piñeiro, 'I censi consegnativi', p. 84.

[81] Vaquero Piñeiro, 'I censi consegnativi', pp. 72–73.

[82] Carter and Goldthwaite, *Orpheus in the Marketplace*, p. 166.

[83] Novi Chavarria, *Sacro, pubblico e privato*, pp. 65–66.

of their niece, Lucia, which the convent loaned back to her uncles at interest — in this way her entry to the convent was paid for through a form of debt financing.[84] The long-term nature of *censi* contracts also made them popular instruments for making perpetual bequests to charitable and religious institutions, for example to say masses. In the seventeenth century, Agnese Ribeira, wife of the governor of Vigevano, left capital in the form of *censi* to the value of 48,000 lire to the city orphanage that she had founded, so providing for its long-term stability.[85]

Similar sorts of contracts could be used to lend money on security of any sort of income stream. In Rome, these included public offices, a form of investment that became popular in the sixteenth and seventeenth centuries.[86] Public officials were able to obtain loans on the basis of selling their future income; or the purchase of an office might be financed like a company, with shareholders providing capital in return for a share of the profits. In 1521, Lucrezia Rocchi invested 50 gold ducats in a 'company' with Francesco Ceccoli, obtaining annual income from the 'tenant' of the office equivalent to 15 per cent interest.[87] Typically such offices were in practice carried out by substitutes, who undertook to pay the 'rent' due to the owners in return for the proceeds.

In Northern Italy, alongside *censi* contracts, mortgage contracts called *livelli* were popular, in which the creditor purchased the title to the property and then leased it back to the debtor.[88] In such contracts, the rights of creditors were better protected, since they formally owned the land. Like *censi*, these were typically employed for safe, long-term investments that brought a modest return, and were therefore particularly popular with women investing dowries.[89] In a sample of Venetian mortgages from 1591, 20 per cent of investors in mortgages were women and they provided 24 per cent of the capital invested. By contrast, women constituted only 12 per cent of those using mortgages to borrow money, and they borrowed relatively small sums (just 11 per cent of the total capital).[90] Comparison can be made with Gayton's data for rural England in the next century, which

[84] Colombo and Dotti, *Oikonomia urbana*, p. 116. See also Strocchia, *Nuns and Nunneries in Renaissance Florence*, p. 25.

[85] Colombo and Dotti, 'Social Configurations of Municipal Debt', p. 62.

[86] Ago, *Economia Barocca*, pp. 191–92.

[87] Esposito, 'Perle e coralli', pp. 254–55.

[88] Corazzol, *Livelli stipulati*, pp. 13–14.

[89] Filippi, 'Patrimonio, redditi e consumi del Convento di Santa Maria della Scala di Verona nel 1680 e nel 1724', p. 71 n. 123.

[90] Corazzol, *Livelli stipulati*, p. 57.

indicate that women constituted around 26 per cent of investors in mortgages.[91] Similarly, women made up a higher proportion of mortgage borrowers (17 per cent), typically linked to short-term needs for significant life events.[92] In both cases, the data tend to confirm women's role as investors rather than entrepreneurs.

With their extensive landholdings as collateral, religious institutions could also offer a sort of deposit banking service to small investors, paying modest returns. The monastery of San Giorgio Maggiore in Venice paid depositors around 5 per cent interest in the late sixteenth century. Those who used mortgage contracts to lend money to the monastery included the widow of a wool-worker who invested 500 ducats, and a wool merchant who invested 10,000 ducats for the dowry of his daughter.[93] Similarly, the hospital of Santa Maria della Scala in fourteenth century Siena functioned as a sort of bank that was particularly popular with women, paying 5–6 per cent interest.[94]

The popularity of these relatively safe forms of investment tends to confirm the picture of most women as passive investors, content with the modest gains that came from long-term investments and preferring to make use of established institutions and agents in order to limit risk.[95] Such conservatism was a rational response to women's need to establish financial security for life, their lack of alternatives in the productive economy, and their goals of transmitting capital to their heirs.

Yet this is not the full picture of women's role as creditors. Women could obtain higher returns through moneylending, typically advancing loans on security of material goods, an activity that was only theoretically limited to the government-regulated pawnbanks. Although there were risks associated with this sort of illegal moneylending, lending money on pledge was relatively secure activity, given that the value of the collateral always exceeded that of the loans. In 1578 the Venetian woman Maddalena received a pair of breeches as pledge against a loan of 40 soldi.[96] She probably worked in partnership with her husband, a second-hand dealer, allowing her to sell off unredeemed pledges easily. Although such loans were often made without any documentation, contracts could also be manipulated to conceal the practice of usury. In fifteenth-century Trapani, the noblewoman Miraglia, a

[91] Gayton, this volume, Table 6.5, p. 160.

[92] Gayton, this volume, Table 6.2, p. 150; pp. 154–58.

[93] Corazzol, *Livelli stipulati*, pp. 97–98.

[94] Piccinni, 'Conti correnti di donne presso l'ospedale senese di Santa Maria della Scala', p. 124.

[95] On women's conservatism, see Fisher, 'Gender Differences in Personal Saving Behaviors', p. 14; Fisher, and Yao, 'Gender Differences in Financial Risk Tolerance'.

[96] Allerston, 'The Market in Second-Hand Clothes', p. 91.

doctor's wife, was involved in various contracts of this sort, involving fictitious sales and loans on pledge, which concealed short-term loans at interest rates from 7 to 28 per cent.[97] Similarly, the expertise of notaries in manipulating contracts helped women to evade the controls on usury in fifteenth-century Rome.[98]

In late medieval Europe, large numbers of Jewish women were involved in small-scale moneylending, often to Christian women.[99] This was a reflection of the particular agency enjoyed by Jewish women to manage their property independently.[100] The case of Richa is a striking example of this sort of activity from late sixteenth-century Venice. She was a female Jewish moneylender, resident in the Jewish ghetto but operating illegally, outside the official pawnbank system. She loaned small sums of money on pledge for short periods of time (from one week to a month), without any documentation. A network of Christian women acted as her agents, connecting Richa to clients throughout the parishes of the city, many of them women.[101] Many Jewish women were also actively involved in managing pawnbanks in partnership with their husbands, as in fifteenth-century Trieste.[102] In fifteenth-century Trapani, Gaudiosa Sammi operated in close partnership with her husband Lucio in variety of commercial and financial operations, and after his death she continued to manage the business with her son.[103] In an analogous case from fifteenth-century Perugia, Rema took over her husband's pawnbank on his death with her son as junior partner — this arrangement probably reflected the practical experience Roma had previously developed in running the bank alongside her husband.[104] Similar cases can be found in fifteenth-century Florence, Como, Pisa, and San Gimignano, reflecting the close involvement of Jewish women in business life.[105] In other cases, however, as in Padua, Jewish women might act as passive investors who entrusted the management of their capital to male relatives who ran the pawnbanks.[106]

97 Mulé, 'Note sulla presenza femminili', p. 170.

98 Esposito, 'Perle e coralli', p. 248. See also Shaw, 'The Informal Economy of Credit'.

99 Jordan, 'Women and Credit in the Middle Ages', p. 46.

100 Lanaro and Varanini, 'Funzioni economiche', pp. 95–96; Sperling and Wray, 'Introduction', pp. 4–5.

101 Archivio di Stato di Venezia [hereafter ASV], Piovego, b.141, 16 Mar 1589.

102 Davide, 'Il ruolo delle donne nelle comunità ebraiche', p. 32.

103 Mulé, 'Note sulla presenza femminili', pp. 176–77.

104 Frank, 'Jewish Women and Property in Fifteenth-Century Umbria', pp. 95, 97, 104.

105 Mulé, 'Note sulla presenza femminili', pp. 177–78.

106 Davide, 'Il ruolo delle donne nelle comunità ebraiche', pp. 40–41.

As the case of Richa suggests, the ties of credit often crossed ethnic boundaries. In fifteenth-century Trapani, various Christian women loaned money to Jews on pledge, as in 1433 when the widow Tommasa loaned 10 onze to the Jew Lucio Sammi on pledge of gold and silver objects.[107] Similarly, the doctor's wife Miraglia loaned money to a Jewish woman in 1463.[108] In this way, Jewish moneylenders might raise their capital from Christian investors, including women.[109] However, other cases suggest that Christian women might more directly involved in moneylending, employing Jews as their financial agents. This was the case of Saretta Galignara in seventeenth-century Venice — she was a wealthy widow who used two male Jewish intermediaries to arrange significant loans (typically a thousand ducats at a time) on pledge of goods, typically silver and gold items.[110]

Women's wealth was concentrated in mobile property rather than land, and this included material goods as well as cash. Particularly for women lower down the social scale, dowries were more likely to consist of material goods — rings, jewels, linens, furniture, and silverware were the main 'repositories of wealth' for households.[111] Goods were a form of savings that might be converted to liquid cash as required: they could be sold relatively easily in the second-hand market, or pawned for cash. Rather than a fixed stock of possessions excluded from circulation, goods were readily used as a means of payment or as collateral.[112]

Material goods could themselves also be loaned out, as typically took place at neighbourhood level, helping those who needed a pledge. Often such loans took place on a friendly basis, without charging a fee, and were unrecorded, but it was also possible to rent goods out at a profit.[113] In seventeenth-century Venice, Marietta Vicentina rented a pair of sheets to Bortolo Filacanevo for one ducat per month, and he then pawned the sheets to raise cash.[114] This was a perfectly legitimate form of credit that could be practised openly, in contrast to the renting out of money. The main risk was that the borrower would fail to return the goods. In

[107] Mulé, 'Note sulla presenza femminili', pp. 169, 172.

[108] Mulé, 'Note sulla presenza femminili', p. 170.

[109] See also Camerano, 'Donne oneste o meretrici?', p. 650.

[110] ASV, Piovego, b.34, 21 May 1670, Menachem Coen vs. Saretta Galignara.

[111] Shepard, 'Crediting Women', p. 16; Sperling and Wray, 'Introduction', p. 6.

[112] Ago, 'Using Things as Money'; Storey, 'Prostitution and the Circulation of Second-Hand Goods in Early Modern Rome; Allerston, 'Clothing and Early Modern Venetian Society'; Matchette, 'To Have and Have Not'; Matchette, 'Credit and Credibility'; Fontaine, 'Il posto delle donne', p. 521.

[113] Allerston, 'The Market in Second-Hand Clothes', pp. 65–67.

[114] ASV, Signori di Notte al Civil, b.340, no.14, 7 Nov 1668.

Rome, it was possible for women creditors to obtain protection for their property by registering such rental contracts with a notary, having the goods appraised by an expert, and with real estate as collateral.[115] More normally, such arrangements were documented privately, with relatively little protection, and only extended to members of the local community. In Venice, creditors were able take their claims to the magistracy of the *Signori di Notte al Civil*, in order to reclaim their property, attempting to prove their case through witness testimony and private documentation. Through such mechanisms, material capital might be invested for profit, and in turn the goods might be used as collateral for cash loans in the pawnbroking sector.

Women played a key role in neighbourhood credit networks, not only as creditors and debtors but also as intermediaries who helped to arrange loans for others. This was a common feature of consumption loans at the neighbourhood level, in which women played a key role.[116] In Florence, female street vendors played an important role as intermediaries enabling elite women to participate in networks of credit and exchange from their homes.[117] Women played a similar role as intermediaries in England, as in the case of Roberta Jones, a laundress and widow who arranged loans for others with the haberdasher and petty moneylender John Pope. More than 84 per cent of Pope's pawnbroking loans (a quarter of his business) were arranged by women.[118] Although the establishment of government-regulated pawnbanks tended to eat into the traditional practices of neighbourhood lending, women continued to play a role in the intermediation of such loans.[119] For borrowers, being seen going to a pawnbank could be a source of embarrassment, which might also damage one's standing with other creditors. As a result, intermediaries played a prominent role in this sort of lending, many of them women. In Bologna, Genoa, and Milan, intermediaries called *montiste*, most of whom were women, advanced money to clients and pawned items on their behalf at the pawnbanks. In eighteenth-century Bologna, their activities came to be regulated — they were not to deposit more than ten pledges per day and they had to deposits sums as guarantees of their correct behaviour.[120]

[115] Esposito, 'Perle e coralli', pp. 252–53.

[116] Jordan, *Women and Credit in Pre-Industrial and Developing Societies*; Fontaine, 'Il posto delle donne'.

[117] Matchette, 'Women, Objects, and Exchange in Early Modern Florence', pp. 247–48.

[118] Lemire, 'Introduction: Women and Credit', p. 8; Lemire, 'Petty Pawns and Informal Lending', pp. 122–23.

[119] Carbonell-Esteller, this volume, pp. 303–04.

[120] Muzzarelli, 'Le donne e i Monti di Pietà', pp. 205–06.

Dowry Litigation and Women's Agency

As previously mentioned, women were typically the creditors of their husbands, primarily through the dowry that they brought to the marriage. These rights were in theory protected in law, with a clear separation between the assets of husbands of wife. In practice, however, relations could be more ambiguous. As Paola Lanaro has emphasized, the formal record of the dowry might be manipulated: for example, the sums recorded as being received for the dowry might not actually be paid in full or on time.[121] It was for this reason that in the mid-fifteenth century, Alberti advised prospective husbands on the need for caution in regard to the dowry, which should be: 'middling in size, certain and prompt' rather than 'large, vague, or promised for an indefinite future'.[122] Insisting that the wife's relatives pay what they had promised might permanently damage relations. Conversely, husbands might falsify the value of dowries they had received, something that Francesco Guicciardini recorded as having done for purposes of tax avoidance.[123] In seventeenth-century Venice, Foscarina Memo was accused of artificially inflating the value of her property, in this way falsifying her own contribution to the partnership. The judges questioned witnesses closely as to whether the prices she had obtained for selling goods given to her by the husband were genuine or had been manipulated.[124]

For this reason, records of litigation can provide insights into the relative contributions of husband and wife to a marriage, and how women might exercise financial agency in practice even within the marriage relationship. Many marital disputes turned on the question of dowry: its precise value might be contested, the groom's family might claim that it had only been partially paid, and the wife might complain that her husband had failed to register and insure the dowry as was his legal and moral duty. Witnesses were often called upon to testify to the reality of the state of relations between the couple, and particularly about the assets that each party had brought to the marriage. Such testimony was essential if the dowry was not formally registered, but could also play a key role if the declared value of the dowry was contested.[125] For example, Foscarina Memo (see above) tried to demonstrate that she was a woman of independent means, as evidenced by the

121 Lanaro, 'La restituzione delle dote', pp. 760–61.

122 Alberti, *The Family in Renaissance Florence*, p. 117.

123 Guicciardini, 'Ricordanze', p. 138.

124 Ferraro, *Marriage Wars in Late Renaissance Venice*, pp. 146, 149.

125 Bellavitis, 'Women, Family, and Property in Sixteenth-Century Venice', p. 182.

fact that she had used mortgage contracts to lend money to the monastery of San Giorgio Maggiore. By contrast, witnesses for the groom's family tried to show that she was a poor woman who was financially dependent upon her husband, and that her dowry was entirely fabricated.[126] In such disputes, the testimony of neighbours, servants, agents, and tradesmen could play a key part in constructing the credit of marital partners.

These issues can be seen in Venice in the case of Lucrezia Gentili, whose fourth husband Iseppo Bindoni brought a complaint against her in court. The couple had married in 1653, but by 1656 Lucrezia had left her husband's house and was involved in litigation with him over her property, in particular the 'gold, silver, coins and goods' that she claimed were hers.[127] The dispute turned on the precise value of her dowry, much of it consisting of material goods that were probably unredeemed pledges, including bracelets, earrings, gold rings, and silver cutlery, the value of which was declared in a 'confession' or receipt made by Iseppo. This sort of informal receipt was an alternative to the proper registration of the dowry with a notary, commonly practised as a way of saving money, although inferior as a form of legal proof. For a wife, this could be problematic, since such documentation might be contested.

Iseppo tried to demonstrate that the receipt was a fabrication, which he had signed solely due to Lucrezia's undue influence over him. In order to show that Lucrezia's dowry was much smaller than stated in the receipt, he presented various witnesses from the neighbourhood, many of them women, who described Lucrezia as a former washerwoman 'from a race of poor and miserable people', who had married first a porter, then a galley musician, and then a 'poor man' called Cipriano Pasini. One woman described how Lucrezia and Pasini had lived miserably 'on one meal a day and her children crying from hunger'. A former landlord described Lucrezia as a poor woman who couldn't keep up with rent payments and had to pawn goods to cover her debts. In contrast to this picture of his wife's poverty, Iseppo tried to show that he was well-off before the marriage, describing his house as being furnished 'with all the things suitable for a gentleman'. Material goods were the visible sign of Iseppo's credit.

Lucrezia defended herself ably, insisting that Iseppo 'came to me with nothing and he had sold everything to second-hand dealers', and that he had been living with a priest with whom he had litigated over the rent. By contrast, she painted a picture of herself as a respectable woman who had brought assets totalling more than 8000

[126] Ferraro, *Marriage Wars in Late Renaissance Venice*, pp. 150–51.

[127] ASV, Piovego, b.33, 7 Aug 1657, Iseppo Bindoni vs. Lucrezia Gentili.

ducats to the marriage. Lucrezia presented herself as a canny female investor. She described how her third husband Pasini had run a mercer's shop in Corfu. Since he was often away in Venice to buy supplies, it was actually Lucrezia who ran the shops, selling goods on credit and lending money at 10 per cent interest to Venetian officers stationed at Corfu. The couple subsequently moved to Venice, where Pasini ran a mercer's shop, and Lucrezia continued to lend money — as she put it, 'I invested money at profit and lent money to people I trusted'. Various witnesses testified to the extent of her investments. One witness described how 'she was a well-off woman equipped with goods and furnishings, and she also made loans of three hundred or four hundred ducats per person'. The nobleman Francesco Grimani described how Lucrezia had lent his mother the sum of 300 ducats on pledge of silver goods, at an interest rate of 10 per cent.

As in the case of Saretta Galignara (see above), Lucrezia made use of various intermediaries, such as the Jewish moneylender Giacob Sorzetto, who described how Lucrezia had loaned him money on pledge of two dresses. Paulina, wife of a salt-fish merchant, similarly described how Lucrezia had given her 200 ducats to lend to her 'friend', paid back with interest after a period of 3–4 months. The second-hand dealer Battista Stabelin described how he sold goods on her behalf, and that her house was filled with 'leather wall hangings [...] beds, mattresses [...] various chains, earrings, bracelets and rings', which were probably pledges. Indeed, her marriage to Iseppo, who was a *comandador* (auctioneer), would have given Lucrezia convenient access to goods put up for public auction, which she could exploit using her networks of women, second-hand dealers and Jews.

Conclusion

Women's capital played a key role in a 'savings revolution' that extended across late medieval and early modern period. In Italy, although the ownership of liquid capital was concentrated in women's hands, it was generally men who actively managed capital in the productive economy. The gendered roles of the economy and household made women into quintessential creditors, obliged to entrust their fortunes to the care of men: to husbands in the form of the dowry, to sons in their business ventures, to governments through investing in public debt, and to merchants, shopkeepers and craftsmen as equity investors. Indeed, much of this investment was carried out on their behalf, as in the case of fathers investing in the dowries of their daughters, or husbands re-investing the capital in their own business affairs. Even as widows, women were often the shareholders and guarantors of the business ventures of male relatives.

When women did obtain direct control of their capital, as in widowhood, their management of wealth tended to be relatively passive, with a preference for well-established, legitimate forms of low-risk investment that secured them a modest income over the long term, such as annuities, mortgages, and public debt. As these avenues for investment opened up across the period, and particularly from the sixteenth century, they appear to have substituted for women's earlier participation in more short-term commercial ventures. Religious and charitable institutions were also favoured channels for investment: they could prosper by catering to women's need for security and support outside their kin groups. For many women, such benefits were often more important than maximizing returns. At the same time, women were also involved in low-level moneylending in the local community. These were often interest-free loans to kin, neighbours, and friends, including goods as well as cash, which cemented women's position in the community and brought benefits in terms of mutual support.

Nevertheless, as recent work has emphasized, this is not the whole picture.[128] There are also examples of women acting in more entrepreneurial roles, including married women as well as widows. Women were often involved in moneylending, motivated not only by neighbourly solidarity, but by profit. Lucrezia Gentili, for example, demonstrated considerable agency in her moneylending activities, first in Corfu and then in Venice, lending significant sums of money on pledge, and making strategic use of her marriage relations to dispose of goods. Sometimes, women were involved in petty consumption loans helping to tide people over a few weeks or months, as in the case of Richa the Venetian Jew, but Saretta Galignara and Lucrezia Gentili are distinctive as Venetian women who lent significant sums of money over longer terms.

When investing capital, women frequently made use of intermediaries or agents. In the formal sector of mortgages, annuities, and government debt, notaries played a key role in helping women to invest their money, broker deals and to ensure that contracts conformed to the usury laws.[129] In the informal sector of neighbourhood credit, women often played a key role in negotiating loans, as in the case of Richa, who used a network of Christian women as her agents to reach into the neighbourhoods of the city. Saretta Galignara on the other hand used male Jewish intermediaries to contract loans and collect payments. Reliance on agents detached women from the day-to-day difficulties of managing money and reduced some of the risks of incrimination. Yet detachment came with its own risks: agents

[128] Petti Balbi, 'Forme di credito femminile'.

[129] Hardwick, *The Practice of Patriarchy*; Esposito, 'Perle e coralli', p. 248.

might exploit their position to defraud investors, and their access to sensitive and incriminating information about moneylending activities gave them the means to pursue a grudge. The extensive archives of litigation reveal something of these tensions, indicating that women might be able to recover assets through legal action, but also the additional costs and delays involved.

Despite the laws protecting the position of women, they often had to struggle hard to assert their rights against the interests of husbands, children, and other kin. In looking for examples of women's financial agency, scholars have given particular attention to the activities of widows, who emerge as the most visible level of women's credit activities through their direct control of these assets. Yet within marriage too, women could exercise financial agency, protected by the clear laws establishing their right to separate property. Cases like that of Lucrezia Gentili reveal something of the negotiation of power within marital relations, and how a mutually advantageous partnership might turn into an acrimonious dispute over the assets that each side had brought to the marriage. The records of marital and contract litigation have considerable potential to reveal more about the informal sector of economy and the ways in which women could also exercise financial agency within marriage, as well as outside it.

Works Cited

Manuscripts

Archivio di Stato di Venezia [hereafter ASV], Piovego, b.141, 16 Mar 1589
ASV, Piovego, b.34, 21 May 1670, Menachem Coen vs. Saretta Galignara
ASV, Signori di Notte al Civil, b.340, no.14, 7 Nov 1668
ASV, Piovego, b.33, 7 Aug 1657, Iseppo Bindoni vs. Lucrezia Gentili

Primary Sources

Boccaccio, Giovanni, *Decameron*, trans. J. M. Rigg (1903; London, 1921)

Secondary Studies

Ago, Renata, *Economia Barocca: Mercato e istituzioni nella Roma del Seicento* (Rome: Donzelli, 1998)

———, 'Using Things as Money: An Example from Late Renaissance Rome', in *Alternative Exchanges: Second-Hand Circulations from the Sixteenth Century to the Present*, ed. by Laurence Fontaine (New York: Berghahn Books, 2008), pp. 43–60

Ait, Ivana, 'Donne in affari: il caso di Roma (secoli XIV–XV)', in *Donne del rinascimento a Roma e dintorni*, ed. by Anna Esposito (Rome: Roma nel Rinascimento, 2013), pp. 53–84

Alberti Battista Leon, *The Family in Renaissance Florence: Books One–Four*, trans. R. N. Watkins (Columbia: University of South Carolina Press, 1969)

Allerston, Patricia Anne, 'Clothing and Early Modern Venetian Society', *Continuity and Change* 15.3 (2000), 367–90

———, 'The Market in Second-Hand Clothes and Furnishings in Venice, c. 1500–c. 1600' (unpublished doctoral thesis, European University Institute, 1996)

———, 'An Undisciplined Activity? Lace Production in Early Modern Venice', in *Shadow Economies and Irregular Work in Urban Europe: 16th to Early 20th Centuries*, ed. by Thomas Buchner and Philip R. Hoffmann-Rehnitz (LIT Verlag Münster, 2011), pp. 63–71

Ambrosini, Federica, 'Penombre femminili', in *Storia di Venezia, vol. VII, La Venezia Barocca*, ed. by Gino Benzoni and Gaetano Cozzi (Rome: Istituto della Enciclopedia Italiana, 1997), pp. 301–23

Angelos, Mark, 'Women in Genoese commenda Contracts, 1155–1216', *Journal of Medieval History*, 20.4 (1994), 299–312

Bellavitis, Anna, 'Dare credito, fiducia e responsabilità alle donne (Venezia, sec. XVI)', in *Dare credito alle donne: presenze femminili nell'economia tra medioevo ed età moderna, Convegno internazionale di studi Asti, 8–9 ottobre 2010*, ed. by Giovanna Petti Balbi and Paola Guglielmotti (Asti: Centro studi Renato Bordone sui Lombardi, sul credito e sulla banca, 2012), pp. 259–67

———, 'Women, Family, and Property in Sixteenth-Century Venice', in *Across the Religious Divide: Women, Property, and Law in the Wider Mediterranean (ca. 1300–1800)*, ed. by Jutta Sperling and Shona Kelly Wray (London: Routledge, 2010), pp. 175–90

Bertoni, Laura, 'Investire per la famiglia, investire per sé: la partecipazione delle donne ai circuiti creditizi a Pavia nella seconda metà del secolo XIII', in *Dare credito alle donne: presenze femminili nell'economia tra medioevo ed età moderna, Convegno internazionale di studi Asti, 8–9 ottobre 2010*, ed. by Giovanna Petti Balbi and Paola Guglielmotti (Asti: Centro studi Renato Bordone sui Lombardi, sul credito e sulla banca, 2012), pp. 51–75

Bezzina, Denise, *Artigiani a Genova nei secoli XII–XIII* (Florence: Firenze University Press, 2015)

Brizio, Elena, 'In the Shadow of the Campo: Sienese Women and their Families (c. 1400–1600)', in *Across the Religious Divide: Women, Property, and Law in the Wider Mediterranean (ca. 1300–1800)*, ed. by Jutta Sperling and Shona Kelly Wray (London: Routledge, 2010), pp. 122–36

Brucker, Gene, *The Society of Renaissance Florence: A Documentary Study* (Reprint edn, New York: Harper & Row, 1998) [1971]

Camerano, Alessandra, 'Donne oneste o meretrici? Incertezza dell'identita fra testamenti e diritto di proprieta a Roma', *Quaderni Storici*, 33.99 (1998), 637–75

Caracausi, Andrea, 'Beaten Children and Women's Work in Early Modern Italy', *Past & Present*, 222.1 (2015), 95–128

Carter, Tim, and Richard A. Goldthwaite, *Orpheus in the Marketplace: Jacopo Peri and the Economy of Late Renaissance Florence* (Cambridge, MA: Harvard University Press, 2013)

Cavallo, Sandra, *Charity and Power in Early Modern Italy: Benefactors and their Motives in Turin, 1541–1789* (Cambridge: Cambridge University Press, 1995)

Cecchini, Isabella, 'A World of Small Objects: Probate Inventories, Pawns, and Domestic Life in Early Modern Venice', *Renaissance and Reformation / Renaissance et Réforme*, 35.3 (2012), 39–61

Chabot, Isabelle, 'Lineage Strategies and the Control of Widows in Renaissance Florence', in *Widowhood in Medieval and Early Modern Europe*, ed. by Sandra Cavallo and L. Warren (London: Pearson Education, 1999), pp. 127–44

——, 'Widowhood and Poverty in Late Medieval Florence', *Continuity and Change*, 3.2 (1988), 291–311

Chojnacka, Monica, *Working Women of Early Modern Venice* (Baltimore: Johns Hopkins University Press, 2001)

Chojnacki, Stanley, 'Getting Back the Dowry: Venice, c. 1360–1530', in *Time, Space, and Women's Lives in Early Modern Europe*, ed. by Anne J. Schutte, Thomas Kuehn, and Silvana Seidel Menchi (Kirksville: Truman State University Press, 2001), pp. 77–96

——, 'Patrician Women in Early Renaissance Venice', *Studies in the Renaissance*, 21 (1974), 176–203

——, *Women and Men in Renaissance Venice: Twelve Essays on Patrician Society* (Baltimore: Johns Hopkins University Press, 2000)

Colesanti, Gemma, and Fiorella Fragnoli, 'Operatrici economiche in Italia meridionale durante il Medioevo', *Mediterranean Chronicle*, 4 (2014), 57–73

——, *Oikonomia urbana: Uno spaccato di Lodi in età moderna (secoli* XVII–XVIII*)* (Milan: Franco Angeli, 2010)

Colombo, Emanuele, and Marco Dotti, 'Social Configurations of Municipal Debt (State of Milan, XVII-XVIIIth Centuries)', *Journal of European Economic History*, 44.1 (2015), 47–83

Corazzol, Gigi, *Livelli stipulati a Venezia nel 1591: studio storico* (Pisa: Giardini, 1986)

Cox, Virginia, 'The Single Self: Feminist Thought and the Marriage Market in Early Modern Venice', *Renaissance Quarterly*, 48.3 (1995), 513–81

Crabb, Ann, 'Gaining Honor as Husband's Deputy: Margherita Datini at Work, 1381–1410', *Early Modern Women*, 3 (2008), 225–31

——, '"If I could write": Margherita Datini and Letter Writing, 1385–1410', *Renaissance Quarterly*, 60.4 (2007), 1170–1206

Davide, Miriam, 'Il ruolo delle donne nelle comunità ebraiche dell'Italia nord-orientale (Padova, Treviso, Trieste e Friuli)', in *Ebrei nella Terraferma veneta del Quattrocento: Atti del Convegno di studi Verona, 14 novembre 2003*, ed. by Gian Maria Varanini and Reinhold C. Mueller (Florence University Press, 2005), pp. 31–43

Della Valentina, Marcello, 'The Silk Industry in Venice: Guilds and Labour Relations in the Seventeenth and Eighteenth Centuries', in *At the Center of the Old World: Trade and Manufacturing in Venice and the Venetian Mainland, 1400–1800*, ed. Paola Lanaro (Toronto: Centre for Reformation and Renaissance Studies, 2006), pp. 109–43

Erickson, Amy Louise, 'Coverture and Capitalism', *History Workshop Journal*, 59 (2005), 1–16

———, 'Possession — And the Other One-Tenth of the Law: Assessing Women's Ownership and Economic Roles in Early Modern England', *Women's History Review*, 16.3 (2007), 369–85

Esposito, Anna, 'Perle e coralli: credito e investimenti delle donne a Roma (XV- inizio XVI secolo)', in *Dare credito alle donne: presenze femminili nell'economia tra medioevo ed età moderna, Convegno internazionale di studi Asti, 8–9 ottobre 2010*, ed. by Giovanna Petti Balbi and Paola Guglielmotti (Asti: Centro studi Renato Bordone sui Lombardi, sul credito e sulla banca, 2012), pp. 247–58

Ferraro, Joanne M., *Marriage Wars in Late Renaissance Venice* (Oxford: Oxford University Press, 2001)

Figliulo, Bruno, 'Lo spazio economico dei mercanti messinesi nel XV secolo (1415–1474)', *Nuova Rivista Storica*, 97.3 (2014), 757–800

Filippi, Vinicio, 'Patrimonio, redditi e consumi del Convento di Santa Maria della Scala di Verona nel 1680 e nel 1724' (dottorato di ricerca, Università degli studi di Verona, 2011)

Fisher, Patti J., 'Gender Differences in Personal Saving Behaviors', *Journal of Financial Counseling and Planning*, 21.1 (2010), 14–24, 77–78

Fisher, Patti J., and Rui Yao, 'Gender Differences in Financial Risk Tolerance', *Journal of Economic Psychology*, 61 (2017), 191–202

Fontaine, Laurence, *The Moral Economy: Poverty, Credit, and Trust in Early Modern Europe* (Cambridge: Cambridge University Press, 2014)

———, 'Il posto delle donne nella piccola economia finanziaria in Europa, in età moderna', *Quaderni*

———, 'Women's Economic Spheres and Credit in Pre-Industrial Europe', in *Women and Credit: Researching the Past: Refiguring the Future*, ed. by Beverly Lemire, Ruth Pearson, and Gail Campbell (Oxford: Berg, 2001), pp. 15–32

Frank, Karen, 'Jewish Women and Property in Fifteenth-Century Umbria', in *Across the Religious Divide: Women, Property, and Law in the Wider Mediterranean (ca. 1300–1800)*, ed. by Jutta Sperling and Shona Kelly Wray (London: Routledge, 2010), pp. 95–108

Fregulia, Jeanette M., 'Stories Worth Telling: Women as Business Owners and Investors in Early Modern Milan', *Early Modern Women*, 10.1 (2015), 122–30

———, 'Widows, Legal Rights, and the Mercantile Economy of Early Modern Milan', *Early Modern Women*, 3 (2008), 233–38

Goldthwaite, Richard A., *The Economy of Renaissance Florence* (Baltimore: Johns Hopkins University Press, 2008)

González de Lara, Yadira, 'The Secret of Venetian Success: A Public-Order, Reputation-Based Institution', *European Review of Economic History*, 12.3 (2008), 247–85

Greif, Avner, 'Contract Enforceability and Economic Institutions in Early Trade: The Maghribi Traders' Coalition', *American Economic Review*, 83.3 (1993), 525–48

Guicciardini, Francesco, 'Ricordanze' in *Selected Writings*, ed. Cecil Grayson (New York: Harper & Row, 1965), pp. 125–70

Hardwick, Julie, *The Practice of Patriarchy: Gender and the Politics of Household Authority in Early Modern France* (University Park: Pennsylvania State University Press, 1998)

Hartigan-O'Connor, Ellen, 'Gender's Value in the History of Capitalism', *Journal of the Early Republic*, 36.4 (2016), 613–35

Homer, Sidney, and Richard Sylla, *A History of Interest Rates* (New Brunswick: Rutgers University Press, 1963)

Ingham, Geoffrey K., *The Nature of Money* (Cambridge: Polity, 2004)

Jordan, William Chester, 'Women and Credit in the Middle Ages: Problems and Directions', *Journal of European Economic History*, 17.1 (1988), 33–62

———, *Women and Credit in Pre-Industrial and Developing Societies* (Philadelphia: University of Pennsylvania Press, 1993)

Kamenaga-Anzai, Yoko, 'Attitudes towards Public Debt in Medieval Genoa: The Lomellini Family', *Journal of Medieval History*, 29 (2003), 239–63

Kirshner, Julius, *Marriage, Dowry, and Citizenship in Late Medieval and Renaissance Italy* (Toronto: University of Toronto Press, 2015)

———, 'Wives' Claims against Insolvent Husbands in Late Medieval Italy', in *Women of the Medieval World: Essays in Honor of John H. Mundy*, ed. by Julius Kirshner and Suzanne F. Wemple (Oxford: Blackwell, 1985), pp. 256–303

Kirshner, Julius, and Anthony Molho, 'The Dowry Fund and the Marriage Market in Early Quattrocento Florence', *Journal of Modern History*, 50 (1978), 403–38

Klapisch-Zuber, Christiane, 'The "Cruel Mother": Maternity, Widowhood, and Dowry in Florence in the Fourteenth and Fifteenth Centuries', in *Women, Family, and Ritual in Renaissance Italy*, ed. Christiane Klapisch-Zuber (Chicago: University of Chicago Press, 1985), pp. 117–31

Koehler, Benedikt, 'Islamic Finance as a Progenitor of Venture Capital', *Economic Affairs*, 29.4 (2009), 89–91

Kuehn, Thomas, '"Cum Consensu Mundualdi": Legal Guardianship of Women in Quattrocento Florence', *Viator*, 13 (1982), 309–34

———, 'Daughters, Mothers, Wives, and Widows: Women as Legal Persons', in *Time, Space, and Women's Lives in Early Modern Europe*, ed. by Anne J. Schutte, Thomas Kuehn, and Silvana Seidel Menchi (Kirksville: Truman State University Press, 2001), pp. 97–115

———, 'Debt and Bankruptcy in Florence: Statutes and Cases', *Quaderni Storici*, 137 (2011), 355–90

Lanaro, Paola, and Gian Maria Varanini, 'Fidecommesso, doti, famiglia: la trasmissione della ricchezza nella Repubblica di Venezia (XV–XVIII secolo)', *Mélanges de l'Ecole Française de Rome. Italie et Méditerranée modernes et contemporaines*, 124.2 (2012), 519–31

———, 'Funzioni economiche della dote nell'Italia centro-settentrionale (tardo medioevo / inizi età moderna)', in *La famiglia nell'economia europea: secc. XIII–XVIII*, ed. by Simonetta Cavaciocchi (Florence: Firenze University Press, 2009), pp. 81–102

———, 'La restituzione della dote. Il gioco ambiguo della stima tra beni mobili e beni immobili (Venezia tra Cinque e Settecento)', *Quaderni Storici*, 135 (2010), 753–78

Laurence, Anne, Josephine Maltby, and Janette Rutterford, eds, *Women and their Money, 1700–1950: Essays on Women and Finance* (London: Routledge, 2009)

Lemire, Beverly, 'Introduction: Women and Credit: A Historical Overview' in *Women and Credit: Researching the Past, Refiguring the Future*, ed. by Beverly Lemire, Ruth Pearson, and Gail Campbell (Oxford: Berg, 2001), pp. 3–14

———, 'Petty Pawns and Informal Lending: Gender and the Transformation of Small-Scale Credit in England, Circa 1600–1800', in *From Family Firms to Corporate Capitalism: Essays in Business and Industrial History in Honour of Peter Mathias*, ed. by Kristine Bruland and Patrick O'Brien (Oxford: Clarendon, 1998), pp. 112–38

Lizzul, Giorgio, 'The Utility of Wealth in the Era of the Public Debt 1300–1500' (unpublished doctoral thesis, University of London, 2017)

Matchette, Ann, 'Credit and Credibility: Used Goods and Social Relations in Sixteenth-Century Florence', in *The Material Renaissance*, ed. by Michelle O'Malley and Evelyn Welch (Manchester: Manchester University Press, 2007), pp. 225–41

———, 'To Have and Have Not: The Disposal of Household Furnishings in Florence', *Renaissance Studies*, 20.5 (2006), 701–16

———, 'Women, Objects, and Exchange in Early Modern Florence', *Early Modern Women*, 3 (2008), 245–51

McGough, Laura, 'Women, Private Property, and the Limitations of State Authority in Early Modern Venice', *Journal of Women's History*, 14.3 (2002), 32–52

McIntosh, Marjorie K., *Working Women in English Society, 1300–1620* (Cambridge: Cambridge University Press, 2005)

Molho, Anthony, *Marriage Alliance in Late Medieval Florence* (Cambridge, MA: Harvard University Press, 1994)

Mueller, Reinhold C., *The Venetian Money Market: Banks, Panics and the Public Debt, 1200–1500* (Baltimore: Johns Hopkins University Press, 1997)

Muldrew, Craig, 'From Credit to Savings? An Examination of Debt and Credit in Relation to Increasing Consumption in England (c. 1650 to 1770)', *Quaderni Storici*, 137 (2011), 391–413

Mulé Viviana, 'Note sulla presenza femminili nel mercato del credito in Sicilia nel XV secolo', in *Dare credito alle donne: presenze femminili nell'economia tra medioevo ed età moderna, Convegno internazionale di studi Asti, 8–9 ottobre 2010*, ed. by Giovanna Petti Balbi and Paola Guglielmotti (Asti: Centro studi Renato Bordone sui Lombardi, sul credito e sulla banca, 2012), pp. 167–78

Munro, John H., 'The Medieval Origins of the Financial Revolution: Usury, "Rentes," and Negotiability', *International History Review*, 25.3 (2003), 505–62

———, 'Usury, Calvinism, and Credit in Protestant England: from the Sixteenth Century to the Industrial Revolution', *University of Toronto, Department of Economics*

Working Paper, 439 (2011), <http://www.economics.utoronto.ca/public/workingPapers/tecipa-439.pdf> [accessed 9 Jul 2013]

Muzzarelli, Maria Giuseppina, 'Le donne e i Monti di Pietà: storia di una relazione di lungo periodo', in *Dare credito alle donne: presenze femminili nell'economia tra medioevo ed età moderna, Convegno internazionale di studi Asti, 8–9 ottobre 2010*, ed. by Giovanna Petti Balbi and Paola Guglielmotti (Asti: Centro studi Renato Bordone sui Lombardi, sul credito e sulla banca, 2012), pp. 195–209

Novi Chavarria, Elisa, *Sacro, pubblico e privato: Donne nei secoli XV–XVIII* (Naples: Alfredo Guida Editore, 2009)

Petti Balbi, Giovanna, 'Forme di credito femminile: osservazioni introduttive', in *Dare credito alle donne: presenze femminili nell'economia tra medioevo ed età moderna, Convegno internazionale di studi Asti, 8–9 ottobre 2010*, ed. by Giovanna Petti Balbi and Paola Guglielmotti (Asti: Centro studi Renato Bordone sui Lombardi, sul credito e sulla banca, 2012), pp. 9–24

Pezzolo, Luciano, 'L'economia', in *Storia di Venezia, vol. VII, La Venezia Barocca*, ed. by Gino Benzoni and Gaetano Cozzi (Rome: Istituto della Enciclopedia Italiana, 1997), pp. 369–433

——, *L'oro dello Stato: Società, finanza e fisco nella Repubblica veneta del secondo '500* (Venezia: Cardo, 1990)

Piccinni, Gabriella, 'Conti correnti di donne presso l'ospedale senese di Santa Maria della Scala: Interessi, patti, movimenti di danaro (1347–1377)', in *Dare credito alle donne: presenze femminili nell'economia tra medioevo ed età moderna, Convegno internazionale di studi Asti, 8–9 ottobre 2010*, ed. by Giovanna Petti Balbi and Paola Guglielmotti (Asti: Centro studi Renato Bordone sui Lombardi, sul credito e sulla banca, 2012), pp. 121–47

Queller, Donald E., and Thomas F. Madden, 'Father of the Bride: Fathers, Daughters, and Dowries in Late Medieval and Early Renaissance Venice', *Renaissance Quarterly*, 46.4 (1993), 685–711

Sambo, Alessandra, 'Strategie d'immortalità tra resistenze private e veti pubblici: Donne e famiglie nella Venezia del Seicento', *Quaderni Storici*, 48.2 (2013), 567–96

Shaw, James E., 'The Informal Economy of Credit in Early Modern Venice', *Historical Journal*, 31.3 (2018), 623–42

Shepard, Alexandra, 'Crediting Women in the Early Modern English Economy', *History Workshop Journal*, 79.1 (2015), 1–24

Sklansky, Jeffrey, 'The Elusive Sovereign: New Intellectual and Social Histories of Capitalism', *Modern Intellectual History*, 9.1 (2012), 233–48

Sperling, Jutta, 'Marriage, Kinship, and Property in Portuguese Testaments (1649–1650)', in *Across the Religious Divide: Women, Property, and Law in the Wider Mediterranean (ca. 1300–1800)*, ed. by Jutta Sperling and Shona Kelly Wray (London: Routledge, 2010), pp. 158–74

Sperling, Jutta, and Shona Kelly Wray, eds, *Across the Religious Divide: Women, Property, and Law in the Wider Mediterranean (ca. 1300–1800)* (London: Routledge, 2010)

———, 'Introduction', in *Across the Religious Divide: Women, Property, and Law in the Wider Mediterranean (ca. 1300–1800)*, ed. by Jutta Sperling and Shona Kelly Wray (London: Routledge, 2010), pp. 1–24.

Spicksley, Judith M., '"Fly with a Duck in thy Mouth": Single Women as Sources of Credit in Seventeenth-Century England', *Social History*, 32.2 (2007), 187–207

———, 'Women, "Usury" and Credit in Early Modern England: The Case of the Maiden Investor', *Gender and History*, 27.2 (2015), 263–92

Storey, Tessa, 'Prostitution and the Circulation of Second-Hand Goods in Early Modern Rome', in *Alternative Exchanges: Second-Hand Circulations from the Sixteenth Century to the Present*, ed. by Laurence Fontaine (New York: Berghahn Books, 2008), pp. 61–75

Strocchia, Sharon T., *Nuns and Nunneries in Renaissance Florence* (Reprint edn, Baltimore: Johns Hopkins University Press, 2013)

Vaquero Piñeiro, Manuel, 'I censi consegnativi. La vendita delle rendite in Italia nella prima età moderna', *Rivista di storia dell'agricoltura*, 47.1 (2007), 57–94

Vitullo, Juliann, 'Femininity in the Marketplace: The Ideal Woman in Fourteenth-Century Florence', *Early Modern Women*, 3 (2008), 211–16

Gold, Ink, and Tears: The Hazards of Credit and the Indebted Widow in Eighteenth-Century Germany

Eve Rosenhaft

This article offers an approach to women's experiences with credit relations that invites attention to elements of challenge and anxiety. At its centre is an account of the ways in which one woman — the middle-class German widow Eva König — negotiated the demands of managing an inheritance encumbered by debt. It gives particular attention to how, in her letters, the gender politics of her situation are reflected in a language that combines business and emotional registers in ways particular to her status and social milieu. Considering the late eighteenth century as a watershed in the emergence of modern commercial and property relations, I argue for closer attention to the ways in which the nexus of vernacular and financial languages of identity and affinity — in this case the uses of the term 'friendship' — has changed over historical time, as changes in social

Eve Rosenhaft is Professor of German Historical Studies at the University of Liverpool (UK). She has held fellowships in Britain, Germany, and the United States. She has published widely on aspects of German social history, including labour, gender, urban culture, and issues of race and ethnicity. Her most recent book publications are *Black Germany: The Making and Unmaking of a Diaspora Community 1884–1960* (Cambridge: Cambridge University Press, 2013 — with Robbie Aitken) and *Slavery Hinterland: Transatlantic Slavery and Continental Europe 1680–1850* (Martlesham: Boydell & Brewer, 2016 — with Felix Brahm). The present article is one of a series of articles on the theme of gender, finance, and middle-class culture in eighteenth-century Germany, including most recently '"All that glitters is not gold, but…": German Responses to the Financial Bubbles of 1720', in *Money in the German Speaking Lands*, ed. by Mary Lindemann and Jared Poley (Oxford and Providence: Berghahn, 2017).

Women and Credit in Pre-Industrial Europe, ed. by Elise M. Dermineur, EER 12 (Turnhout: Brepols, 2018), pp. 203–226.
BREPOLS ✠ PUBLISHERS DOI 10.1484/M.EER-EB.5.115754

structure and accompanying shifts in gender relations transformed the terms of economic subjectivity.

The study of women and credit brings together two fields of scholarship whose initial impulses were critical of complacent assumptions about both the pre-industrial past and the contours of 'modernity', but in which the general trend of scholarship has tended to be at least functionalist and often optimistic or celebratory.[1] Credit relations were never unproblematic, though; they called for active management — what Jürgen Schlumbohm has characterized as 'strategies of loosing and binding',[2] and as relations of trust they also implied a degree of risk. Mischa Suter expresses the delicacy of the balance when he characterizes credit as a 'riskante Vorleistung' (a payment in advance incurring a degree of risk) which opens up a space for 'Unwägbarkeiten' ('imponderable' conditions and outcomes).[3] The purpose of this essay is to consider the 'down sides' to credit relations as they affected women in their particular circumstances, and specifically the situation of indebtedness. My strategy here is to explore the possible meanings of the combination of 'women' and 'credit' at the margins, or at the point where women's competence might have been tested or their allegiances stretched. This might help to re-centre discussion on woman-specific practices and experience, given the extent to which the scholarship has 'normalized' women as financial actors.[4]

One way to think about 'margins' is to make explicit the network model that underlies a functionalist reading of early modern credit relations.[5] If we picture credit relations in terms of networked households, and even if we accept that kin and non-kin relationships overlap in these networks, individual households and families themselves constitute both crucial nodes in wider networks, and independent sets of relations which may be in tension with the purposes of the wider network and in any case are governed by distinct dynamics and sets of rules. In this sense, the bounds of the family constitute one margin, or horizon, of a set of

[1] Muldrew, *The Economy of Obligation*, pp. 4–5; Fontaine, 'Makeshift, Women and Capability', pp. 56–72.

[2] Schlumbohm, 'Zur Einführung', pp. 7–14.

[3] Suter, 'Jenseits des "Cash Nexus"', p. 90.

[4] Cf. Fontaine, 'Women's Economic Spheres', pp. 15–30, esp. pp. 27–30. In her recent book, *Silent Partners,* Amy Froide has explored the place of risk and loss in the experience of early modern women investors, with particular reference to the dimensions of women's life course and their complex relationships with male relatives and advisers that I address here; see especially Chapters 3 and 6.

[5] Cf. Lipp, 'Aspekte der mikrohistorischen und kulturanthropologischen Kreditforschung'; Gestrich and Stark, eds, *Debtors, Creditors, and their Networks*.

credit relations, and this makes practices of *innerfamilial* credit and indebtedness particularly interesting. The relevance to women of such an approach should be clear, since life course within family is clearly something that structured the ways in which women could and did exercise financial agency. Moreover, when the family functions both as credit network and as the primary locus of individual socialization, the ambivalent mix of affect and material interest that underlies most relationships between debtors and creditors comes into sharp focus.[6]

What I want to explore more closely here is a second 'margin': the point of particular stress represented by the transition in status from wife to widow. This was in principle a moment of crisis for the entire network, because a widow's capability to exercise her newly gained capacity as independent actor was one of those 'imponderables' to which Mischa Suter refers. It was a situation that called for the readjustment of existing relationships among creditors, kin, and others. Among other testing changes was the fact that as part of her inheritance, debts which a woman might not have incurred or had any role in managing passed from her husband's 'account' to hers.

I am interested in the broadly emotional dimensions of this situation: that is, in the ways in which women debtors expressed their needs and their anxieties about self and others. It is, again, Mischa Suter who has most recently articulated the value of exploring the discourses of self that emerge from conversations about credit, arguing from nineteenth-century sources that with the emergence of modern liberal capitalism debt became part of the social dynamics that shaped characteristically modern subjects.[7] But early modern historians have for some time been aware of the negotiation of credit relations as a forum for the articulation of gendered subjectivity. Scholarship on risk and failure in business history, and especially on bankruptcy, has explored the languages that the law and occupational and associational cultures made available to male debtors.[8] In the case of women, the record is patchier. Discourses of shame and honour were notoriously gendered, but the historians' observation about the sexualization of women's 'creditworthiness' that frequently features in the exchange of insults around credit transactions has now become so familiar that we may overlook the 'dead air' that it implies: how — for example — might credit as a *positive* measure of 'character' have been associated with perceptions and self-perceptions of financial competence, success, and failure in the case of women?[9]

[6] See for example Fontaine, *The Moral Economy*, p. 283.

[7] Suter, *Rechtstrieb. Schulden und Vollstreckung im liberalen Kapitalismus 1800–1900.*

[8] Safley, 'Business Failure and Civil Scandal'; Fisher, 'Bankruptcy in Early Modern German Territories', pp. 173–84. See also Ditz, 'Shipwrecked: or, Masculinity Imperiled'.

[9] E.g. Muldrew, '"A Mutual Assent of her Mind"', p. 53. Cf. Finn, *The Character of Credit.*

In the German case, the silence is most felt in the case of wives and widows of the middling sort who do not figure in the records of riot and litigation. As Daniel Rabuzzi has observed, merchant women might or might not have been equipped to manage credit relations, but in any case they 'wrote little self-reflectively about their commercial activities or even about their attitudes toward commerce generally' — with the notable and endlessly productive exception of the Jewish businesswoman Glückl von Hameln (1646–1724).[10] The case study below draws on a set of ego-documents, letters between a merchant widow and her fiancé written between 1770 and 1776. Before turning to that study, though, it will be useful to set out the situation that prevailed in the German lands in respect of women and credit.

Widows and Credit in the Holy Roman Empire

We have learned not to exaggerate the helplessness of widows. The German case echoes the wider European picture here, although it has been argued that the fragmentation of jurisdiction even within territorial states and the relative autonomy of municipalities and even villages was the key peculiarity of the Holy Roman Empire that both enabled and constrained women in particular ways.[11] By the eighteenth century, the forms of gender guardianship and the legal incapacities that persisted in general terms in each of the many legal codes in force within the Empire had been modified in many places to enable married women to work and trade in their own right as well as in partnership with their husbands: this applied everywhere to those involved in the buying and selling of goods at various levels (*Handelsfrauen*, *Kauffrauen* or *Kaufmänninnen*).

Widows of all classes enjoyed a particular degree of independence, and the still relatively limited research on personal credit in German-speaking Europe reflects their competence to manage that.[12] Among weavers in the putting-out system in Württemberg, Sheilagh Ogilvie finds widows well versed in playing terms of credit

[10] Rabuzzi, 'Fading Images, Fading Realities?'.

[11] Beachy, 'Women without Gender', and Ogilvie, *A Bitter Living*, p. 75.

[12] In addition to works cited elsewhere in the notes, see Deuter, 'Schulden und Privatkredit im 18. Jahrhundert am Beispiel des Bamberger Heinrichsviertels', pp. 137–84. Individual studies of rural credit relationships have challenged a long-standing assumption that urban actors were normally at the heart of credit networks; many of these are localized in Switzerland and Austria, for example Khull-Kholwald, *Der Adel auf dem Land und sein Kredit*. Wider studies that give attention to credit practices within particular status and occupational groups include: Brakensiek, *Fürstendiener*; Klingbeil, *Ein Stand für sich? Lokale Amtsträger in der frühen Neuzeit*.

and interest to their own benefit.[13] In the case of the salaried service middle classes who constituted a numerically and ideologically significant fraction of the middling sort, it is clear that a woman without a husband — a 'Frau vom Stand' barred by the code of respectability from earning an income through work — was expected to rely on the management of cash for her livelihood beyond any direct support she might receive from family members. The ideal was a widow who could live from the interest on capital reserved by marriage contract or fixed on her by her husband (a legacy or jointure) or her father (a dowry).[14] And in some German territories by the eighteenth century widows were granted explicit rights to manage their dowry for themselves.[15] As a result, investment of some kind was central to the lives of these women, and relatively underdeveloped capital markets left most of them dependent on local forms of credit.[16] A recent study of personal credit in Hanover between 1550 and 1750 shows that over the two centuries some 12 per cent of identifiable lenders were women, including married women but with widows in a majority.[17] In the university town of Göttingen, where the total proportion of women among creditors was around 13 per cent, widows were responsible for some 70 per cent of the funds lent by women in the first half of the eighteenth century, much of it in the form of mortgages.[18]

The changes to custom and law that enabled German women as economic actors left them exposed as debtors, however. Indeed, change was generally driven by the demands of creditors seeking access to the otherwise protected assets of wives and widows, which became more urgent with the increased use of bills of exchange.[19] While it was possible in most jurisdictions for women to enter into credit relations in their own name or as co-signatories with their husbands, the price was explicit renunciation of their *weibliche Gerechtigkeiten* — the immunity from claims on their personal property that they enjoyed in respect of their sex.[20] In mercantile

[13] Ogilvie, *A Bitter Living*, p. 238.

[14] Brakensiek, *Fürstendiener*, p. 248; Möhle, *Ehekonflikte und sozialer Wandel. Göttingen 1740–1840*, p. 92.

[15] Fontaine, 'Women's Economic Spheres', p. 20 (citing Claudia Opitz).

[16] Gestrich and Stark, 'Introduction', in Gestrich and Stark, eds, *Debtors, Creditors, and their Networks*, pp. 1–10 (3).

[17] Sturm, *'wat ich schuldich war'*, pp. 66–71, 87.

[18] Winnige, 'Vom Leihen und Schulden in Göttingen. Studien zum Kapitalmarkt', pp. 252–320.

[19] Beachy, 'Women without Gender'.

[20] For Hanover, see Sturm, *'wat ich schuldich war'*, p. 86.

communities like Hamburg, where my case study is situated, widows enjoyed the least protection from their husbands' creditors.

The Indebted Widow Eva König

Eva König was born Eva Katharina Hahn in Heidelberg. Her father was a *Kaufmann* — a merchant engaged in long-distance trade, probably in textiles. In 1756 she married Engelbert König, a textile merchant from Hamburg; he died in 1769, leaving her a widow at thirty-three with four children aged from one to thirteen. Both the Hahns and the Königs were exemplars of an urban middling milieu in which mercantile family businesses remained the economic core of households whose younger sons increasingly made careers in the professions or civil service. The Königs were active members of the cultural élite in Hamburg, not only a cosmopolitan commercial centre but the capital of the German enlightenment; among the friends they made there in the 1760s was the critic and dramatist Gotthold Ephraim Lessing. After her husband's death Eva became close to Lessing and they were betrothed in the autumn of 1771, marrying in 1776. She died of puerperal fever in 1778. Almost all we know about her comes from her correspondence with Lessing, which was published by Lessing's brother in 1789.[21] The original letters have not survived, and there exist only a handful of other manuscript letters from her.

Although Engelbert König died unexpectedly, it is unlikely that he died intestate; however, no will has survived. Similarly, we have no evidence for the character of the Hamburg merchant house that Eva inherited. The letters make clear that the intention was always that it should be wound up, the remaining stock sold, and the proceeds returned to the estate.[22] The sum of goods and capital in the estate was sufficient for Eva to anticipate an 'Erbteil' (portion of the inheritance).[23] The principal asset that she inherited, though, was a pair of factories which Engelbert König had set up in Vienna in the 1760s: a 'Hamburg-style' silk manufacture, which specialized in introducing new luxury textiles to the Austrian market, and an 'English style' wallpaper factory. With twenty-three looms in 1762, its first year of operation, and a further thirteen working and employing a total of thirty-five men

[21] The definitive critical edition of the letters is still *Meine liebste Madam: Gotthold Ephraim Lessings Briefwechsel mit Eva König 1770–1776*. In the following, the letters are referred to only by date, but all references are to this edition. Except where otherwise noted, the letters are from Eva König to G. E. Lessing.

[22] 25 November, 10 and 19 December 1771; Nuremberg, [6 March] 1772.

[23] 13 December 1771.

and twenty-eight women a decade later, the textile plant flourished, to become one of the largest in private hands in the Austrian empire.[24]

By law and custom Eva had full capacity to dispose of this inheritance in the interest of herself and her children. Where there were minor children, a Hamburg widow was customarily understood to have full rights of guardianship and management of the estate. Increasingly often, one or more guardians was appointed, and guardians were commonly named in the father's will, but in merchant families a man who trusted his wife to take over the business could and would designate her as the children's guardian and manager of the estate.[25] The actions of Eva and the rest of the family suggest that this was the case with the Königs.

Eva's most recent biographer, Petra Oelker, plausibly represents her as a competent businesswoman, not only a merchant wife but the daughter of a merchant widow who had socialized with other independent women traders.[26] However, the inheritance of the factories presented her with a challenge that went beyond her legal rights or personal competence, because with the manufactures she inherited her husband's debts. These included loans made towards the operation of the factories and were owed both to family members and to outsiders (she uses the terms 'die Meinigen' — 'my people' — and 'Fremde' — 'strangers', respectively). She characterized her eldest brother Johann Georg Hahn, a Heidelberg merchant, as her principal creditor, and her brother-in-law, Friedrich Wilhelm König, was also a creditor of the Vienna manufactures. Among the others with claims on the firm was a certain Herr von Wagener, in Vienna, who called in his debt in November 1771 when his own company was being dissolved. One of her four Hamburg creditors was 'the Jew P.', probably Israel or Lazarus Popert, both wealthy manufacturers.[27] And there were incidental commitments like a 1200-Mark surety for the debts of Friedrich Christoph Wurmb, for which she was liable when he declared bankruptcy in December 1771.[28] Since she reported that she owed her uncle Johann Conrad

[24] Blume, 'Engelbert Königs Wiener Fabriken', pp. 1–2; Deutsch, *Die Entwicklung der Seidenindustrie in Österreich 1660–1840*, pp. 104–05, 108.

[25] Trummer, *Das Hamburgische Erbrecht*, 2 vols. vol. 1, pp. 351–53. For an example from another jurisdiction, see the Will of Christian Andreas To der Horst, 1749, Stadtarchiv Braunschweig D I 7 Nr 10, pp. 613–25.

[26] Oelker, '*Ich küsse Sie tausendmal*'.

[27] 23–25 December 1771. Individuals, including family members, are rarely given their full names in Eva König's letters; they are identified in the explanatory notes to *Meine liebste Madam*.

[28] 25 November 1771. On the role and obligations of the guarantor (*Bürge*), see Sturm, '*wat ich schuldich war*', pp. 96–102. Women could act as guarantors in their own right; it is not clear whether Eva König had provided the surety for Wurmb in her own name or whether it formed part of her negative inheritance.

Kaltschmidt 10,000 Gulden plus four years' interest, and he was not the greatest of her creditors, her total debts must have been very substantial.[29] When she did her accounts at the end of 1771, having received all the business papers from Vienna after some delay, she reckoned that she would need 15,000 Marks to tide her over while she sorted things out, and this seems to have been in addition to the demands of her creditors.[30] The process of liquidating Eva's inheritance only ended in 1774; her debts were on the way to being discharged in 1776.

Dealing with her creditors was Eva's first responsibility as widow and heiress. Germanic law dictated that creditors had first claim on an estate before the residue was shared out among the heirs, and under Hamburg law, the wife's personal assets, both property brought into the marriage and her dowry, could be called on to repay debts.[31] There does not appear to have been any protection for the interests of minor children against the claims of creditors in Hamburg law, apart from a provision that gave the widow and dependent children a period of grace before the creditors could enforce their claims.[32] This would be in keeping with the practice in other mercantile jurisdictions, such as the Baltic ports where Lübeck law was in force; there, as a disincentive to bankruptcy, the widow of a bankrupt who had minor children could only extinguish claims on her future earnings and assets by renouncing her own claim on her dowry and other extant property.[33]

Eva's central preoccupation was whether and how to dispose of the factories, which might provide a good income in the long term but whose sale could be a source of capital to meet short-term needs. These decisions were complicated by unanticipated demands on her material and psychological assets. The obligations associated with debt constituted a network that involved people with varying and sometimes multiple claims on her good faith, and mobilizing to satisfy her creditors — as a precondition for moving on — called for the creation of new sets of connections and obligations. If we have come to see women's involvement in credit networks and other financial operations as a matter of routine in spite or because of the real and imagined obstacles to their economic agency, Eva König's case shows that engagement with debt in managing the transition from wife to indebted widow (and back to free agent) was anything but routine; rather it was freighted with risk and anxiety. Moreover, the fact of being a woman meant that both creditors and family and friends perceived her and their own scope for action in gendered terms,

[29] 28 December 1774.

[30] 10 December 1771.

[31] Trummer, *Das Hamburgische Erbrecht*, pp. 108–12.

[32] Trummer, *Das Hamburgische Erbrecht*, pp. 25, 77–85.

[33] Rabuzzi, 'Women as Merchants in Eighteenth-Century Northern Germany', p. 450.

so that negotiating the gender politics of her position added to the emotional stress inherent in the situation and called for particular kinds of self-representation.

Eva presents herself in her letters as someone familiar with the world of business and experienced in the kinds of networking it called for. The Vienna manufactures were managed on site by König's factor Cornelius Hornbostel, but on a brief visit to Vienna in the autumn of 1770 she inspected the works herself as a matter of course and observed that they were going well.[34] In March 1772, after much deliberation, she moved to Vienna. Living on the site of the textile factory, she took over its management and finally succeeded in selling both the textile and the wallpaper factories in 1774. She sold the textile factory to Hornbostel and a partner, netting 26,500 Gulden from the sale. One source names the interest income on this sum as 500 Reichstaler (reflecting an investment at 3 per cent), which would have guaranteed her a respectable living.[35] But the buyers would only take over the business if it was backed up by a state subsidy. Eva's application for a grant to the Austrian Imperial Ministry of Commerce, the only one of her business letters to have been published, reads in part:

> Sollte aber auch diese meine untertänigste Bitte unerhört bleiben, so wäre ich jetzt (da die Mantinitaft einzuführen erlaubet worden, worauf [...] ich mich seit einiger Zeit verlegt habe) um so mehr gezwungen [...] das in so schönem Flor stehende Werk zurtrümmert aus der Hand zu schlagen und so viele aus der Fremde hergezogene Leute brotlos zu machen, auch das Herzeleid zu erleben, meine Familie, die mir bis jetzt so treu beigestanden, zu verkürzen, der ich ohnedies mit meinen vier Kindern zur Last falle.[36]

> But should my humble request remain unheard, I would now (since permission has been granted for the import of Mantini taffeta, which [...] I have been producing for some time) be all the more compelled to [...] leave the flourishing enterprise in ruins and make so many men brought in from abroad unemployed, and also suffer the pain of failing to repay my family, which has so far stood by me so faithfully, and instead becoming a burden to them along with my children.

That the author of the letter is a woman becomes clear only in the closing reference to the threat of personal dependency; otherwise she writes confidently and

[34] 4 October 1770.

[35] Henneberg and Henneberg, *Geschichte der Familie Henneberg (Braunschweig)*, p. 211. Eva's daughter Amalia married into the Henneberg family. Cf. Hamburg, ? April 1776, in which she anticipates an income of '4 to 500 Tlr Louis d'Or' if her capital is invested at 3 per cent.

[36] Cited by Blume, 'Engelbert Königs Wiener Fabriken', p. 2.

unsentimentally — if in the familiar conventions of deference — about *her* business: She is someone with *personal* responsibility for a business, its employees, and her adult relatives.

Eva's letters also show her as experienced in managing relations of credit. As late as May 1776, with their marriage approaching, she reproaches Lessing for being too sensitive to accept a loan from her to relieve him of a momentary embarrassment.[37] Frequent references to credit operations, mainly the circulation of bills of exchange (*Wechsel*), to some of which she was party in her own name, constitute the background music to the conversation about her current financial problems. Just before Christmas 1771 she reports to Lessing on the situation of their mutual friend Johann Friedrich Schmidt, facing bankruptcy with a debt of 7000 Marks. She is concerned about Schmidt's circumstances, particularly since his wife is clearly oblivious to any problems. But the Schmidts' situation also provokes reflection on her qualities as debtor and creditor: Eva had been an early party to a chain of *Wechsel* associated with Schmidt's debts, though her name no longer featured there; his principal creditor had now lost patience and all payments were frozen. Eva had two thoughts: first, she remembered how her hand had 'trembled' as she signed the *Wechsel* in the first place — an anxiety now confirmed by the failure of this particular credit network. Still more worrying, though, was the possibility that Schmidt might have come to her for help; his creditor, being a long-time associate, would not be insisting on payment if Schmidt were not facing insolvency, and in ignorance of that Eva probably would have made Schmidt a further loan — thereby worsening her own circumstances.[38]

A similar reflection on her own character in the context of past and present debts, which places her agency in a rather different light, appears in her account of her dealings with 'the Jew P'.[39] Popert had agreed to write off 40 per cent of her debt and to wait for payment of the remainder, on condition she could find someone to stand surety. Eva's first instinct was: 'der Jude muß für sein Mißtrauen bestraft werden' ('the Jew has to be punished for his lack of trust'); she would accept his terms but avoid paying him any more than she could afford. She acknowledged that this had nothing to do with personal animosity; he had always been generous to her, and in fact had recently helped her out to the tune of 1500 Gulden by buying a *Wechsel* that she held on an Augsburg merchant house and taking the loss when that business went into liquidation. But she thought that Popert could

[37] 19/31 May 1776.

[38] 20 December 1771.

[39] 21–23 December 1771.

afford to take another loss, acknowledging that her attitude was simple 'Eigensinn' ('pig-headedness').[40] Her reason for citing the incident was to allay Lessing's fear that her good nature and conscience might lead her to act against her own interests: 'Es ist wahr, ich handle gern aufrichtig und redlich, meinem Charakter, meinen Grundsätzen gemäß; doch daß ich in dem Fall, worin ich jetzt bin, meinem Vorteil entgegen stehen sollte, bloß um den Schein von Eigennützigkeit zu vermeiden, keineswegs!' ('It's true, I prefer to act in an upright and honest fashion, as suits my character and my principles; but that in my present circumstances I should resist acting to my own advantage just to avoid seeming selfish — by no means!').[41]

This is an example of the 'split personality' that Laurence Fontaine attributes to the early modern businessman, 'someone whose interest required that he be at the same time coldly calculative and warmly compassionate'.[42] Fontaine points out that this duality was unavoidable, particularly given that credit relations typically involved multiple communities to which the businessman stood in different relations. In other respects, too, we can see Eva König executing a very typical tightrope walk between competing claims. We find her constantly weighing up the respective interests of 'Meinige' and 'Fremde' for example — such that her relatives were the last of her creditors to be satisfied.[43] What, then, is gender-specific about her situation and her response?

Key to Eva König's situation was the fact that despite her legal capacity as an independent actor, and her manifest self-confidence, she was unable to escape a degree of reliance on men, and notably on her male relatives. They enjoyed a superior power to act in the world and a claim to guide her actions which were implicit in her status within the family as well as in status-specific codes that limited the options available to a 'Frau vom Stand'. In the first instance, the men around her weren't much help. Lessing advised her to stay well and cheerful at all costs and comfort herself with the thought that none of it was her fault.[44] Since her brother Johann Georg and her brother-in-law were also her principal creditors, it is perhaps

[40] Lessing did not comment on this, but the author of *Die Juden* and *Nathan der Weise,* plays critiquing contemporary antisemitism, would have recognized the perverse logic of citing both moral superiority to the Jew (at a time when lack of trust was viewed in Christian theological terms as a sin against God and one's fellow-man) and his actual financial power to justify one's own failure to act in good faith. On the theological uses of Vertrauen/trust, see Rosenhaft, 'How to Tame Chance', pp. 24–25.

[41] 21–23 December 1771.

[42] Fontaine, *The Moral Economy*, p. 283.

[43] 11 November 1775.

[44] GL to EK, 20 November 1771.

not surprising that they couldn't agree on a solution, and on one occasion her middle brother David, a professor of physics in Utrecht, plunged her into depression by saying that if (or when) she fell into destitution he would of course support her for the rest of her life.[45] Clearly David had some confidence in her competence, though, since in spite of his undisguised anxiety he asked whether she hat 'Muth und Lust' — courage and desire — to move to Vienna and manage the factory herself; in the event, it seems to have been a family conference that finally persuaded her to embark on her second, more extended visit to Vienna a few weeks later.[46]

Her exasperation with her dependence on men nevertheless finds expression in repeated complaints about her brother-in-law. Friedrich Wilhelm König was Engelbert König's younger brother, a minor civil servant in Hamburg. A year younger than Eva and unmarried, he had the scope for action that she lacked and possibly a degree of legal authority; he may have been the executor of Engelbert's will, and it is possible that in his own judgement he was protecting the interests of his nieces and nephew when he repeatedly failed (or refused) to act as Eva expected. As she saw it, he was simply being irresponsible — or as she put it in one of only two uses of the key term 'honour' in her letters, he simply would not do 'was er anders seiner Ehre wegen hätte tun müssen'[47] ('what you would have expected him to do for the sake of his own honour'). At the end of 1771 the business of the Wurmb bankruptcy left her 'nahe dabei, alle Contenance zu verlieren' ('on the verge of losing all patience') at Friedrich Wilhelm's failure to drum up the money necessary to cover her obligations.[48] And by early 1773 she was no longer hesitating to use terms like 'nichtswürdig' ('good-for-nothing') and 'unwürdig' ('unworthy') in relation to him and his actions: Her relatives had agreed that the profits from the sale of her Hamburg warehouses (in the end, she was not quite sure how they had been sold) could be used to pay off her 'stranger' creditors, on the condition that they would nevertheless agree to let their investments lie in the Vienna manufacture until she could bring it into profit, and she had instructed Friedrich Wilhelm to solicit the agreement of the 'strangers' on the basis of a valuation of the factory. Instead, he had sent the valuation to her brother (copy to Eva), with the suggestion that the family creditors might accept less than their paper claim while the 'strangers' were

[45] 11 December 1771.

[46] 28 December 1771 and 7 January 1772.

[47] 7 January 1772. The second use is in reference to Lessing in the context of his own salary negotiations: February/March 1776. In the letters 'honour' is never used in connection with Eva or any other woman.

[48] 19 December 1771.

paid more. Eva's one consolation at that point was that in fact she had already told her own brothers what was going on, so they were not in a position to be taken advantage of by Friedrich Wilhelm's machinations.[49]

In the end, the men in Eva's life did provide a supportive framework that enabled her own actions, and that she acknowledged in emotive terms. She was never less than appreciative of Johann Georg's support, and he made an important contribution by suggesting, as a way out of the initial impasse, that she find an independent adviser. That role was played by Johannes Schuback, four years her senior and founder of a Hamburg merchant house which is still in existence, and it was largely through his interventions that Eva was able to negotiate the entangled interests of 'Meinige' and 'Fremde'. (Of Schuback, Lessing observed to Eva that he was pleased 'daß sich nun ein Mann dabei interessiert, der hoffentlich von dieser Seite mehr Kaufmann ist, als Sie'[50] ['that a man is now taking an interest who I hope is more of a businessman than you']). In late 1774 Schuback persuaded Eva's uncle to suspend her obligation to him by writing over the debt to her children until such time as there were no longer any claims against her and she could reclaim it as a gift. As she expressed it, her relief at the lifting of the debt was not more intense than her satisfaction in hearing from Schuback that her uncle had expressed the love of a father for her, in spite of having children of his own.[51] (It was in connection with this arrangement that Lessing, otherwise careful to avoid influencing Eva's financial decisions, ventured his sole piece of unsolicited advice; in May 1776 he urged her never to make any claim on that capital — for reasons he could only impart face-to-face.)[52]

Nevertheless, I think we can identify in Eva's letters a degree of psychological stress arising from the constraints particular to her situation as middle-class widow. At the same time we can recognize in her choice of words (Lessing called Eva a 'fertige Briefschreiberin'[53] — an accomplished letter-writer) ways of describing the particular mix of business and personal relationships that reflect a historical moment in which languages of affinity and obligation were being renegotiated, with particular consequences for the injection of values of sentiment into middle-class culture. It is a significant feature of that conjuncture that both men and women engaged in the language of sentiment, but it is certainly true that women had privileged access

[49] 26 January 1773.

[50] GL to EK, 16 December 1771.

[51] 18 December 1774.

[52] GL to EK, 2 May 1776. For an example of a characteristically supportive but unemphatic reply to one of Eva's direct questions, see his letter of 3 December 1772.

[53] GL to EK, 10 June 1770.

to it in the context of emerging middle-class gender norms. This is clear among other things in the uses to which Eva König puts the term 'friend' and the affect that attaches to it in different cases, including the terms in which she invokes questions of risk, trust and confidentiality.

The multiplicity of meanings that the term 'friend' had in the early modern period is well known. Across a range of regional and linguistic contexts we find the word applied to blood relatives (including in statutes governing inheritance), patrons, and business associates — indeed, to each and all of the multiple communities involved in credit networks — at least as often as it signifies an affectionate relationship with non-kin, although the notion of friendship as a union of hearts and minds shared by moral equals was already present in European culture by the seventeenth century.[54] In milieux in which women exercised independent political or business agency, the term in all its meanings could be applied to women as well as men, in spite of evidence of an early sexualization of 'friend' as applied to women in real or presumed erotic relationships.[55]

The phrase Johann used in encouraging Eva to find an independent adviser was 'einen redlichen Freund zu Rate ziehen' — seek advice from an honest friend. 'Friend' here denotes a functional role in an essentially business context, but in Eva's presentation Johannes Schuback becomes something more, in a narrative that begins with a powerful sense of risk and uncertainty and climaxes in a celebration of disinterested attachment. The choice of adviser, who in fact acted as her agent as the business went on (in parallel and sometimes in tension with her brother-in-law), was her own, and her choice was itself a business decision that *reinforced* her capacity to make strategic choices. But the social dynamics that informed her interactions with Schuback as with her male relatives were necessarily gendered.

Of her decision to approach Schuback Eva writes,

> Hierzu war aber nicht allein ein redlicher, sondern auch ein einsichtsvoller und verschwiegener Mann erfordert. Die Schwierigkeit war: wo finden wir den? Endlich fiel mir ein Mann ein, der hier, auswärts, und besonders am Wiener Hofe, dafür passieret; ich kannte ihn aber nicht einmal von Person. Doch wagte ich es, und ersuchte ihn schriftlich um seinen Beistand.[56]

[54] Tadmor, *Family and Friends in Eighteenth-Century England*; Fontaine, *The Moral Economy*, esp. Chapters 8–10; Sabean, *Kinship in Neckarhausen, 1700–1850*, pp. 42–45; Grüne, 'Freundschaft, Privatheit und Korruption', pp. 289–90; Jahncke, 'Patronage, Freundschaft, Verwandtschaft'.

[55] Gowing, 'The Politics of Women's Friendship'; Schleuning, *Hof, Macht, Geschlecht*, pp. 300–17; D'Cruze, 'The Middling Sort in Eighteenth-Century Colchester', p. 189.

[56] 10 December 1771.

> But for this purpose I needed a friend who was not only honest but also wise and discreet. The problem was: where to find him? At last I thought of someone who passes for such here, abroad and especially at the court in Vienna; but I didn't even know him to look at. Nevertheless, I took a chance, and wrote to ask for his help.

Here Eva is using the language of risk: the term 'wagen' is now commonly translated as 'dare', but in the eighteenth century it was intimately associated with gambling — cognate with 'wager'. Eva and her fiancé Lessing were regular buyers of lottery tickets. And here, too, she was taking a chance. In engaging Schuback Eva was readjusting her personal-and-business connections in a way that, among other things, gave her access to Schuback's own networks — not least his familiarity with the situation in Vienna, where he was involved in business and enjoyed the confidence of the Empress Maria Theresa. Although Eva was probably personally acquainted with his brother, she knew Johannes only by reputation.[57] And her approach to him incurred multiple risks — from the immediate risk of embarrassing rejection to the more serious long-term one that her trust in him might prove to have been misplaced. The language of gambling recurs in this correspondence, and Eva's subsequent comments in some ways chart the highs and lows of the gambler or speculator.

In the first instance, though, her trust proved to have been well placed:

> Diese Epoche hat mir einen aufrichtigen Freund erworben, der mit solchem Eifer für mich sorget, daß er gestern halb eilf in der Nacht noch einen Weg von einer halben Stunde in meinen Angelegenheiten machte. Gegen Sie kann ich ihn nennen, sonst will er noch nicht genannt sein — es ist Herr Johannes Schuback.[58]

> In these days I have gained an upright friend, who is so earnest in his care for me that last night at half past ten he walked half an hour's distance on my business. I can name him to you, though he doesn't want to be named otherwise — it's Herr Johannes Schuback.

What Schuback did at their first meeting was to look over her accounts and ask her what *she* wanted to do. He agreed with her own plan, which was to open her

[57] On Schuback, see his entry in Kopitsch and Brietze, eds, *Hamburgische Biographie*, vol. 2, p. 383; Möring, *1757–1957. 200 Jahre Johannes Schuback & Söhne Familie und Firma in Hamburg*, pp. 49–100. Neither personal nor business papers from this period in the history of the firm seem to have survived. Schuback was a better-established businessman than the Königs and there is no evidence that Eva paid him a fee for his help.

[58] 10 December 1771.

books to her creditors and ask that they extend the deadline for repayment until the Vienna business could be sorted out. Here a second discourse inflecting trust emerges: the emphasis on confidentiality and the risk associated with breaching it. We see it here even in the question of identifying her adviser, whose own reputation was at stake in the affair. It was also central to the question of how much she should reveal about her circumstances. She repeatedly asked Lessing to keep her letters to himself: 'Auf die Verschweigenheit kömmt es hauptsächlich an, sonst bin ich gewiß verloren'. ('Discretion is the key thing, otherwise I am surely lost'.)[59] The *appearance* of transparency was itself an element in the negotiation of trust between any debtor and creditor, while every debtor had an interest in keeping control of information about his or her actual situation. The fact that Eva was a woman and her confidants men gave a particular inflection, I think, to the danger she perceived of being 'lost' or ruined.

The question of who knew what is linked to another use of the term 'friend' in a letter of November 1772. At that point, Eva had been in Vienna overseeing the manufactures for seven months, and the business was going better than ever. This was partly because those of the investor-creditors whom she characterized as 'friends' had in fact refrained from pulling out their capital. The overall result was that she faced a real choice between selling off the factories and making a new start with the capital, and keeping the business going in order to ensure that her creditors were fully satisfied. Schuback thought it best to sell up and offered to manage the resulting capital on her behalf, and (with her permission) sought the permission of her creditors to do so. While 'die meisten Fremden' (most of the strangers) among them agreed, it was her 'friends' who were reluctant to give Schuback the necessary powers. As Eva explained, they did not and could not know the nature of her arrangement with Schuback.[60] Here 'friend' is being used in the mixed sense of a business associate with whom one shares a relationship of trust and who can be expected to have one's interests at heart; among them were presumably the 'die ältesten Freunde' ('oldest friends'), named only as R. and M., who feature six months later as the only non-family creditors yet to be satisfied.[61]

What Eva learned to value in Schuback, beyond his manifest business competence and good connections, was the way he combined material disinterest — equal

[59] 13 December 1771.

[60] 19 November 1772.

[61] 21 June 1773. The editors of the letter edition propose that the two creditors, whom Eva identifies only by their initials, were members of the Hamburg elite, one a merchant and one a lawyer.

detachment from Eva's finances and from her family — with a demonstrated commitment to her wellbeing and energy and discretion in pursuing it: 'Ist das nicht ein redlicher Mann? [...] Er tut so viel für mich, daß er mich öfters vor Dankbarkeit stumm macht, und tut es so stille, daß ich erst, wenn die Sache entschieden ist, erfahre, daß er es getan hat'.[62] ('Is that not an honest man? [...] He does so much for me that he often leaves me speechless with gratitude, and he does it so quietly that I only learn when the business is decided that he has done it'.) But the confidence Eva had placed in Schuback gave him a real, if unsought, power over her peace of mind. In December 1771 she writes

> Nie habe ich Gott mit muntererem Eifer gedankt, als für den Freund, den er mir in Herrn Schuback zuwies. Er ist der edelste, der rechtschaffenste Mann; allein so sorglich, so nachdenkend, wie ich leider! selbst bin. Alle möglichen Unglücke, die nur kommen können, sagt er mir vor. Er fürchtet, daß das Kapital in der Wiener Fabrik wie im Lotto lieget [...]

> I have never had reason to thank God more cheerfully than I thank Him for the friend he has sent me in Herr Schuback. He is the noblest, the most upright man — but also as inclined to worry and ponder as I (alas) am. He sets before me all the possible misfortunes that might arise. He is afraid that the capital is about as safe in the Vienna factory as in the lottery [...]

This left Eva mentally negotiating between her sense of her own competence and her trust in Schuback, a tension with consequences for her state of mind:

> Für mich, die das Werk kennet, ist zwar wenig Wahrscheinlicheit, daß diese betrübte Prophezeiung in Erfüllung kommen könne, oder werde; allein denken Sie selbst, wenn einem so was so öfters widerholet wird, so wird man zuletzt betäubt, und trauet seinem eigenen Urteile nich mehr. Am Tage bin ich meiner mächtig; wenn ich aber in der Nacht auf einen solchen Gedanken komme, so weiß ich ich nicht wieder heraus zu finden.[63]

> As for me, who knows the factory after all, I don't think it very probable that these dark prophecies are likely to be fulfilled; but you can imagine that when you hear that sort of thing repeated time and time again you grown numb in the end and don't trust your own judgement any more. In daylight I am completely in control, but when such a thought comes to me at night I can find no way out.

[62] 3 January 1772.

[63] 13 December 1771.

While still unknown, or in prospect, Eva's adviser was an 'honest friend', a sense of 'friend' that implies trust and support without express sentimental attachment. In Eva's letters Schuback makes a progress from business friend to intimate, and the progress was complete when Eva and Lessing married at the Schubacks' country house. The evolution of their relationship is thrown into relief by the parallel story of a 'friend' who turned out to be little more than a business partner, the investor-creditor von Wagener whose calling in of his debts features in the letters as a moment of emotional as well as financial crisis. In November 1771, reporting von Wagener's action, she wrote to Lessing: 'Ich wollte gerne in dem elendesten Winkel der Welt Wasser und Brod essen, wenn ich nur aus dem Labyrinth einmal heraus wäre!'[64] ('I would gladly be living on bread and water in the vilest corner of the world, if only I could escape from this labyrinth!') Von Wagener presented a puzzle to both Eva and Lessing, since he was a long-standing 'friend' of Eva's husband's. They socialized regularly, and von Wagener had promised with tears in his eyes to help Eva in any way he could, since her husband had helped to forestall a lawsuit which would have ruined him.[65] Lessing put his finger the contradiction: 'So will er Ihnen diese Freundschaft noch nach [König's] Tode sehr teuer bezahlen lassen'.[66] ('He's certainly expecting you to pay a high price for that friendship now that [König] is dead'.)

The tears marked von Wagener as a man of feeling, acting in accord with a code of sensibility which by the 1770s had embedded in it a friendship discourse that was entirely sentimental, and that by the nineteenth century had become the dominant one among Germany's educated classes. In this new vision of friendship the meaningful border in terms of language and practice was not the one that separated affection and interest, but the porous barrier between platonic and erotic intimacy — not least as friendships between men and women based on moral equality became thinkable.[67] Friedrich Gottlieb Klopstock, one of the leading poets of sentimental friendship, belonged to Lessing and Eva's Hamburg literary circle, and that sense of 'friend' is deployed quite self-consciously in their published correspondence. In the months preceding their betrothal in the Autumn of 1771 we see them using it to 'feel out' each other's intentions: Lessing calls Eva his 'liebe Freundin'

[64] 14 November 1771.

[65] 25 November 1771.

[66] GL to EK, 20 November 1771.

[67] Schmidt, 'Das Verhältnis von Freundschaft und Liebe im 18. Jahrhundert', in Schmidt and others, eds, *Freundschaft und Verwandtschaft*, pp. 115–43; Nenon, *Aus der Fülle der Herzen*.

('dear friend') in the very first letter, but Eva replies only with the closing formula 'Ihre ergebene Dienerin' ('your devoted servant'); only after some back-and-forth in the deployment of such formulas does Eva declare herself, and that in the relatively ambiguous role of friendly adviser, having told him not to work too hard: 'Diesen Rath gibt Ihnen Ihre beste Freundin und ergebene Dienerin' ('This advice is from your best friend and devoted servant').[68] Her last use of 'Dienerin' is on 7 May 1771, after which she always signs as 'Freundin', often 'aufrechte Freundin' ('sincere friend'). The importance that Eva attributed to the display of emotion in everyday contexts is similarly apparent elsewhere in her letters, in a parallel thread in which she puzzles over the behaviour of a woman friend whose style of coping with the death of her child is businesslike rather than emotional.[69]

Von Wagener's adherence to the code of sensibility should have predicted a degree of altruism on his part, and on reflection Eva could not bring herself to believe that he would insist on her ruin. In January 1773 she was in fact able to reach an accommodation with him. But the persistent emotional power of that initial shock is apparent in her account of their last meeting:

> [Eben], weil es so gelang [...] so griff es mich mehr an, als wenn der redliche Mann stürmisch und hart gewesen wäre. In dem letzten Falle hätte ihm mein freies Gewissen die Spitze geboten. Allein er zeigte nichts als Mitleid und Eifer, zur baldigen Endschaft meiner Sache das Seinige beitragen zu wollen, und also können Sie leicht denken, daß ich trauriger von ihm ging, als ich zu ihm kam. Ich war so matt, wie ich zu Hause kam, daß ich alle mögliche Anstrengung brauchte, um nur mit einigen Zeilen an S[chuback] den Ausgang dieses Geschäfts melden zu können.[70]

> [Precisely] because it was so successful [...] it hit me harder than if that honest man had been stormy and intransigent. Then my conscience would have been free to face him down. But he showed me nothing but sympathy and eagerness to make his own contribution to bringing my business to a rapid conclusion, and so you may well imagine that I went away in a sadder frame of mind than when I had arrived. I was so exhausted when I got home that I had to make the greatest effort even to write a few lines to Schuback to report the outcome of the business.

Reflected here is not only the stress incurred by being reminded of the lived tension between business and affection, but the mental constraint imposed by the

[68] Letters dating from 10 June to 30 September 1770.

[69] 19 December 1771.

[70] 26 January 1773.

condition of indebtedness. Eva uses the term 'free' here advisedly, although her 'debtor's prison' is entirely psychological. She spent the next week in bed — not the first time she had found the situation physically debilitating; at the beginning of the correspondence she wrote of being exhausted by 'diese Auftritte — an die ich nicht gewöhnet bin' ('these comings and goings, which I'm not used to').[71]

Conclusion

The expression of mental strain in physical debility in this case is not unique to Eva's letters; her brother David's letter of 1771, in which he asked whether she had 'Muth und Lust' to travel to Vienna, ended with the (less than encouraging) observation: 'Mein Schlaf ist durch diese Sorgen, die ich mit aller Anstrengung nicht abschütteln konnte, weggenommen, und meine Gesundheit ganz zerrüttet'[72] ('These worries, which I cannot shake off however hard I try, have robbed me of my sleep and completely ruined my health'). The language of anxiety, like the discourse of sensibility, was one available to both men and women. Similarly, there is an uncanny echo of Johann Georg Hahn's advice to his sister in a work published ninety years later; a Victorian book of financial advice to women recommends that they 'seek a sensible and upright Friend, who is a good man of business'.[73] This complicates the business of identifying what is either gender- or period- (or indeed place-) specific about Eva König's experience or the languages she deploys. Here we might begin by observing that the author of the Victorian advice book was herself a woman: although the language does not appear to have changed, the speaker has, as has the medium through which she addresses her listeners.

In his own micro-study of the mentality of a Swiss (male) debtor, Mischa Suter adduces a clear distinction between economic and personal relations, such that the use of economic language allows for distancing from the more tangled problems of family life. He sees his subjects making choices between different 'registers of legitimation' rather than following 'the scripts dictated by tradition'.[74] We might ask how far it was possible for a woman like Eva König to distance herself from the emotional claims of her family, but the notion of a 'script' is helpful here, in the sense of the combinations of words available for self-representation. In the longer

[71] 10 December 1771.

[72] Cited in 28 December 1771.

[73] 'A Banker's Daughter' [Emma Galton], *A Guide to the Unprotected*, p. 13.

[74] Suter, *Rechtstrieb*, p. 140.

term, it does seem to be the case that changes in vernacular discourses of friendship which emphasized sentimental bonds were associated the decreasing use of 'friend' as a transparently commercial term. And 'friend' may stand here for a complex of words — including shame and honour, but also (even) risk and trust — the history of whose affective valence and gendered associations as well as of their functions in the formal and informal negotiation of credit relations remains to be explored over the *longue durée*. Eva König's situation was liminal in the sense that it marked a crisis at the porous border between family and business relations; at the same time, as widowhood was a normal moment in most women's life course, the particularities of her situation were typical for women of her social and marital status ('Frauen vom Stande' on the threshold of respectable widowhood). It is of wider significance for a history of women and credit because it occurred at a transitional moment in the move from mercantile to manufacturing cultures and in the growth of new middling social groups asserting new and gendered visions of human personality and action. In these circumstances, the capacities of the *Kaufmännin* increasingly had to be exercised in the language of bourgeois femininity, while the personality of the business*man*, too, was subject to renegotiation.

Works Cited

Manuscripts

Braunschweig, Stadtarchiv, D (Testamenta)

Primary Sources

Meine liebste Madam: Gotthold Ephraim Lessings Briefwechsel mit Eva König 1770–1776, ed. by Günter Schulz and Ursula Schulz (Munich: Beck, 1979)

Secondary Studies

'A Banker's Daughter' [Emma Galton], *A Guide to the Unprotected in Every-Day Matters Relating to Property and Income* (London: Clay and Taylor, 1863)

Beachy, Robert, 'Women without Gender: Commerce, Exchange Codes, and the Erosion of German Gender Guardianship', in *Family Welfare: Gender, Property and Inheritance since the Seventeenth Century*, ed. by David Green and Alastair Owens (Westport: Praeger, 2004), pp. 195–215

Blume, Heinrich, 'Engelbert Königs Wiener Fabriken', *Reichspost* (Vienna), 30/187 (10 July 1923), pp. 1–2

Brakensiek, Stefan, *Fürstendiener—Staatsbeamte—Bürger* (Göttingen: Vandenhoeck and Ruprecht, 1999)

D'Cruze, Shani, 'The Middling Sort in Eighteenth-Century Colchester', in *The Middling Sort of People: Culture, Society and Politics in England, 1550–1800*, ed. by Jonathan Barry and Christopher Brooks (Basingstoke: Macmillan, 1994), pp. 181–207

Deuter, Franziska, 'Schulden und Privatkredit im 18. Jahrhundert am Beispiel des Bamberger Heinrichsviertels', in *Stiftungen, Fürsorge und Kreditwesen im frühneuzeitlichen Bamberg*, ed. by Mark Häberlein and Michaela Schmölz-Häberlein (Bamberg: Bamberg University Press, 2015), pp. 137–84

Deutsch, Helene, *Die Entwicklung der Seidenindustrie in Österreich 1660–1840* (Vienna: Conegen, 1909)

Ditz, Toby, 'Shipwrecked: or, Masculinity Imperiled: Mercantile Representations of Failure and the Gendered Self in Eighteenth-Century Philadelphia', *Journal of American History*, 81 (1994), 51–80

Finn, Margot, *The Character of Credit: Personal Debt and English Culture, 1740–1914* (Cambridge: Cambridge University Press, 2003)

Fisher, Paul, 'Bankruptcy in Early Modern German Territories', in *The History of Bankruptcy: Economic, Social and Cultural Implications in Early Modern Europe*, ed. by Thomas Max Safley (Abingdon: Routledge, 2013), pp. 173–84

Fontaine, Laurence, 'Makeshift, Women and Capability in Preindustrial European Towns', *Female Agency in the Urban Economy: Gender in European Towns 1640–1830*, ed. by Deborah Simonton and Anne Montenach (Abingdon: Routledge, 2013), pp. 56–72

———, *The Moral Economy: Poverty, Credit, and Trust in Early Modern Europe* (Cambridge: Cambridge University Press, 2014)

———, 'Women's Economic Spheres and Credit in Pre-Industrial Europe', in *Women and Credit*, ed. by Beverly Lemire and others. (Oxford: Berg, 2001), pp. 15–30

Froide, Amy M., *Silent Partners: Women as Public Investors during Britain's Financial Revolution, 1690–1750* (Oxford: Oxford University Press, 2017)

Gestrich, Andreas, and Martin Stark, eds, *Debtors, Creditors, and their Networks: Social Dimensions of Monetary Dependence from the Seventeenth to the Twentieth Century* (London: German Historical Institute, 2015)

———, 'Introduction', in *Debtors, Creditors, and their Networks: Social Dimensions of Monetary Dependence from the Seventeenth to the Twentieth Century*, ed. by Andreas Gestrich and Martin Stark (London: German Historical Institute, 2015), pp. 1–10

Gowing, Laura, 'The Politics of Women's Friendship', in *Love, Friendship and Faith in Europe, 1300–1800*, ed. by Laura Gowing and others (London: Palgrave Macmillan, 2005), pp. 131–49

Grüne, Niels, 'Freundschaft, Privatheit und Korruption: Zur Disqualifizierung sozialer Nähe im Kräftefeld frühmoderner Staatlichkeit', in *Varieties of Friendship: Interdisciplinary Perspectives on Social Relationships*, ed. by Eric Anton Heuser and others (Göttingen: Vandenhoeck & Ruprecht, 2011), pp. 287–308

Henneberg, Richard, and Bruno Henneberg, *Geschichte der Familie Henneberg (Braunschweig)* (Giessen: Hof- und Universitäts-Druckerei, 1909)

Jahncke, Gabriele, 'Patronage, Freundschaft, Verwandtschaft: Gelehrtenkultur in der frühen Neuzeit', in *Freundschaft und Verwandtschaft: Zur Unterscheidung und Verflechtung zweier Beziehungssysteme*, ed. by Johannes F. K. Schmidt and others (Konstanz: UVK, 2007), pp. 181–200

Khull-Kholwald, Martin, *Der Adel auf dem Land und sein Kredit: Der Schuldschein als zentrales Finanzinstrument in der Steiermark (1515–1635)* (Vienna: LIT, 2013)

Klingbeil, Thomas, *Ein Stand für sich? Lokale Amtsträger in der frühen Neuzeit* (Hannover: Hahn, 2002)

Kopitsch, Franklin, and Dirk Brietze, eds, *Hamburgische Biographie*, 6 vols, vol. 2 (Göttingen: Wallstein, 2003)

Lipp, Carola, 'Aspekte der mikrohistorischen und kulturanthropologischen Kreditforschung', in *Soziale Praxis des Kredits. 16.–20. Jahrhundert*, ed. by Jürgen Schlumbohm (Hannover: Hahn, 2007), pp. 15–36

Möhle, Sylvia, *Ehekonflikte und sozialer Wandel: Göttingen 1740–1840* (Frankfurt a.M: Campus, 1997)

Möring, Maria, *1757–1957: 200 Jahre Johannes Schuback & Söhne Familie und Firma in Hamburg* (Hamburg: Hanseatischer Merkur, 1957)

Muldrew, Craig, *The Economy of Obligation: The Culture of Credit and Social Relations in Early Modern England* (Basingstoke: Macmillan, 1998)

———, '"A Mutual Assent of her Mind"? Women, Debt, Litigation and Contract in Early Modern England', *History Workshop Journal*, 55 (Spring 2003), 47–73

Nenon, Monika, *Aus der Fülle der Herzen: Geselligkeit, Briefkultur und Literatur um Sophie von La Roche und Friedrich Heinrich Jacobi* (Göttingen: Vandenhoeck & Ruprecht, 2005)

Oelker, Petra, *'Ich küsse Sie tausendmal': Das Leben der Eva Lessing* (Berlin: Claassen, 2005)

Ogilvie, Sheilagh, *A Bitter Living: Women, Markets and Social Capital in Early Modern Germany* (Oxford: Oxford University Press, 2003)

Rabuzzi, Daniel A., 'Fading Images, Fading Realities? Female Merchants in Scandinavia and the Baltic', *Histoire Sociale / Social History*, 68 (2001), 354–70

———, 'Women as Merchants in Eighteenth-Century Northern Germany: The Case of Stralsund, 1750–1830', *Central European History*, 28 (1995), 435–56

Rosenhaft, Eve, 'How to Tame Chance: Evolving Languages of Risk, Trust and Expertise in Eighteenth-Century German Proto-Insurances', in *The Appeal of Insurance*, ed. by Geoffrey Clark and others (Toronto: University of Toronto Press, 2010), pp. 16–42

Sabean, David Warren, *Kinship in Neckarhausen, 1700–1850* (Cambridge: Cambridge University Press, 1998)

Safley, Thomas Max, 'Business Failure and Civil Scandal in Early Modern Europe', *Business History Review*, 83 (Spring 2009), 35–60

Schleuning, Regina, *Hof, Macht, Geschlecht: Handlungsspielräume adeliger Amtsträgerinnen am Hof Ludwigs XIV* (Göttingen: Vandenhoeck & Ruprecht, 2016)

Schlumbohm, Jürgen, 'Zur Einführung', in *Soziale Praxis des Kredits. 16.–20. Jahrhundert*, ed. by Jürgen Schlumbohm (Hannover: Hahn, 2007), pp. 7–14

Schmidt, Johannes F. K., 'Das Verhältnis von Freundschaft und Liebe im 18. Jahrhundert', in *Freundschaft und Verwandtschaft: Zur Unterscheidung und Verflechtung zweier Beziehungssysteme*, ed. by Johannes F. K. Schmidt and others (Konstanz: UVK, 2007), pp. 115–43

Sturm, Beate, *'wat ich schuldich war': Privatkredit im frühneuzeitlichen Hannover (1550–1750)* (Stuttgart: Steiner, 2009)

Suter, Mischa, 'Jenseits des "Cash Nexus": Sozialgeschichte des Kredits zwischen kulturanthropologischen und informationsökonomischen Zugängen', *WerkstattGeschichte*, 53 (May 2010), 89–99

——, *Rechtstrieb: Schulden und Vollstreckung im liberalen Kapitalismus 1800–1900* (Konstanz: Konstanz University Press, 2016)

Tadmor, Naomi, *Family and Friends in Eighteenth-Century England: Household, Kinship and Patronage* (Cambridge: Cambridge University Press, 2001)

Trummer, Carl, *Das Hamburgische Erbrecht*, 2 vols (Hamburg: Perthes-Besser & Maucke, 1852)

Winnige, Norbert, 'Vom Leihen und Schulden in Göttingen. Studien zum Kapitalmarkt', in *Göttingen 1690–1755: Studien zur Sozialgeschichte einer Stadt*, ed. by Hermann Wellenreuther (Göttingen: Vandenhoeck & Ruprecht, 1988), pp. 252–320

Never-Married Women and Credit in Early Modern England

Judith M. Spicksley

Credit in Early Modern England

This article begins with a discussion of the credit activities of women in early modern England in general, before moving to look more specifically at those of never-married women, through examination of a sample of 323 never-married women's probate inventories from the diocese of Lincoln between 1547 and 1700. A further sample of 1024 male wills from the same diocese in which testators left bequests to one or more daughters is used to demonstrate a shift away from livestock towards cash portions for daughters from the late sixteenth century. The article considers what might have been driving increased levels of formal lending from the early seventeenth century, and what the impact of that lending might have been on the local economy and on the never-married women involved.

Credit in every economy takes a number of forms depending on the level of commercial activity, the extent of monetization, and the laws that regulate it. In their study of credit in peasant societies, Firth and Yamey claimed that the concept of credit exists in all societies, even in those with economic structures that are non-monetary in nature. This implies that credit constitutes a fundamental element in the creation and maintenance of any socio-economic system.[1] In England

[1] Firth and Yamey, 'Capital', p. 29.

Judith M. Spicksley is a Lecturer in Economic History in the Wilberforce Institute at the University of Hull.

Women and Credit in Pre-Industrial Europe, ed. by Elise M. Dermineur, EER 12 (Turnhout: Brepols, 2018), pp. 227–252.
BREPOLS PUBLISHERS DOI 10.1484/M.EER-EB.5.115755

in the early modern period, credit appears as an indispensable part of everyday life, with up to 90 per cent of yearly household transactions being carried out on credit.[2] This credit took a number of forms — trade credit, money owed for purchases, overdue wages and rent, informal moneylending, and loans guaranteed by some type of formal credit arrangement — although their relative importance is not always easy to discern. Probate inventories and accounts, which provide the primary evidence for credit holding in the sixteenth and seventeenth centuries, do not always reveal enough information to establish categorically what the nature of that credit was. The historiography of credit in early modern England has sometimes fudged this issue too.[3]

In addition, it seems likely that the general level of indebtedness had increased since the late medieval period. Debts including the delayed payment for goods or services, the informal extension of cash, the pawning of goods, and the forward selling of agricultural products are visible in medieval documents, as is the lending of money at interest, although its use was circumscribed by the church until the sixteenth century.[4] But the need for credit expanded dramatically as a result of population growth which increased the number of the landless, and rising inflation which lowered the real wage.[5] The lack of circulating *specie* was a further problem.[6] This frequently meant that men and women who relied on wage labour or engaged in petty trades lived with the near-constant threat of shortfalls in income; for these groups delayed payments and short-term loans were a vital part of the way house-

[2] Muldrew, *The Economy of Obligation*, p. 117. This estimate is based on a sample of probate records from King's Lynn.

[3] While Swain and Holderness suggested that on average around 40 per cent of testators in the Midlands were in possession of some form of credit across the early modern period, they did not establish the proportions of the different types testators held. Holderness, 'Credit in English Rural Society', p. 102; Swain, *Industry*, pp. 189–90.

[4] Jordan, *Women and Credit*, pp. 32–38; Schofield and Mayhew, eds, *Credit and Debt*, p. 30; Kermode, 'The Trade of Late Medieval Chester', p. 299; Briggs, *Credit and Village Society*; Clark, 'Debt Litigation', pp. 247–79.

[5] The population of England grew from around 2.8 million in 1541 to over 5.3 million by 1657. It fell back slightly afterwards to hover around 5 million until the early eighteenth century. Wrigley and Schofield, eds, *Population History*, pp. 531–33. Food prices more than trebled between 1540 and 1640 and the cost of industrial and other consumption goods more than doubled. See Munro's revisions at <https://www.economics.utoronto.ca/wwwfiles/archives/munro5/ResearchData.html> [accessed 19 April 2016]; Clark, *English Prices* <http://gpih.ucdavis.edu/Datafilelist.htm> [accessed 19 April 2016].

[6] See Spicksley, 'Usury Legislation', p. 284; Muldrew, '"Hard Food"', p. 88.

holds made shift to survive.[7] Since goods functioned as a store of value it is hardly surprising to find there was a growth in pawning too, especially in urban areas.[8] The spill-over effects of operating within an expanding economy that relied heavily on credit were seen in the attempts by individuals to manage the likely pitfalls by raising the symbolic as well as material value of credit on the one hand, and by creating estimates of actual 'worth' on the other.[9]

The rising demand for credit in the form of cash loans was in some respects matched by an increase in its supply, as attitudes towards moneylending underwent significant change. Although the medieval church had considered the taking of interest on cash loans illegal, under Roman law it had been possible to enter into interest-bearing loans where both the lender and the borrower shared the risks, and by the beginning of the sixteenth century at least, a revised definition of interest-bearing lending had gained papal support. In England, although 'forebearance' or compensation at a rate of 10 per cent had been legal under Henry VIII, all interest-bearing lending was declared illegal under Edward VI and remained so under Mary, even though the Crown was a significant borrower of money. It was not until Elizabeth's Act Against Usury of 1571, which began the process of redefining usurious practice as the taking of interest at an excessive rate (as defined by statute), that 'use' at a rate of 10 per cent gained popular support.[10]

William Harrison may have been wont to scoff at those with a little capital who put it out at 'use', but he appears to have identified a society-wide movement in which many of those with cash at hand chose to extend it for profit from the late sixteenth century.[11] There are difficulties in testing this theory since there is no

7 Lemire, *The Business of Everyday Life*, p. 16.

8 Boulton, *Neighbourhood and Society*, pp. 88–92; Lemire, 'Petty Pawns', pp. 112–38.

9 In Muldrew's *The Economy of Obligation*, it was the credit of individuals as indicated by their social standing and reputation that provided the key to their market participation as it offered the promise of trustworthiness and fair dealing. Muldrew, *The Economy of Obligation*, pp. 2–3. But if reputation could help secure trade credit, evidence of financial worth remained important. Alexandra Shepard has argued that 'judgements informing credit relations were principally based on assessments of a person's "worth", in terms of the net value of moveable goods' (Shepard, 'Crediting Women', pp. 15–16). The credit economy was managed through knowledge of the items households possessed as much as by the persons they contained; Shepard, *Accounting*, pp. 35–81.

10 Spicksley, 'Women, "Usury" and Credit', p. 268.

11 According to Harrison's much-cited critique usury was 'perfectly practiced almost by every Christian and so commonly that he is accounted but for a fool that doth lend his money for nothing'. Harrison, *The Description of England*, p. 203. See also Jones, *God and the Moneylenders*; Kerridge, *Usury*.

neat recoverable division between what we might conceptualize as co-operative informal interest-free 'community' lending and more profit-oriented individually-driven 'productive' or formal lending. Holderness argued that 'the taking of interest at an equitable rate had become well established, and may indeed have been normal by 1630–1650 within English rural society', but because it did not gain clear legal support until the mid-seventeenth century, payments of interest were not always recorded.[12] Even formal lending agreements evaded discussions of interest rates, and we cannot be entirely sure that all the bonds (one of the most common methods of securing lending) recorded on inventory schedules were indicative of formal lending agreements. Such documents functioned more broadly as general deeds of contract, 'whereby any man confesseth himselfe by his writing orderly made, sealed and delivered to give any thing unto him with whom he so Contracteth'; in other words, they did not apply uniquely to cash loans.[13]

The value of interest-bearing lending to the economy and society of early modern English is easily demonstrated. While probate documents demonstrate the involvement of a broad middling band of male and female testators in the borrowing and lending of money, surviving household and estate accounts of those of higher social standing evidence comparable levels of elite engagement in the process. The records of Lady Alice Le Strange, for example, reveal that the family borrowed heavily to fund their daughter Elizabeth's £3500 marriage portion, and also stepped in to settle their son Nicholas's debts. The ability to borrow enabled them in addition to undertake significant improvements to their Norfolk estate and re-establish financial stability in the 1650s after the disastrous plundering of the bulk of their sheep flock by Parliamentarian forces in the 1640s.[14] The benefits of interest-bearing lending did not escape the attention of early modern public institutions either. Churchwardens lent out the cash they had acquired from deceased parishioners at statutory rates for the benefit of the poor, while charitable annuities provided further support for those in need.[15] Companies looking to trade and

[12] Holderness, 'Widows in Pre-Industrial Society', p. 442; Lemire, 'Petty Pawns', p. 121. The Le Strange accounts, for example, offer no mention of interest rates until 1654. Griffiths, ed., *Her Price*.

[13] Bills or obligations were similar legal documents, relating more specifically but not exclusively to transfers of cash. See West, *Symbolaeographia*, sects 31, 146, 147. Informal loans, undertaken without formal credit instruments, could nevertheless have been secured by the exchange of pawns.

[14] Griffiths, ed., *Her Price*, pp. 71–80.

[15] See for example, Palmer, ed., *Tudor Churchwardens' Accounts*, pp. 73, 75, 79, 82; Spicksley, ed., *Business and Household*, pp. 32–33; McIntosh, *Poor Relief*, p. 262.

settle overseas promised creditors the opportunity to make a substantial profit from the investment of their capital, and by the later seventeenth century those involved in the development of towns and cities were canvassing those with capital for funds to develop their urban environments, supporting a significant urban renaissance in the provinces.[16] The English state too recognized the benefits that borrowing from its subjects could deliver, securing its increasingly expensive global ambitions by recourse to publicly funded debt.[17] Extending the concept of 'rent' to the newest form of economic asset promised to deliver benefits to individuals, groups and organizations in a wide range of social, economic and political contexts.

Women and Credit

Before moving to examine the significant increase in the engagement of never-married women in the formal extension of cash during the seventeenth century, this section engages with the historiography of women and credit in the early modern period more generally. In the 1920s, Tawney's vision of early modern English society was one of a world of small property-owners — tradesman, peasant farmers or small masters — who needed credit to tide them over difficult periods. This led him to characterize the moneylender as a local *man*, 'a monopolist — "a money-master" — a maltster or a cornmonger, "a rich priest" [...] the solitary capitalist in a community of peasants and artisans'.[18] Work undertaken since then has confirmed that the clergy were active in the extension of credit, along with merchants, retailers, tradesmen, and yeomen;[19] the gentry too appear as participants in this trend, and the fact that individual gentlewomen were active as lenders prior to marriage

[16] Spicksley, 'Usury Legislation', p. 295; Todd, 'Fiscal Citizens'; Froide, *Silent Partners*, Introduction; Borsay, *The English Urban Renaissance*, pp. 16–28, and for the construction of walks and gardens see pp. 162–72.

[17] Todd, 'Fiscal Citizens'; Froide, *Silent Partners*, pp. 62–64.

[18] Tawney, *Religion*, pp. 155–56. Shipley, 'Thomas Sutton', pp. 456–76.

[19] Holderness, 'The Clergy as Moneylenders'; North, 'Merchants and Retailers', p. 299; and see for example the probate records of Thomas Anthony Brooke als Butson, yeoman, 1623/4; Nicholas Langbridge [clothmaker], 1625; and John Trickey, weaver, 1658, in Wyatt, ed., *Uffculme*, pp. 44, 47–48, 89. Peter Spufford revealed the extensive and vital nature of rural credit in the sixteenth and seventeenth centuries as well as the high levels of 'deliberate borrowing', and a 'very striking growth' in secured debt between the 1580s and the 1620s. Spufford, 'Long-Term Rural Credit', pp. 216–19.

has been known for some time.[20] Nor were they the only women to do so. We now know that women of all marital estates and a wide range of socio-economic statuses were engaged in some form of credit provision in the early modern period. Holderness's work in the 1980s, for example, outlined the heavy involvement of widows in all forms of credit, and the extent of this involvement has been supported by more recent research.[21]

Wives too were deeply embedded in the lending economy. Beverly Lemire's work, in which married women not only appear as lenders, but as brokers of credit, has revealed the involvement of this group in securing loans for household members as well as friends and neighbours by acting as guarantors.[22] Wives then had an important role to play in providing 'the support networks that enabled households to get by in the face of haphazard income streams and a limited cash flow'.[23] Their activities are usually presented as examples of small scale, day-to-day operations at the lower end of the credit market, a function of their relatively lower access to economic resources.[24] But even within this framework, moneylending may have been as much an economic as a social activity. In his *Discourse upon Usury*, written in 1572, Thomas Wilson allowed both the Doctor and the Lawyer to be critical of wives and provincial women who demanded interest on small loans of money.[25]

[20] Heal and Holmes, *The Gentry*, pp. 125–27; Spufford, 'Long-Term Rural Credit', p. 224; Tittler, 'Money-Lending', pp. 249–63; Spicksley, ed., *Business and Household*; Griffiths, ed., *Her Price*, pp. 72–81; Laurence, 'Lady Betty Hastings', pp. 533–40.

[21] Holderness, 'Widows in Pre-Industrial Society'; Hodges, 'Widows of the "Middling Sort"', pp. 318–321; Lemire, 'Petty Pawns'; Lemire, *The Business of Everyday Life*.

[22] The extension of small loans without formal security was a function of reputation and trust, in which more established members of the community would arrange and secure the loans of those whose 'credit' was insufficient. See Lemire, 'Petty Pawns', p. 120, and pp. 123–24 for the activities of widow and laundress, Roberta Jones, as guarantor; and Lemire, 'Introduction', pp. 3–14.

[23] Shepard, 'Minding', p. 55; and see McIntosh, 'Women, Credit, and Family Relationships', pp. 143–63. Cathryn Spence's recent study of women and debt litigation in the Scottish courts has revealed how extensively married women in particular were engaged in networks of debt and credit in early modern Scotland. See Spence, *Women, Credit, and Debt*.

[24] For women's reduced access to resources see Lemire, 'Petty Pawns', p. 120.

[25] The Doctor mentions women who put out their husband's money at use 'with the retorne many tymes of the shillinge peny for a moneth, which is one hundred for an other by the yere'. The Lawyer criticises the activities of provincial women: 'even weomen, yea and goodman hoyden of the countrey, in whome a man woulde thinke were no crafte or subtiltie to live, can aske the shillynge pennie for a weeke, whiche in a yeare amounteth to foure shillynges and foure pence, besydes the principall'. Wilson, *A Discourse*, pp. 297, 211.

Alexandra Shepard's detailed micro-study of the dispute between two married women in London in the early eighteenth century, moreover, provides evidence of a pro-active, market-based, business-oriented approach to lending amongst wives too.[26] Her example may prove to be more the exception than the rule — it may have been more common for married couples to collaborate in the organization of credit than for married women to operate alone — but it is significant because it indicates that despite suspending their legal personality (as *feme covert*), marriage did not prevent women from moving into the profitable lending market as an occupation.[27]

Older studies of female lenders tended not to characterize them as women 'whose fundamental business (and perhaps livelihood) was moneylending', but for whom credit emerged as part and parcel of their accompanying commercial activities, a function of their occupations as alewives and innkeepers, for example; widows were thus primarily understood as seeking to supplement their earnings by putting out spare cash at interest.[28] For many women this may indeed have been the case. Nevertheless, credit was 'a mechanism that enabled many to get by and a few to flourish', and there is no doubt that for some at least it did constitute a major element of their income, even if it was not their only source of wealth.[29] Nor was it something they neglected to exploit. From the purchase of early lottery tickets in the sixteenth century, to the 'putting out' of cash at interest, to the holding of shares in chartered and joint stock companies, to investment in private and public finance — at both local and national level — women, regardless of their marital estate, were prepared to invest their cash in the hope of a profit.[30] We should not be surprised. As Alexandra Shepard has recently made clear, it was the role of the female head of the household to guard, manage and expand the assets under her

[26] In an early eighteenth-century testamentary dispute concerning the business activities of two London pawnbrokers, Elizabeth Carter and Elizabeth Hatchett, it was claimed that the latter 'had borrowed £300 to set herself up in "Employment" as a moneylender'. Shepard, 'Minding', p. 63.

[27] For collaboration between married couples see Lemire, 'Petty Pawns', 120. Spence's study too reveals much about the relationship between coverture and credit in early modern Scotland. See Spence, *Women, Credit, and Debt*; McIntosh, 'Women, Credit, and Family Relationships', pp. 151–53.

[28] Jordan, *Women and Credit*, p. 20.

[29] Lemire, 'Introduction', p. 4; and see for example Spicksley, ed., *Business and Household*; and the discussion of the widow Janet Fockart in Spence, *Women, Credit, and Debt*, p. 143.

[30] Shepard, 'Minding', 68; Todd, 'Fiscal Citizens'; Froide, *Silent Partners*, 'Introduction'; Spicksley, 'Usury Legislation', p. 297.

control.[31] Such management did not begin with marriage, however, but with preparation for marriage and the move into adulthood.

Never-Married Women and Credit

If never-married women appear little different from their married and widowed contemporaries in terms of their overall engagement with credit, the form that credit took was not the same. On the one hand, it seems that few never-married women offered trade credit, probably because fewer appear to have been directly engaged in commerce before the later seventeenth century. We know that population pressure and fears about the cost of bastard children encouraged towns to restrict the working opportunities of never-married women as well as their capacity to live independently in the late sixteenth and early seventeenth centuries, and girls rarely received a formal apprenticeship. There are occasional references to overdue wages and some examples of amounts owed for goods or livestock in the inventory material, but the fact that never-married women rarely owed debts themselves is suggestive of a generally low participation in commercial or business activities.[32] In relation to moneylending, however, that rate is likely to have been much higher. The experience of Margaret Prater, a thrifty Romford servant in the sixteenth century in the work of McIntosh, may well have been characteristic of the involvement of many never-married women in the informal extension of cash.[33] In Lincolnshire too, never-married women were already significant as informal lenders before 1600, and continued to engage in this type of lending across the seventeenth century. Like Sarah Fell of Swarthmoor Hall, some were also likely to have been providing day to day credit facilities, although our evidence for this at present is rather limited. Fell, daughter of the Quaker Margaret Fell Fox, and step-daughter of George Fox,

[31] Shepard noted that although married women's involvement in brokering credit, is often characterized 'as "informal", and principally associated with networks of female solidarity', in reality, 'married women's borrowing and lending activities stemmed from their responsibilities for asset management within their households, which were understood as a form of enterprise'. 'Minding', p. 55. In addition, McIntosh has revealed that 'family ties pulled many women into credit relationships'. McIntosh, 'Women, Credit, and Family Relationships', p. 159.

[32] Analysis of 152 single women's probate accounts is able to provide additional confirmation of their primary function as creditors: less than 14 per cent of the sample recorded any evidence of borrowing. Probate inventories rarely record debts owed by the testator, but accounts provide evidence of debts paid from the deceased's estate. Spicksley, '"Fly with a Duck in thy Mouth"', p. 206; Spufford, Brett and Erickson, eds, *Probate Accounts*, p. xxviii.

[33] McIntosh, 'Moneylending', p. 568.

regularly recorded lending a few shillings to named local individuals for a short period of time; occasionally she herself was the borrower, on similar terms. In addition, she accepted small sums 'to lay by' for safekeeping, until such time as the owners required they be returned, acting in the manner of a quasi-banker.[34] This may help explain why a small number of never-married female householders were in possession of relatively large amounts of cash.[35] Yet most never-married women with

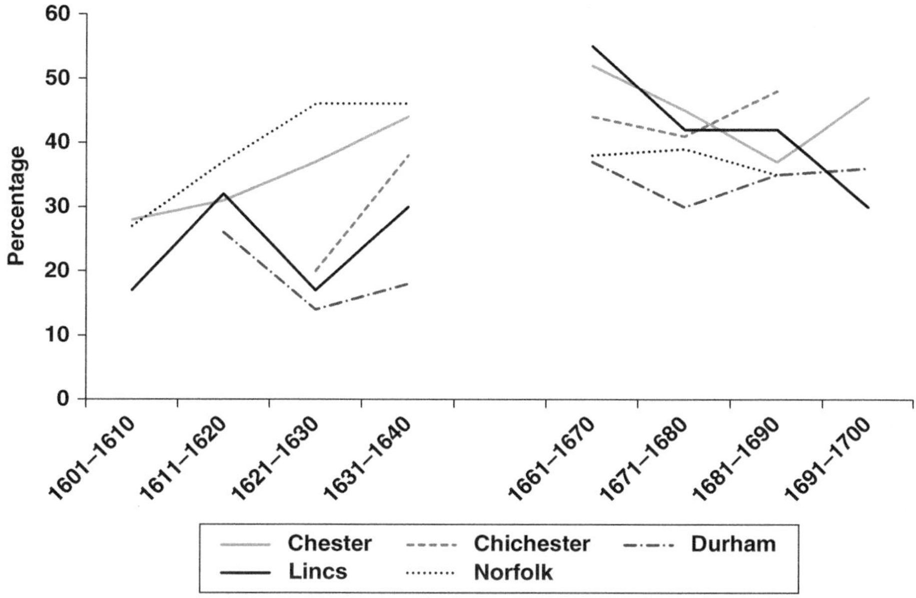

Figure 9.1. Never-married women's formal lending, 1601–1700. *Source:* Chester Record Office Consistory Court probate records 1601–1700; West Sussex Record Office Chichester Consistory Court probate records, 1619–1698; Durham University Library Durham Consistory Court probate records 1611–1700; Lincolnshire Archives INV records 1601–1700; Norfolk Record Office Consistory Court probate records, 1605–1687. The 1640s and 1650s were excluded because of the very small number of documents.

[34] Spicksley, '"Fly with a Duck in thy Mouth"', p. 193; Penny, ed., *The Household Account Book*, pp. 18, 27, 63, 75, 135, 139, 169, 326, 351. Sometimes larger amounts were deposited. Henry Watson left £10 with Richard Cholmeley 'to kepe for him untill he nede it'. Cholmeley, *The Memorandum Book*, p. 90. These monies may have been lent out in the meantime.

[35] Across the seventeenth century in Lincolnshire five women held £50 or more in cash, only one of whom was lending; in Cheshire there were also five women who had £50 or more in cash, but all five were lending; in Durham only two women, both lenders, held the same amount; in Norfolk the number was four, again all lenders.

cash appear to have been more interested in its role as an asset on which money itself could be made. A study of probate material taken from five English counties across the seventeenth century has revealed evidence of a general shift by never-married women towards higher levels of formal debt, that is, debt secured by recognized credit instruments such as bonds, bills, 'specialties', mortgages, and statute debts.[36]

Informal loans, provided without legal protection, remained an important part of the portfolio of lending such women offered, and some who lent formally ran informal loans alongside. Although, as noted earlier, it is difficult to establish the extent to which interest was charged on some formal as well as informal loans, the decision to increase the security of loan repayment is in itself indicative of a change in attitudes. The rise in formal lending was neither consistent nor uniform, but the pattern was clear. By the end of the seventeenth century women in all areas of the study were more deeply engaged in formal lending than they had been at the beginning. The highest levels of credit may well have been offered during the wartime Interregnum, for which we have very few records, and the fall back afterwards in every county under consideration bar one suggests that considerable amounts of capital were lost during that period. Moreover, with the exception of Lincolnshire, formal lending once again was expanding by the final decade of the century.

The women in the probate sample were not from the poorest sectors of early modern society. The church discouraged probate for estates valued at or below £5, although inflation over the course of the late sixteenth and early seventeenth century meant that in real terms, the sample was extending downwards over the period as a whole.[37] Nevertheless, the fact that some women, including servants, were lending relatively small amounts may have brought them into the probate process; appraisers responsible for the preparation of the inventory were instructed to include debts owed to the testator.[38]

We know from the detailed accounts of Joyce Jeffreys, an elderly Herefordshire spinster of lower gentry status, that she at least had a very significant amount of

[36] See also Spicksley, '"Fly with a Duck in thy Mouth"', pp. 192–93.

[37] Arkell, 'The Probate Process', p. 12. Probate inventories in a study of English households undertaken by Overton, Whittle, Dean, and Hann for the period 1600–1750 covered around 50 per cent of the population; the richest 10 per cent and the poorest 40 per cent were excluded. See Overton, Whittle, Dean, and Hann, *Production*, p. 26. However, survival rates vary, with a norm of perhaps 20–30 per cent of the population. See Arkell, 'Interpreting Probate Inventories', pp. 73–74. Overton suggested that 28 per cent of the adult male and widowed female deaths in Lincolnshire in the late seventeenth century produced an inventory. Overton, 'English Probate Inventories', p. 209.

[38] Swinburne, *Briefe Treatise*, § vii, 218^{v}; Spufford, 'Long-Term', p. 213.

cash out on loan. In her best year, 1639–1640, Jeffreys's records suggest that this may have amounted to as much as £4800.[39] The bulk of her lending consisted of formal debts secured on bills, bonds, statute debts and mortgages; the accounts also reference two examples of pawn and there is evidence of the use of named sureties.[40] Hester Pinney, a spinster from Dorset who moved to London at the age of twenty-four to run the family lacemaking business, invested in mortgages, lottery tickets, and public securities to secure her future finances. In the 1720s and 1730s she was investing her capital in the Bank of England and South Sea Company annuities.[41] Bills, bonds, and 'specialties' were the most common debt instruments to appear in the probate documents, although the use of mortgages was also in evidence, and appears to have expanded in the later seventeenth century.[42] This may have been part of a broader social trend. In Juliet Gayton's work on the borrowing patterns of customary tenants in five Hampshire manors between 1645 and 1705, just over a quarter of the lenders were never-married women.[43]

Trying to recover who may have been in receipt of this credit at any sort of quantitative level is difficult, given the restricted amount of information that inventories usually provide on debtors. In the Durham group — which had the fullest amount of detail — we see never-married women lending to yeomen, butchers, merchants, tanners, and a range of other craftsmen, tradesmen, and professions including a beer brewer, captain, clerk, glazier, glover, vicar, and curate.[44] Jeffreys's accounts are much more illuminating, and lend support to the Durham findings: she lent her capital out on a variety of social and occupational levels, counting members of the rural aristocracy and the gentry, urban officials (including mayors and aldermen), individuals from the professional and clerical sector, and a range of craftsmen and tradesmen among her debtors. Jeffreys's lending activities were closely linked to the location of her business dealings. As well as her local dealings in and around the city of Hereford, Jeffreys had estates at Wharton, Broadward, and Tarrington, which were between six and fifteen miles away, and she had also lent money to her

[39] Spicksley, ed., *Business and Household*, p. 37.

[40] Spicksley, ed., *Business and Household*, pp. 86, 91–92, 139.

[41] Sharpe, 'Woman's Worth', pp. 178–79; Froide, *Silent Partners*, p. 189.

[42] Mortgaging of property provided the landed gentry with an opportunity to maintain and improve their social status by engaging in conspicuous consumption from the late seventeenth century. See Borsay, *The English Urban Renaissance*, p. 202.

[43] Of the seventy-eight lenders identified, twenty (25.6 per cent) were never-married women and ten (12.8 per cent) were widows. Gayton, 'Tenants, Tenures and Transfers', pp. 236–37.

[44] Spicksley, '"Fly with a Duck in thy Mouth"', p. 197.

London tailor.[45] That attorneys and other individuals with knowledge clearly acted to link lenders with borrowers at some distance is clear from cases brought by individuals in the central courts.[46] Nevertheless, a considerable proportion of never-married lenders with less expansive credit portfolios and more restricted interests appear to have demonstrated that there was some truth in Francis Bacon's claim that creditors disliked sending monies 'farre off' or putting it with strangers.[47] Thus around a third of never-married women appear to have provided some form of credit to family members, both male and female, which, while it was less than the 40 per cent of individuals Holderness indicated had been extending credit to their kin, exceeded the 17 per cent found by Wrightson and Levine in Terling.[48] That there was room for considerable variation is demonstrated by the fact that although Jeffreys was related to over seventy individuals in her accounts either by birth or marriage, only ten of her relatives were in her debt.[49] Finally, it is also interesting to note the impact of gender on lending practices. In her work on Southampton, Amy Froide found that women rarely lent money to each other at interest, and this was also the finding of a larger probate sample.[50] There most women who specified their debtors had loaned money to local men and male relatives, and once again Jeffreys' accounts demonstrate a parallel trend. Only eight of the 145 debtors listed in her accounts were female, and of those, only Joan Rod alias Norman and Elizabeth Chippe (bound with her brother Thomas) owed over £10.[51] The remainder appear to have been granted informal loans with no apparent interest and no set date for repayment. Where women were concerned, Jeffreys's lending seems to have been more characteristic of the small scale, informal type of credit behaviour that had been a constant of female practice for some time.

[45] 18 per cent of her debtors lived over fifteen miles away, 46 per cent resided at between six and fifteen miles distant, and the remaining 36 per cent lived within five miles of Hereford. All distances are approximate and have been calculated as the crow flies. Assuming the debtors without specified locations were from Hereford changes the comparative percentages to: nought to five miles 53 per cent; six to fifteen miles 34 per cent; over fifteen miles 13 per cent. Spicksley, ed., *Business and Household*, pp. 33 and n. 130.

[46] Spicksley, '"Fly with a Duck in thy Mouth"', p. 197.

[47] Bacon, *The Essayes*, Number 41 'Of Usurie', p. 246.

[48] Spicksley, '"Fly with a Duck in thy Mouth"', p. 198; Holderness, 'Widows in Pre-Industrial Society', p. 441; Wrightson and Levine, *Poverty*, p. 100. See also Spufford, 'Long-Term Rural Credit', pp. 223–26.

[49] Spicksley, ed., *Business and Household*, pp. 33–34.

[50] Froide, *Never Married*, p. 135.

[51] Spicksley, ed., *Business and Household*, pp. 31–32.

The Lincolnshire Sample

In this final section I have taken a collection of the wills and inventories of never-married women in Lincolnshire between 1547 and 1700 to investigate first, what factors were instrumental in driving the increased levels of formal lending and second, what the impact of that lending was. Lincolnshire in this period was an agrarian county, characterized by a large number of rural villages linked to a network of small market towns with a few larger urban centres. Most of the work on credit to date has focused on either the urban or the rural experience, but here, in addition to total levels of lending, it has been possible to separate and compare the two. As Figure 9.2 reveals, there was an overall increase in the proportion of never-married women engaged in some type of lending over the period, as levels rise from 37 per cent before 1600 to 64 per cent after 1659. There is no evidence of formal lending prior to 1600, but in the period 1600–1659, 29 per cent of the sample were engaged in formal lending, a figure that rises to 43 per cent after that date. The pattern of formal lending in Lincolnshire thus maps neatly onto the national pattern as formal lending, a major driver in the growth of credit provision, undergoes expansion. The proportion of those engaged *only* in informal lending, which

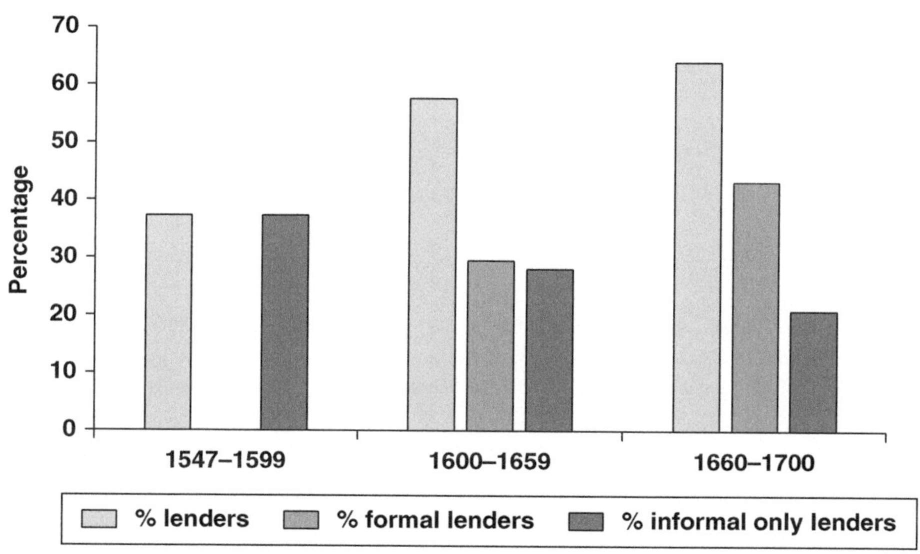

Figure 9.2. Lending status of never-married women in Lincolnshire, 1547–1700. *Source:* Lincolnshire Archives [LA] INVS 1547–1700. There are 323 women in the probate inventory sample.

stood at 37 per cent of the sample before 1600, has by the later seventeenth century fallen to 21 per cent.[52]

Figure 9.3 demonstrates that changes in the pattern of lending tended to be similar across rural and urban areas. Total levels of lending grew, as did the proportion of women engaged in formal lending, although both trends were more marked in towns and cities. In the period 1660–1700, only 23 per cent of urban women were not engaged in lending, compared with 40 per cent in the countryside. Over the same period 68 per cent of urban women had become involved in the formal extension of capital, as opposed to 35 per cent in rural areas. The rise in informal lending in urban areas in the early seventeenth century is not a feature of rural experience, however, and in addition deviates from the general national trend. The sample is small — only 24 per cent of the Lincolnshire sample is urban — but it does speak to Lemire's argument about the particular value of credit in urban areas.

That never-married women become increasingly visible as lenders from the late sixteenth century is a function at least in part of a contemporaneous fall in the rate

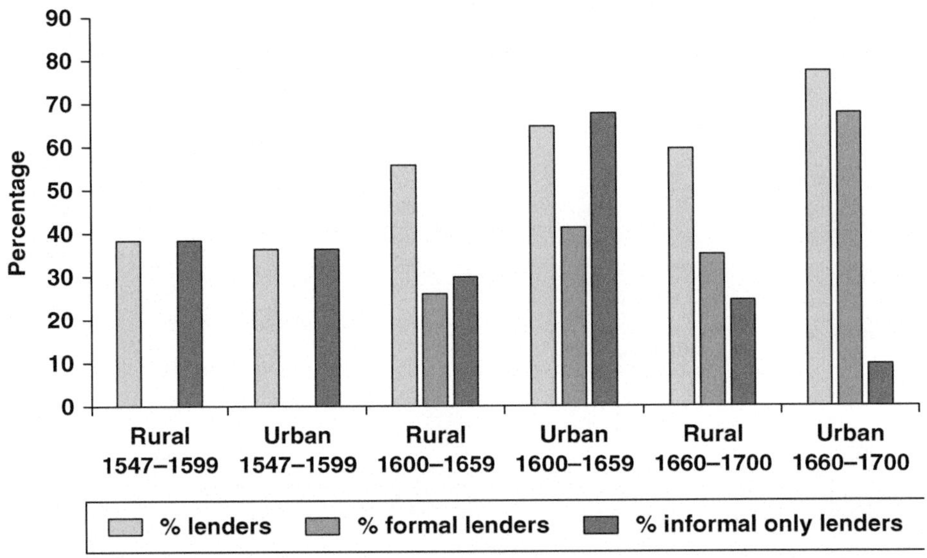

Figure 9.3. Lending status of never-married women in Lincolnshire by location, 1547–1700. *Source:* Lincolnshire Archives [LA] INVS 1547–1700. There are 323 women in the probate inventory sample.

52 Lenders were categorized as 'formal' if they held debt securities and 'informal' if they did not. The small number of women who held both appear in the 'formal' category. This means the proportion of women engaged in informal lending is an underestimate.

of marriage. This fall is visible from the 1570s, and by the 1630s the celibacy rate amongst 40–44 year olds had reached 20 per cent; the rate continued to climb until the later seventeenth century, peaking at 27 per cent for that cohort in the 1680s.[53] But there was a further major socio-institutional change that appears to have raised the profile of never-married women as capital investors. The Act Against Usury of 1571 operated to make it more attractive for fathers to leave gifts of cash to their orphaned daughters and request that these be 'put out' at interest until those daughters reached their majority.[54] We can see this shift in Figure 9.4 below.

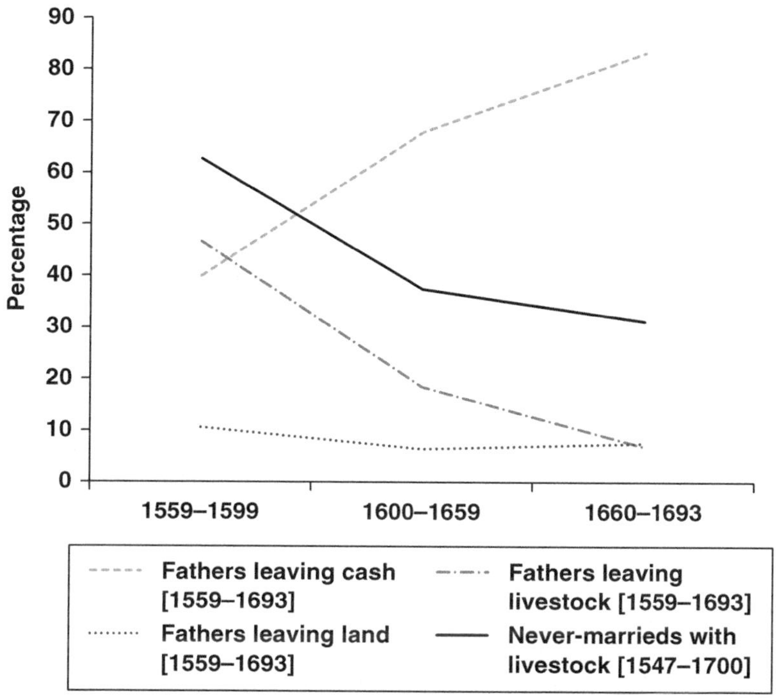

Figure 9.4. Testamentary practice and possession of livestock in Lincolnshire, 1549–1700. *Source:* LA LCC Wills, 1570–1693; LA INVS, 1547–1700. The Wills sample consists of 1024 male testators who left bequests to one or more daughters; the figure represents the bequests that were left to the eldest daughter only. The INV sample contains 323 never-married women's probate inventories.

[53] Wrigley and Schofield, *Population History*, p. 260.

[54] Though encouraging lending at interest more generally, the Act of 1571 gave interest-bearing lending explicit legal authority in the case of orphans, allowing payments 'according to the ancient rates or customs of the city of London, or any other city where like order is for the custody of orphans and their goods'. 13 Eliz. I, *c*. 8.

This figure reveals the marked upward trend in the proportion of fathers who bequeathed cash to their eldest daughters between the late sixteenth and late seventeenth centuries, more than doubling from 40 per cent to 82 per cent in this period.[55] The proportion of fathers leaving livestock to their eldest daughters had compared favourably with cash legacies in the late sixteenth century, but fell away dramatically afterwards from a high of 46 per cent at that point to a mere 7 per cent by the end of the seventeenth.[56] To what extent then was the Act Against Usury the primary cause of this shift in practice?

First, as far as it is possible to see, the changing composition of the male will sample does not appear to have had a marked impact, although this is difficult to check accurately because of the large and fluctuating number of wills that carried no occupational designation.[57] Shifts in the level of livestock holding by fathers could, however, provide at least part of the explanation, and there is evidence to support the idea that livestock holding was declining in urban and some rural areas in the seventeenth century.[58] If we turn to Lincolnshire more specifically, we can see individual cases of difficulty. In 1586, for example, the vicar of Legsby and Stainton by Langworth, Hamlet Marshall, reported a general sheep rot across the county. He had lost most of his own sheep, and there had been in addition great storms, resulting in the drowning of many cattle or their death from lack of fodder.[59] The general trends in livestock holding — a reduction between the 1590s and the 1630s, with a move to smaller herds — have been explained by reference to a run of very good harvests with very low prices followed by a run of very wet years when stock

[55] A similar trend is evident amongst younger daughters and sons in the Lincolnshire wills.

[56] Though 71 fathers bequeathed both cash and livestock to their daughters between 1549 and 1693, the proportion doing this also fell over the period in question 13.5 per cent to 1599; 6.6 per cent to 1659; and 3.2 per cent to 1693.

[57] 51 per cent of male wills in the sample for the period 1559–1599 had no designation, falling to 13 per cent for the period 1660–1693. The fastest growth in the early seventeenth century is among the yeomen, craft/trade and labouring groups. However, the proportion of yeomen leaving their daughters cash was already high in the later sixteenth century, and actually fell back in the early seventeenth, while amongst labourers, levels of cash gifts remained virtually unchanged. Husbandmen too increased their bequests of cash in the early seventeenth century, but their proportional presence in the sample falls back slightly. Only in the craft/trade sector do we see a proportional increase in the use of cash bequests as well as in their presence in the sample.

[58] Shammas, *The Pre-Industrial Consumer*, p. 30. Everitt, 'Farm Labourers', pp. 182–83. Everitt also indicated that the percentage of peasant labourers holding cattle fell in eastern England between 1560–1600 and 1610–1640; see pp. 178–79.

[59] Hill, *Tudor & Stuart Lincoln*, p. 86.

succumbed to disease; by the Restoration, however, there were signs of recovery in almost every region.[60] There were also problems in accessing pasture. Drainage of the fens drastically reduced the amount of pasture available for the inhabitants of Hareby, for example, resulting in a decline in the number of sheep kept on the fen from 360 to 'very few'; in Mavis Enderby only one eighth of the former 1000 sheep could be pastured on the fens after drainage.[61]

Enclosure too may have been a factor. A petition to enclose the village of Bassingham by the vicar there in 1629 had complained about the insufficient amount of pasture that was available given the recent rise in population. This had not only resulted in weak animals but led to the death of all the young sheep and 200 of the cattle in 1628.[62] If enclosure was 'in full swing' in Lincolnshire between 1600 and 1700, the attendant loss of common rights in meadows in particular could have been significant.[63] It was possible, however, for never-married women, who had always experienced very low levels of landholding, to pasture their livestock with employers, relatives or friends. Thus Margaret Forte of Haxey in the Isle of Axholme left a single cow to Nicholas Forte in her will in 1576, which she noted was already in his hands, while the will of Isabell James, in service in Great Grimsby, revealed that she had a ram at the house of John Crowston in 1612.[64]

There may also have been ongoing commercial concerns. Sheep farming had been a staple of the Lincolnshire economy since the medieval period, but rising wool prices peaked in 1594 and fell for much of the 1600s; the impact of this was not helped by the government ban on wool export in 1614 in an attempt to assist the struggling textile industry.[65] Small sheep farmers in the sheep-corn areas of Lincolnshire were amongst those who complained most vociferously to Parliament.[66] But while incidents such as these would have knocked confidence in animal

60 Thirsk, *English Peasant Farming*, p. 193.

61 Thirsk, *English Peasant Farming*, p. 118.

62 Johnston, '17th-Century', p. 8.

63 Kain, Chapman and Oliver, *Enclosure Maps*, p. 20. Ross Wordie believed that far more land had been enclosed in the seventeenth century than earlier or later (24 per cent as opposed to 2 per cent in the sixteenth, 13 per cent in the eighteenth and 11.4 per cent in the nineteenth centuries); cited in Thirsk, 'Introduction', p. 2.

64 Lincolnshire Archives (LA) LCC Wills 1576–7/51^{v}, Margaret Forte of Haxey, 1576; LA LCC Wills 1612/558, Isabell James, Great Grimsby, Lincolnshire, 1612.

65 Shammas, *The Pre-Industrial Consumer*, p. 30. For prices see Clark's price and wage series above.

66 Thirsk, *The Rural Economy*, p. 184.

husbandry, it is not clear that livestock on balance had become a poorer form of investment. Lending out £1 at a rate of 10 per cent in the late sixteenth and early seventeenth century could produce a return of 2s. per year; cows, which were selling for around 22s. in the later sixteenth century, could be rented out for around 4s. per year.[67] Sheep were occasionally rented out too, but more commonly held for their wool and offspring. The mean average cost of a sheep was around 3s. in the later sixteenth century. Thus £1 would buy at least six sheep, which — with lambing at a 0.5 per cent success rate and maturity within a year — would produce a further six sheep in three years, a profit of 6s. 8d. per year.[68] Wool from six sheep might make 10s. per year, although this does not take into account the costs of pasturing, tithes, medicines, or clipping.[69] The most optimistic calculations then suggest that livestock still represented a good investment in the late sixteenth and early seventeenth century, and though declining access to pasture would have been a cause for concern, the speed of the shift away to cash for daughters indicates there were additional forces at play.

The impact of this shift in inheritance practice was of major importance in the economic development of the seventeenth century. Inheritance was not the only way in which women could access capital: servants could extend any savings they had made from their wages too. In Lincolnshire eight of the twelve servants in the sample were lending, six of them formally, of amounts ranging between 10s. 6d. with £23. But a 'best guess' estimate of the amount that could have been available through bequests to eldest daughters in Lincoln, calculated from demographic information in 1563 and 1702, suggests a figure of £1912 available at the first date rising to £13,838 at the second (the modern equivalent of a rise from £400,000 to nearly £1,800,000).[70] The actual total may well have been considerably higher, given that this does not take account of bequests of cash to younger daughters or

[67] The average price for livestock has been calculated from the inventory entries of Lincolnshire never-married men and women between 1549 and 1575. There are relatively few prices for livestock rentals. See LA INV 83/727 John Dawson of Whaplode, 1593, 4s p.a. for one cow; LA INV 98/242 John Burton [no location] 1605, 9s 8d for two cows; LA INV 80/248 Hannah Couke of Wigtoft, 1591, 10s for two cows.

[68] Lambing rates were likely to have been between 0.6 and 0.8 per ewe where sheep were carefully managed, but lower elsewhere. Griffiths, ed., *Her Price*, p. 32. The calculation would also depend on the age at which ewes were allowed to lamb.

[69] Yorkshire servants in the 1640s paid 18d. per sheep per year for pasturing. Woodward, ed., *The Farming and Memorandum Books of Henry Best*, p. 140. For tithes see Tarver, 'The Due Tenth'.

[70] Spicksley, 'Usury Legislation', p. 290 and n. 82.

sons.[71] The impact of the shift on never-married women themselves could also have been significant. Wealth levels among those who were lending rose between the late sixteenth and late seventeenth century, and more especially amongst formal lenders where that rise was above the rate of inflation.[72] Indeed, relative to other creditors, their lending — as a proportion of their total assets — appears to have been higher than that of any other social group.[73] The bulk of their wealth, therefore, was in the form of cash assets. There were some benefits to this, inasmuch as a number of women should have been able to live independently through living off their interest. Donald Woodward argued that for around £5 a year an adult male in the later seventeenth century could have enjoyed a relatively nutritious diet.[74] To obtain this, women would need to have invested £84 at the prevailing rate of 6 per cent, and been in receipt of the interest due. However, of the fifty-four women who were involved in formal lending from 1660, only twelve, or 22 per cent, held more than £84 in debt, and the records do not provide information on how regularly they received payments of interest. This included a number of wealthy gentlewomen, including Mrs Bridget Phillips of Gainsborough who held debts to the value of £400 in 1687, and Mrs Jane Farmery of Northorpe who was owed over £235 in 1691; both were in possession of mortgages.[75] Thus while the Lincolnshire community at large was poised to benefit from the huge amount of capital made available via the lending activities of never-married women, the effect on the lives of the majority of the latter was likely to have been more muted.

Conclusion

In early modern England, and regardless of their marital status, women were involved in the provision of credit, both in the form of delayed payment for goods

[71] See Habakkuk, *Marriage*, pp. 3–4, 117, for the shift to cash portions for younger aristocratic and gentry sons; Spicksley, 'Usury Legislation', p. 281 n. 30 for the shift to cash portions for first-named sons in Lincolnshire.

[72] Despite arguing that inventories were not 'a reliable guide to the total wealth of any individual, nor can they be used for comparative analysis of relative wealth', Moore added a useful condition: 'unless [...] the person concerned owned little or no land', never-married women rarely held land. Cited in Arkell, 'Interpreting Probate Inventories', p. 95.

[73] Spicksley, '"Fly with a Duck in thy Mouth"', p. 203.

[74] Woodward, *Men at Work*, p. 216.

[75] LA INV 187/151 Bridget Phillips of Gainsborough, 1687; INV 190/105 Jane Farmery of Northorpe, 1691.

or services, and the lending of cash, informally and for profit. As such, they were likely to have seen their involvement expand from the later sixteenth century under the pressure of demographic and economic expansion that was not matched by an increase in the supply of specie.[76] But these were not the only factors at play. From the late sixteenth century institutional changes in the form of the Act Against Usury encouraged never-married women especially, and more specifically in urban areas, to engage in the formal credit market. Women were then able to improve the security of their lending and safeguard their assets. In this too, they were part of a broader social movement that included men and women from a wide range of status groups with capital at hand. Beyond the informal brokering of household credit, women of every marital status were cognisant of, and active participants in, the rapidly growing credit market, although within that group never-married women appear as a special category: both the level of their lending, as a proportion of those involved, and its value — relative to their total wealth — were exceptional.

Peasants in a monetary economy have the option of saving in cash or goods. Peasant saving is not a decision of the individual alone, however, but guided 'by the general set of ideas and values current about capital accumulation' in the particular society in question. Different preferences emerge in response to the possibility of exchanging such goods for cash, attitudes towards the asset as a form of currency, storage of the asset and competing demands for it.[77] After 1571 the confirmation of cash as a legitimate form of investment for orphans and a rising demand for capital in the early modern economy shifted testamentary preferences for daughters in particular away from livestock towards money. We know that the impact of that lending had significant economic ramifications, providing new opportunities for borrowers to invest in production opportunities as well as those in consumption, and never-married women may have been instrumental in addition in encouraging the general acceptability of cash as a form of asset.[78] The impact on their own lives, however, appears to have been less momentous. Independence for never-married women was only possible for those with the largest loans whose debts were regularly serviced, or for those who had significant additional income-generating activities.

[76] Muldrew argued that the period from 1550 represented the 'most intensely *concentrated* period of economic growth before the late eighteenth century', Muldrew, *The Economy of Obligation*, pp. 20–21.

[77] Firth and Yamey, 'Capital', pp. 23–24.

[78] Spicksley, 'Women, "Usury" and Credit'.

Works Cited

Manuscript Sources

Lincolnshire Archives (LA) INVS 1547–1700
Lincolnshire Archives (LA) LCC WILLS 1547–1700

Primary Sources

Bacon, Francis, *The Essayes or Counsels, Civill and Morall* (1625)

Cholmeley, R., *The Memorandum Book of Richard Cholmeley of Brandsby 1602–1623*, North Yorkshire County Record Office Publications, 44 (1988)

Harrison, William, *The Description of England*, ed. by Georges Edelen (Ithaca: Cornell University Press, 1968; Dover ed., 1994)

Penny, N., ed., *The Household Account Book of Sarah Fell of Swarthmoor Hall* (Cambridge: Cambridge University Press, 1920)

Swinburne, Henry, *A Briefe Treatise of Testaments and Last Willes* (1591)

West, William, *Symbolaeographia: The Art, Description or Image of Instruments* (1592)

Wilson, Thomas, *A Discourse upon Usury*, ed. by Richard H. Tawney (London: Frank Cass, 1925)

Wyatt, Peter, ed., *The Uffculme Wills and Inventories 16th to 18th Centuries*, Devon and Cornwall Record Society, new series, 40 (1997)

Secondary Studies

Arkell, Tom, 'Interpreting Probate Inventories', in *When Death Do Us Part: Understanding and Interpreting the Probate Records of Early Modern England*, ed. by Tom Arkell, Nesta Evans, and Nigel Goose (Oxford: Leopard's Head Press, 2000), pp. 72–102

———, 'The Probate Process', in *When Death Do Us Part: Understanding and Interpreting the Probate Records of Early Modern England*, ed. by Tom Arkell, Nesta Evans, and Nigel Goose (Oxford: Leopard's Head Press, 2000), pp. 3–13

Borsay, Peter, *The English Urban Renaissance: Culture and Society in the Provincial Town, 1660–1770* (Oxford: Clarendon Press, 1989)

Boulton, Jeremy, *Neighbourhood and Society: A London Suburb in the Seventeenth Century* (Cambridge: Cambridge University Press, 1987)

Briggs, Chris, *Credit and Village Society in Fourteenth-Century England* (Oxford: Oxford University Press, 2009)

Clark, Elaine, 'Debt Litigation in a Late Medieval English Vill', in *Pathways to Medieval Peasants*, ed. by J. A. Raftis (Toronto: Pontifical Institute of Medieval Studies, 1981), pp. 247–79

Clark, Gregory, *English Prices and Wages, 1209–1914*, Global Price and Income History Group, University of California, Davis: < http://gpih.ucdavis.edu/Datafilelist.htm>

Everitt, Alan, 'Farm Labourers', in *Rural Society: Landowners, Peasants and Labourers 1500–1750, Chapters from the Agrarian History of England and Wales*, Volume 2, ed. by Christopher Clay (Cambridge: Cambridge University Press, 1990), pp. 161–230.

Firth, Raymond, and B. S. Yamey, 'Capital, Saving and Credit in Peasant Societies: A View from Economic Anthropology', in *Capital, Saving and Credit in Peasant Societies* ed. by Raymond Firth and B. S. Yamey (London: Allen and Unwin, 1964), pp. 15–34

Froide, Amy, *Never Married Singlewomen in Early Modern England* (Oxford: Oxford University Press, 2005)

———, *Silent Partners: Women as Public Investors during Britain's Financial Revolution, 1690–1750* (Oxford: Oxford University Press, 2017)

Gayton, Juliet, 'Tenants, Tenures and Transfers: The Landholding Experiences of Rural Customary Tenants in Some Hampshire Downland Manors, 1645–1705', unpublished PhD thesis, University of Exeter, 2013

Griffiths, Elizabeth, ed., *Her Price Is above Pearls: Family and Farming Records of Alice Le Strange, 1617–1656*, Norfolk Record Society, 79 (2015)

Habakkuk, John, *Marriage, Debt and the Estates System: English Landownership 1650–1950* (Oxford: Clarendon Press, 1994)

Heal, Felicity, and Clive Holmes, *The Gentry in England and Wales, 1500–1700* (Basingstoke: Macmillan, 1994)

Hill, J. W. F., *Tudor & Stuart Lincoln* (Cambridge: Cambridge University Press, 1956)

Hodges, Mary, 'Widows of the "Middling Sort" and their Assets in Two Seventeenth-Century Towns', in *When Death Do Us Part: Understanding and Interpreting the Probate Records of Early Modern England*, ed. by Tom Arkell, Nesta Evans, and Nigel Goose (Oxford: Leopard's Head Press, 2000), pp. 306–24

Holderness, B. A., 'The Clergy as Money-Lenders in England, 1550–1700', in *Princes and Paupers in the English Church 1500–1800*, ed. by Rosemary O'Day and Felicity Heal (New Jersey: Barnes and Noble, 1981), 195–209

———, 'Credit in English Rural Society before the Nineteenth Century, with Special Reference to the Period 1650–1720', *Agricultural History Review*, 24.2 (1976), 97–109

———, 'Widows in Pre-Industrial Society: An Essay upon their Economic Functions', in *Land, Kinship and Life-Cycle*, ed. by Richard M. Smith (Cambridge: Cambridge University Press, 1984), pp. 423–42

Jones, Norman L., *God and the Moneylenders: Usury and the Law in Early Modern England* (Blackwell: Oxford, 1989)

Johnston, J. A., '17th-Century Agricultural Practice in Six Lincolnshire Parishes', *Lincolnshire History and Archaeology*, 18 (1983), 5–14

Jordan, William Chester, *Women and Credit in Pre-Industrial and Developing Societies* (Philadelphia: University of Pennsylvania Press, 1993)

Kain, Roger J. P., John Chapman, and Richard R. Oliver, *The Enclosure Maps of England and Wales 1595–1918: A Cartographic Analysis and Electronic Catalogue* (Cambridge: Cambridge University Press, 2004)

Kermode, Jenny, 'The Trade of Late Medieval Chester,1500–1550', in *Progress and Problems in Medieval England: Essays in Honour of Edward Miller*, ed. by Richard Britnell and John Hatcher (Cambridge: Cambridge University Press, 1996), pp. 286–307

Kerridge, Eric, *Usury, Interest and the Reformation* (Aldershot: Ashgate, 2002)

Laurence, Anne, 'Lady Betty Hastings, Her Half-Sisters, and the South Sea Bubble: Family Fortunes and Strategies', *Women's History Review*, 15.4 (2006), 533–40

Lemire, Beverly, *The Business of Everyday Life: Gender, Practice and Social Politics in England, c. 1600–1900* (Manchester: Manchester University Press, 2005)

———, 'Introduction. Women, Credit and the Creation of Opportunity: A Historical Overview', in *Women and Credit: Researching the Past, Refiguring the Future*, ed. by Beverly Lemire, Ruth Pearson, and Gail Campbell (Oxford: Berg, 2001)

———, 'Petty Pawns and Informal Lending: Gender and the Transformation of Small-Scale Credit in England, circa 1600–1800', in *From Family Firms to Corporate Capitalism: Essays in Business and Industrial History in Honour of Peter Mathias*, ed. by Kristine Bruland and Patrick O'Brien (Oxford: Clarendon Press, 1998), pp. 112–38

McIntosh, Marjorie K., 'Moneylending on the Periphery of London, 1300–1600', *Albion*, 20.4 (1988), 557–71

———, *Poor Relief in England, 1350–1600* (Cambridge;: Cambridge University Press, 2012)

———, 'Women, Credit, and Family Relationships in England, 1300–1620', *Journal of Family History*, 30 (2005), 143–63

Muldrew, Craig, *The Economy of Obligation: The Culture of Credit and Social Relations in Early Modern England* (Basingstoke: Macmillan, 1998)

———, '"Hard Food for Midas": Cash and its Social Value in Early Modern England', *Past and Present*, 170.1 (2001), 78–120

Munro, John H., Revision of the Phelps Brown Hopkins' Basket of Consumables Commodity Price Series and Craftsmen's Wage Series, 1264–1700 (nd), at <https://www.economics.utoronto.ca/wwwfiles/archives/munro5/ResearchData.html>

North, Christine, 'Merchants and Retailers in Seventeenth-Century Cornwall', in *When Death Do Us Part: Understanding and Interpreting the Probate Records of Early Modern England*, ed. by Tom Arkell, Nesta Evans, and Nigel Goose (Oxford: Leopard's Head Press, 2000), pp. 285–305

Overton, Mark, 'English Probate Inventories and the Measurement of Agricultural Change', in *Probate Inventories: A New Source for the Historical Study of Wealth, Material Culture and Agricultural Development*, ed. by Ad Van Der Woude and Anton Schuurman (Utrecht: HES Publishers, 1980), pp. 205–16

Overton, Mark, and others, *Production and Consumption in English Households, 1600–1750* (London: Routledge, 2004)

Palmer, Anthony, ed., *Tudor Churchwardens' Accounts*, Hertfordshire Record Society, 1 (1985)

Schofield, Phillip, and Nick Mayhew, *Credit and Debt in Medieval England, c. 1180-c. 1350* (Oxford: Oxbow Books, 2002)

Shammas, Carol, *The Pre-Industrial Consumer in England and America* (Oxford: Clarendon Press, 1990)

Sharpe, Pam, 'A Woman's Worth: A Case Study of Capital Accumulation in Early Modern England', *Parergon*, 19.1 (2002), 173–84

Shepard, Alexandra, *Accounting for Oneself: Worth, Status, & the Social Order in Early Modern England* (Oxford: Oxford University Press, 2015)

———, 'Crediting Women in the Early Modern English Economy', *History Workshop Journal*, 79 (2015), 1–24

———, 'Minding their own Business: Married Women and Credit in Early Eighteenth-Century London', *Transactions of the Royal Historical Society*, Sixth Series, 25 (2015), 53–74

Shipley, Neal R., 'Thomas Sutton: Tudor-Stuart Moneylender', *Business History Review*, 50.4 (1976), 456–76

Spence, Cathryn, *Women, Credit, and Debt in Early Modern Scotland* (Manchester: Manchester University Press, 2016)

Spicksley, Judith M., ed., *The Business and Household Accounts of Joyce Jeffreys, Spinster of Hereford, 1638–1648*, British Academy, Records of Social and Economic History Series, 41 (Oxford: Oxford University Press, 2012)

———, '"Fly with a Duck in thy Mouth": Single Women as Sources of Credit in Seventeenth Century England', *Social History*, 32.2 (May 2007), 187–207

———, 'Usury Legislation, Cash and Credit: The Development of the Female Investor in the Late Tudor and Stuart Periods', *Economic History Review*, 61.2 (May 2008), 277–301

———, 'Women, "Usury" and Credit in Early Modern England: The Case of the Maiden Investor', *Gender and History*, 27.2 (August 2015), 263–92

Spufford, Peter, 'Long-Term Rural Credit in Sixteenth and Seventeenth-Century England: The Evidence of Probate Accounts', in *When Death Do Us Part: Understanding and Interpreting the Probate Records of Early Modern England*, ed. by Tom Arkell, Nesta Evans, and Nigel Goose (Oxford: Leopard's Head Press, 2000)

Spufford, Peter, M. Brett, and Amy Louise Erickson, eds, *Probate Accounts of England and Wales*, British Record Society, 112 (1999), 213–28

Swain, J., *Industry before the Industrial Revolution: North East Lancashire 1500–1640*, Chetham Society, third series, 32 (1986)

Tarver, Ann, 'The Due Tenth: Problems of the Leicestershire Tithing Process 1560–1640', *Transactions of the Leicestershire Archaeological History Society*, 78 (2004), 97–107

Tawney, Richard H., *Religion and the Rise of Capitalism* (1926; Harmondsworth: Penguin, 1961)

Thirsk, Joan, *English Peasant Farming: The Agrarian History of Lincolnshire from Tudor to Recent Times* (London: Routledge and Kegan Paul, 1957)

———, 'Introduction', in *Agricultural Change: Policy and Practice 1500–1750*, Chapters from the Agrarian History of England and Wales, ed. by Joan Thirsk, Volume 3 (Cambridge; Cambridge University Press, 1990)

——, *The Rural Economy of England: Collected Essays* (London: Hambledon Press, 1984)

Tittler, Robert, 'Money-Lending in the West Midlands: The Activities of Joyce Jefferies, 1638–1649', *Historical Research*, 67 (1994), 249–63

Todd, Barbara, 'Fiscal Citizens: Female Investors in Public Finance before the South Sea Bubble', in *Challenging Orthodoxies: The Social and Cultural Worlds of Early Modern Women Essays Presented to Hilda L. Smith*, ed. by Sigrun Haude and Melinda S. Zook (Farnham: Ashgate, 2014), pp. 53–76

Woodward, Donald, ed., *The Farming and Memorandum Books of Henry Best of Elmswell, 1642,* British Academy, Records of Social and Economic History Series, 8 (Oxford: Oxford University Press, 1984)

——, *Men at Work: Labourers and Building Craftsmen in the Towns of Northern England, 1450–1750* (Cambridge: Cambridge University Press, 1995)

Wrightson, Keith, and David Levine, *Poverty and Piety in an English Village: Terling 1525–1760* (Oxford: Clarendon Press, 1995)

Wrigley, E. A., and Roger S. Schofield, eds, *The Population History of England 1541–1871: A Reconstruction* (Cambridge: Cambridge University Press, 1981; pbk edn, 1989)

Credit, Strategies, and Female Empowerment in Early Modern France

Elise M. Dermineur[1]

'I do not wish them [women] to have power over men; but over themselves'
—Mary Wollstonecraft, *A Vindication of the Rights of Woman*

Introduction

In 2006, Muhammed Yunus and the Grameen Bank, a financial institution specializing in microcredit, won the Nobel Prize for peace 'for their efforts to create economic and social development from below'.[2] Many had believed that the development of microcredit institutions could contribute to the reduction of poverty, stimulate development, and empower women. By now, we know that the microcredit miracle did not occur and has not fulfilled its promise.[3] But despite the

[1] The author would like to acknowledge the generous financial support of Riksbankens Jubileumsfond.

[2] 'The Nobel Peace Prize 2006'. *Nobelprize.org*. Nobel Media AB 2014. Web. 8 May 2017. <http://www.nobelprize.org/nobel_prizes/peace/laureates/2006/>.

[3] See for instance Duflo, Banerjee, Glennerster, and Kinnan, 'The Miracle of Microfinance?'.

Elise M. Dermineur is an associate professor of history at Umeå University and a Pro Futura Scientia Fellow at the Swedish Collegium for Advanced Study in Uppsala. Dermineur's publications include articles published in the *Journal of Social History*, *The Journal of Interdisciplinary History*, *Traverse Revue d'Histoire — Zeitschrift für Geschichte*, *Social Science History*, among others. In 2017, she published *Gender and Politics in Eighteenth-Century Sweden*, a political biography of the Swedish queen Lovisa Ulrika (1720–1782).

Women and Credit in Pre-Industrial Europe, ed. by Elise M. Dermineur, EER 12 (Turnhout: Brepols, 2018), pp. 253–280.
BREPOLS PUBLISHERS DOI 10.1484/M.EER-EB.5.115756

critics, microcredit is still a widespread form of exchange in developing countries and even in developed regions worldwide.[4]

In pre-industrial Europe, microfinance was also widespread. Most pre-industrial European dwellers in search of capital turned to informal or semi-informal credit markets, lending and borrowing small or substantial amounts, either for their investments or to make ends meet. Before the advent of commercial and savings banks, finding funds occurred mostly at the local level through networks of acquaintances or brokered relations. In fact, most exchanges in pre-industrial Europe took place via credit. Debt and credit were, to a great extent, embedded in society.

Women's empowerment and credit activities are often considered part of the same package. This association has been increasingly reinforced thanks to the recent attention given to the microcredit revolution in developing countries. Today, most microfinance institutions give preference to female borrowers. About 95 per cent of the Grameen Bank's clients are women.[5] Many believe that female access to loans engenders their subsequent empowerment.[6] In pre-industrial Europe, on the other hand, this picture appears to be more nuanced. Chris Briggs has shown that in medieval England, for instance, credit networks brought little empowerment to women in traditional communities. This is because, he argues, too few women acted as *independent* lenders and borrowers. No significant impact ensued from their financial activities.[7] Yet, as many contributions in this present volume show, it seems that the proportion of female borrowers and female moneylenders gradually increased across Europe from 1500 onwards, with more or less regularity and homogeneity. Here and there, historians have begun to report female credit endeavours; it has become clear that urban and rural women not only took part in credit activities but also that their activities were of significance.[8] Across Europe, their marital status often determined their freedom of action in such markets.

[4] Bhatt and Tang, 'Making Microcredit Work in the United States'.

[5] Wahid, 'The Grameen Bank and Women in Bangladesh', p. 95.

[6] Several economists support the positive correlation between credit activities — especially lending — and female empowerment. Recently, however, this assumption has been challenged. Ester Duflo and Abhijit Banerjee, for instance, have shown that, despite the fact that most micro-borrowers are women, they do not seem to enjoy any form of empowerment. The two economists explain this is because these women do not use the capital borrowed to invest in profitable activities but, rather, to overcome difficulties. Banerjee and Duflo. *Poor Economics*, p. 171.

[7] Briggs, 'Empowered or Marginalized?'.

[8] See for instance Hanawalt, *The Ties That Bound*, p. 151. Jordan, *Women and Credit*. Laurence and others, eds, *Women and their Money*. Lemire and others, eds, *Women and Credit*.

The recent investigations made by scholars have therefore revealed that women were active in these premodern credit networks. This has encouraged historians such as William C. Jordan, for example, to question the social importance of credit networks with high female participation.[9] Building upon this analysis, this article is concerned with the impact of credit activities on women's lives. What did their involvement mean for the community and for their household? Was credit a factor in female emancipation and empowerment? In attempting to answer these questions, I examine the role of women in rural and local credit markets in eighteenth-century France. The emphasis is placed particularly on their role as creditors *and* debtors, but also, and above all, on the social consequences of their involvement in such transactions. Through the examination of about 2000 loan contracts (1730–1790) from two rural manors located in the south of Alsace — the seigneurie of Delle and Florimont — it is possible to reconstruct women's socio-economic networks and show that their position both as lenders and borrowers was far from negligible, thereby supplying some answers to the many questions that remain regarding women and credit. As 'there is something distinctive and significant about women's roles in credit', their contribution was critical.[10] To appreciate the role played by women in financial exchange, it is essential first to review their actions within the framework of the local credit market, secondly as debtors, then as creditors, with special reference to their marital status, and finally to question their social empowerment. Crossing the results of our investigation regarding notarial loan contracts with other sources allows us to sketch some features of the early modern empowerment framework.

Female Borrowers and Female Lenders in Eighteenth-Century France

Local Credit Markets

In early modern France, as in other European regions, various circuits of credit coexisted.[11] Urban and rural dwellers could invest their savings or locate available funds either through informal circuits or through the institutional credit market. Informal credit activities were mostly private agreements contracted between a lender and a borrower, with no institutional intercession. These transactions were often oral, sometimes registered privately in writing in a *livre de raison,* or on a

[9] Jordan, 'Women and Credit in the Middle Ages'.

[10] Jordan, *Women and Credit*, p. 1.

[11] On this see especially Hoffman and others, *Priceless Markets*.

loose piece of paper. Most of these small exchanges elude us; they do not appear in the archives except in probate inventories, which give an incomplete picture, at a given time, of an individual's credit standing, i.e. at his death.[12] On the other hand, historians have been able to gather more information regarding the institutional credit market. Creditors and borrowers could agree on a loan and register their transaction through the intercession of a notary. These notarial registers constitute the backbone of my investigation.

I have compiled and examined notarial registers for two rural Alsatian manors.[13] From 1730 to 1790, the registers of the seigneurie of Delle and the seigneurie of Florimont are continuous and offer vital information regarding local credit activities and credit networks. The sample covers a total of 2085 notarial deeds. In the seigneurie of Delle, the registers contain a total of 1463 loans, while in the seigneurie of Florimont, the registers account for 622 contracts (see Table 10.1). The volume exchanged in both seigneuries throughout the period did not reach a high ceiling compared to larger towns. In Paris, for instance, in the eighteenth century, millions of *livres* were exchanged on an annual basis.[14] But our sample is nonetheless consistent with other rural areas in terms of volume exchanged.[15]

Table 10.1. General overview of the credit market in the seigneuries of Delle and Florimont 1730–1790 (in livres).

	Seigneurie of Delle	**Seigneurie of Florimont**
Number of contracts	1463	622
Volume	442,573	304,534
Average loan	302.5	489.6
Median loan	200	200

In both seigneurie, *obligations* contracts were largely preferred over any kind of annuity at the notary's office. Registering a loan transaction with the notary — against a fee — allowed both parties to secure their transaction, especially in the

[12] On this issue, see notably Lindgren, 'The Modernization of Swedish Credit Markets'.

[13] I have used the notarial registers of the seigneurie of Delle and the seigneurie of Florimont at the Archives Départementales du Territoire de Belfort (ADTB hereafter); 2E 4/155–159, 2E 4/194, 2E 4/222–223, 2E 4/245–246, 2E 4/257–258, 2E4/279–280.

[14] Hoffman and others 'Redistribution and Long-Term Private Debt'. See especially the graph on page 260.

[15] Nuits-Saint-Georges's volume of exchange can be compared to the seigneurie of Delle and Florimont for instance. See Rosenthal, 'Rural Credit Markets and Aggregate Shocks', p. 292.

context of uncertainty about the repayment capacity of peasants. Increasingly, throughout the eighteenth century, official authorities such as the notary represented indisputable guarantors and intermediaries, and peasants gradually resorted to their services more and more often. The deed itself followed specific legal norms and gradually standardized the transactions. The contract traditionally contained the following information: the date, the names of both parties, their marital status, their place of residence, sometimes their professions and their kinship relations if any; the amount lent and received, and the interest fee (5 per cent was the common legal norm and cap in early modern France); the duration of the loan; the guarantees and mortgages promised, and often the name of one or several guarantors.[16]

Participation in the local credit market was theoretically open to everyone with available savings to invest or anyone who sought credit, provided that they had enough social and economic capital to back the loan. Women could participate legally in these financial exchanges. Their marital status, however — especially for married women — limited their freedom of action. Female minors could borrow and lend money with the legal assistance of their father or a male guardian. Unmarried women over twenty-five years-old — the age of majority — could also engage their assets and seek capital with the assistance of a male relative or a guardian. However, it appears that this rule was not always consistently enforced. Most of these unmarried women, who had reached their majority, appeared at the notary's office on their own. Married women could not legally borrow or extend money without their husbands' permission. But equally a husband could not engage his wife's assets without her consent. Married couples had to agree on financial transactions, since a loan involved their responsibility as borrowers and their mutual assets as creditors. Finally, a widow could legally manage her assets as she wished. Her legal capacity resembled those of men; Scarlett Beauvalet Boutourye pinpoints this phenomenon as the widow's 'retrieved legal capacity'.[17]

Women as Borrowers

Philip Hoffman and his co-authors note that 'if influential women could readily lend, it is true that they still had difficulty borrowing'.[18] In general, throughout early modern France, women had a narrower access than men to resources that

[16] Lending money was a risky activity and guarantees were almost always sought to secure the transaction. Debtors pledged their land, livestock, upcoming harvests, houses and dependent buildings and so on. A third party underwriter could be added to the deal.

[17] Beauvalet-Boutouyrie, *Etre Veuve*.

[18] Hoffman and others, 'Information and Economic History', p. 91.

included financial markets, labour opportunities, inheritance, and legal rights. Regional distinctions and legal norms could accent this discrepancy further. Without adequate assets, guarantees and social capital, women had difficulty in locating available funds and securing transactions. In the seigneurie of Delle, however, women (regardless of their marital status) signed 684 loans (46.75 per cent) and borrowed a total of 226,655 livres (51.2 per cent of the total exchanged), while in the seigneurie of Florimont, female borrowers signed 353 deeds (56.7 per cent of the total) for 128,055 livres borrowed (42 per cent of the total). In other words, women, in both seigneuries, borrowed almost half of the capital available. But if we consider these figures more closely, it appears that marital status played a key role in the allocation of funds (see Table 10.2). Unmarried women and widows represented the minority of borrowers, while the proportion of married couples in need of credit increased throughout the century to reach a significant proportion in the final decade.[19] Very little information was provided regarding the purpose of the loan. Some transactions were in real money, delivered in cash, while other were delayed payment agreement.

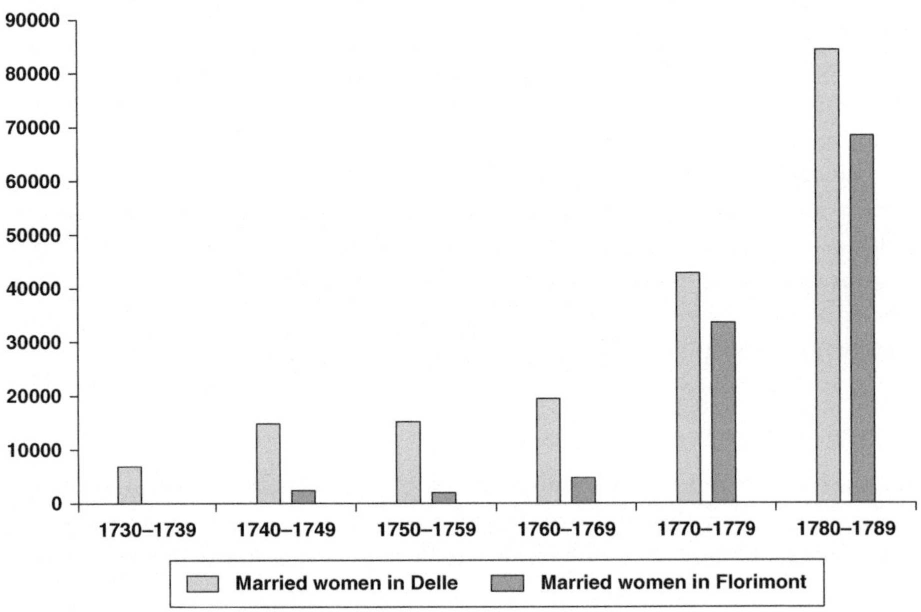

Figure 10.1. Married Women as debtors in the Seigneurie of Delle and Florimont, 1730–1790 (Volume of Exchange).

[19] Unmarried women or single women, in this article, refers to a group of women who are over twenty-five years old and unmarried. Their status might have been transitory — they would eventually marry — or permanent.

Table 10.2. Overview: women borrowing money in the seigneurie of Delle and Florimont, 1733–1789.

	Unmarried women		**Married couples**		**Widows**		**Groups**		**Men**	
	D	F	D	F	D	F	D	F	D	F
Number of loans subscribed	20	11	567	291	84	40	13	11	779	269
Volume borrowed	3956	1945	183,407	111,008	34,230	10,565	5062	4537	215,918	176,479
Mean	197.8	176.8	323.5	381.5	407.5	264.1	389.4	412.5	277.2	658.2
Median	116	178	200	208	200	167	207	279	180	200

D: Seigneurie of Delle

F: Seigneurie of Florimont

In the period we note the increasing share of married couples in the volume of exchange, with a rapid increase starting in the 1760s and continuing onwards (see Figure 10.1). How can we explain that, quite suddenly, male debtors included their wives in these deeds? Not only did married couples seek more funds but there were also gradually more of them doing so in the credit market. This phenomenon could be observed in both seigneuries and the shift seemed to have occurred at the same time. In Delle, 567 married couples sought credit (38.75 per cent) for a total of 183,407 *livres* (41.44 per cent) throughout the period. While they represented only 29.04 per cent of the borrowers in the 1730s, this became 47.41 per cent in the last decade of the *Ancien Régime*. In the seigneurie of Florimont, the same pattern applied. 291 married couples (46.78 per cent) signed loans at the notary for a total volume of 111,008 *livres* (36.45 per cent), their proportion increasing in number throughout the eighteenth century; while only 15.6 per cent in the first period of our sample, this became 47.4 per cent in the last decade. In both seigneuries, the increase of married debtors was constant, but seems to have taken off in the late 1760s as Figure 10.1 shows.

Contextual conditions, and factors such as rampant inflation, high demographic pressure, fragmentation of land, etc., undoubtedly pushed more and more people to locate available funds in the credit market. Indeed, if we look at the figures closely, the volume of exchange increased rapidly in the last two decades of the *Ancien Régime*. As already stated, the notarial documents rarely specify the purpose of a loan. It is extremely difficult for us to uncover what purpose a loan served. But how and why did married couples become the main debtors in the second half of the eighteenth century? Why did this particular group of debtors come to monopolize almost half of the capital available in the credit market? There are several possible explanations for this phenomenon.

First, peasants gradually placed more trust in the person of the notary to secure their transactions; as repayment could be sought in court, it was essential to keep track of financial transactions with official documents. This new confidence in the figures of authority may partially explain the increasing number of people who signed a deed at the notary's office (see Table 10.1), but this still does not explain why it was specifically married couples who abruptly became the main borrowers after the 1760s.[20]

The central explanation may lie in the fact that peasants had increasingly mortgaged a good deal of their land in order to secure their transactions, possibly in the seventeenth and at the beginning of the eighteenth century.[21] Some pieces of

[20] More on this phenomenon in Dermineur, 'Trust, Norms of Cooperation, and the Rural Credit Market'.

[21] Dermineur, 'Female Peasants, Patriarchy, and the Credit Market'.

land had been mortgaged for considerable periods of time. Creditors had no control over, and no information on, what land had been mortgaged or not, since no method of tracking this had been established — even if the intercession of notaries could be helpful to inform them in this matter. In the meantime, the numbers of default proceedings at court dramatically increased after 1760s.[22] In this context of lack of information and trust deficit, creditors were eager to secure their investments through new guarantees.

In the 1730s and 1740s, most of the loans contained specific mortgage guarantees, usually a specific plot of land, while at the end of the period the notary laconically inscribed on most contracts that the debtor(s) would mortgage '*tout ses biens tant meubles qu'immeubles*.'[23] Third party underwriters were gradually added to the deed, while it is possible women's lineage property — especially their dowries — became even more interesting to creditors. Indeed, as we have already noted, there was a dramatic increase in the number of married women who were involved in loan deeds after the late 1760s. Husbands and wives borrowed together and therefore offered greater guarantees to their creditors. Mortgaged lands no longer seemed to represent enough of a guarantee, and married women's property (mostly un-mortgaged plots of land and cash either inherited or owned through dowries) now seemed to represent an additional and greater guarantee in the eyes of creditors. Finally, creditors could legally seek repayment by turning to the widow for her share of the debt in the case of her husband's death.[24] After 1760, peasants not only had to add their wives and their wives' lineage property to the deed, but also had to find, in most cases, a third-party underwriter to reassure lenders.

We might legitimately ask whether married women were forced to sign loans alongside their husbands. Considering the traditional and patriarchal characteristics of rural societies, this question appears to be justified. A few examples can help us to better understand the extent of household partnerships. In April 1770, André Duprez and his wife borrowed 200 livres from the local judge in order for the couple to buy two new bulls for their farm. In January 1778, Pierre Joseph Rouge, a retired cavalryman, consented to extend credit to a couple of peasants, Ignace le

[22] On this point, see especially Dermineur, 'Trust, Norms of Cooperation, and the Rural Credit Market.'

[23] 'All his movable and immovable goods'.

[24] In the case of a husband borrowing money on his own, the repayment passed to his heirs upon his death. His wife, then, was responsible for a third of the debt but could refuse the inheritance and let down the creditor(s). His children were responsible for the other two-thirds. But in the case that a husband and wife signed a loan together, she was responsible for half of it and had to reimburse the creditor(s). See Dermineur. 'Widows' Political Strategies'.

Jeune and his wife Marie Catherine Surlet, in order for them to build a new house. In August 1780, Jean Baptiste Girardin and his wife Sophie Erard bought, with deferred payment, several items for their inn from a merchant. These three examples illustrate the partnership that existed between husband and wife within their households. As peasant households have always had to turn to creditors to pay their taxes, buy new lands or just for subsistence purposes, credit was most definitely an integral part of the household's experience. The partnership existing between spouses represented in fact a form of survival strategy, in which the household prevailed over the individual.

Women had always contributed to the household income in one way or in another. Signing an official deed at the notary held them responsible for half of the debt. Some historians have underlined the fact that, given their property was at stake, signing was an indication of submission. Instead, I think that women turned to become critical business partners at this point. The fact that women's lineage property and assets were at stake did not represent a reinforcement of patriarchy, but rather a breach of it, as women retained the right not only *not* to sign the deed if they did not want to, but were also able to withdraw their assets, by requesting a legal separation of property before the judge, if they considered that the financial situation of their household was endangered by their husband's decisions.[25] This is a key moment, therefore, when the erosion of patriarchy as a societal model began. Men were no longer in command of their households. Their guarantors possessed external control over the household's husbandry of resources, and their wives had to play a more critical role in the household management. From this point on, economic partnerships between spouses became even stronger and could be regarded as a survival strategy to cope with indebtedness. I believe this is a form of empowerment; women gaining more weight in their role of household partner. New economic conditions, such as those described in this here, made married women an important household component and associate. I will return to this point.

If women had access to the credit market as borrowers, they also played a key role in the extension of credit as lenders. Marital status, once again, remains a key tool of analysis.

Women as Creditors

In a common assumption, financial transactions in early modern Europe were traditionally associated with the manly sphere of business and trade, and almost

[25] On this topic see especially Hardwick, 'Seeking Separations'.

automatically excluded women. Supposedly, women were less well connected than men, had no legal access to public positions, and had less incentive and opportunity regarding commercial transactions, which in turn diminished their chances of meeting potential business partners. Historians have nonetheless found evidence that women were involved in credit markets, as this volume demonstrates.

If we know little about the role of female creditors, we know even less about the involvement of women in rural credit markets. The monetization of exchange entered slowly into the mechanisms of the local economy in the early modern period. Women's access to capital was more complicated than in urban areas, because of the specificities of household and labour structures that were more commonly shared and mutualized. In rural areas, the household prevailed over the individual, especially in regards to the management of resources and consumption strategies. Men, as heads of their families, thus tend to appear more in the sources. Nonetheless, in the seigneurie of Delle, female investors, regardless of their marital status, signed 278 contracts (19 per cent of the total contracts) for a volume of 83,453 livres (18.8 per cent of the total exchanged), while in the seigneurie of Florimont female investors appeared in 136 deeds (21.9 per cent) for a volume of 81,035 livres (26.6 per cent).

In order to examine the female contribution to the credit market, we are bound to divide women into categories according to their marital status. Marital status, indeed, not only determined the credit capacity of women but also determined their social position within the community; it is therefore a key tool of analysis.

Unmarried women and widows represented the majority of the women who extended credit in both seigneuries. Intriguingly, unmarried women ranked first among female creditors.[26] In the seigneurie of Delle, 152 contracts were signed by unmarried women out of a total of 1463 contracts (10.4 per cent) for a total amount of 32,948 livres out of 442,573 livres in total (7.44 per cent). Similar figures are found in the seigneurie of Florimont, where unmarried women signed 59 contracts (9.48 per cent) for a total of 31,062 livres (10.2 per cent). In the seigneurie of Delle, 78 contracts were signed by widows (5.3 per cent) for a total amount of 32,628 livres (7.37 per cent). In the seigneurie of Florimont, widows signed 44 contracts (7.07 per cent) for a total amount of 25,125 (8.25 per cent). The proportion of married women as moneylenders was quite low in both seigneuries. The capital they extended reached 4 per cent of the total volume in Delle and 7.36 per cent in Delle. For the purpose of this article, the focus is especially on unmarried women and widows.

[26] Amy Froide states that in Southampton single women loaned out more money than widows. Froide, *Never Married*, p. 133.

Table 10.3. Marital status and the allocation of capital in the credit market of the seigneuries of Delle and Florimont, 1733–1789.

	Seigneurie of Delle				**Seigneurie of Florimont**			
	N	*V*	*Median per contract*	*Mean per contract*	*N*	*V*	*Median per contract*	*Mean per contract*
Single women	152 (10.4%)	32,948 (7.44%)	162.5	216.7	59 (9.48%)	31,062 (10.2%)	200	526.4
Married couples	48 (3.3%)	17,877 (4%)	200	372.4	24 (3.85%)	22.415 (7.36%)	200	933.9
Widows	78 (5.3%)	32,628 (7.37%)	200	418.3	44 (7.07%)	25,125 (8.25%)	336.5	571.2
Groups	3 (0.2%)	1072 (0.2%)	200	357.3	9 (1.4%)	2433 (0.8%)	259	270.3
Men	1182 (80.8%)	358,048 (80.9%)	200	303.1	483 (77.6%)	222,823 (73.1%)	200	461.3
Total	1463	442,573			622	304,534		

Entering into the credit market as a creditor supposes sufficient financial means. In traditional societies, we might ask where the money came from that these women possessed. Where did they find the necessary resources to have surplus to invest and lend? Answering this question will help us in turn to determine if whether or not women were empowered by moneylending.

Unmarried Women

Marguerite Duprez was a domestic in the town of Delle.[27] She had emigrated there from her native village of Saint-Dizier-l'Evêque, located only a few kilometres away. In 1777, still unmarried, she loaned money to Joseph Tallon (120 Livres) and in 1784 to Pierre Michelat and his wife (220 livres), both from Saint-Dizier-l'Evêque.[28] She thus kept an existing bond with her native community. Incidentally, she continued lending money there after she married. In 1788, Marguerite Duprez and her husband, lent 255 livres to Madelaine Michelat, also from the same village.

Like Marguerite Duprez, many single women invested their wages as rural domestics in the local credit market. Sheilagh Ogilvie estimates that 'between the ages of 25 and 45, about one quarter of unmarried women still lived as servants'.[29] In the seigneurie of Delle and Florimont, young men and women often worked as domestics in wealthy farms or shops before establishing a household of their own. If a few young men worked as apprentices in artisan shops in villages and neighbouring towns, some young women could find employment as qualified workers in market-based sectors, especially in textile production. These qualified workers, however, often had to emigrate to larger towns. This did not prevent them maintaining strong ties with their native village, as our example shows. As Laurence Fontaine puts it, female servants were at the heart of a system of capital redistribution.[30] The capital amassed by these female domestics could not be kept safely at home; it was

[27] On this, see especially Dermineur, 'Single Women'. When we refer to early modern single women, we target the group of women to have reached reproductive age, who were able to work, who remained single for some time — this period could be more or less long depending on several factors — or who never been married at all. All these women had in common the fact they had lived without the authority and social protection of a husband.

[28] ADTB 2E4/279 and 280.

[29] Ogilvie, *A Bitter Living*, p. 271.

[30] Fontaine, *Pauvreté, Crédit et confiance dans l'Europe préindustrielle*, p. 156.

undoubtedly more secure invested in the credit market. I have found evidence that male domestics also invested their wages in the credit market.

Another source of capital for unmarried women was constituted in property and money they might inherit. Judith Spicksley shows that this revenue motivated most of the single women involved in lending activities in her British sample in the seventeenth century.[31] The seigneuries of Delle and Florimont were both located in a region where partible inheritance was the norm. The parental patrimony was shared equally among the heirs — the children — regardless of gender. This legal norm, therefore, contributed greatly to the independence of women, and certainly benefitted unmarried women deprived of an income or family assistance since they could use their share in case of necessity. It is difficult, however, to estimate precisely in which cases and on what occasions single women chose to invest their inherited capital in the credit market.

We might therefore wonder whether single women with regular incomes, such as domestics and rural workers, and/or with inheritance possibilities, were constrained to extend credit to their relatives. Because they lacked the support of a spouse and were in a vulnerable position — presumably more so than other community members — were single women constrained to extend credit to their relatives? Were they in a position to resist such demands? We certainly do lack points of comparison to answer this complex question. In Paris, Hoffman found that only 3 per cent of the borrowers and creditors were blood related. In rural areas, this percentage was higher, given the stronger norms of cooperation, solidarity, and endogamy. In England, Holderness found that 40 per cent of lenders and borrowers were blood related, while Wrightson and Levine counted 17 per cent of loans contracted by family members in a British village.[32] In the seigneurie of Delle, 7.4 per cent of all transactions were between members of the same family, while this rate reached 8 per cent in Florimont. In both seigneuries, women, regardless of their marital status, were more likely to extend credit to their relatives than did men, but they lent small amounts of money in comparison with the overall median. In Delle, 10.6 per cent of single women extended credit to their relatives, while 23.7 per cent did so in Florimont — but in this seigneurie, they were also less numerous, which in turn biases the significance of this percentage. As a point of comparison, Spicksley found that a third of single women lenders provided credit for family and kin.[33]

[31] Spicksley, '"Fly with a Duck in thy Mouth"', p. 198.

[32] Holderness, 'Widows in Pre-Industrial Society', p. 441. Wrightson and others, *Poverty and Piety*, p. 100.

[33] Spicksley, '"Fly with a Duck in thy Mouth"', p. 198.

While these figures were slightly higher than average, nothing indicates that family members took advantage of the incomes of single women, especially when we compare them to other groups (see Table 10.4 below).

Compared to male creditors, single women did extend credit more often to their relatives. This can be explained by the fact that, unlike men, they lacked commercial connections and public visibility. They lent money to people in their direct circle of interaction without necessarily being constrained to do so. The fact that unmarried women took the precaution to register their transactions before the notary reinforced the argument that a loan to a family member had to be repaid. It would be valuable to compare these results with informal transactions.[34]

Table 10.4. Same family contracts in the seigneuries of Delle and Florimont, 1730–1790.

	Same family contracts		**Volume**		**Median**	
	D	*F*	*D*	*F*	*D*	*F*
Single women	16/152 (10.5%)	14/59 (23.7%)	4,106	4,946	151	195
Married couples	11/48 (22.9%)	2/24 (8.3%)	6,154	236	150	118
Widows	3/78 (3.8%)	5/44 (11.3%)	545	1,531	200	240
Groups	1/3 (33.3%)	2/9 (22.2%)	672	735	672	368
Men	77/1181 (6.51%)	27/483 (5.6%)	25,578	10,608	179	288
Total	108/1463 (7.4%)	50/622 (8%)	37,055 (8.4%)	18,057 (5.9%)	174.5	249.5

When we closely examine the network of debtors of single women, it appears that these women chose to extend capital principally to men (48.7 per cent in Delle, 44 per cent in Florimont) and married couples (respectively 39.5 per cent and 35 per cent), denoting a safe strategy on their part. Indeed, in the case of married couple debtors, both spouses guaranteed the loan. If one of the borrowers died, the other was still accountable for that share of the debt along with the heirs, increasing the safety of the capital investment. Men were also sought-after borrowers as they could easily bring collateral and mortgages to secure the transactions. Amy Froide has highlighted the same lending strategy on the part of single women in

[34] Informal transactions were private agreements contracted outside the notary's office. These exchanges can be tracked thanks to probate inventories.

Bristol. There, women also overwhelmingly extended capital to men (ten out of twelve loans).[35] Despite the strong norms of solidarity and cooperation in traditional communities, it seems that single women were also careful investors.

Single women, indeed, protected their capital and did not lend blindly. On 9 September 1743, Marie Agathe Maraget lent 60 *livres* in cash to her neighbour Nicolas Charbonnier. She secured her transaction by asking Charbonnier for a specific piece of land to be mortgaged (an orchard in this case), and she also required a guarantor.[36] On March 1745, Jeanne Preney extended money to one of her relatives, Maurise Preney, and her husband Jean Pierre Bernard. She delivered to them the amount of 100 *livres* in cash. The money presumably came from her wages; she was employed by the village priest as a domestic. In order to secure the transaction, and perhaps because she feared she would not retrieve her capital for some reason, she asked for the mortgage of a meadow and a piece of arable land.[37] Many examples such as these ones can be found. Most single women tightly secured their transactions and diversified their portfolios.

Widows

Anne Marie Monnier was married to the *laboureur* Nicolas Jeantine. Perhaps because her husband was overwhelmed with farm tasks, or perhaps because she was extending credit on her own money, she, alone, was present before the notary on November 1771 and on June 1777. On the first occasion, she extended credit for a total of 500 livres to Pierre Jacquet and Marie Anne Liron, a married couple living in her village of Suarce.[38] A few years later, in 1777, she agreed to renew an old obligation and to extend a new loan to Catherine Frin, the widow of Henri Werther, in order to rebuild her house destroyed by a fire. Anne Marie Monnier lent Catherine Frin 880 *livres*.[39] She delivered the money to her clients, and her husband countersigned the deeds later; but on this occasion too, he left her to go alone to the notary.

When Monnier's husband passed away in 1779, at fifty years old, she did not remarry and managed her property in her own name as head of her household.[40] She continued to extend credit to her neighbours and friends. But in 1783,

[35] Froide, *Never Married*, p. 135.

[36] ADTB 2E4/157.

[37] ADTB 2E4/157.

[38] ADTB 2E4/443 15 novembre 1771.

[39] ADTB 2E4/444 13 juin 1777.

[40] ADTB Registre paroissial 095 E dépôt GG 1–5.

perhaps feeling she could not work any longer, she invested a considerable amount of money in the credit market, presumably in order to secure a regular income for her retirement. Like her, widows were often eager to invest in the credit market to secure a fixed income, especially if they had no offspring.[41] She extended a total of 3173 *livres* to ten different borrowers, all living in her village, thus spreading risk.[42] Most of the capital repayment deadlines were on demand, indicating her willingness to receive fixed amounts of money from the interest every year. The transactions were all risk-limited as all the borrowers lived in her village, most of them were married (if one spouse died, the other was still responsible for his or her share of the debt), the repayment date was on demand, meaning she could withdraw her capital anytime (with notice) if needed, and she diversified her investment in lending her capital to ten different debtors, thus spreading the risk. Most of the widows extending credit sought an annual return worth their investments; especially aging widows who attempted to diversify their income.

In practice, a widow regained full legal capacity but in theory her access to labour, resources, lands, and money remained extremely difficult.[43] Julie Hardwick states that 'widows often found it difficult in daily practice to take advantage of the autonomy their legal position promised'.[44] But some widows, the wealthiest among them, however, had enough resources to invest in the credit market, like Anne Marie Monnier. Most of these women inherited part of the community property assets and/or had funds of their own. For instance, widows got back their dowries and could also have inherited from their parents — partible inheritance was the rule there. This has prompted scholars to recognize the centrally important role of widows in local economies, at the heart of the redistribution system for its active members.[45]

Many widows did extend money in the credit market in order to secure their old age.[46] This strategy was quite common in urban areas for wealthy widows.[47] In

[41] In Württemberg, widows also invested in state mortgages. See Sabean, *Property, Production, and Family*, p. 47. Laurence Fontaine has noted the same thing among early modern French widows. Fontaine, *L'économie morale*, p. 157.

[42] ADTB $2^E4/445$.

[43] Scarlett Beauvalet-Boutourye is quite positive about the status of widows in this era and talks about 'la capacité retrouvée'; Beauvalet-Boutourye, *Etre Veuve*, p. 195.

[44] Hardwick, 'Widowhood', p. 133.

[45] Jordan, 'Women and Credit in the Middle Ages', p. 47.

[46] See also Rosenhaft, 'Did Women Invent Life Insurance?'.

[47] See Zuijderduijn's article in this volume for more details on female investors and life insurance.

the seigneurie of Delle, seventy-eight widows (5.3 per cent) extended credit for a total of 32,628 *livres* (7.4 per cent), while in the seigneurie of Florimont forty-four (7.07 per cent) lent out money for a total of 25,125 *livres* (8.2 per cent). Some of these women extended credit several times throughout the period. During the eighteenth century, the participation of widows in the credit market was quite irregular, with the exception of the seigneurie of Florimont in which they gradually came to participate more in terms of number and volume. It is worth noting that their loans were on average no smaller than those of men.

Where did the loans made by widows go? Who were widows' clients? Just like unmarried women, securing their capital was certainly the main preoccupation of widow investors. Indeed, widows first lent to men (almost 50 per cent in Delle and 60 per cent in Florimont in terms of volume) and to married couples (55 per cent in Delle and 35 per cent in Florimont in terms of volume). In terms of risk-taking, widows, like other female creditors, took minimal risks and tightly secured their transactions. Protecting their capital for their old age appears logical. Laurence Fontaine suggests that widows were very active in proximity lending.[48] This pattern is similar to what we have observed among unmarried women. Capital extended to their neighbours was high, but no higher than any other category.

Credit Activities and Female Empowerment

As unmarried women and widows invested their money in the credit market of their local communities, we might ask whether they benefitted in any way from these activities. Were these women empowered? And if so, how? Can we measure empowerment? But first, let us sketch the contours of 'pre-industrial empowerment' and outline the framework in which women could find freedom of action.

Characteristics of Early Modern Empowerment

Modern microcredit activities are often associated with the notion of empowerment and emancipation. Countless studies have asked whether or not microfinance does empower women. Despite this scholarly and political interest, there is no clear consensus among scholars about what modern empowerment is supposed to encompass and entitle. Empowerment can be roughly defined as the power or

[48] Fontaine, *L 'économie morale*, p. 159.

the ability to influence decision making.[49] It could also be a process of becoming more influential within one's household or/and community. Jo Rowlands also argues that empowerment includes the process that leads people to perceive themselves as able and entitled to make decision.[50]

If we consider the sphere of microcredit, for example, women are supposed to gain financial independence, assertiveness, respect, and autonomy both within their household and within their communities. Ultimately, these female beneficiaries of microcredit are also supposed to contribute to economic development. This definition remains a bit blurry and the means to achieve empowerment is often vague. This has lead Serene Khader to note that, 'though donor agencies and academics routinely describe empowerment as a development goal, there is little agreement of what type of life changes constitute empowerment and why such changes are ultimately valuable'.[51]

Early modern or pre-industrial empowerment was, in essence, not intrinsically different. The term 'empowerment', and the concept itself, were of course not used or referred to by contemporaries. I believe that the notion of 'pre-industrial empowerment' implied a transformative dimension, a change in the distribution or application of power. It was an improvement of one's situation, a challenge in a certain power dynamic. A person or a group, an institution, or a situation, could empower a group or an individual. The process itself could take place in practice without necessarily being formally identified by the agents as such, i.e. as empowering. What differed from our contemporary society was perhaps the way early modern society was organized and structured. When we consider women in the early modern period, we refer to a group of individuals who traditionally had less power, influence, authority, and economic and political opportunities than men. Across Europe, not only did countless institutions, organizations and markets legally bar access and deny rights to female members, but pre-industrial consciousness and norms validated this de facto biological sex order and, therefore, discrimination. As a result, pre-industrial female empowerment was deeply connected with the challenge of patriarchy.[52]

For the purpose of this article, I tentatively sketch a framework assessing the empowerment of early modern female creditors. How can we assess the

[49] On empowerment see especially Bacqué and Biewener, *L'empowerment*; Duflo, 'Women, Empowerment'; Pitt and others, *Does Micro-Credit Empower Women?*

[50] Cited in Parpart and others, 'Rethinking (Em)powerment', p. 11.

[51] Khader, *Adaptive Preferences*, p. 173.

[52] On this see especially Dermineur, 'Anatomy of Early Modern Patriarchy'.

economic and social effects of lending activities? What are the factors we need to look at? It is difficult, for obvious reasons, to assess the social impact of credit activities, above all for the early modern period. Points of comparison, at this stage, are still greatly missing. What follows is an attempt to bring some key elements to the debate. In order to do so, marital status is once again a useful tool of analysis.

Single Women and Autonomy

As previously explained, single women creditors did play a dynamic role in the local economy, increasingly extending more capital throughout the eighteenth century. If their participation in the local credit market corresponds to an increasing economic need for liquidity and funds, we can nonetheless suppose that these women benefitted from their lending activities. I believe that the involvement of more single women in the credit market corresponded to a community need, rather than to an active involvement on women's part in financial activities.[53] Single women had increasingly greater access to cash because of their service-oriented labour and their savings capacity (most of these female servants were rural servants, and benefitted from room and board, amplifying their saving capacity). The service-oriented labour market expanded in the eighteenth century. These female domestics represented, therefore, potential creditors. We can argue that their participation in the credit market was sought out; especially in an economy where cash remained scarce.

We might ask what kind of social benefits these single women lenders obtained. Rosenthal observes that 'quantitative analysis of credit activity suggests that individuals used these markets to invest their savings and withdrew their funds when they needed to provide for their children'; in the case of single women, it is likely they withdrew their money in order to get married, demonstrating a certain independence from their families, opportunities in the labour market, and an appreciation for investment and protection of their assets.[54] Marie Margueritte Beuné is a good example. She lent 512 livres in May 1745 to three different creditors, thus diversifying her investment. In November 1747, she married Antoine Betevy

[53] In northern Sweden and in Finland, Tiina Hemminki has shown that the first savings banks' main clients were in fact female domestics. Her dissertation is in Finnish, the English title is 'Wealth, Credit, and Trust: The Lending Relationships of Peasants on Both Sides of the Gulf of Bothnia 1796–1830'.

[54] Rosenthal, 'Rural Credit Markets and Aggregate Shocks', p. 305.

and could count on her returns from the credit market to increase her dowry and her new household's capital.[55] Her assets were thus protected and returned a small profit into the bargain. Thanks to their wages invested in the credit market, female domestics showed independence and assertiveness.

These women, who invested their savings and domestic wages in the credit market, might have been able to relieve their parents of part, or perhaps all, of their endowment at marriage. Several marriage contracts in the area mentioned cash in the dowry provision.[56] We still lack data on this critical issue and can only hypothesise. If we consider the inheritance system — partible in this region — and if we suppose that some brides were able to provide for their own dowry, then we might reconsider the traditional pattern of inheritance. Indeed, in regions of partible inheritance historians have asserted that, in practice, daughters were often excluded from their parent's inheritance after they had been endowed at marriage, while their brothers would be endowed *and* receive their share of the family property at the deaths of their parents, creating an inheritance practice that was highly discriminatory and based solely on gender.[57] In the case that some women were able to provide their dowries themselves, there was no obstacle to them accessing their parent's property and inheriting the same share as their brothers. While this is an interesting hypothesis, more data and research could help to verify it.

A second hypothesis could also be developed. We might suggest that these single women had more freedom to choose their life partner thanks to their ability to negotiate loan contracts, their access to resources and their possible dowry provision. To date, historians know very little about the choice of marriage partner in traditional communities. This issue would also need more data and research but could prove to be significant.

Widows and Promised Independence

I have shown elsewhere that women in general, and widows in particular, did benefit from a change in legal norms in the second half of the eighteenth century, and this related to their involvement in the credit market.[58] This is very clear in marriage contracts. Indeed, an increasing proportion of marriage contracts allocated the

55 ADTB 2E4/ 157.

56 Dermineur, 'Women in Rural Society', Chapter 3.

57 See especially Derouet, 'Le Partage des Frères'.

58 Dermineur, 'Widows' Political Strategies in Traditional Communities'.

surviving spouse — in most cases the widow — a greater share of the couple's estate and greater protection. This development became particularly visible after 1760. In the seigneurie of Delle and Florimont, we see that the provisions stated in these contracts *became* increasingly favourable to women, and especially to widows.[59] The division of community property, which traditionally entitled a widow to a third of the community property in this region, was increasingly modified by the soon to be wed couples, granting *half to each spouse*.[60] It is worth noting that, in the majority of cases, the surviving spouse was in fact the wife.[61] Therefore, the increasing protection afforded to the surviving partner did intentionally protect widows.

Additionally, other new legal provisions were progressively introduced in these marriage contracts, which further protected widows. The provision of the survivor's benefits embraced a broad range of possibilities, usually deliberated upon and negotiated by the contracting parties themselves.[62] Among the types of insurance available for the surviving spouse, we find the following: the dower, a discretionary provision which could be unilateral, usually in favour of the widow; mutual donation, which was egalitarian regardless of sex; provisions in case there were children and in case there were none; usufruct, unilateral or mutual; and a possible combination of several of these features, along with other gifts that did not respond to clear legal norms but rather to specific familial situations. All these changes, I argue, were directly related to the increasing participation of women in credit activities. Protecting the widow's assets and patrimony was beneficial to her household, her social capital, but also to creditors.

One reason for the legal improvement of the condition of widows could lie, paradoxically, in the difficult economic situation that was emerging in the eighteenth century, and in the greater involvement of women in the credit market. First, the equal share of the community property, and the adoption of new legal measures protecting widows, could be a direct consequence of economic change. Indebtedness, indeed, grew substantially in the eighteenth century, especially in its second

[59] About this specific region see especially Bouvalot, *Coutumes de la Haute-Alsace*; Storti, 'Coutume de Ferrette et/ou coutume du comté de Belfort'.

[60] In my sample, this new provision was progressively applied in the 1720s and gradually came to be used by the majority of betrothed couples; in the 1760s it was at 53.13 per cent and it continued to grow until finally it came to dominate the marriage contracts of the 1780s at 81.4 per cent.

[61] For figures see Maillard, 'Les Veuves Dans La Société Rurale'.

[62] As many studies have by now shown, the surviving spouse was in most cases the woman. See for example, Maillard, 'Les Veuves Dans La Société Rurale'.

half.[63] In this particular region, like elsewhere in early modern France, peasants increasingly borrowed more money and had difficulty in meeting their repayment deadlines. Many of them, then, proceeded to associate their wives to the loan, in order to bring greater, and new, guarantees to the deeds and to reassure creditors; as a consequence, wives then became accountable for half of the debt. As a husband and a wife borrowed money together, the loan was secured through their borrowing capacity as a couple, that is, through the property held in common, and through the lineage property of each (including women's dowries).[64] Leaving the widow half of the community property could potentially discharge the heirs of a greater debt, and above all made the wife fully responsible and accountable for her actions, transforming her into a joint economic partner, while reassuring potential creditors and business partners.[65]

This informal legal evolution did not originate directly in the involvement of widows in the credit market but, rather, in the involvement of women in general in the extension of credit. Moreover, the strategies adopted by peasants to secure the position and status of widows did not originate from widows alone, but were most probably the result of a consensus reached in the community, derived from other complex social and economic strategies employed by peasants in order to cope with external economic effects, such as growing indebtedness. As previously stated, widows' capital could benefit the active population greatly in a system of capital redistribution.

The association of women with the economic viability of the household and farm did force a crack in the traditional paradigm of patriarchy, allowing for the survival of the family and of the *lignée*. Everyone in the community contributed to combatting the effects of indebtedness, and to the search for, and creation, of capital. Women, regardless of their marital status, became associated with this process, more by necessity than by will. Wives were increasingly associated with their husbands in the search for capital in the credit market, thus becoming key economic partners. Widows were similarly solicited to extend credit, just as single women did.[66] Everyone in the community participated in the effort to ensure its survival

[63] See among others Fontaine, *L'économie morale*; Grenier, *L'Economie d'Ancien Régime*. And for this particular area see especially Boehler, *Une Société*; Dermineur, 'Female Peasants, Patriarchy'.

[64] Dermineur, 'Women in Rural Society'.

[65] More on this here: Dermineur, 'Les Femmes et Le Crédit'; Dermineur 'Trust, Norms of Cooperation, and the Rural Credit Market'.

[66] See especially Dermineur, 'Single Women'.

and to cope with indebtedness. Such a consensus is not surprising, as norms of cooperation and reciprocity were high in traditional communities.[67]

Both the enhancement of access to resources for widows and their participation in the credit market improved their living conditions and certainly contributed to their empowerment both socially and economically. Measuring and evaluating empowerment proves to be extremely difficult, but we can observe the effects of these changes for widows here and there in other documents. For instance, it appears that widows did serve progressively more often as guarantors to back loans in the credit market, indicating the social credit they benefitted from.[68] We also see that, towards the end of the eighteenth century, widows were more numerous in negotiating the marriage contracts of their children. About 24 per cent of brides had their marriages arranged solely by their widowed mother. Alyson Poska has found similar figures in early modern Galicia.[69] Widows who negotiated the marriages of their children played a key role in the negotiation process and their authority was asserted more or less with force, depending on how successful they were. Widows similarly appeared less often before judges in the last decades of the eighteenth century, perhaps indicating that their status and greater access to resources preserved them from conflict.[70]

These are the indications of some of the changes affecting women in general. We need to be extremely careful in arguing that these new conditions were in fact an effect of female empowerment resulting from women's increasing key role in credit activities. Causation, effect, and correlation can easily be intermingled. Future studies on this topic will help us to clarify the social effects of female participation in credit markets.

Conclusion

Thanks to their credit activities, female creditors benefitted from some social improvement in their status. In a common assumption, the female sex and marital

[67] See Dermineur, 'Trust, Norms of Cooperation, and the Rural Credit Market'.

[68] Dermineur, 'Women in Rural Society'.

[69] Poska, *Women and Authority*, p. 119: 'In my examination of approximatively 300 marriage and dowry contracts in the province of Ourense, only about one-third of the brides had two living parents at the signing of the marriage contracts'. 'More than 28% of brides had their marriages arranged and/or dowries arranged solely by their widowed mothers'.

[70] Dermineur, 'Women in Rural Society'.

status constituted a fundamental barrier to independence, emancipation, privileges, and social prerogatives, especially in pre-industrial rural communities. But, thanks to women's involvement in the credit market and their lending activities, women fulfilled a key social function, rewarded in turn by greater social freedom, especially regarding marriage, an important stage in life not only for women but also for their families. First, investing their wages and savings in the credit market might allow these women to relieve their families of part — or all — of the dowry. By doing so, perhaps single women could, in turn, freely choose their future spouse. More work remains to be done in this area to back up this idea. Widows who extended credit could also enjoy greater social credit and a more recognized position as heads of their households. Finally, the activities and gradual presence of women in the credit market also had an important impact on the social fabric and the interaction of women with their families and towards men. To some extent, a proportion of these women were necessary actors in the credit market, a social and public sphere in which, in a traditional assumption, they were not expected to interact. As this study has shown, women could be empowered by credit activities. I believe, however, that a number of factors needed to come together in order for empowerment to crystallize in practice.

More research on this topic will shed more light on these critical issues. In particular, the cross-examination of notarized loans and informal loans may reveal more about women's role and activities in rural credit markets.

Works Cited

Manuscripts

Archives Départementales du Territoire de Belfort, 2E 4/155–59, 2E 4/194, 2E 4/222–23, 2E 4/245–46, 2E 4/257–58, 2E4/279–80

Primary Sources

Bouvalot, Edouard, *Coutumes de la Haute-Alsace dites de Ferrette* (Colmar: Barth et Held-Baltzinger, 1870)

Secondary Studies

Banerjee, Abhijit V., and Esther Duflo, *Poor Economics: A Radical Rethinking of the Way to Fight Global Poverty* (New York: Public Affairs, 2011)

Bacqué, Marie-Hélène, and Carole Biewener, *L'Empowerment, une Pratique Emancipatrice* (Paris: La Découverte, 2013)

Beauvalet-Boutouyrie, Scarlett, *Etre Veuve Sous l'Ancien Régime* (Paris: Belin, 2001)

Bhatt, Nitin, and Shui-Yan Tang, 'Making Microcredit Work in the United States: Social, Financial, and Administrative Dimensions', *Economic Development Quarterly*, 15.3 (2001), 229–41

Boehler, Jean-Michel, *Une Société Rurale en Milieu Rhénan: la Paysannerie de la Plaine d'Alsace (1648–1789)* (Strasbourg: Presses Universitaires de Strasbourg, 1995)

Briggs, Chris, 'Empowered or Marginalized? Rural Women and Credit in Later Thirteenth- and Fourteenth-Century England', *Continuity and Change*, 19.1 (2004), 13–43

Dermineur, Elise M., 'Anatomy of Early Modern Patriarchy', in *Revisiting Gender in European History, 1400–1800*, ed. by Elise M. Dermineur and others (New York: Routledge, 2018), pp. 10–28

———, 'Female Peasants, Patriarchy, and the Credit Market in Eighteenth-Century France', *Proceedings of the Western Society for French History*, 37 (2009), 61–84

———, 'Les Femmes et Le Crédit Dans Les Communautés Rurales Au 18e Siècle', *Traverse Revue d'Histoire — Zeitschrift Für Geschichte*, 2 (2014), 53–64

———, 'Single Women and the Rural Credit Market in Eighteenth-Century France', *Journal of Social History*, 48.1 (2014), 175–99

———, 'Trust, Norms of Cooperation, and the Rural Credit Market in Eighteenth-Century France', *Journal of Interdisciplinary History*, 45.4 (2015), 485–506

———, 'Widows' Political Strategies in Traditional Communities: Negotiating Marital Status and Authority in 18th c France', in *Gender and Political Culture, 1500–1800*, ed. by James Daybell and Svante Norrhem (Farnham: Routledge, 2016), pp. 123–39

———, 'Women in Rural Society: Peasants, Patriarchy and the Local Economy in Northeast France, 1650–1789', unpublished PhD dissertation, Purdue University, 2011

Derouet, Bernard, 'Le Partage des Frères. Héritage Masculin et Reproduction Sociale en Franche-Comté aux XVIIIe et XIXe Siècles', *Annales. Économies, Sociétés, Civilisations*, 48.2 (1993), 453–74

Duflo, Esther, 'Women, Empowerment and Economic Development', *Journal of Economic Literature*, 50.4 (2012), 1051–79

Duflo, Esther, and others, 'The Miracle of Microfinance? Evidence from a Randomized Evaluation'. Working Paper. National Bureau of Economic Research, May 2013. <https://doi.org/10.3386/w18950>

Fontaine, Laurence, *Pauvreté, Crédit et confiance dans l'Europe préindustrielle* (Paris: Gallimard, 2008)

Froide, Amy M., *Never Married: Singlewomen in Early Modern England* (Oxford: Oxford University Press, 2005)

Grenier, Jean-Yves, *L'Economie d'Ancien Régime: Un Monde de L'échange et de L'incertitude* (Paris: Albin Michel, 1996)

Hanawalt, Barbara A., *The Ties That Bound: Peasant Families in Medieval England* (Oxford: Oxford University Press, 1989)

Hardwick, Julie, 'Seeking Separations: Gender, Marriages, and Household Economies in Early Modern France', *French Historical Studies*, 21.1 (1998), 157–80

———, 'Widowhood and Patriarchy in Seventeenth Century France', *Journal of Social History*, 26.1 (1992), 133–48

Hemminki, Tiina, 'Wealth, Credit, and Trust: The Lending Relationships of Peasants on Both Sides of the Gulf of Bothnia 1796–1830', unpublished PhD dissertation (in Finnish), University of Jyväskylä, Finland, 2014

Hoffman, Philip T., and others, 'Information and Economic History: How the Credit Market in Old Regime Paris Forces Us to Rethink the Transition to Capitalism', *The American Historical Review*, 104.1 (1999), 69–94

———, *Priceless Markets: The Political Economy of Credit in Paris 1660–1870* (Chicago: University of Chicago Press, 2001)

———, 'Redistribution and Long-Term Private Debt in Paris, 1660–1726', *The Journal of Economic History*, 55.2 (1995), 256–84

Holderness, B. A., 'Widows in Pre-Industrial Society: An Essay upon their Economic Functions', in *Land, Kinship and Life-Cycle*, ed. by Richard M. Smith (Cambridge: Cambridge University Press, 1984), pp. 423–42

Jordan, William Chester, *Women and Credit in Pre-Industrial and Developing Societies* (Philadelphia: University of Pennsylvania Press, 1993)

———, 'Women and Credit in the Middle Ages: Problems and Directions', *Journal of Economic History*, 4 (1988), 33–62

Khader, Serene, *Adaptive Preferences and Women's Empowerment* (New York: Oxford University Press, 2011)

Laurence, Anne, and others, eds, *Women and their Money, 1700–1950: Essays on Women and Finance* (London: Routledge, 2008)

Lemire, Beverly, and others, eds, *Women and Credit: Researching the Past, Refiguring the Future* (Oxford: Berg, 2001)

Lindgren, Håkan, 'The Modernization of Swedish Credit Markets: Evidence from Probate Records', *The Journal of Economic History*, 62.3 (2002), 810–32

Maillard, Brigitte, 'Les Veuves Dans La Société Rurale au XVIIIe Siècle', *Annales de Bretagne et Des Pays de l'Ouest*, 106.1 (1999), 211–30

Ogilvie, Sheilagh, *A Bitter Living: Women, Markets, and Social Capital in Early Modern Germany* (Oxford: Oxford University Press, 2003)

Parpart, Jane L., and others, 'Rethinking (Em)powerment, Gender and Development: An Introduction', in *Rethinking Empowerment: Gender and Development in a Global/Local World*, ed. by Janes L. Parpart (London: Routledge, 2002), pp. 3–21

Pitt, Mark, and others, *Does Micro-Credit Empower Women? Evidence from Bangladesh* (Washington: World Bank, 2003)

Poska, Allyson M., *Women and Authority in Early Modern Spain: The Peasants of Galicia* (Oxford: Oxford University Press, 2006)

Rosenhaft, Eve, 'Did Women Invent Life Insurance? Widows and the Demand for Financial Services in Eighteenth-Century Germany', in *Family Welfare: Gender, Property and Inheritance since the Seventeenth Century*, ed. by David Grenn (London: Praeger, 2004), pp. 163–94

Rosenthal, Jean-Laurent, 'Rural Credit Markets and Aggregate Shocks: The Experience of Nuits St. Georges, 1756–1776', *The Journal of Economic History*, 54.2 (1994), 288–306

Sabean, David W., *Property, Production, and Family in Neckarhausen, 1700–1870* (Cambridge: Cambridge University Press, 1991)

Spicksley, Judith M., '"Fly with a Duck in thy Mouth": Single Women as Sources of Credit in Seventeenth-Century England', *Social History*, 32.2 (2007), 187–207

Storti, Marie-Lyse, 'Coutume de Ferrette et/ou coutume du comté de Belfort', *Revue d'Alsace*, 132 (2006), 205–44

Wahid, Abu, 'The Grameen Bank and Women in Bangladesh', *Challenge*, 42.5 (1999), 94–101

Wrightson, Keith, and others, *Poverty and Piety in an English Village: Terling, 1525–1700* (Oxford: Oxford University Press, 1995)

Women and Money: Credit, Debt, and Status in the Eighteenth-Century London Court of Exchequer

Margaret Hunt*

Introduction

Debt and credit have always been as much about immaterial things as about money or goods. For hundreds of years 'debt', 'credit', and their cognates and equivalents in other European languages, have been used to speak about personal character, trust, and duty or responsibility to God, to one's family, to one's master or employer, as much or more than about money or other tangibles lent or owed.[1]

But whether they pertain to material or immaterial things, debt and credit imply some sort of contract or prior agreement to fulfil certain terms. That prior

* I should like to thank Amanda Collins, Henry Horwitz, Dana Rabin, Rachel Weil, and Maria Ågren for their assistance with and comments on earlier drafts of this paper.

[1] For example, the Oxford English Dictionary divides its lengthy discussion of the word 'debt' into two broad categories 'a sum of money or a material thing' and 'a thing immaterial'.

Margaret Hunt (margaret.hunt@hist.uu.se) is professor of history at Uppsala University and the author of several books including *The Middling Sort: Commerce, Gender and the Family in England 1680–1780* (1996) and *Women in Eighteenth-Century Europe* (2010). She has recently co-edited (with Philip Stern) a collection of primary documents on late seventeenth-century India entitled: *The English East India Company at the Height of Mughal Expansion: A Soldier's Diary of the 1689 Siege of Bombay* (2016). In addition she has published essays on the British law courts, sharia law, the Royal Navy, the history of sexuality, and other topics. At present she is at work on a 'biography' of a single seventeenth-century English East India Company ship.

Women and Credit in Pre-Industrial Europe, ed. by Elise M. Dermineur, EER 12 (Turnhout: Brepols, 2018), pp. 281–300.
BREPOLS PUBLISHERS DOI 10.1484/M.EER-EB.5.115757

agreement can be an actual business contract, written or unwritten. Or it can be more akin to a social contract: a set of duties and responsibilities accruing to or enforced upon some group in return for something else —usually basic maintenance. Unlike with a business contract the terms of these often asymmetrical social exchange may not need to be spoken or spelled out, but they are nevertheless capable of being strongly, even brutally enforced. Alternatively, as discussed in this article, arrangements and agreements can oscillate between money and intangible benefits and deficits, and they can do so not just in a metaphorical sense (though the different understandings of credit and debt frequently did bleed over into each other), but in day-to-day practice.

The English Court of Exchequer, one of the central equity courts up to its abolition in 1880, was often a staging area for movement and oscillation between the two species of obligation. This article uses a series of cases from the Court of Exchequer during the reigns of Anne (1703–1714), George I (1714–1727) and George II (1727–1760) to examine the way relatively poor women parsed the value of their own work, both paid and unpaid. What did they think their work was worth, in terms both of monetary rewards and less tangible benefits? And how did their work fit with and help constitute the social arrangements that made up their lives? It concludes that women like these exploited the fluid boundaries between paid and unpaid work in an effort to enhance their bargaining power. Moreover, they used the language of credit and debt, especially deferred debts, as a vehicle both to quantify what they believed they were owed and to demand that payment be legally enforced. The central equity courts (Chancery and Exchequer) were headquartered in Westminster, which in the early modern period was a separate city, though today it has been merged into London. These two courts heard large numbers of cases involving women litigants in the early modern period. Indeed, by the late eighteenth century about 20 per cent of plaintiffs in equity were women. In an earlier essay I estimated that around 69,000 women from all over England and Wales initiated suits in equity over the course of the eighteenth century, most of them pertaining to debt and credit, business disputes, tithes, family quarrels (especially over inheritance), and marriage settlements.[2] The present article is not a systematic study of this very large body of evidence. Rather it analyses in some

[2] For a fuller discussion of women suing in equity, including the numbers, types of suits, marital status of plaintiffs, etc. see Hunt, 'Wives and Marital "Rights"', pp. 110–12. That discussion is heavily reliant on statistical and other data provided by Henry Horwitz in his indispensable handbook, *Chancery Equity Records and Proceedings*, see especially pp. 36–37. See also Horwitz, *Exchequer Equity Records and Proceedings*. The percentage of female defendants is unknown.

depth a small number of exemplary debt cases brought by poor female litigants from London and Middlesex, so as to make some qualitative generalizations about the complex relationship among early modern London women between paid work, family duty, and the language of debt and credit.

In late seventeenth- and early eighteenth-century London, as we now know, most women, whether married, single or widowed, worked at least part of the time for wages or other remuneration, and they engaged in a wide range of types of work. Nevertheless, it is also the case that they were more likely than men to be concentrated in a fairly narrow range of occupations and those occupations were often associated with food, drink, making and mending clothes, housework, or care for others.[3] Moreover the relationship of women's work to a money wage was unstable. Women 'sold' housecleaning, food preparation, child-, elder- and sick-care, the making and mending of clothes, and sex for money. They also did these things as part of the complex barter systems of favours and duties performed and expected, of emotional connection, of symbolic capital, of security or its lack, that so often constituted women's lives as daughters, wives, mothers, sisters, and dependent or semi-dependent relations.

Contracts

Before looking at individual cases we need to think a little about the social context of debt, credit, and exchange, both in their tangible and intangible forms. One heuristic device for thinking about a great many, though surely not all, social transactions, is the notion of different kinds of contracts. Two broad types of contracts shape most of the cases described in the next part of this article, and they epitomize, in their ideal form, at any rate, two very distinct ways of thinking about work.

The first often goes by the name 'status contract'.[4] A status contract derives its form, and a good deal of its content, from the *relative status* of the parties to the

[3] The most nuanced discussion of London women's work is Erickson, 'Married Women's Occupations in Eighteenth-Century London', pp. 267–307. Especially revealing figures on women's workforce participation come from an article by Earle, 'The Female Labour Market in London'. According to his data some 60 per cent of London married women, 83 per cent of spinsters, and 85 per cent of widows reporting being wholly or partially maintained by paid work between 1680 and 1720 (see especially p. 337).

[4] The notion of the status contract comes, somewhat altered, from Kingdom, *What's Wrong with Rights?* Another way to think about these arrangements, focused on a slightly later period, is Steedman, *Labours Lost.*

agreement, which is typically asymmetrical. In early modern England the archetypal status contract was the marriage contract. It was conceived as a bargain but the rights and responsibilities of the two parties were different. Specifically, the subordinate party, the wife, 'agreed' to obey her husband and give over all her movable property to him. At the same time the superior party, the husband, took on the duty of partially supporting the wife. One of the central features of this sort of contract, and of most status contracts, was the partial setting aside of monetary exchange relations. In the marriage contract, whether written, verbal or merely implied, a woman, largely unconditionally, bestowed her labour, sexual services, and the fruit of her reproductive powers on one man free of monetary charge. But because the status contract described a hierarchical relationship, it gave the husband extensive rights to define what his wife's duty should be, and to punish or 'correct' her, including through the use of violence, if she failed to fulfil them.[5] By contrast the man's duties were more vague and discretionary. He was supposed to provide basic subsistence and a place to live for his wife and for their children and local authorities were sometimes prepared to enforce this (though it was never easy to define what basic subsistence was). But a wife was not permitted to 'correct' her husband's behaviour in the way he could hers, and in practice, except in very egregious cases of violence or neglect, there were few formal checks on a husband's behaviour. It is symptomatic of the nature of marriage that a husband and wife, though they might 'owe' each other all kinds of duties and obligations, could never sue each other for debt. Status contracts took many other forms in the early modern period, but their terms almost always included (a) a status differential and the implied right of the superior party to discipline the inferior one; (b) the exchange of service, loyalty, etc., not primarily for money but for basic support; and (c) wide discretionary powers for the superior party in the relationship. Apprenticeship, with its lengthy period of unpaid service to a skilled craftsman in return for room and board and the opportunity to learn a trade, fits well under the rubric of the status contract. We should also include less formal 'contracts', in which, for example, an unmarried woman 'offered' her labour and her obedience to a more successful relative in return for board and a roof over her head.

Quite different from the status contract is a contract based explicitly on monetary exchange. This is a contract, usually written or verbalized, in which one party agrees to provide certain goods or services in return for *money*, and in which the prior status of the contractors is largely irrelevant to the transaction. For example,

[5] Hunt, 'Wives and Marital "Rights"'; Hunt, 'Wife Beating, Domesticity and Women's Independence'.

if a gentleman-householder contracts with a poor widow woman in his neighbourhood to do his laundry for him in return for a few shillings a year, and — very importantly — she is capable of going to court to enforce payment, we can say that their manifestly unequal status in the world either is not germane to the transaction or is actually (if only temporarily) abrogated by the contract. Obviously we would not want to take this too far. An enforceable money contract may be the one egalitarian moment in a sea of inegalitarian power relations, and it does not *necessarily* spread its influence very widely beyond the transaction itself. It is worth reflecting, for instance, that laundry work was and is dangerous and backbreaking work, involving caustic and toxic cleaning agents, large vats of boiling water, and heavy lifting. In the early modern period (indeed into the twentieth century) it was associated with high rates of injury both to women and children, and low life expectancy. We may suspect, too, that were the gentleman-householder to fail to honour his side of what, almost certainly, would have been only a verbal bargain, the widow might not be able to bear the expense, the loss of time, or the damage to her reputation that a court case might involve.

What is the significance of this social and transactional diversity? For one thing, the fact that more than one kind of contract was notionally available had the effect of expanding people's rhetorical opportunities. As we will see, in the context of the court, and presumably in everyday life as well, women, in particular, moved rather freely, and often quite creatively, between status contracts and money exchange contracts, depending upon which seemed to serve their immediate interest. Let us move then to the law courts where some of these complicated negotiations took place.

Cases in Equity

The two central equity courts in England were the Court of Chancery and the Court of Exchequer. Procedures in Chancery and Exchequer were almost identical, as were the types of cases litigants brought there. Equity law developed in the late middle ages as a way to lessen what was perceived as the harshness, the inflexibility, and the inaccessibility of the common law, and this seems to have made it slightly more attractive to women and others likely to live in subordination. Indeed, already by the late sixteenth century, equity had a somewhat exaggerated reputation for being 'the special friend of women'.[6] It needs to be stressed, however, that

[6] Erickson, *Women and Property*, pp. 5–6; Cioni, *Women and Law in Elizabethan England*, pp. 1–17.

equity was never intended fundamentally to overhaul hierarchy. Rather it sought to remedy its worst abuses in the interest of rendering the overall structure more legitimate and hence more robust. 'Equity' never meant 'equality'.

It is often assumed that the equity courts were too costly to attract any but rich litigants. But it cost less than a pound to file a bill and if one's total assets were less than five pounds one could petition to initiate (or defend) a case *in forma pauperis*, which meant one was forgiven most court costs. Most of the cases discussed in this article were people litigating *in forma pauperis*. It was also possible for a group of people to make a single complaint and share the cost. Moreover, the really expensive part of suing in equity courts was when a case dragged on. But during the reign of Anne about 85 per cent of cases originating in London and Middlesex were dropped shortly after the bill (or the bill and answer) were filed, in other words, at the pleading or preliminary stage. That is because suits were being initiated as a way to coerce or embarrass the defendant or defendants into coming to terms rather than with the intention of pursuing the case to the bitter end. This is frustrating for the researcher because it means that there is no way to know the outcome of the vast majority of Exchequer cases. The upside is that it draws our attention to the tactical choices of humbler litigants. This paper focuses on a group of cases in which relatively poor women sued in Exchequer taking advantage of the *in forma pauperis* provision. And all of these cases were indeed dropped before they got to the deposition stage or to a hearing in court, signalling that the parties had settled or that the action had moved to a different court. This means we do not know the final outcome in any of them, so we cannot evaluate how successful women's strategies were. All that can be said is that these litigants (or their legal counsel) viewed these as viable ways to fight a case.

Women in the Court of Exchequer

A great many of these cases are 'family' cases — suits between relatives or people who had known one another, often for decades. This means that they are suffused by that singularly mercenary rancour so characteristic of disputes between people who might, in better times, be expected to love or at least like each other. In 1704 or 1705 Anne Walters of St Paul's, Covent Garden, a midwife, sued out a bill in equity in the Court of Exchequer against one Abraham Godfrey Hankowitz, a chemist, and his wife.[7] According to Walters, Hankowitz had, about twelve years

[7] National Archives, Kew, Public Record Office E 112/826 suit no. 154 (Exchequer Bill) Anne Walters v. Abraham Godfrey Hankowits et uxor (London and Middlesex, 1704).

before, prevailed upon her to come and live with him and his wife during the later stages of the latter's pregnancy. Because the wife remained sickly, Walters was asked to remain with the family on a permanent basis to help with nursing and housekeeping. Walters later alleged that she moved in with the Hankowitzes reluctantly, because she was worried that this new situation might prove incompatible with her midwifery practice and she did not want to 'lose the laying and bringing to bed of several persons of good fashion and quality'.[8] But she ultimately agreed on condition (she later claimed) that Hankowitz pay her five shillings a week wages and give her the freedom to carry on her midwifery practice out of their home. Thereafter she nursed Mrs Hankowitz through a number of miscarriages and serious illnesses, helped to supervise her medication, sat through the night with her when her life was despaired of, and so on. Anne Walters was not modest about her contribution: in her view, the sick woman's recovery 'was and ought to be ascribed, next under God and the Ability and medicines prescribed to her [*sic*] by her physicians, to the care, fidelity, labour, pains and watchings of your oratrix [Ann Walters]'. Anne Walters also took care of the Hankowitzes' son who contracted a disease 'very apt to infect such persons as attend upon and are conversant with people sick of that disease'.[9] So contagious was this sickness that the child was abandoned by all except Anne Walters

> who out of a tender regard to the said child and a just sense of her duty attended upon the said child during its sickness [...] and sometimes lying with it in its illness thereby exposing [her] to great Hazard and danger of her life, wearying her out with continual troubles and watching notwithstanding [she] [...] cheerfully went through all these labours and inconveniences to do her duty and preserve a good conscience.

At some point, Walters also took the child off to the country to speed its recovery, thereby losing the opportunity to assist at the childbirth of several women, 'being by this means defrauded by Mr Hankowitz and his wife of several sums of money' she would otherwise have earned.

After some years of this, Abraham Hankowitz and his wife returned to their native land (Germany) on business, leaving Walters to oversee the household. But

[8] Here and in all other quotes from early modern documents spelling has been modernized, abbreviations are written out, and punctuation (generally absent from the originals) has been quietly inserted so as to enhance readability. The legalism 'said' as in 'the said Child' has been removed except when it contributes to greater clarity.

[9] The child was described at one or another time as having contracted spotted fever, measles, and small pox.

after the couple's return, they broke all their promises to her, failed to pay her what they owed her (according to Walters, five shillings a week for twelve years and an additional £11 she had lent them), and also forced her to do work she was not contracted to do, such as cooking. The Hankowitzes also began claiming Anne Walters was not a servant at all, but a long-time lodger, and they threatened to arrest her at the common law for non-payment of room and board.

This case is representative of a good many equity cases brought by relatively poor women in the Court of Exchequer in the late seventeenth and early eighteenth century. Such cases very routinely featured attempts to translate types of work most often associated with women into commodity or cash terms, and they often hinged on whether the relationship between the plaintiff and the defendant(s) 'justified' the plaintiff demanding money for her work, and consequently redefining herself into a creditor in a debt/credit relationships. Thus, in Walters v. Hankowitz the central question was what status Anne Walters had in the household; Anne Walters claimed she was a servant and was therefore owed money for her services; while the Hankowitzes claimed she was a lodger and therefore actually owed money to them.

Let us try to look at this case as Anne Walter's contemporaries might have done. An early eighteenth-century onlooker might well suspect that Walters originally entered the Hankowitz household *not* as either a lodger or a servant, but as an unmarried female, quite likely a relative,[10] who needed a place to live. But Anne Walters does not fit the received picture of a helpless or dependent female relative. Instead, at least according to her, she was a professional, whose midwifery skills were in some demand. Given Mrs Hankowitz' poor state of health and frequent lyings-in, we can imagine that Anne Walters was a quite decided asset around the house. Perhaps her services were initially provided in exchange for room and board. Perhaps she made enough money delivering other women's children that the Hankowitzes asked her to pay something toward her upkeep. Or perhaps Anne Walters demanded some sort of additional salary from the start (beyond simply room and board) from the Hankowitzes in return for her services. Whatever the original agreement may have been (if any) Anne Walters lived for twelve years with the Hankowitzes. We cannot hope to reconstruct in detail the slow buildup of irritation, the jockeying for advantage, the emotional ambivalence, and the failed negotiations that finally tore this household apart. All we know is that, at some point, relations deteriorated so far that the Hankowitzes tried to arrest Anne Walters for debt and Walters retaliated by suing out a bill in Exchequer in which she sought

[10] There are hints in the case that Anne Walters and the Hankowitzes were kin.

to attach a precise money value to the 'work' she claimed she had done over those twelve years. But how does one easily assign a price to sleeping with a sick (and dangerously contagious) child when its own family has effectively abandoned it? What is it worth in money terms to watch through the night with someone who might die before daybreak? Such acts are hard to reconcile with the money exchange contract and the process of commodification more generally — and still less with the language of credit and debt — because they are things women have traditionally done within the family, not for money but out of love and a sense of duty.

Let us look at another dispute centred on status, money, and debt. In 1716 John Richardson, a 'gentleman' of St Mary Newington Butts in Surrey, sued one Ann Salter of London for a string of expenses supposedly incurred by him for which she was refusing to reimburse him. Salter had recently had Richardson arrested in an effort to force him to return £100 he had allegedly borrowed from her. But Richardson claimed in his bill of complaint in Exchequer that the money he had paid out on Anne Salter's behalf more than compensated for the £100 she had 'deposited' with him. He appended to his bill a long list of items allegedly supplied to Salter, including clothes, shoes, and gloves, 'four ounces of green Tea', some inexpensive jewellery, and £10 for her room and board in several Essex towns.[11]

When the subpoena was served on Salter she petitioned the Court of Exchequer to admit her as a pauper litigant. In her brief and pointed *in forma pauperis* petition she told the court:

> That some years ago the Plaintiff [John Richardson] made his addresses to your Petitioner [Ann Salter] to Marry him, and by that means prevailed with your Petitioner to lend him £100 pretending he would make great advantages of it [i.e., invest it well] and that he would pay her Interest for the same.
>
> That the Plaintiff afterwards basely marrying another, and refusing to pay your Petitioner her money, your Petitioner brought her action [for debt] against him in the Sheriff's Court, London. [A]nd the Plaintiff, just as your Petitioner had summoned her case for Trial, caused your Petitioner to be served with a Subpoena out of this Honorable Court [of Exchequer] and has filed a Long Bill against your Petitioner though in truth he has no just cause of Complaint against your Petitioner.[12]

[11] E 112/979 suit no. 245, John Richardson v. Anne Salter (London and Middlesex, 1716). A similar case involving ex-lovers and lodging was E 112/1231 suit no. 3276, Mary Sky v. William Newton (London and Middlesex, 1755). E 185/16 is Sky's *in forma pauperis* petition.

[12] Anne Salter's *in forma pauperis* petition is at E 185/16. It is signed in a rather uncertain hand and dated 22 Nov. 1717.

Salter's answer to Richardson's bill went into a good deal more detail about their relationship. She had become acquainted with Richardson about ten years before. According to her, she had never deposited money with him to buy her wearing apparel, pay her debts or buy food. But

> The Complainant [John Richardson] using frequently to visit and write letters to her and pretending a great deal of Love and Affection to this Defendant and this Defendant believing his intention to be real [?] and good did admit him to visit her from time to time.

Having become intimate with John Richardson ('visit [...] from time to time' was probably meant to convey that the two were having sexual relations), Ann Salter was one day sitting and talking with her sister, Elizabeth, in Richardson's presence. Ann had recently gotten hold of a note for £100 drawn on a London goldsmith, and her sister having about £250, the two sisters began 'consulting together about joining their Stock and setting up in some trade together to get their living and improve their fortunes'. However, John Richardson immediately spoke up, saying 'that no Woman that he pretended to court for his wife [...] should follow a trade for he could do without it'. He advised Ann not to put her money into starting a business but instead to lend him the £100 and he would give her a bond for it and pay her interest.

Anne Salter did lend Richardson the money, but 'the complainant [John Richardson] continuing his Addresses to and conversations with [her] and she believing him to be sincere and that she should become his wife did not take a Bond of him'. That proved to be a mistake because sometime after that John Richardson 'without any just cause and contrary to many solemn promises and engagements' broke things off with Anne Salter, married another woman and 'absconded' and refused to meet with Salter or return the £100 plus interest. Disgusted, Anne Salter took action in Sheriff's Court to recover her money. Richardson then counter-sued her in the Court of Exchequer in order (she claimed) to get out of giving her her money back. Ann Salter provided an item-by-item disclaimer of Richardson's inventory of the debts she supposedly owed him. Richardson did present her with 'six (but not twelve) yards of Silver ribbon' but 'he told her [it] was for a Valentine's gift'. It was true that Richardson had brought her a piece of holland (a type of linen cloth); he had, however, neglected to mention in his inventory that he had asked her to sew him some shirts with it:

> and this Defendant did make him nine shirts therewith and there being about three or four ells left, this defendant believes the complainant did tell [her] that she should have that [in return] for making his shirts and [she] believes that same [cloth] was

> not worth above three shillings and nine pence per Ell, and that the making of the same shirts was worth more than the three or four ells of Holland which he gave her aforesaid.

Though Richardson did help her with her rent to the tune of about £3, he also 'used to come and sometimes bring his friends with him and Drink it out [entertain them] so that this Defendant conceives she ought not to be charged therewith'. And the silk he gave her was a present 'to make her a gown and petticoat for her Wedding Suit and therefore this Defendant is advised she ought not to be charged therewith'. Now obviously Salter is trying, with some success, to paint her former fiancé as a complete cad. Charging her for Valentine's day gifts and her wedding dress? When the engagement turned sour and Richardson broke the 'contract', goods, services, and loans that had been conceived of within the context of a marriage-about-to-happen, that is, within a régime of emotions and impending coverture, all suddenly gained monetary value. Both parties conspired in this effort. But because this *was* an aborted engagement, not everything could be explicitly stated. Thus, one crucial 'commodity' that had no precise price-tag in Richardson v. Salter was Anne Salter's sexuality. Yet the practice of men giving women money, help with living expenses, and gifts (especially gifts of clothes and jewellery) after having enjoyed their sexual favours was very thoroughly ingrained in eighteenth-century gender relations. So powerful was this convention that it became part of Salter's (or her lawyer's) strategy to acknowledge the intimate nature of the plaintiff's relationship with the defendant precisely so as to demonstrate how much more likely it was that Richardson had given her *quid pro quo* 'gifts' than that he was merely paying out money on her behalf in the expectation that he would be reimbursed. It is for this reason that her plea oscillated between claims more appropriate to a status contract (a marriage about to happen), and claims that would have been completely inconsistent with such as contract — such as her insistence on providing a precise valuation of the labour she put in to sewing Richardson's shirts.[13]

Both Walters v. Hankowitz and Richardson v. Salter revolve around a shift from some sort of status contract (in the case of Richardson and Salter, one that closely resembled marriage, but, crucially, was not *actually* one) to an attempt by one or both parties to reinterpret the relationship in the context of monetary exchange. Let us look for purposes of comparison at a true marriage, in this case

[13] Other lovers were less reluctant to put a price on their chastity. See e.g., E 185/16 (*in forma pauperis* petition), Duboys v. Aldegond, Walsh and Rabeau (London and Middlesex, 1706). The bill is missing in this case.

one somewhat higher up the social ladder (though in this case we should probably presume that all the figures are somewhat inflated). Anne Greenwood, the widow of a grocer, married Edward Hearne, who may have been a wholesaler, in around 1682. Before her remarriage she had been 'a widow of a very considerable fortune' with many excellent marriage prospects, or at least so she asserted in her bill.[14] In time Edward Hearne, who claimed to have a great fortune, won out over the competition. Sadly for Anne, it was not until after the marriage had taken effect that she discovered that, in reality, Edward Hearne was a man of 'mean and low condition'. Moreover, it soon became evident that Hearne had married her for her estate rather than for love, for

> no sooner [had he] got your Oratrix's[15] fortune into his hand but he grow very outrageous, beating and bruising [her] in a very outrageous manner, in so much that your Oratrix hath often despaired of her life by his, the said Edward Hearne's insolent carriage.

After several years of marriage. Edward Hearne, having acquired as many of his wife's effects as he could (to the tune, she claimed, of upwards of £1000), abandoned her and refused thereafter to maintain her so that she was forced to rely on the charity of relatives. Adding insult to injury. around 1692 Edward Hearne made several trips to the East Indies, where (Anne Hearne claimed) he acquired an estate of above £5000. But despite his 'great acquisitions' Hearne would not allow his wife so much as a farthing for her maintenance, even though she had brought her husband a large fortune.

Here we see how a status contract, such as marriage, could inhibit some kinds of money claims while encouraging others. Anne brought her husband £800 when she married him. Her effects were worth £1000. Edward Hearne made £5000 in the East Indies, and so forth. But Anne Hearne did not and could not claim any monetary compensation for her labour during her coverture, even though her bill of complaint suggests that she continued to work as a grocer after her marriage to Hearne, only to see him pocket her profits. The appeal to equity in Hearne v. Hearne was based not upon credit and debt (as a wife Anne Hearne could not actually sue her husband for debt), but upon an affirmation of the status differential

[14] E 112/826 suit no. 163, Anne Hearne by Roger Robertson, Clerk and Rector of Hanwell, Middlesex her *procheine amy* v. Edward Hearne (London and Middlesex 1703). This case is discussed in a slightly different context in Hunt, 'Wives and Marital "Rights"'.

[15] The 'orator' or 'oratrix' (the female form) is the person making a plea (Anne Hearne herself).

between the two parties. Anne Hearne appealed to the paternalistic impulses of the court to make her husband to pay her some basic maintenance. She did not and could not ask to be recompensed for the value of her labour.

Depending on what they perceived to be their interests, women in the Exchequer cases were perfectly willing to couch their claims in either status contract terms or monetary exchange contract terms — or some combination of the two. But there were plenty of cases in which women saw advantages in claiming the money relation rather than the status one. Brewer v. Rutland (1703) is a case in point. John Brewer's father, who was also Mary Rutland's maternal grandfather, left Mary a legacy of £200 to be paid when she reached the age of eighteen. However, when she reached her majority, Brewer (presumably the executor of the estate) claimed he could not afford to pay her her legacy. After a few years Mary Rutland sued her uncle for the money in the Court of Exchequer, and he retaliated by filing a cross-bill alleging that *she* owed *him* a substantial sum of money for costs incurred in bringing her up (he had apparently taken her into his home on the death of her father). Rather implausibly, Brewer's bill for bringing up Mary Rutland came to £193, which would have left her a mere £7 from her legacy. But Mary's answer to the cross-bill disputed this account. She may technically have been a ward, but Mary claimed that she had not been brought up at anything close to the standard of the rest of Brewer's family. Rather she had been kept as a servant to clean, make beds, and wait on Brewer's own children. The occasional sums of money Brewer sent her way (which, in his bill, he had claimed were advances on her inheritance) Mary viewed as payment for services rendered. The clothes Brewer claimed to have bought for her were, in reality, hand-me-downs from his wife and of little value. They were also given to Mary Rutland only conditionally. So, at one point, she was given a petticoat, but 'the Complainant [John Brewer] or his wife [...] took the petticoat again before half worn out from this defendant and caused cushions to be made thereof'.[16]

Brewer v. Rutland makes explicit the way in which the meaning of a contract could shift depending upon whether the injured party was a ward or a servant. Brewer was asking the court to resolve the question of whether or not the labour he demanded of Rutland was commensurate with what one might reasonably expect in the 'status contract' between a householder and an orphaned, semi-dependent niece he had agreed to take into his family. It was in Brewer's interest to formulate the issue in this way because the solicitude which English law and custom showed for the autonomy of the male household head allowed him considerable latitude

[16] E 112/826 suit no. 165, John Brewer v. Mary Rutland (London and Middlesex, 1703).

in fulfilling his side of the 'contract'. Also to Brewer's benefit was the traditional expectation that unmarried female relations would offer their labour up for the disposition of the male in whose home they resided. The *only* reason this case ever came to court at all was because Brewer failed to pay Rutland's legacy, not because he and his family allegedly exploited her labour. By contrast, it was very much in Mary Rutland's interest to recast the relationship in terms of a money exchange contract and herself as the Brewer's creditor While in his household she had been treated neither as a member of the family nor as a 'paying guest'. Rather, she had been forced to dress in worthless hand-me-downs and to wait on people. As far as she was concerned, her labour more than compensated both for the (low) quality of the support she received, and for Brewer's intermittent payments. The cost of her 'upbringing' should not, therefore, be taken out of her legacy.

How far would women go to claim money value for their work? It seems that they would go very far indeed. Two final cases illustrate this point. The first is Paine v. Lloyd (1709). James Paine was a mariner who, on or around June of 1704, went on a voyage to the West Indies, leaving his wife, Martha, with one child and pregnant with another. Six months later his wife died in childbirth, though the child survived. After Martha died her spinster sister, Mary Lloyd (the defendant in the case) took upon herself 'the rule and management' of the household, put out the children to nurse, and then let out the house to lodgers. On Paine's return in 1708 his sister-in-law (as Paine tells it)

> pretended she had not only taken a great deal of pains in looking after your orator's house and family since the death of your orator's wife but also laid out a great deal of money in paying for the children's clothes, [wet]-nursing and maintenance in all amounting about thirty pounds and [she] used abundance of plausible language to gain your orator's belief of the same.[17]

James Paine signed a bill promising to reimburse Mary Lloyd £30 for what she had paid out. He would later say that he would have been perfectly willing to pay 'had such her pretenses been real and she been so true and faithful a friend to your orator and his family as she pretended'. But, as he went on to argue, that was far from the case. Apparently Mary Lloyd had 'confederated' with several other woman friends to carry away an assortment of his household goods, including a down bed, a sheet, a brass kettle, 'a fine broadcloth petticoat', Martha's wedding ring, and all her wearing apparel and linen to the value (he claimed) of £50 or more. Paine also alleged

[17] E 112/826, suit no. 1355, James Paine v. Mary Lloyd (London and Middlesex, 1709). The 'orator' was the petitioner. This case is discussed in a slightly different context in Hunt, 'Women and the Fiscal-Imperial State', p. 32.

that Mary Lloyd had taken in rent from some lodgers that should have gone to him as Martha's husband. Later he also claimed to have been 'credibly informed' that Mary, instead of helping and assisting his wife, 'usually beat and abused her sister in a very cruel and barbarous manner'. Paine refused to pay Lloyd's demand for £30 and, since she held his bond, she had him arrested for debt at the court of Queen's Bench. Paine then sued in Exchequer for an injunction to stop the Queen's Bench suit.

Mary Lloyd's answer in the Exchequer case, coupled with a cross-bill against Paine that she also filed, tell us a considerable amount about the way women supported themselves in the early eighteenth century in the absence of a man. They also contain rare evidence about some of the ways poor women exchanged care and service among themselves. According to Mary Lloyd, when John Paine went to sea, he left his wife Martha with 'only 4 pence and a farthing or some such insignificant sum'. Consequently, Martha asked her sister Mary to come and live with her and 'to give her what assistance she could under such her unhappy circumstances'. Mary consented, and in order to help her sister out financially, arranged for a 'gentlewoman lodger' and a 'nurse child' to come live with them. In addition, Mary worked for her sister 'as a servant', presumably ministering to the lodger and the 'nurse child' as well as doing other household work. Because the two women were in such dire financial straits, Mary was never paid for these services, but she claimed she 'deserved' £4 per annum wages 'and she would have had as much in other places and not have done so much work'.

After her sister's death, Mary Lloyd took care of the two children and 'bargained and put them out to nurse and paid for nursing thereof for upwards of three years' which came to a total of £15 8s. 6d. She denied having carried away any of John Paine's goods. A few things of little value had been given to a female relation 'who had watched and been at great pains with the complainant's wife in the time of her illness' and the petticoat was (she claimed) given to Mary Lloyd herself by her dying sister who declared, before several witnesses, that 'she [Martha] had nothing else worth her [Mary's] acceptance and which she gave to this defendant as an acknowledgement for some part of this Defendant's kindnesses to her'. Other furniture was seized for the rent by the landlord. Paine's wife never had a wedding ring of her own but 'borrowed a ring for that purpose of one Mr Lang's Daughter'. The missing sheet had actually belonged to Mary Lloyd's then master (she had by this time taken on a paying job) and she took it off her own bed and lent it to her sick sister because '[at] the laying in of the Child on which she died [Martha] had but one sorry old sheet on her bed'.[18]

[18] E 112/826 suit no. 1355, Paine v. Lloyd, and suit no. 1356 (cross-bill), Lloyd v. Paine. The story is told here on the basis of both the bill and cross-bill and their respective answers.

Mary Lloyd was seeking to establish several things in her plea. First, Paine had violated his marriage vows by going off to sea for such a lengthy period without making proper provision for the support of his wife and her children. Hence, it was unjust for him to insist on the letter of the law of coverture (by which all his wife's goods and income belonged to him) since he had not upheld his part of the bargain. Having, as it were, dispensed with the status contract, Mary Lloyd moved aggressively into the language of exchange. She 'deserved' £4 a year for working for her sister as a servant[19] and would have received it elsewhere. It was unreasonable for John Paine to try to recoup money from her for the nurse child they had taken in or the lodger or lodgers she had been instrumental in finding, because she had maintained them with her own labour, and she and her sister and her sister's child had needed the money to survive. The missing household furnishings and clothes had made their way into the economy of makeshift and swapping, with some going to pawn, some for the rent, and some to reward neighbours for their help in a time of crisis. All this is mixed in with more emotional details (though still couched in the language of obligation and exchange), most notably her sister's deathbed bestowal of her best petticoat on her 'as an acknowledgement' of her kindness and many services.

There is a tendency, even today, to see women, especially women acting in a maternal or quasi-maternal capacity, as somehow more detached from the market than men. It is for that reason that one may feel a certain discomfort at the spectacle of a woman going to court to sue a much younger relative for the cost of lodging, food, clothing, washing, and schooling ever since his infancy. The final case, Cross v. Cross (1736), revolves around just such attempt to retrospectively 'commodify' women's 'caring' work. The trouble began when Charles Cross, a brazier, has his aunt, a widow named Anne Cross, arrested for debt. Anne Cross was understandably aggrieved at this, because her nephew had been orphaned quite young, and she and her husband had taken him in and raised him. So she retaliated by suing her nephew in Exchequer. There she made a series of expansive claims about what Charles Cross 'owed' her for her trouble in bringing him up. Anne Cross also wanted Charles to pay back money she claimed she had 'lent' him to set up in trade and to reimburse her for having kept house for him once he was out of his apprenticeship. Charles Cross, for his part, refused to pay her on the grounds that, while a child, he never made any promise to repay money spent on his upbringing. He also suggested in his plea that his uncle, who was also his godfather, and who, by this time, had been dead for sixteen years, 'would have been kind to him' and

[19] Other sources from the period suggest that most woman servants made between £1 and £6 per year, depending on the board arrangements. For a valuable account of servants and their contracts see Steedman, *Labours Lost*.

emphatically would *not* have expected payment for his keep as a child. And though he acknowledged that Anne Cross had raised him, he nevertheless justified his having earlier had her arrested for debt by using the now familiar claim that she had stayed with him in the capacity of a lodger, not a housekeeper.[20]

Conclusion

How did eighteenth-century women think about the worth of their work and their place in the universe of credit and debt?[21] Historians tend to see subordination, whether in marriage or in some other dependent or semi-dependent status, as *the* normative state for women in the early modern period. And there is a persistent suspicion in the historical literature that women themselves might have had difficulty breaking free of the miasma of submission, self-abnegation, and apparent political nullity that subordination imposed on them. But the Exchequer cases suggest that both married and unmarried women were more discursively entangled in the world of debt and credit, more conversant with monetary exchange contracts, and more willing to talk about their work in contractual terms than this older model implies. They were also quite capable of reconceiving 'status contracts' — when they were found wanting — in more 'commodified' terms. Since all of these cases were settled out of court we do not know whether this gambit would actually have convinced the judges, but the intentions of the litigants are clear. They were seeking to undermine precisely that aspect of status contracts — the expansive discretionary power given to the higher status party in the contract and the difficulty of enforcing the contract in court — that so often posed problems for women and other lower status groups.

It may be that for some women marriage plus coverture was less *the* normative state than a hiatus in a larger pattern of monetary exchange transactions. As we have seen, marriage involved the suspension of monetary contract relations with *one* person, the husband, and to a lesser extent his children (mothers are not, ordinarily, supposed to charge their children for services rendered either). Almost every other labour transaction we see seems to have involved money, valuations, and the language of credit and debt. Women seem to have had a clear sense of the worth of their labour, and one does not get the sense that they gave much of themselves away for free. Nor did they have many compunctions, at least in retrospect, about 'charging' for anything and everything they possibly could.

[20] E 112/1001 suit no. 1457, Charles Cross v. Anne Cross (London and Middlesex, 1736).

[21] For an important recent discussion of this issue see Shepard *Accounting for Oneself*.

Is the highly commodified and contractual world of work suggested by these cases merely a product of the adversarial atmosphere of the court? Court cases do put things in inordinately stark perspective, and they undoubtedly put pressure on litigants to translate their anger and disappointment into money claims. But the ubiquity of relations of credit and debt, and the widespread practice of imprisonment for debt, must, if anything, have had an even more central role.[22] Exchequer litigants, who in many cases were defending themselves against a pre-emptive claim by someone else, were desperately in search of a peg to hang their cases on; they were doing their utmost to transform themselves from vulnerable debtors to empowered creditors. Given that virtually the only asset most of these women had was their labour, is it any wonder that they worked especially hard to emphasize its monetary value?

But in the final analysis I do not think that the women who pleaded their cases in Exchequer, or Chancery, or numerous smaller or more local venues were so very different from contemporaries who never made it to court. The stories they tell, about the exchange of gifts and services between people who expect to marry, the disposition of a dying woman's clothes, conflicts over whether a person is a lodger or a servant, are situations from real life. No doubt full of fabrications and wishful thinking, these little scenarios of family economics and household politics nevertheless speak volumes about both the immaterial and in-kind benefits women expected to derive from social and family relationships, including hierarchical ones. They also show us many instances where women litigants used the language of money and obligation — credit and debt — instrumentally to highlight those instances where more immaterial bargains — usually within some sort of status contract — had not been fulfilled. In many respects the world of today looks different from that of two hundred and fifty years ago. And yet, women in the modern day continue to have a different relationship to money than men. It is true that men also found themselves in status contracts — such as apprenticeships — and that these bargains too, sometimes went badly wrong. Nevertheless it is still the case that women were and are expected to do more for less money than men, both within the family and without. And even today when they work for pay their work is more likely to resemble what they are 'supposed' to do at home for free than does the work of their brothers, husbands, and sons. In the end, we in the early twenty-first century are linked to women and men of the eighteenth by the fact that the 'currencies' with which we transact our public and private lives still have much to do with gender, and that continues to be true whether those currencies consist of money, actionable credits and debts, or less quantifiable mediums of exchange.

[22] Muldrew, *The Economy of Obligation*.

Works Cited

Manuscripts and Archival Sources

National Archives, Public Record Office, E 112 (Exchequer bills and answers); E 185 (petitions to file *in forma pauperis*); E 134 (Exchequer depositions)

Secondary Studies

Cioni, Maria L., *Woman and Law in Elizabethan England with Particular Reference to the Court of Chancery* (New York: Garland Publishing, 1985)

Earle, Peter, 'The Female Labour Market in London in the Late Seventeenth and Early Eighteenth Centuries', *Economic History Review*, 2d ser., 42 (1989), 328–53

Erickson, Amy Louise, 'Married Women's Occupations in Eighteenth-Century London', *Continuity and Change*, 23 (2008), 267–307

———, *Women and Property in Early Modern England* (London: Routledge, 1993)

Horwitz, Henry, *Chancery Equity Records and Proceedings, 1600–1800: A Guide to Documents in the Public Record Office*, Public Record Office Handbook 27 (London: HMSO, 1995)

———, *Exchequer Equity Records and Proceedings, 1649–1841*, Public Record Office Handbook 32 (Richmond: Public Record Office, 2001)

Hunt, Margaret R., 'Wife Beating, Domesticity and Women's Independence in Eighteenth-Century London', *Gender and History*, 4 (1992), 10–33

———, 'Wives and Marital "Rights" in the Court of Exchequer in the Early Eighteenth Century', in *Londinopolis, c. 1500-c. 1750: Essays in the Cultural and Social History of Early Modern London*, ed. by Mark S. R. Jenner and Paul Griffiths (Manchester: Manchester University Press, 2000), pp. 107–29

———, 'Women and the Fiscal-Imperial State in the Late Seventeenth and Early Eighteenth Centuries', in *A New Imperial History: Culture, Identity and Modernity in Britain and the Empire, 1660–1840*, ed. by Kathleen Wilson (New York: Cambridge University Press, 2004), pp. 29–47

Kingdom, Elizabeth, *What's Wrong with Rights? Problems for a Feminist Politics of Law* (Edinburgh: Edinburgh University Press, 1991)

Muldrew, Craig, *The Economy of Obligation: The Culture of Credit and Social Relations in Early Modern England* (New York: St. Martin's Press, 1998)

Shepard, Alexandra, *Accounting for Oneself: Worth, Status, and the Social Order in Early Modern England* (Oxford: Oxford University Press, 2015)

Steedman, Carolyn, *Labours Lost: Domestic Service and the Making of Modern England* (Cambridge: Cambridge University Press, 2009)

Women, Small Credit, and Community: Barcelona in the Eighteenth Century*

Montserrat Carbonell-Esteller

Credit practices were extremely widespread in eighteenth-century Catalonia and served as a common part of the adaptive household strategies and economies of working people. The discontinuity of individual and family incomes gave rise to a dynamic of successive bouts of indebtedness that forced them to enter the informal credit market. The circuits of the informal credit market expanded, linking individuals to one another in a long chain of successive indebtedness that was often transmitted from generation to generation. For different European cities in the early modern period, various studies based on an analysis of inventories have shown that at the time of death it was very common to have outstanding debts and outstanding credits, with the debtor and creditor often being the same person.[1]

Informal credit became a common mechanism for day-to-day survival. The purchase of foodstuffs, clothing, and medicine often entailed access to credit and

* The author thanks the Centre d'Estudis Antoni de Capmany HAR2015–64769-P and the project HAR2014–57187-P for their financial help.

[1] Fontaine, *L'économie morale*.

Montserrat Carbonell-Esteller is senior lecturer, Department of Economic History, Institutions, Policy and World Economy, University of Barcelona and member of the Institut Interuniversitari d'Estudis de Dones i Gènere (Iiedg). She works on economic and social history, with a special focus on late eighteenth-century and early nineteenth-century Spain. Her main research areas are history of poverty, poor relief and welfare, family and survival strategies, microfinances, and urban history with special reference to gender.

Women and Credit in Pre-Industrial Europe, ed. by Elise M. Dermineur, EER 12 (Turnhout: Brepols, 2018), pp. 301–320.
BREPOLS PUBLISHERS DOI 10.1484/M.EER-EB.5.115758

its use. 'Trust' was a risk that sellers took on in exchange for building a loyal and regular clientele. Such purchases often went hand in hand with the practice of leaving pledges as collateral against future payment of the debt incurred. In this way, informal credit mechanisms ensured continued access to basic necessities and credit became a common practice that enabled the household economy to function.[2] Credit passed through the hands of shopkeepers, craftsmen, masters, and servants who ensured a regular flow of credit through a network of contractual, customary, and reciprocal relations. The informality of this type of credit practice lay precisely in the ambiguity of the mutual obligations linking debtor to creditor. The effectiveness of credit relations of this sort was underwritten by the local community, which exerted various forms of control to ensure that trust and respective obligations were not violated.[3]

In the Barcelona of the late eighteenth century, the factory system developed very early, with new textile industries devoted to the production and printing of cotton textiles (*indianas*, or calicoes). In the second half of the century the city's population almost tripled thanks both to immigration and to natural population growth. The economic, social, and demographic transformation that took place explains the urban densification, the increase in rents, the rise in food prices, and the generalization of poverty and inequality, in a world in which labour opportunities for men and women, boys and girls, increased exponentially as the industrial city gradually came into existence.[4]

For the city of Barcelona and Madrid, in the eighteenth and early nineteenth centuries, informal networks of credit are becoming a subject of focused research.[5] Grocers' and apothecaries' inventories seem to be a suitable source to begin investigating informal credit and consumption levels in the period. Lists of debtors and creditors and the multitude of items pledged as collateral against debts turned the premises of apothecaries into veritable warehouses of hugely varied objects and belongings.[6] By studying the stocks of merchandise and of items deposited as collateral and kept stored in these shops, it is possible to obtain a significant approximation of the type and levels of consumption in the period. While it is true, however, that the subject of informal credit networks in the city of Barcelona in the eighteenth and early nineteenth centuries is now being addressed, the aspects relating

[2] Tebbutt, *Making Ends Meet*; Tomkins, 'Pawnbroking and the Survival Strategies'.

[3] Muldrew, *The Economy of Obligation*.

[4] Mora-Sitja, 'Labour Market Integration'.

[5] Torra, 'Las botigues de teles de Barcelona'; López de Barahona, 'Estrategias de supervivencia'.

[6] Spence, 'Women, Gender and Credit'.

to moneylending, including lawsuits and litigation that it generated, still remain practically unexplored.

Credit for the Poor and the Community

The recourse to collateral-based credit was a common practice among working families. Indeed, eighteen-century Barcelona saw an early attempt to formalize credit practices surrounding consumption. One example of this effort comes in 1751 with the creation of the Mont de Pietat de Nostra Senyora de l'Esperança i Salvació de les Ànimes de Barcelona (henceforth 'the Mont de Pietat'), which was an institution that specialized in the lending of money in exchange for the deposit of items pledged as collateral. The Mont de Pietat operated as a sort of pawnshop storing pledges in the form of collateral and *formally* establishing the obligations of debtor and creditor under by-laws approved by royal authority. At the same time, it was also a pious institution whose origins were tightly bound up with a charitable institution in Barcelona called the Casa del Retir, which was dedicated to helping repentant prostitutes and destitute women. As shall be seen shortly, the Casa del Retir was financed in part from profits generated by the Mont de Pietat. The network of charitable services and the intertwined nature of specialized institutions, which was a prototypical feature of the *Ancien Régime*, are plain to see. The functions of credit and assistance crisscross in the origins of this type of institution, which was to culminate in the late nineteenth and early twentieth centuries in the emergence of the savings bank and the generalization of their use among the working classes.[7]

This attempt to formalize credit practices, however, must be understood as part of a secular process to combat moneylending and control the profits that it generated. This is why the royal decree to set up the Mont de Pietat laid out the need to regulate credit practices so that people would not use informal avenues that might devolve into abusive moneylending. The text is quite telling on the issue: 'Given the notorious usury being exacted in that City (Barcelona), by which secured loans are granted at monthly interest rates of a Spanish *real*, a *real* and a half, and two *reales* a month per doubloon; and seeking to extinguish these pernicious abuses'.[8] The formalization of credit reduced the power of the city's most sought-after moneylenders, but it also quite probably weakened the networks of informal credit that

[7] Nadal i Sudrià, *Història de la Caixa*.

[8] *Constituciones del Real Monte de Piedad*.

had developed with long-standing community practices, including moneylending. Aspects relating to the web of moneylending practices, increasingly institutionalized credit, and the potentially growing precariousness of informal networks are deserving of in-depth study. However, they go beyond the scope of this article, which will focus on working households and their use of the recourse to collateral-based credit.

Branches of the Mont de Pietat offered two types of services: *credit* in exchange for objects pledged as collateral; and *provision* for which individuals deposited their savings. This type of institution brought together two types of survival strategy that varied by size and timeframe: a medium and long-term strategy in the case of provision and a day-to-day strategy in the case of small loans incurred in exchange for collateral. Among the users of the Mont de Pietat were, on the one hand, people who deposited small sums to be accumulated for their old age, as in the case of widows, and, on the other hand, young unmarried women who were saving for a dowry to enter the marriage market. The savings and guaranteed immunity of funds deposited in the institution, therefore, secured resources to be activated in the future.[10] In addition, there were families who often turned to the Mont de Pietat for small loans obtained by pledging objects, which in most cases were modest articles of clothing, raw wool, or metal objects. The Mont de Pietat as a collateral-based lending entity was part of the adaptive strategies of working families in eighteenth-century Barcelona.

Between Financial Returns and Charitable Assistance

The key to how this institution operated is the fact that its financial help (credit) was funded with the deposits of pious individuals. The supply of funds largely determined the number and value of loans granted. The mechanisms in play in this lending institution basically depended on the aspects set out below, namely the value and number of deposits, the interest rate, the loans and the donations. Deposits, which could be withdrawn freely with prior notice, were not permitted to yield financial returns or interest under the by-laws of the Mont de Pietat. In practice, however, the deposited funds did attract an interest rate of between 2 and 2.5 per cent until the 1770s.[9] Thus, the Mont de Pietat was defined in 1764 as *mixed*, indicating that the institution drew on the funds of the devout, which did

[9] Sant Cugat del Vallès, Arxiu Nacional de Catalunya (ANC) Fons del Mont de Pietat de Ntra. Sra. Esperança, Llibre de Comptaduria, any 1764, Llibre 165.

not yield returns, and on funds bearing interest. The weakness of this early lending institution, however, was precisely the ambiguity of interest on deposited and borrowed capital. In the last quarter of the eighteenth century, this was to spark a controversy that would mark the evolution of the institution. Funds ceased to flow when interest on deposits was banned.

Charitable assistance involved the provision of an amount of money as a function of a pledged item without, in principle, charging an interest rate. The items pledged as collateral could be jewellery, silver objects (e.g., candlesticks, cutlery, buttons, and little boxes), clothing made of silk, linen, wool, hemp, or cotton, and raw materials for textiles. Other metals such as copper were also accepted. Land, furnishings, deeds of transfer, letters of credit, and promissory notes were not allowed as collateral. If, after six months and a day, the loan had not yet been repaid, the object pledged as collateral was put up for public auction on the subsequent Sunday morning. Nevertheless, the regulations set out in the institution's by-laws were not always followed to the letter. The short time span established to repay loans points to the dynamism of small credit for consumption and the enormous responsiveness of household economies in the short run.

Under the by-laws, the maximum value of loans was set at fifty-six Catalan *libras*, which was equivalent to 1120 *reales de ardite*. However, the board of the Mont de Pietat had latitude to set the optimal maximum based on the institution's potential liquidity. As a result, loans were effectively greater than fifty-six Catalan *libras* throughout the eighteenth century, although in years in which the Mont de Pietat experienced difficulties, the loan limit was once again reduced to the original amount.[10] Under the institution's by-laws, pieces of jewellery were the most highly preferred collateral, securing a loan worth two-thirds of their appraised value, while pieces of clothing secured loans at only half their appraised value.

It was also stipulated that anyone who had pledged an object as collateral could not obtain an additional loan until the first loan had been repaid. However, this condition was not always kept in practice either. For example, on 4 January 1764, Joseph Ballasca, a shoemaker and resident of Abaixadors Street in the parish of Santa Maria del Mar, pledged a gold earring to secure a loan of seventy-five *reales de ardite*. A few weeks later, on 1 February, he pledged a silver spoon, fork, rosary, and chain. Then, in March of the same year, he pledged a pair of gold buttons, two gold rings, and a little silver bell in exchange for 120 *reales de ardite*.[11] These three loans

[10] This measure was applied from the Junta General on 30 December 1785. ANC, Fons Mont de Pietat, *Llibre d'acords*.

[11] ANC, Fons Mont de Pietat, Llibre de Comptadoria. Any 1764. Llibre 165.

enabled him to withstand the winter of 1764, the worst in many years. On the following 12 July, Joseph Ballasca repaid the loans and recovered the pledged objects. While not everyone's fortune proved as good as his, Ballasca's case illustrates the collateral-based lending practices that were enormously widespread and rooted in the day-to-day lives of families of craftsmen in Barcelona in the final third of the eighteenth century.

Donations flowed into the Mont de Pietat when the borrower repaid the loan and recovered the pledged collateral, a transaction that transpired in an office called the 'Treasury', or when a purchaser acquired the object at public auction, which would be held in the 'Hall of Almonedes'. In effect, a donation represented the interest on borrowed funds and therefore constituted the Mont de Pietat's profits, though under the lending institution's by-laws such donations were supposed to be voluntary in nature. The ambiguity and controversy over this aspect played out in parallel with the conflict over interest on loan capital. The institutional dynamic and the controversy surrounding the legitimacy of interest on capital became a recurring issue in Catholic Europe.

Paradoxically, such donations or alms were the profits arising from these credit operations. They became the only funds available to defray the institution's expenditures (salaries, employee bonuses and interest on deposits), to increase the capital of the Mont de Pietat to cope with the demand for loans and, lastly, to help the Congregation of Nostra Senyora de l'Esperança to maintain the Casa del Retir in Barcelona, as stipulated in the by-laws and in the royal decree of 1764. This institutional doubling, which was typical of the Catholic countries of southern Europe and, in the case before us, is embodied by the board of the Mont de Pietat and the Congregation, led to many conflicts throughout the eighteenth century. Once again, these conflicts bear witness to the struggle between the laity and the clergy to wrest control of institutions providing charitable assistance, which in this case also included lending institutions.

Women and Pawn-Broking Institutions in the Eighteenth Century

The operation of the Mont de Pietat generated a kind of circle in which its financial returns determined the influx of its deposits, its deposits permitted the granting of a given volume of loans, and the donations generated by these loans made it possible to pay returns, which once again attracted or discouraged an influx of deposits. The weight of moral and ideological conceptions regarding moneylending and interest-bearing loans blocked the way towards the formalization of credit. The effectiveness and flexibility of informal networks probably also saw their popularity continue. Such secular lending practices made it possible still to cope with the discontinuity of income through 'economies of improvisation' typical of pre-industrial working families and featuring women in a key role.[12]

To a large extent, the controversy over returns on deposited funds and interest on borrowed money marked the trajectory and dynamic of the institution. On repeated occasions, the controversy led to appeals being made to the monarch, requesting a change in the by-laws to legalize interest. By the late 1760s, the conflict over the issue led to a suspension of new deposits. This, in turn, raised doubts over the viability of the Mont de Pietat as a credit institution owing to the lack of funds on hand to meet the demand for loans. The heyday of the institution coincides with the years in which it offered a return of 2 or 2.5 per cent, a rate at which funds flowed in and loans or assistance expanded greatly. This expansionary period spanned from the institution's founding until the year 1767, in which new interest-bearing deposits were suspended until the controversy over financial returns could be resolved. Finally, in May 1770, the board took the decision to return all interest-bearing deposits together with the respective interest due, within a period of six months.

Throughout the 1770s, various attempts were made to obtain funds and cope with the demand for loans, but none appears to have met with success. Deposits continued to flow in but with minimal intensity and interest continued to appear in the annual accounts but reduced to a minimal amount. From the 1770s, the Mont de Pietat appears to have entered into a near-dormant phase, throughout which the controversy over interest-bearing deposits and donations, together with the clash between laity and clergy in the institution and in the Congregation of Nostra Senyora de l'Esperança, stifled the potential development of an institution of credit and social provision that would not reappear until the early twentieth century.[13] The formalization of collateral-based credit, which had successfully been developing for two decades, proved unsustainable in the final quarter of the eighteenth century. Piety as an alternative driver for the depositing of funds did not work, possibly because there were other more profitable alternatives or other newly created institutions that better met the interests of depositors.[14]

[12] Hufton, *The Poor of Eighteenth-Century France*, and King and Tomkins, eds, *The Poor in England 1700–1850*.

[13] Nadal i Sudrià, *Historia de la Caixa* ; Rumeu de Armas, *Historia de la Previsión*.

[14] The creation in 1776 of two banks, the Banc de Canvis de Barcelona, that lasted a few years, and the Bank of Lost Funds, which remained until 1808, can help explain the lack of vitality of the Institution in this time. See Castañeda, 'Sector financer'. In the year 1785 was created the Monte Pio General para Viudas, Pupilos e Impedidos, this can contribute to explain the fall of loans and deposits. The widows were very assiduous among the clients of the credit institution. See *Kalendario i guia de forasteros*.

The lack of funds prevented the Mont de Pietat from meeting the demand for credit from those in need. The dynamic between loans and deposits is clear. In 1751, the year of its founding, the Mont de Pietat recorded 808 loans, a figure that would continue to rise until the year 1766, when it reached the maximum influx of families in need and a total of 9975 items pledged in collateral. While families pledging objects as collateral may have repeated the operation various times throughout the year, bearing in mind that each of the nearly 10,000 instances affected a family, the numbers involved in this sort of credit were very high for a city of roughly 70,000 inhabitants. The figure began to decline in 1767 and by 1772 had fallen to 2910 collateral-based loans. A plausible hypothesis for the decrease is that borrowers were turning to a new credit institution created that year in Barcelona, the Mont de Pietat for Widows. It should also be determined, however, whether the effectiveness of informal networks of credit challenged the institutionalization of collateral-based credit. In any event, from then on, the Mont de Pietat lacked the dynamism of preceding periods and it entered into a dynamic of difficult subsistence, though after a variety of mergers and transformations, it has persisted to the present day. The resilience of this collateral-based credit institution has been tried and tested.[15]

How prevalent were women as credit applicants, i.e., as borrowers? What gender bias is reflected in these credit institutions? This study enables us to observe how the prevalence of women varies according to the dynamic of the institution and the context. If we observe the rate of feminization of borrowing coming to the Mont de Pietat in search of credit, we can see the following. At the time of founding, the prevalence of women seeking credit is quite high. It appears that a defining trait of the new institution was its charitable assistance to families in need. As a result, the presence of women was common, just as it was more generally in the city's institutions that provided assistance.[16] As funds flowed in attracted by the interest offered by the Mont de Pietat and the new credit institution successfully took root in the city, the number of men using its resources grew and the rate of feminization of borrowing fell (see Table 12.1). The prosperous institution drew the attention of people who could bring better pledges as collateral and obtain better loans and the negotiating ability of men in the valuation of the pledges appears to be greater. Women's presence in the new and successful bank for the poor declined and they turned toward more peripheral institutions like the Mont de Pietat for Widows or they resorted to the informal collateral-based credit market. The tendency of formal banking appears to have been to drive away the

[15] Carbonell-Esteller, '*Montes de Piedad* and Savings Banks'.

[16] Carbonell-Esteller and Marfany, 'Gender, Life Cycle, and Family "Strategies"'.

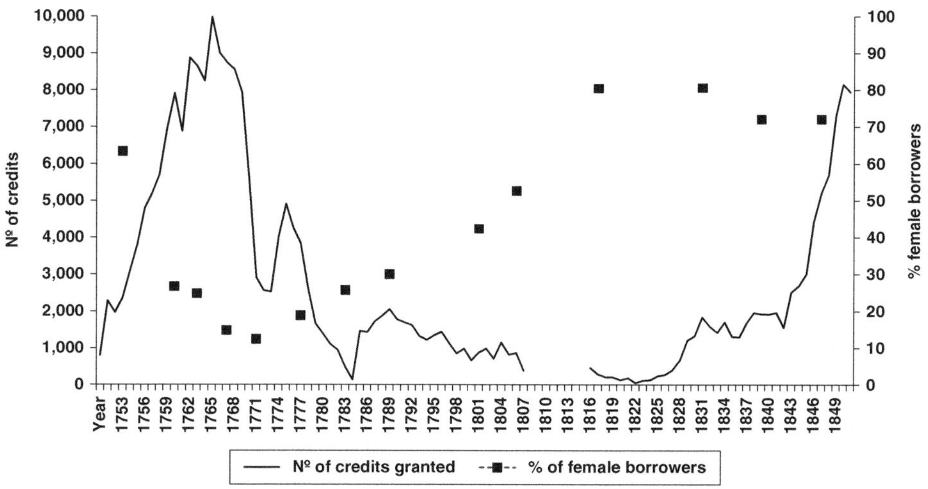

Figure 12.1. Number of credits and percentage of female borrowers, Barcelona, 1751–1842. *Source: Balances bimensuales 1751–1842* and *Llibres de Comptaduria (1851–1842)* ANC, Fons Mont de Pietat de Nostra Senyora de l'Esperança de Barcelona.

poorest of the poor.[17] However, when institutional and political problems led to the prohibition of interest on capital and the institution's ability to lend dwindled, the scarcity of credit and the meagreness of loans forced the poorest individuals, among whom women were particularly prominent, once again to become the borrowers par excellence. The success or weakness of the small-loan institution has a clear gender bias.

Ultimately, the formalization and institutionalization of this sort of credit was a process of enormous complexity. The present study shows that the institutionalization of small credit has had, and probably still has, a gender bias. Certainly, the use of this credit type had a clear gender bias. The conflicts over interest on deposits and the low level of funds deposited in the Mont de Pietat curbed the supply of credit from the mid-1770s onwards. Indeed, the new mechanism for depositing funds at an uncertain rate of interest lay beyond people's economic expectations. Also, the effectiveness of long-standing informal networks of credit probably challenged the viability of the new institution with its hugely diminished capital. Giving a convincing response to this hypothesis would require in-depth research into both public and private credit in the city. Here, however, we focus exclusively on examining the use made of a collateral-based institution at a time of crisis: the winter of 1764.

[17] Carbonell- Esteller, '*Montes de Piedad* and Saving Banks'.

Resorting to Microcredit during a Period of Crisis

The winter of 1764 was exceptionally harsh in Catalonia, particularly in the city of Barcelona.[18] That year, however, the city's Mont de Pietat had full coffers and a strong lending capacity. The institution's vitality went hand in hand with a declining representation of women among its borrowers: the rate of feminization among borrowers was only 25 per cent (see Figure 12.1). To observe the behaviour of urban small credit and the mechanisms that come into play in the survival strategies of working people, 624 cases of objects pledged as collateral have been selected for the month of January that year.[19]

Looking at the distribution of borrowers by gender, we see a predominance of men among those applying for credit from the Mont de Pietat in January 1764. Only a fifth of all borrowers were women, with slightly more than half of these being widows. It seems plausible to state that behaviour differs by gender among practices in informal credit networks and institutionalized credit. Melanie Tebbutt, referring to the case of England in the late nineteenth and early twentieth centuries, has shown that women more typically turned to networks of informal collateral-based credit linked to the purchase of daily provisions.[20] By contrast, the consulted documentation suggests that the institutionalization of credit practices, when the institution enjoyed a sound lending capacity, led to a greater influx of men seeking loans. As a result, it appears that success in the formalization of credit practices was accompanied by the masculinization of their use. The formal banking sector tended to drive out the poorest of the poor. Those with the worst assets to pledge as collateral signified greater risk for the institution. Accordingly, the appraised value of pledged objects was lower and the granted loan was very small. As a result, the poorest of the poor tended to turn to the traditional credit market.

Turning to the distribution of collateral-based credit by amount borrowed, small loans predominate. More than half of the pledged items correspond to the range between 50 and 149 *reales*, and these account for half of all moneys borrowed. Nearly a third of the sample are loans in the lowest range, between one and forty-nine *reales de ardite*. Therefore, 80 per cent of the loans relate to small-credit operations. Bearing in mind that the standard wage for an unskilled labourer in 1764, according to Vilar's data, was 7 sous and 6 diners and that in the period

[18] Vilar, *Catalunya dins l'Espanya moderna*, and Simon Tarrés, 'Barcelona i Catalunya'.

[19] The data have been distributed in six groups according to the value of the loan. The first group between 1 and 49 reales de ardites until the last between 1000 and 6000 reales de ardites.

[20] Tebbutt, *Making Ends Meet*, and Tomkins, 'Pawnbroking and the Survival Strategies'.

1752–1753 the daily wages for a master builder and a skilled builder were 14 and 12 sous, respectively, most loans ranged up to a maximum of fifteen days' wages in value.[21] As a result, the recourse to small collateral-based loans from the Mont de Pietat was an option practised by the working classes purely for subsistence, to stretch their money for day-to-day survival. With time, it also became a recourse for the least fortunate. Women securing credit from Barcelona's Mont de Pietat in January 1764 had a greater representation in the smallest loans, which ranged from 0 to 49 reales (five days' wages for an unskilled labourer), and in the medium-sized loans, which ranged from 150 and 499 reales (between fifteen and thirty days' wages for an unskilled labourer).

Table 12.1. Distribution of credits according to value and borrowers by gender. Mont de Pietat de Barcelona, 1764. Author: ANC, Fons Mont de Pietat de Nostra Senyora de l'Esperança, *Llibre de Comtaduria* 1764.

Nominal value (reales de ardites)	**Day's wages of a construction worker**	**Borrowers**	
Microcredits		*% Women*	*% Men*
1–49	>5	42.8	28.5
50–99	5<10	39.5	39.4
100–49	10<15	9.4	26
Small credits			
150–299	15<30	6.7	3
Larger credits			
300–999	30<100	0.6	2.6
1000–6000	>100	0.6	0.4

Turning to the distribution of loans by type of pledged collateral, we can see that the sort of object deposited with the Mont de Pietat is an indicator of the borrowers' creditworthiness, their material level of belongings, and, consequently, their level of consumption. Men and women borrowers who had better objects to pledge as collateral could secure greater credit. By contrast, those with the fewest belongings, who pledged linens, smocks, breeches, copper pots, and raw wool, were the ones with the least ability to secure credit, but also the ones who operated best

[21] Vilar, 'Transformaciones económicas'.

with their resources because they repaid their debt, recovered their pledges and returned for new loans secured against the same objects. Credit and consumption were intertwined.[22]

Looking at the distribution of pledged collateral by type of object, we find a clear correlation between large loans and jewellery and the smallest loans and clothing. As the value of the loan rises, the percentage of jewellery and mixed collateral (jewellery and clothing) grows at the expense of pledges made up exclusively of clothing. Interestingly, we observe the presence of jewellery in the group of quite small loans of between 50 and 149 *reales*, where women abound but there are also men depositing a gold wedding ring. It is also in this loan category where the maximum percentage of mixed pledges (clothing and jewellery) is concentrated. Focusing on the type of objects pledged as collateral, we observe a striking level of diversification of consumption among the working classes. Possessing some ring or medallion, often inherited, probably signified an investment for working people that could be translated at a given moment into a key element for survival. Networks of solidarity among these people were often forged out of flows in the transmission of modest, but strategically crucial, objects and women played a fundamental role here. Reciprocity-based relational networks accompanied credit practices within the community.

As the value of the loan rises, the amount of gold dwindles and the amount of silver increases, and vice versa. This explains why people of higher standing pledged silver cutlery, dishware, and candlesticks. They would typically do this through male or female servants who went on their behalf to the Mont de Pietat. By contrast, the least fortunate, as noted earlier, would typically deposit a gold ring. In effect, the value and type of pledged objects indicates a material wealth and consumption level that differs according to the specific social and economic status of the men and women borrowing money. Different patterns of behaviour can also be distinguished in the pledging of clothing as collateral, though these loans always fall below 300 *reales de ardite* in value. Clothing pledged as collateral sometimes combined two or more raw or woven fabrics. That is, a loan might be secured by two or more distinct pieces of apparel. Wool, which appears to be the most popular material, is concentrated in the smallest loans. Hemp is distributed equally among the smallest and medium-sized loans, indicating that it was a common material, but also one that was prized. Cotton and calicoes, though not highly represented, are concentrated in the small loans. Silk appears in the bands of higher loans secured

[22] Francois, *A Culture of Every Day Credit*; Murhem, 'Credit for the Poor'; Montenach, 'Legal Trade and Black Markets'; Lemire, Pearson, and Campbell, *Women and Credit*.

with clothing, because it was the most prized material, had the greatest value and involved the highest level of consumption.

Turning to the distribution of borrowers by occupation, the documentation only gives the profession of the borrower in 63.6 per cent of the sample. The most represented occupational sectors, from highest to lowest, are textiles and garments, agriculture, construction, metalworking, and fishing and sailing. Taking into account that most borrowers with a declared trade are Barcelona residents, the percentages of occupations among the Mont de Pietat's borrowers have been weighted for representativeness by comparing them to the proportion represented by their trades within the active population of Barcelona taken as a whole in 1764.With all the caveats that are required, the property registry, or cadastre, of 1764 has been utilized to prepare an approximate index for this purpose. The index has only an indicative value because not all professions are represented in the property registry, nor are all individuals employed in each profession represented. In only a few sectors has it been possible to weight the data. For example, in the case of peasant farmers, market gardeners, and domestic servants, weighting has not been possible. It has been possible, however, to confirm that the textiles and garments sector was the one to generate the most applications for credit from the Mont de Pietat. It is likely that the families tied to the textile sector had greater access to clothing or raw material to pledge as collateral, enabling them to obtain credit more easily and thus linking this kind of household production with credit practices.

So far, we know that textile, agriculture and construction workers were the primary clients of the Mont de Pietat. Next, it is necessary to see whether the act of pledging belongings to obtain credit was a step downwards in a process of impoverishment that translated into an inability to repay loans and, therefore, into the definitive loss of the pledged object; or whether, by contrast, it was a strategy or tactic to get through times of hardship, after which the borrowed money was repaid and the object in question recovered.

Looking at the percentage of failures to repay loans, we find that the number of instances when a loan could not be repaid and the pledged item was lost to be very high according to the analysed sample. Nearly half of the clientele of the Mont de Pietat let go of their strategic belongings at a low price and therefore forcibly. The definitive loss of a pledged item very likely signified a further step downwards in the process of pauperization. In the late eighteenth century, Antoni de Capmany explained that in times of economic hardship working families lost their possessions cheaply. The text is quite telling: '[when a craftsmen] resorted to the protection of the Hospital [...] we must suppose that he had already sold off all of his household goods, his finest jewels and perhaps the tools of his trade, because this humble recourse must be seen as the saddest of extremities for a skilled labourer's self-respect'.[23] In effect, the recourse to small loans by means of pledging objects as collateral was one of the first mechanisms that came into play to keep from falling into destitution.

The highest levels of success in recovering pledged objects were concentrated in the band of smaller loans. The significance of the percentage of failure in recovering pledged objects, however, depends as well on the size of the loan. It was difficult, though not impossible, for someone pledging a ring with emeralds and diamonds to become so impoverished that he or she could not reclaim it. Such a person might have much greater resources to bring to bear, from goods to personal relations, that would distance him or her from those who lost what little they had. As a result, the significance of the loss of higher loans, in general terms, indicates impoverishment understood as a loss of wealth rather than as pauperization that would lead implicitly to destitution.

The percentage of pauperization and impoverishment can also be seen to grow, broadly speaking, as the value of the loan rises. The failure to recover pledged objects and to repay loans increases as the loans become larger, because higher loans are the hardest to repay. So the optimal strategy, taking into account the possibility to return repeatedly to the Mont de Pietat, appears to have involved applying for what the borrower knew he or she could repay, leaving the door open to repeat the operation on other occasions. Ultimately, the behaviour of the clientele of the Mont de Pietat becomes logical: those less able to bear indebtedness applied for small loans, those with a greater ability to take on indebtedness applied for big loans, with the former showing a greater adaptive ability in relation to adverse circumstances. In view of the data, one might ask whether it was more profitable to have good creditworthiness or to operate precisely — as did those applying for the smallest loans — in relation to the few resources available.

Looking at the rate of success or failure in the repayment of loans and the recovery of pledged items by occupational sectors, we find the following: the sectors with the highest success rate are broadly those most represented in the smallest loans (textiles, agriculture, and construction), whereas the sectors that fail to repay loans and lose pledged objects as well as the opportunity to apply for additional loans are commerce and food. The latter two sectors appear to be the most shaken at a time of subsistence crisis in an urban context, to which may also be added their lack of experience operating in this type of very short-term survival strategy.

Ultimately, the adaptive capacity of working families and individuals successfully developed short-term strategies to cope with their needs. The distribution of

[23] Capmany i Montpalau, *Discurso económico*.

pledged loans by amount borrowed and by type of pledged objects, as well as the success rate in repaying loans and recovering pledged objects, has clearly demonstrated that the resort to this type of credit, through the formalization of such a practice in an institution of this nature, proved to be one of the viable options taken by a significant portion of Barcelona's working families, particularly in the textile and construction sectors. The concentration of 80 per cent of the loans in the highest band of fifteen days' wages for an unskilled construction worker, along with the ability to repay loans and recover pledged collateral, shows the adaptive capacity of working people's household economies in adverse circumstances. Lastly, a level of diversification of consumption is clearly evident and should not be underestimated even in the band of small loans as this range of credit brings together various types of clothing, raw material, objects, and jewellery. The predominance of men among the borrowers turning to the Mont de Pietat has suggested the hypothesis that the formalization and institutionalization of credit practices masculinized their use. At the same time, the networks of solidarity and reciprocity forged among kin and farther afield were sustained above all by women. This latter point is supported by the transmission of objects — ones that could be pledged as collateral — in the wills of working women. These aspects need to be given a systematic treatment over a broader time period and compared with other types of notary and parish documentation. However, such an effort would exceed the scope of these pages, which are limited to a look at the use of collateral-based credit in adaptive household economies in a context in which such practices were becoming institutionalized and amid a period of scarcity and hardship in the city of Barcelona, such as the harsh winter of 1764.

Women and the Transmission of Objects Pledged as Collateral

The habit of cultivating reciprocity among workers was transmitted from generation to generation. Among the wills of working women in the second half of the eighteenth century in Barcelona, examples abound of women who leave highly diversified bequests of clothing, rings, or silver buttons to various relatives and — to a lesser degree — to acquaintances, thus consolidating kinship networks as a key resource to cope with survival and uncertainty. Women thus appear to have played a significant role in the networks forged around credit.

From the wills of working people, particularly those of women, who had the least to bequeath in terms of quantity and value, we can see an enormous diversification of heirs and a wide dispersion of assets given as bequests. A woman might leave a bequest to her direct nieces, to nieces of a sister of hers or of her husband, or to other relatives with whom she did not necessarily have a direct relation — in most cases, residing in very distant villages. She could leave each of them objects, such as clothing, linens, or a silver button, or she might leave money. However modest, each of these objects had a key strategic importance because, as has been seen, the practice of pledging objects as collateral for survival purposes was extremely widespread among workers in the second half of the eighteenth century.

Even more significant, however, is the enormous dispersion of the few assets belonging to these women. This indicates their wish to consolidate kinship bonds and sometimes also bonds of friendship or with neighbours. The secular practice of cultivating kinship bonds was primarily carried out by women, becoming one of the main avenues of provision against future calamities and the tendency of family units to fragment in times of hardship.

The case of Maria Blanch i Gubern, a Barcelona women dedicated to spinning silk in the late eighteenth century, offers an extremely telling example of the practice of leaving bequests.[24] Widow of the linen weaver Joan Blanch since 1760, Maria Blanch first created a will in 1773. She was probably childless, though this is not known for certain. In her will (which she amended twice, first in 1777 and again in 1780), Maria Blanch made an extremely careful list of her scarce assets to bequeath. She was possibly related to most of the women on her list. Though their surnames do not confirm kinship, the information that comes out of the dense relational network shown in the document indicates this was the case. She distributed her assets as follows: to Antònia and Maria Vigo, unmarried daughters of a miller, she left the small sum of two libras ten sous each on the condition that their whereabouts could be ascertained; to Maria Capmany, Francisca and Eulària Ribó (all three residents of Sant Genís d'Horta), Isabel Pujol (resident of Sabadell) and Catarina Bladas (resident of Sant Quirze), all nieces of hers, she left 'all the clothing and linens in my use' in addition to an empty box with lock and key that went to Maria Capmany; to her deceased husband's niece Francisca T., whose surname is not recorded, she left serge skirts that were currently pledged as collateral and she forgave her debts; to her sister-in-law Lluïsa Blanch, she left three *libras* that should, if Lluïsa predeceased her, pass to Magdalena Blanch, her daughter-in-law; she left her chemises or smocks 'to whomever should attend her in her final illness'; and finally she left a silver peseta each to the Hospital de la Santa Creu, the Hospital de la Misericòrdia, and the Infants Orfes.

[24] Barcelona, Arxiu Històric de Protocols de Barcelona (AHPB) Fons comercial. Llibre de tot el que es paga, 1782 B-244. Ramon font Alier, Testaments, 1762–1784 (25 d'ocubre de 1773) fol. 313; 1777, fol. 386; 1780, fol.: 481. I am grateful to Marta Vicente for providing this document.

This example shows that an unskilled working woman such as Maria Blanch named in her will ten women, all relatives, among whom she distributed her used clothing and some cash. Most strikingly, her will is not exceptional. Wills of this kind, in fact, were a common practice among Barcelona women.[25] This aspect supports the hypothesis that women played a key role in the maintenance of informal networks of welfare provision and solidarity.

Reciprocity may not be the sole aim pursued in this approach to wills. Often the exercise of the benefactor's patronage toward the beneficiaries also served to tighten the bonds among people, establishing a hierarchy that enabled benefactors to consolidate their status and make it visible. These ties of non-institutional patronage became profitable for the group, invigorating and enriching its relational network before civil or ecclesiastical authorities or before other corporate bodies. In the case of the working woman Maria Blanch leaving money to the poor of three hospitals, the gesture was possibly made with an expectation of some privilege (or advantage) in life or at the time of burial. It would not be unusual for Maria Blanch to anticipate the possibility in old age of going to stay at either the Hospital de la Misericòrdia or the Hospital de la Santa Creu. As a result, leaving a bequest to these institutions might safeguard the chances of her admittance on good terms, for example, to the Misericòrdia infirmary or to the same hospital's Casa de Sant Rafael, to which elderly women who were not beggars could pay for admittance. If nothing else, being on good terms with these institutions could be useful when requesting the admittance of some relative of hers. Therefore, patronage relations also entailed an exchange of reciprocities, with which even the humblest were not unfamiliar.[26]

The practice of bequests among working people consolidated kinship networks as a form of long-term welfare provision. The transmission of objects — humble ones that were nevertheless strategically crucial because they often became collateral — forged bonds that linked together eighteenth-century workers in a relation of reciprocity and provision. Credit practices carried out within the community contributed to ensuring the survival of its members. Particular forms belonging to the *moral economy* persisted without succumbing before the ascendance of the profit economy. The role of women, the support networks forged by them, and their know-how in managing survival — the collection of information, the exchange of complicity and reciprocity, and their ability to negotiate to obtain appraisals of clothing and to secure credit — were crucial elements in gaining access

[25] Vinyoles, *La vida quotidiana a Barcelona*.

[26] Levi, 'Reciprocidad'; Fontaine, *L'économie morale*.

to available resources. Weaving relationships of interdependence allowed in many occasions to overcome situations of vulnerability. The *agency* of women developed as the options and choices in survival strategies grew more varied in the Barcelona households of the eighteenth century.

Works Cited

Manuscript and Archival Sources

Barcelona, Arxiu Històric de Protocols de Barcelona (AHPB). Fons comercial. Llibre de tot el que es paga, 1782 B-244. Ramon font Alier, Testaments, 1762–1784

Sant Cugat del Vallès, Arxiu Nacional de Catalunya (ANC), Fons del Mont de Pietat de Nostra Senyora de l'Esperança i Salvació de les Ànimes de Barcelona, *Llibres de Comptaduria.* Llibre 165

Sant Cugat del Vallès, Arxiu Nacional de Catalunya (ANC), Fons del Mont de Pietat de Nostra Senyora de l'Esperança i Salvació de les Ànimes de Barcelona, *Llibre d'acords*

Primary Sources

Capmany i Montpalau, Antoni de, *Discurso económico-político en defensa del Trabajo mecánico de los menestrales* (Madrid: Imprenta Sancha, 1788)

Constituciones del Real Monte de Piedad que su Magestad Catholica ha erigido en la Ciudad de Barcelona la Ilustre Congregación de Nuestra Señora de la Esperanza y Salvación de las almas, para alivio de los necesitados y subsistència de la Real Casa del Retiro ... (Barcelona: Imprenta de Francisco Surià, Impressor, en la calle de la Paja, 12 abril 1764)

Kalendario i guia de forasteros de Barcelona (Barcelona: Viuda Piferrer, 1786)

Secondary Studies

Carbonell-Esteller, Montserrat, '*Montes de piedad* and Savings Banks as Microfinance Institutions on the Periphery of the Financial System of Mid-Nineteenth-Century Barcelona', *Business History*, 54.3 (2012), 363–80

Carbonell-Esteller, Montserrat, and Julie Marfany, 'Gender, Life Cycle, and Family "Strategies" among the Poor: The Barcelona Workhouse, 1762–1805', *The Economic History Review*, 70.3 (2017), 810–36

Castañeda, Lluís, and Montserrat Carbonell-Esteller, 'Sector financer i mercat de capitals al primer terç del segle XIX', in *Història Econòmica de la Catalunya Contemporània,* ed. by Jordi Nadal, and others(Barcelona: Edicions 62, 1991), v, pp. 338–51

Fontaine, Laurence, *L'économie morale: Pauvreté, crèdit et confiance dans l'Europe préindustrielle* (Paris: Gallimard, 2008)

Francois, Marie, *A Culture of Everyday Credit: Housekeeping, Pawnbroking and Governance in Mexico City, 1750–1920* (Lincoln: University of Nebraska Press, 2006)

Hufton, Olwen, *The Poor of Eighteenth-Century France* (Oxford: Oxford University Press, 1974)

King, Stephen, and Alannah Tomkins, eds, *The Poor in England 1700–1850: An Economy of Makeshifts* (Manchester: Manchester University Press, 2003)

Lemire, Beverly, Ruth Pearson, and Gail Campbell, *Women and Credit: Researching the Past, Refiguring the Future* (Oxford: Berg, 2002)

Levi, Giovanni, 'Reciprocidad mediterránea', *Hispania,* LX/1, 204 (2000), 103–26

López de Barahona, Victoria, 'Estrategias de supervivencia y redes informales de crédito entre las clases populares madrileñas del siglo XVIII', in *La historia como arma de reflexión: estudios en homenaje al profesor Santos Madrazo,* ed. by Francisco Javier Hernando Ortego, José Miguel López García, and José Antolín Nieto Sánchez (Madrid: Universidad Autónoma de Madrid, 2012), pp. 37–40

Mora-Sitja, Natalia, 'Labour Market Integration in a Pre-Industrial Economy: Catalonia, 1772–1816', *Oxford Economic Papers,* 59 (2007), 156–77

Montenach, Anne, 'Legal Trade and Black Markets: Food Trades in Lyon in the Late Seventeenth and Eartly Eighteenth Centuries', in *Female Agency in the Urban Economy: Gender in European Towns, 1640–1830,* ed. by Deborah Simonton and Anne Montenach (New York: Routledge, 2013), pp. 17–34

Muldrew, Craig, *The Economy of Obligation: The Culture of Credit and Social Relations in Early Modern England* (London: Palgrave, 1998)

Murhem, Sophia, 'Credit for the Poor: The Decline of Pawnbroking 1880–1930', *European Review of Economic History,* 20 (2015), 198–214

Nadal i Sudrià, *Història de la Caixa de Pensions* (Barcelona: Edicions 62, 1991)

Rumeu de Armas, Antonio, *Historia de la previsión social en España. Cofradías, Gremios, Hermandades, Montepíos* (Madrid: Instituto Nacional de Previsión, 1944)

Simon Tarrés, Antoni, 'Barcelona i Catalunya Durant la crisi de subsistències de 1763–64', *Quaderns d'istòria,* 1 (1995), 95–108

Spence, Cathryn, 'Women, Gender and Credit in Early Modern Western European Towns', in *The Routledge History Handbook of Gender and the Urban Experience,* ed. by Deborah Simonton (London: Routledge, 2017), pp. 21–32

Tebbutt, Melanie, *Making Ends Meet: Pawnbroking and Working-Class Credit* (London: Methuen, 1984)

Tomkins, Alannah, 'Pawnbroking and the Survival Strategies of the Urban Poor in 1770s York', in *The Poor in England 1700–1850: An Economy of Makeshifts,* ed. by Stephen King and Alannah Tomkins (Manchester: Manchester University Press, 2003), pp. 166–98

Torra, Lidia, 'Las botigues de teles de Barcelona: Aportación al estudio de la oferta de tejidos y del crédito al consumo (1650–1800)', *Revista de Historia Economica-Journal of Iberian and Latin American Economic History,* 21 (2003), 89–105

Vilar, Pierre, *Catalunya dins l'Espanya moderna* (Barcelona: Edicions 62, 1966, vol. III)

———, 'Transformaciones económicas, impulso urbano y movimiento de los salarios: Barcelona del siglo XVIII', in Vilar, Pierre, *Crecimiento y desarrollo* (Barcelona: Ariel, 1974), pp. 209–10

Vinyoles, Teresa, *La vida quotidiana a Barcelona vers 1400* (Barcelona: Fundació Vives Casajuana, 1985)

Women and Credit in the Area of Santiago de Compostela at the End of the Old Regime (1770–1805)

Francisco Cebreiro Ares*

Introduction

In 1786 the 'heirs' of Maria Caneda, a baker established in the street of *Entremuros* in Santiago, filed a lawsuit for the properties she had bequeathed before her death in the parish of San Pedro de Loureda. Through this lawsuit we gain interesting

* This article is set within the wider scope of doctoral research on monetary relations and credit in Galicia, in the Northwest of Spain, between 1760–1820, and operates under the framework provided by the Spanish Ministry Program for research: 'Culturas urbanas: Las ciudades interiores en el noroeste ibérico, dinámicas e impacto en el espacio rural' (*Urban Cultures: Inland Towns and Cities from the Northwest of Spain and Portugal, their Dynamics and their Impact on Rural Areas* HAR2015-64014-C3-3-R). It aims to make a contribution to the work on women's studies by scholars who have preceded me in the department of History of the University of Santiago de Compostela, especially Serrana M. Rial and Ofelia Rey Castelao. I want also to give thanks for the time and work spent by Elise M. Dermineur and Juliet Gayton on reviewing the English version of this article. Any remaining errors are my own.

Francisco Cebreiro Ares is a postdoctoral researcher at the University of Santiago de Compostela (Galicia, Spain) His main lines of research concern the monetary and financial history of the eighteenth century from a social perspective, with special attention to such topics as silver bullion and exchange flows of bills, rural credit, and commercial urban credit.

Women and Credit in Pre-Industrial Europe, ed. by Elise M. Dermineur, EER 12 (Turnhout: Brepols, 2018), pp. 321–344.
BREPOLS PUBLISHERS DOI 10.1484/M.EER-EB.5.115759

insights into how money and property were managed by women at the time, and also into what her neighbours had to say about her activity.[1]

As it turns out, Maria Caneda was married to a carpenter by the name of Tomás García, who after a time left her a widow. In the subsequent inheritance trial, several witnesses came forth and testified that María Caneda was indeed a most 'prosperous' woman. Bernardo Rodríguez, carpenter and an associate of Maria's late husband, testified that she had managed the bread oven single-handedly, and in his own words, 'her husband would give her the full salary of his work'. Similarly, her neighbour Coleta Vidal, claimed that she had heard talk among the neighbours that Maria had bestowed each of her daughters with one hundred *ducados* (1100 *reales de vellón*) as dowry. She had also handsomely helped her sons in their monetary affairs: one of them received money to pay off a lawsuit against a woman who was suing to get her son recognized, and the other received money to pay off his duty to serve the Spanish army in Italy.

Another carpenter, Fernando Martínez, declared that he had once been doing some jobs in Maria's house, and she had brought him a drink in nothing but a two-handled 'tembladeira' (silver goblet). Tomás Fachal, sculptor and an associate of María's two sons, Miguel and José, mentioned that she possessed two small antique silver boats, which decorated her house. Finally, Benito Roma, who had been one of Maria's customers, stated that: 'People said [...] that the aforementioned baker María Caneda had money or lent it to others, though he himself had never borrowed from her'.

Such statements, mixing fact and gossip, cannot be easily isolated from the traditional view of millers and bakers as wealthy speculators. However, and importantly for this study, they fully illustrate the role of women in credit across the eighteenth century in Galicia and provide a typical example for further analysis.

Indeed, the study will aim to analyse the forms, frequency, and circumstances in which women accessed credit at the end of the eighteenth-century in Santiago de Compostela, and its evolution during the early years of the following century. In order to do this, the study has been divided into three sections.

The first section gives a general overview of the role of women in the Old Regime economy of Galicia, based on previous available studies and adding my own

[1] Archivo Histórico Universitario de Santiago de Compostela (AHUS), Municipal, Pleitos Antiguos, Civil, 1786. *José, Juan y Gregorio García con D. Antonio Buján sobre partija de bienes*. Unless stated otherwise, all monetary values are expressed in *reales de vellón*, which was the monetary main unit of accounting during the eighteenth century in Spain. Its multiple, the *ducado*, and submultiple, the *maravedí*, have the following equivalence: (1 *ducado* = 11 *reales*) and (1 *real* = 34 *maravedies*).

contribution and examples from my dataset. Thus, this section is focused on women and their access to money, through inheritance, salary, and savings. The second section discusses conditions and types of mortgage credit in Santiago de Compostela and its hinterlands, with subsections on the *census* and the *obligations* market, with special attention on mechanisms of female alienation from the *census* markets.[2] After this analysis, the volume of women's participation in urban and rural credit is determined, and in the third section and conclusion a first overview of women's role in credit in this region of Galicia (Spain) is presented. Finally, some hypotheses are proposed to understand their increasing participation in credit at the end of the century.

The Role of Women in the Economy of Eighteenth-Century Galicia

Until fairly recently, historiography had not given much attention to the history of credit as regards gender in pre-industrial societies. Even in the case of Galicia, where we can find several studies on the role of women in the economy of early modern times, credit relations have remained, for the most part, unexplored.[3]

In Serrana Rial's in-depth analysis of the notarial activity of women in Santiago de Compostela and its area of influence, the importance of credit-based transactions is identified. Women's activity registered by a notary in the mid-eighteenth century was much lower than their demographic proportion. Indeed, only 21 to 24 per cent of notarial deeds had women as the main actors, when in fact more than half the population were women.

Moving down into the specific types of acts carried out by women, credit related deeds are one of the least frequent to be found. Notwithstanding this, we should also note two facts: the first, that credit deeds — and powers of attorney — were the notarial activity with the highest increase rate, from the middle to the end of the eighteenth century (from 4.2 to 7.1 per cent); and secondly, and more importantly, credit deeds are the notarial activity in which general percentages and women's percentages tend to be similar (only −0.6 to −0.1 per cent of difference between credit deeds in general and women's credit deeds).

[2] *Census* was one of the notarial forms of credit under the Spanish Crown. See below in this article, '*Notarial credit forms and "markets"*'.

[3] Jordan, *Women and Credit*; Lemire, Pearson, and Campbell, eds, *Women and Credit*; and Lemire, *The Business of Everyday Life*. For the Galician case: Rey Castelao and Rial García, *Historia das mulleres en Galicia*, p. 105; and Poska, *Women and Authority*.

Structures and Determining Factors for Women to Access Money

Moving on from the registry office records, which represent a portion of the economic activity of the time, the following paragraphs will point out some structures and the evolution of some of the factors that influenced women's role in money and credit in Galicia, more specifically in the area of Santiago de Compostela during the eighteenth century.

In Galicia, four factors have been found to be the most important, allowing women to take part in credit activities, both as creditors and debtors. These factors include: i) inheritance regimes, more specifically the so called *mellora.* ii) the high rate of male migration; iii) the rise of women heading households mainly in urban areas, but also in rural settings; iv) the increasing monetization of dowries. All these factors are strongly interconnected and operated as a whole.

Inheritance and Discrimination through the *mellora*

As previous historiography has noted, Galicia cannot be simplified with a single demographic and socioeconomic set of features, valid for the entire territory.[4] It is the result of a variety of circumstances (environment, society, and economy among other features) and customary practices carried out indoors and within the general Castilian legal framework. This was possible because, in practice, Castilian law (outside the nobility) was far more flexible than has been alleged, since it endorses inheritance shared evenly between the heirs regardless of gender.

The *mellora*, or 'improvement', was the name for an inheritance regime that gave a larger share of the inheritance-goods to a single daughter — or son — who remained in the parental home, and took care of the elderly and the property. In some of the wealthiest and most populous regions of Galicia, this pattern tended to give preference to women, rather than to men. As a result, households tended to be matrilineal and residences, matrilocal. This inheritance pattern operated across an extended area of Galicia including the old province of Santiago de Compostela.[5]

Male Migration

As Eiras Roel and Rey Castelao have shown previously, this inheritance pattern was often the result of a high rate of male migration. Indeed, Galician menfolk moved

[4] Eiras Roel, 'Mecanismos autorreguladores', pp. 51–72.

[5] More information about *mellora* in Rial García, 'Mujer y actividad económica', p. 154.

to Portugal and Cadiz, generally on a mid-term basis period, and the Indies.[6] Eighteenth-century wills show that the distribution of inheritance towards women was the result of the *mellora*. But it also came about when there were no sons remaining at home.[7] This migration also had a remarkable effect on other monetary transactions: indeed, mothers and wives of young Galician men working abroad managed their monetary remittances, acquired land, and granted credit, more often than not to their kinsfolk.[8]

Women as Head of Urban and Rural Households

As a result, an significant proportion of women headed households both in rural and urban areas. These women, some of them also spinsters or widows, who found themselves living alone in rural areas would generally hold smaller households, with less land and fewer cattle than a man in a similar situation might have.[9] It is also interesting to note how, in these areas where migration was so common, illegitimate offspring of women in these circumstances was quite frequent, and therefore, better tolerated than in other regions. This entailed the added issue of extra mouths to feed with comparatively fewer resources. As Dubert pointed out, one of the most noteworthy alterations in the eighteenth-century urban demography of Santiago de Compostela, was precisely the rise of the household headed by a woman without a man by her side (henceforth called 'women alone').[10]

Progressive Monetization of Dowries

The eighteenth century also shows a progressive monetization in dowries, which might have been the paradoxical result of the process of peasant impoverishment. The tendency to endow brides-to-be with money rather than goods is a general pattern in Galicia throughout this century.[11] In the case of the Santiago region, the progressive monetization of dowries is absolutely clear across the mid-seventeenth

[6] Rey Castelao, 'Movimientos migratorios en Galicia'; Pascua Sánchez, 'Los Gallegos en el Cádiz'.

[7] Rial García, 'Mujer y actividad económica', pp. 158–61.

[8] Saavedra Fernández, 'Mecanismos informáis'.

[9] Rial García, *Mujer y actividad económica*, pp. 206–31.

[10] Dubert García, *Los comportamientos de la familia*, pp. 55–61.

[11] Lugo, and Terra de Montes (Pontevedra). Sobrado Correa, 'El sistema dotal', p. 15. and Fernández Cortizo, 'Matrimonio y régimen dotal', pp. 46–47. See also Zuijderduijn, this volume.

century through to the mid-eighteenth. Money, as a specific part of dowries, rose, and could be seen in 12.6 to 23 per cent of the dowry contracts. This meant that dowries of perishables and household equipment dropped while those in coinage rose. Specifically, dowries of cereals decreased from 45 to 19 per cent, and cattle declined from 92 to 46 per cent. In consequence, peasants had less real estate and cattle, but more money to deal with. The bulk and value of dowries also underwent changes at the same time. If in the seventeenth century the average was 444 *reales*, in the eighteenth century it decreased to 350 *reales*.[12]

Thus, it is safe to say that in the seventeenth century, money was more exclusive, socially restrictive, and higher in value than in the following century. Indeed, the second half of the eighteenth century saw monetization developing under the umbrella of impoverishment and inflation. The dominant figure is the impoverished peasant, but frequently acting in the market, as owner of less cattle, property, and cereal than in the past, because he was forced to sell it. In general, this needy peasant transmits less value for more money. This process would finally push women, just like their male counterparts, into the 'money chains'.

As a result of these factors, it becomes important to investigate two main lines of research. The first is the phenomenon of the will as dowry for servants, often women, and the second is the question of safeguarding women's savings.

Wills as dowry. It should be assumed that most house servants, and even apprentice artisans, were not paid even yearly. A common practice of the time was for servants to receive back payment for their work at the time of their master's death, often by receiving real estate and other goods through their master's wills. Such testamentary practices usually included the back wages, and household goods, on the assumption that the former servant would establish a new household of his or her own. From this perspective, many townsfolk's wills might be seen as minor dowries in favour of their former servants to be used as they pleased.

Although the economic and social relevance of this phenomenon has already been pointed out, it is not yet possible to quantify its monetary impact in the city and region. Let it suffice, for the moment, to present an appropriate example. In July of 1777, Juan Antonio González de Estrada made out a will with a notary as witness. The testator had been born in Labastida (Álava, Basque Country), and was Master Surgeon of the Royal Hospital of Santiago de Compostela.[13] In his will, he left six thousand *reales* to his sister in Labastida. Regarding his servant, María González, who had waited on him for over fifteen years, he stated:

[12] Burgo López, 'Niveles sociales y relaciones matrimoniales', pp. 183–85.

[13] AHUS, *Protocolos de Santiago*, 5.987, fol. 76^{r}.

> and it is my will, that she should be given the wages for each of the years [fifteen] that she has been in my service, and two hundred *reales*, and fifty gold doubloons, one piece of linen from my large chest, the two beds with all the bedclothes, all the kitchenware, foodstuff, one desk and chest of her choice, four Moscovian stools, four paintings of her choice, a necklace with a diamond cross and the eight thousand *reales* worth participation I have in the business of Mr Domingo de Otero from the Villars Street.[14]

Through the will of her master, María González set up a household of her own, and more importantly, she became a capitalist associate of Domingo Otero. Unfortunately, it is not possible yet to determinate how common this practice actually was. However, it should be considered as another way in which a servant woman could obtain capital, and then potentially offer credit to others. Nevertheless, the question may be asked: where and how did women of lower social standing keep their money?[15]

Safeguarding women's savings. One answer may be found in one of the most detailed post mortem inventories, at least as regards coinage, that was discovered in the Compostelan notarial records. Indeed, on 20 September 1781, when the legal heirs of one of the Capellans of the Royal Hospital of Santiago were executing the will of Mr Gregorio Rial, they were forced to stop and enquire after Mrs Benita Suárez Mosquera.[16] In a small lead box, property of the Chaplain, they found twenty thousand *reales* and the following note, in the handwriting of the deceased:

> I, Mr Gregorio Rial, do hereby certify that all the money contained in this lead box is the property of Benita Suárez Mosquera, single woman and neighbour of San Cosme de Portomeiro, who gave it to me to keep safe, and return to her whenever she needed it. Today there are only two thousand seven hundred and thirty nine *reales* and a half.
> [23 January 1770]

The same manuscript described the eleven cash transfers that the Chaplain had made to Benita over the past eleven years. The remaining coins were, perhaps unfortunately for María Benita, delivered to Mr Domingo Romero.

[14] The terms 'Mr' and 'Mrs' are used throughout the article as translations of the Spanish terms 'don' and 'doña', which indicate social, rather than marital, status.

[15] Fontaine, *The Moral Economy*, p. 129.

[16] AHUS, Hospital Real, *Sección Escrituras* nº63, *Prego de Parga* 1777–83, fol. 409r.

Table 13.1. Coins property of Benita Suárez in the postmortem inventory of Gregorio Rial (1781). *Source:* AHUS, HR, Escrituras n°63, Prego de Parga 1777–1783, f. 411.

Number	Coin type	Value (rsdv)
2	Gold four *doblones* with premio	160
76	Small gold *escudos*	1615
1	Silver half *peso*	10
6	Silver five *pesetas*	30
4	Silver *reales*	8
89		1823

It is not possible to determine whether this case was frequent or not. However, it does illustrate an example of a woman alone operating with a mechanism to safeguard her savings in cash.

Notarial Credit Forms and 'Markets'

As several scholars have pointed out, monetary circulation and credit in pre-modern societies was multiform and multilayered. Credit mirrored the very complexity of society. Historians tend to work with a partial view of the facts, as most transactions were carried out orally, though sometimes they are fortunate enough to find the full chain of events that culminates in the written sources. The few studies concerning credit in the Galicia of the Old Regime outline three major types of notarial credit: *censos consignativos*, *obligaciones* and *ventas de rentas.*[17]

i. *Censos* were the traditional form of mortgage credit under the Spanish Crown and in its empire. Substantially, it was a formal long-term debt (undetermined), with a yearly 3 per cent interest fixed by Crown' laws, until the full amount of the borrowed capital was repaid. The *censo* was the legally and socially accepted form of credit, recognized, and endorsed by the Catholic Church and the Spanish Crown. Moreover, *censos* were regarded

[17] Blanc, 'La complexité monétaire en France' pp. 81–111; Fontaine, Postel-Vinay, Rosenthal, and Servais, *Des personnes aux institutions*. On the notarial typology of Galician credit, see Ferreiro Porto, 'Fuentes para el estudio de las formas del crédito', pp. 289–306. Regarding *obligations,* see especially Dermineur, this volume.

as the classical form of institutional credit, and were often used by the clergy, nobility, hospitals and other charitable institutions.

ii. *Obligaciones* were a public act of acknowledgement of debt, registered by a notary. *Obligaciones* included all types of credit, with or without guarantees, with a huge variability in length and time, and spread across all strata of society. In many cases it was not even 'new' monetary credit; the *obligación* often made reference to pre-existing debts, goods already delivered, and the like. Given the breadth and generality of its legal definition, the *obligación* was in fact an umbrella term that covered a wide variety of activities. It is also possible to follow certain cases of oral credit through to written sources through the mechanism of the *obligación*.[18]

iii. *Ventas de renta* were strongly related to peasants and generally involve strong usury, even extortion. Through this act, one person (usually a peasant) sold an amount of rent, usually cereals, for a certain price (the credit) with a piece of land as collateral. Like the *censos*, the rent, acted as an interest rate, which in this case was a floating interest rate, as a of cereal price fluctuations. It was not uncommon for the peasant to be unable to repay his debt, or redeem the deed.[19]

For the main source of data, we have considered each of these three types of notarial deeds linked to credit registered by the *Registro de Hipotecas* or Mortage Registry in the Galician town of Santiago de Compostela between 1770–1805.[20] This major institution was first established by Royal Law or *Real Pragmática* on 31 January 1768, and continued its work until tax changes were introduced in 1829–1830. In the specific case of Santiago de Compostela, the mortgage office register was first established in August 1768. This source allows for various lines of study of credit relationships, following the work of Greenow for Guadalajara (México).[21] The dataset extracted from it includes almost 900 contracts over thirty-five years.

The remainder of this article, and its statistical analysis, is based on the notion of 'women alone'. This means women who were independent from the legal and economic point of view, with no need for a tutor to operate before a notary. The

[18] See for example, Dehouve, 'La réglamentation du crédit'.

[19] Rey Castelao, *Aproximación a la historia rural*, pp. 149–53.

[20] AHUS, *Fondo Contaduría de Hipotecas* (FCH), books 206–222, years 1768 to 1846.

[21] Greenow, *Credit and Socioeconomic Change*. For the Galician case see Cebreiro Ares, 'El Registro de Hipotecas'.

term 'women alone' was developed by British and French historians in the 1980s. In this study the category of 'women alone' was found to be mostly single women over twenty-five years old and widows, but also the wives of migrants, and women acting as legal guardians for their sons and daughters.[22]

Throughout the period of study, men were the creditors in 80 to 90 per cent of cases. Percentages below 80 were seen only in the second and third five-year term (1775–1784). Moreover, as the nineteenth-century approached, there is evidence of an increasing variety in the types and combinations from the perspective of gender. Towards the end of the eighteenth century, more women were involved in credit transactions as creditors, but much far, as debtors.

For the purposes of this work only the *censos* and *obligaciones* will be considered, given the fact that between them they cover 92 per cent of the amount involved. There is also another reason that makes it possible to leave out the *ventas de renta*. The point is that at the end of the eighteenth century most of them were indeed rents transferences between *rentiers*, and not a mechanism for (new) credit.

The *Census* Market

Generally speaking, the *census* market was no place for a woman without a man, as only twenty-six cases of women alone as debtors and creditors were found throughout in the full thirty-five years of study. However, women were strongly relevant if their menfolk were to make any benefit at all in that area because of the central role of dowry as mortgageable property. Indeed, joint operations of men and women as debtors account for 37.2 per cent of the overall debt.[23] However, if the amount of credit given to institutions (415,000 *reales*) is deducted, as it should be for this study, then the figure rises to 50 per cent. By the same calculation, and leaving aside the institutional offers of *census* credit (891,243 *reales*), women alone accounted for only 8.2 per cent of the overall amount as debtors, but 14.2 per cent as creditors. However, this figure is not fully representative, since one single *census* accounts for the considerable sum of 61,000 *reales*, and proves the importance of social status in *census* markets, as will be shown. This *censo* will also be described at some length later. A significant point is that partnerships of husband and wife as *census*

[22] Wall, 'Women Alone'; Hufton, 'Women without Men'; Wall, Robin, and Laslett, eds, *Family Forms in Historic Europe*. Rial, 'Las mujeres "solas"'.

[23] They represent 70 per cent of all annuities in fifteenth-century Holland. See Zuijderduijn this volume, pp. 95–120.

creditors were rare, while they were the most frequent type of debtors. This was due to the central role of dowries as real estate goods for married women which could be offered as security for a mortgage, and the secondary public role of married women to lend as they needed the clear consent of their husbands to act regarding property or, the support of a local judge in the absence of her husband.

Table 13.2. Women's position in the *census* credit markets of the Santiago de Compostela Registers 1770–1804 (*reales de vellón*).

	DEBTORS				CREDITORS			
	Women alone		**Men and women**		**Women alone**		**Men with women**	
	no.	*Amount*	*no.*	*Amount*	*no.*	*Amount*	*no.*	*Amount*
1770–1774	4	55,400	9	27,422	0	0	0	0
1775–1779	1	3300	21	205,333	1	3300	0	0
1780–1784	1	1951	7	57,173	1	4400	0	0
1785–1789	5	13,500	25	94,569	3	15,300	1	4000
1790–1794	5	14,299	16	133,619	3	20,000	1	5000
1795–1799	1	11,000	7	37,900	1	61,000	0	0
1800–1804	0	0	6	47,150	0	0	3	21,150
Total	17	99,450 (8.2%)	91	603,166 (50%)	9	104,000 (14.2%)	5	30,150 (4.1%)

In the first period (1770–1784), although some women did have access to the *census* market as borrowers, the typical credit situation for them was found to be in patrician (nobility and upper urban groups) social positions. The second period, after 1785, shows the trouble many households encountered in managing money under the high inflation rates.

For example, on 5 January 1772, Gonzalo Fernandez Reguera, acting as proxy for Mrs Ana Josefa de Soto y Altamirano, received a *census* of 44,000 *reales* (a significant amount for the time) from Andrés Losada y Sotomaior. The said Andrés Losada y Sotomaior was in the process of setting up a prosperous *mayorazgo* for Mr Pedro de Otero Vermúdez, by investing the remittances Pedro's uncle sent him from the Philippines.[24] Mrs Ana Josefa was the widow of Mr Ramon Nicolás

[24] *Mayorazgo* allowed the nobility to make their property inalienable.

Torrado y Riazos, who held the post of *Regidor Perpetuo*, which was municipal nobility at its highest rank. She mortgaged their country home of Santa Maria de Asados, twelve town houses, and a considerable number of other properties.[25] To do all this, she needed the approval of the Royal Audience of A Coruña.[26]

Within the pattern of credit set in the elevated ranks of urban society, the most impressive in terms of quantity was the case of Juana Tomasa Valdivieso y Camaño as creditor. When she became the beneficiary of the Dean of Santiago de Compostela Cathedral, Mr Policarpo Mendoza, she then became owner of one of the largest *census*-inheritances of the century in the city. Among her many financial dealings, she agreed to credit the Spanish monarchy with 61,000 *reales*, a fabulous sum for the urban economy of Santiago. This would be repaid through revenues from the tobacco monopoly.[27]

The possibilities for women alone to become borrowers by a *census* in the rural areas seems to have been quite limited. Considering the extent to which peasant women had access to credit, no more than five cases were found. Two of them were the *census* granted to two peasant women from the area of Padrón by the shrine of *Nuestra Señora de la Merced* (Our Lady of Mercy) in Bandín. In 1772 and in 1773 Serafina de la Fuente and Michaela Chico, received 200 *reales* each from the shrine. As guarantee, Serafina mortgaged several pieces of land, while Michaela did the same with her house (the inheritance she had received from her parents), and two other plots of land.[28] Another case, which is specially pertinent since it involves women in both roles, urban creditor and rural debtor, is the case of Mrs Maria Antonia Suárez de la Peña widow of Mr Domingo Nieves, of the town of Santiago de Compostela. In 1787 she lent the modest amount of 500 *reales* to Tomasa de Ferros, spinster, from the parish of San Simón de Ons de Cacheiras. Tomasa mortgaged two pieces of land of three *ferrados*.[29]

Female Alienation from the *Census* Market and its Mechanisms

There were at least two mechanisms operating which could exclude or limit women's access to the *census* market: one concerned institutions, and the other was set in the dynamics of marriage and property. The first of these limiting mechanisms operated

25 AHUS, FCH., b.207, Mateo González de Mourentán, 5–1–1772.

26 Fernández Vega, *La Real Audiencia de Galicia*.

27 AHUS, FCH, b.213, Manuel Hacha Patiño (Coruña), 8–8-1796.

28 AHUS, FCH, b.207, *Giro*, 20–12-1772 and 24–21-1773.

29 AHUS, FCH, b.212, *Giro*, 19–18-1787, escritura Manuel Antonio Colmelo.

to bar peasant women from obtaining credit from institutions. The records of notary Mr Doldán y Aldao, from the School of Orphans of Santiago de Compostela, nicely show the intricate process of accepting a woman's offer for *census*.[30]

The most frequent procedure for peasants to get credit from urban institutions involved a mediator. He would obtain offers for *census* from those living outside the town walls who needed cash. The procedures were then always easily carried out by the mediator with the crediting institution (hospital, cathedral, religious foundation, etc.) and involved no further research on the mortgageable property by the creditor.

The only example in which a more complex process was found, involved sisters Ms Antonia and Josefa Portas. They lived in Magariños, a small country area of the parish of San Salvador de Sietecoros (30 km south of the town). First of all, like any other solicitants, they presented an inventory listing all the mortgageable properties they owned. This included a house, with a wine-cellar, a kitchen, and thirteen pieces of land, which all added up to fifteen *ferrados*, a comparatively hefty amount of property for the area. In their case, however, the Bishop of Tanes, who managed the orphanage, required that their declaration of property be officially certified, with witnesses. Therefore, the local judge of the jurisdiction of Quinta y Cordeiro — where the Portas sisters lived — was requested to intervene, and he certified the property together with witnesses. Thus, Francisco San Marco de Besa, Juan Fernández, and Silvestre Portas each provided a long and detailed assessment of each piece of land. Futhermore, Ignacio Caietano Torreiro, Pedro Figueira, and Francisco San Marco Verde were requested to do the same once again. All in all, there were six assessments for the same lot of property. The entire process took a month, from 1 December 1776 to 8 January 1777, after which the sisters did obtain 3000 *reales* from Orphanage.[31] This example shows how complicated it could be for independent peasant women to access urban institutional credit, even if they were clearly wealthy in terms of real estate.

The second mechanism relating to marriage is well known and remains operational even today. In this case, a husband and wife would borrow against a mortgage on the wife's property. If the couple wanted to relend money later on, the husband almost always did it on his own. The wife's role in credit transactions was limited to providing extra guarantees for the creditors.

[30] See for example the Mexican case: Von Wobeser, *El crédito eclesiástico en la Nueva España*.

[31] AHUS, Protocolos de Santiago, 5987, the memorial starts at fol. 3^r, the *interrogatorio*, fol. 23^r. The *ferrado* is the galician unit measure of land (for Santiago region, approx. 750 m^2).

A case like this was documented by notary Andrés Varela Vaamonde on 3 June 1779. In a first deed, retired army sergeant Mr José Blanco mortgaged his property, together with his wife, Mrs Maria Ana Gonzalez. The heavy mortgage included three houses and a considerable amount of land, as guarantee for the 7700 *reales* loaned to them by Mr Alberto Rosendo.

Not much later, the sergeant, this time on his own, loaned 2200 *reales* (from the previous amount of 7700) to a peasant called Pascual Pardiñas, from San Martín de Laraño. The practice of chained credit through *census* deeds was not uncommon; in fact, it was a practical tool to obtain a rent to help pay for the interest of the first credit. It is obvious that Mrs Maria Ana Gonzalez was not necessary for the second operation. She was jointly responsible for paying the first, and we hope, for enjoying the income from the second one.[32]

To end this section, it is safe to state that the position of peasant women in the *census* market was weak: we find few cases, for values, and with fairly onerous terms in mortgaging. Although women did theoretically have the option for credit via the *census*, in practice it could be extremely difficult to obtain, except when they were part of privileged urban spheres of society.

The *Obligations* Market

In contrast with the *census*, *obligations* were a flexible and comprehensive deed, which covered multiple economic relations. Given its official nature, the Registry only shows some of these relations — those who were voluntarily presented by the creditor, something that was generally conditioned by social status. This could be one of the explanations for the absence of women in the first ten years. Similarly, their role as creditors is also rare.

A general overview of women's position in the *obligation* markets (Table 13.3) shows some similarities but, most of all, differences with the census market (Table 13.2). Partnerships of men and women as joint creditors were even more unusual than in the census (less than 3 per cent of the cases of *census* and 1 per cent of the total amount of debt). Independent women in credit were far more frequent as signers of *obligations*, especially after 1780: as debtors, they appeared in fifteen cases of *census* against fifty cases of *obligations*. As creditors, women operated in nine cases of *census* and thirty of obligations.

On the one hand, it is clear that the role of women as debtors rose from 1785, onwards and very strongly in the first years of the nineteenth century. On the other

[32] AHUS, FCH, b. 213, Andrés Varela Vaamonde 3-6-1799, fol. 274^{v} and fol. 279.

hand, women's role as creditors clearly improved from 1780 and, in particular, from 1795–1804, dates of rising prices, commercial turbulences, and expenditure problems of the Spanish Treasury.

Table 13.3. Women's position in the *obligations* credit markets of Santiago de Compostela Registers 1770–1804 (*reales de vellón*).

	DEBTORS				CREDITORS			
	Sole women		**Men and women**		**Sole women**		**Men and women**	
	no.	**Amount**	**no.**	**Amount**	**no.**	**Amount**	**no.**	**Amount**
1770–1774	0	0	9	69,939	3	2709	0	0
1775–1779	0	0	12	162,524	1	1515	1	2000
1780–1784	3	13,081	20	85,708	4	22,644	2	2120
1785–1789	10	19,877	20	83,637	2	1900	1	2200
1790–1794	8	74,179	29	178,533	2	11,058	3	15300
1795–1799	8	32,854	31	124,813	9	102,853	0	0
1800–1804	21	46,265	44	459,353	9	27,142	1	700
Total	50 (15%)	186,256 (7.2%)	165 (49.5%)	1,164,507 (44.9%)	30 (9%)	169,821 (6.5%)	8 (3%)	22,320 (<1%)

The *obligacion* encompassed a wide range of social circumstances, especially compared to the *census*. As an example, we find the remarkable case of a woman alone as creditor who carried out two credit operations. Juana Pereiro, a neighbour of the borough of San Andrés Apóstol of Santiago de Compostela, can be considered a good early example of the woman alone in the town in the mid eighteenth century. Just like Mrs Benita Suárez Mosquera, she was able to build up considerable capital, and had to find a way to manage it. On 21 January 1774 she decided to lend the significant amount of 10,500 *reales*, for one year, to Mr Andres Gil, patron of the boat San José y Ánimas, from the seafaring village of Muros. The credit was granted with the ostensible goal of 'trading at Sea'. This operation is rare in 'the capital market' of Santiago de Compostela. It is quite unusual to find so clear an investment in sea trade. Indeed, some months later, she lent 2000 *reales* to Mr Custodio Álvarez, goldsmith of the town, which she gave in 'one hundred silver *pesos fuertes*'. This coinage is the sign of dealings with sea trade. To carry out the operation, the goldsmith even had to introduce some personal guarantee of payment.

Thus, we have silversmith Mr Alberto Rey, bookseller Mr Geronimo del Reino and smith Mr Manuel Alvarez. Mrs Juana undoubtedly wielded her power.[33]

It seems that granting credit was not unusual for Juana Pereiro. Given the fact that she was in a position to demand guarantees to her affluent customers, it seems legitimate to infer that she must have operated on a general basis in the networks of credit, the very type that is not reflected in the official source, the Registry.

Regarding women alone as debtors in urban settings, there was the case of Ms Teresa Rey. She retailed small metal tools (*quincallería*) in the main market-square of the town, the *Plaza del Campo*. In a certain notarial deed she asserted her responsibility for 1030 *reales* worth of goods taken on credit (*productos al fiado)* from the shop of Mr Diego Andrés García y Cía. To guarantee payment she mortgaged half of her house. The deed included a clause whereby 3 per cent interest would be charged if she had not repaid the entire debt within a year.

Credit, women, and textile production would indeed become a frequent triangle, both in Santiago de Compostela and in many other European cities. The *obligation* signed by Ms Maria Requeijo with prominent merchant Mr Juan Antonio García Parada is a good example of such interaction.

On 13 December 1785, Maria, a spinster over twenty-five years old, recognized a debt for 1144 *reales* which she had contracted with merchant Mr J. A. García Parada. She stated that the debt had been preceded (in April of the previous year) by:

> 120 pounds cloth of fine linen, at the price of 12 *reales* a pound, for 1344 *reales*, *was given on credit by Josefa Varela, wife to García Parada, but she (Maria) resold it to Cristina Antonia de Santa María* (...) For her good name she (Maria) was paying 200 *reales* now and acknowledging a 1144 debt (my italics).

The deed meant that she 'had to' mortgage her house in the neighbourhood of Basquiños and repay at the rate of 200 *reales* a year.[34]

It also appeared that some lenders even specialized in loans to widows, as a specific line of business. Such is the case of apothecary Mr Bernardo Bedoya, at the Royal Hospital, who made several credits to women at the turn of the nineteenth century. Indeed, his responsibilities as apothecary would put him in frequent business contact with women, since women were the daily providers of food,

[33] AHUS, Protocolos Santiago, 5792, Ramón Romero Pimentel y Leis, 1774, fol. 8^{r} and fol. 48^{r}–49^{r}.

[34] AHUS, FCH, 13-12-1785, ante Domingo Antonio Rodríguez, fol. 44^{v}.

groceries, wine, or other necessary services for the hospital. Such connections could easily have evolved into borrowing or lending.

Businesswomen, or *comerciantas*, also took on a conspicuous role in credit transactions. More often than not they were widows of merchants who continued with the business affairs of their late husbands with the support of their servants and aides. However, in some cases, they became noticeable promoters on their own account. Such were the cases of Mrs María García de la Mata, widow of merchant Mr Antonio Freire, Mrs Josefa López de Azevedo, widow of Mr Antonio and Mrs María García, widow of Mr Gregorio de Robles.

Focussing on the case of Maria Garcia de la Mata, who was one of most prominent creditors of the 1790s, she not only gave credit to her clients, but also to lawyers, like Mr Manuel Pérez Lapido, who owed her 5036 *reales*.[35] There are several reasons to highlight the credit she signed on 12 August 1796 in favour of Mr Juan Antonio Lorenzo, dweller in the village of A Garda, on the border with Portugal and 130 km south of Santiago de Compostela. The amount was truly grand, 52,500 *reales*, that was delivered in 'good coins of gold and silver' at a 6 per cent interest rate. As far as we know, investments of capital from Santiago in other cities were unusual and Mrs Maria requested that the deed of obligation include a clause whereby Mr Juan Antonio should repay in 'good gold and silver coins, the same as those he received, because she needed these coins for her monthly remittance (she) sent to Madrid'. This meant that Maria García de la Mata was connected to the bullion market of the court which collected gold and silver coins from the provinces.[36]

As other studies have pointed out, it was not unusual for the women servants of a household to lend cash to their masters. As an example, we have the case of Ms Maria Vicenta de la Iglesia in 1788. When she moved her service from the household of Miguel de Yllobre and Maria Antonia de la Torre to that of Mr Domingo Vieites, she requested that her previous masters formalize the loans she had given them, which added up to 900 *reales*.[37]

Within the town walls women as creditors were to be found in the merchant and trading businesses, but also from the aristocracy, equally capable of lending considerable amounts. One example is Ms Rosa Elme who in 1803 lent 10,700 *reales* to merchant Marcos Gacio.[38] At the same time we also find women as

[35] AHUS, FCH, b. 213, 8–7-1796, Florencio de Barcia.

[36] AHUS, FCH, b. 213, 12-8-1796, Francisco Antonio Pedrero de Barros.

[37] AHUS, FCH, 24-4-1788, Domingo Antonio Varela.

[38] AHUS, FCH, 20-1-1803, Giro, Francisco Xavier Gándara, fol. 1^r.

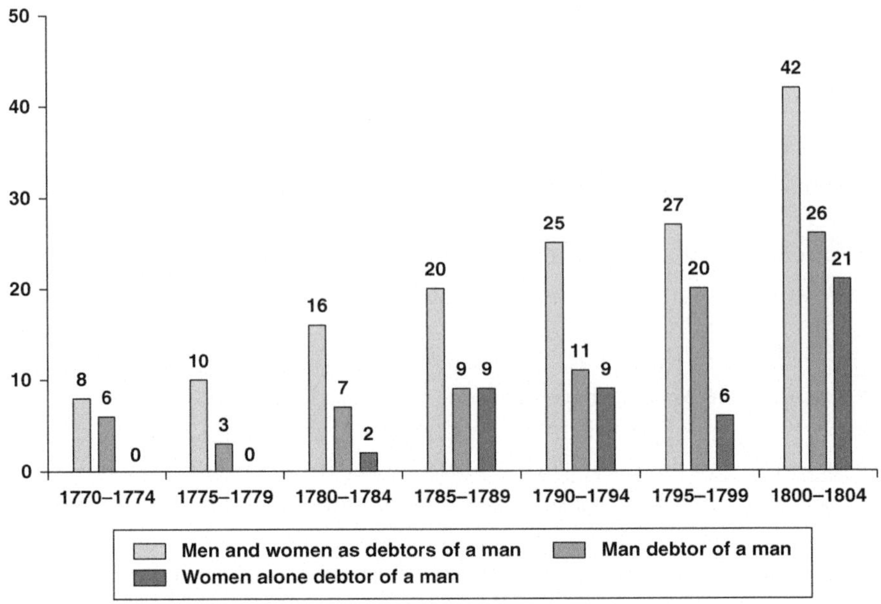

Figure 13.1. Most frequent gender positions in *obligations* markets (number of cases).

creditors for minor sums, such as the 850 *reales* that Ms Bernarda Moreda gave to Mr Bartolomé Sánchez and his wife Mrs Juana de la Torre in 1804.[39]

Returning to a general perspective, Figure 13.1 shows that this area of economics was dominated by men, but also subject to certain changes over time, with two noteworthy features:

i. The most frequent type of debtor was that composed of individuals of both sexes, where married couples represented the great majority. However, there were also widows with their offspring, and parents-in-law with their daughters-in-law, acting as joint-partners, which highlights the importance of dowry as mortgageable property.
ii. From 1780 onwards, women alone (single, married, or widowed) took on a prominent role as individual debtors, particularly in rural areas. This upsurge could be the result of the strong inflationary forces at the end of the eighteenth century, coupled with the response of creditors who endeavoured to continue providing goods to rural areas in a generalized context of poverty. Geography is a relevant aspect in this process, given that the Registry shows

[39] AHUS, FCH, 8-2-1804, Giro, José Antonio Mallo, fol. 2[v].

an increase in credit connected to the rural and provincial districts outside the town, where female work was closely linked to linen yarning.

To illustrate this phenomenon, three *obligations* have been found, signed in March 1802 by three women from the parishes of Santa Eulalia de Oza and San Julian de Sales (5.5 and 9 kms south of Santiago de Compostela). The three deeds were signed by three single women, all over twenty-five years of age, in benefit of merchant Mr Miguel Seco from Pontecesures, a village close to Santiago and Padrón, on the other side of the river Ulla. These women signed and accepted a debt of Baltic linen, taken on credit from the merchant's shop.[40]

They are relevant inasmuch as they portray a common social pattern from the region of the Ulla, while giving an insight into the networks of female solidarity working in the context of credit. The most complex of the three were signed by Maria, Vicenta, and Francisca de Castro, three sisters from Laraño. They formally recognized a linen debt for 1614 *reales* and sixteen *maravedíes*. The sum included 243 *reales* and twenty-five maravedíes for an *arroba* of linen that the sisters had lent to Simón Rodriguez, a neighbour of San Andres de Yllobre. It also included 115 *reales* and 17 *maravedíes*, from a linen debt of Ms Maria Antonia Cao, spinster from San Julian de Sales, and for whom the sisters guaranteed payment. The full amount was quite substantial for peasantry. They had to mortgage their large house with two floors, kitchen, wine cellar, stables, orchard, plus a sizeable rural property: four and a half *ferrados*, forty *cuartillos* of cropland and six *ferrados* of *toxal* (gorse-land).

This case shows how inheritance, migration, and property concurred with the newly established trade in Baltic linen, geared around the Atlantic. Interconnected through credit, single women, wives of émigrés, neighbours, and sisters helped each other to take the floor in financial business chains, sometimes even placing themselves above the ever-dominant male. In rural areas, women as creditors were certainly less numerous — at least as far as the official or notarial channels of credit are concerned.

Conclusion

From the analysis of the quantitative data in this study, it seems that registered female mortgage credit activity was clearly lower in proportion than the presence of women in the population. However, the specific case studies show that women in

40 AHUS, FCH, b. 214, Giro, Andrés Constela, 10, 12 and 18, 3-1802.

Galicia were in fact participating fully in the monetary economy at the end of the Old Regime. This apparently contradictory situation raises two questions:

The first is how to consider the role of independent women in credit: they represented 5 to 14 per cent of respectively creditors and borrowers, and 60 per cent of the borrowers, if we were to count joint men and women's operations. These figures present a strong contrast with commonplace daily credit in rural areas. In this case, women's presence was far stronger, since 20 to 40 per cent of the customers buying on credit were women, operating individually.

The second is what are the driving forces behind the rising pattern in women's participation in the notarial credit market as debtor, mainly in *obligaciones*, the credit type that is the least formally regulated of the three (Figure 13.1).

To answer the first question two main variables need to be taken into consideration: the structural elements of the economy outlined in section 1, and the level of visibility (publicity) of the credit transactions. In this article, it has been shown that the structures which allowed independent women to access money (inheritance, domestic service salaries, linen manufacturing, monetization of dowries, and migrant remittances) should be related — when we shift to credit analysis — to the level of publicity involved in the act of (registered/documental) credit. Indeed, independent women's participation in credit appears to be spread out — in its different stages — as follows: mortgage registry accounts for 5 to 15 per cent; notarial credit is estimated to be 20 to 25 percent; and 30 to 40 per cent of the cases come from oral credit and the private books of shops.

Another conclusion which can be drawn from this first question is that the role played by 'women alone' must have been considerably larger than previously thought, especially in those areas that are most difficult for historians to penetrate. From an urban point of view, it is necessary to write the history of the prominent noblewomen and women merchants who play a crucial role in Compostelan urban community. From a rural point of view, the combination of male migration and *mellora* inheritance regimen or, in other words, the *mellora* as a social response of strong male migration rates, put the women of the Compostelan region in a new and unusual position. They had money remittances to deal with and the necessity of gaining access to the land and credit markets. But if it was a positive effect in the middle of the century and early 1770s, it became a troubled position in 1780–1790 when inflationary pressures lowered the purchasing power of money and those women with smaller household were sunk in debt chains. The metaphor of the iceberg seems relevant, to explain the visible part of notarial credit as the necessary, sometimes heroic, often tragic, condition of the women as a whole.

Regarding the second question, the hypothesis is supported that women in credit became crucial in the context of the end of the eighteenth-century

European crisis, and the necessary restructuring of circuits of capital accumulation. This materialized through a *double movement*: first, the property of wives, daughters and mothers acquired more significance, as a result of inflationary pressure, which hardened mortgage conditions. Secondly, the elites were more inclined to interact with women as suitable and new partners, even in the hitherto exclusive field of the public register — indeed, it was necessary to rebuild the economic structures which had been dissembled by first, the Atlantic Wars (since 1780) and secondly, the problems of Spanish Treasury (1790–1808).

Finally, the results are indeed far from suggesting a positive linear approach to presenting pre-modern credit markets as an early arena for women's empowerment. Even taking the more exceptional cases into consideration, it has been shown that in general, women acted in conjunction with their fathers, fathers in-law, sons, uncles or grandsons. In other cases, they were fallen women, with illegitimate offspring and clearly disadvantaged in credit chains where property, wealth and status were the main keys to success. If women became more relevant in credit markets at the end of the Old Regime it was due to inflationary forces and the legal rights they had regarding property.

Works Cited

Archival Sources

Archivo Histórico Universitario de Santiago de Compostela (AHUS)
Municipal Records
Pleitos, Documentos antiguos
Mortgage Register Records
Fondo Contaduría de Hipotecas (FCH), books 206 to 214
Hospital Real
Sección Escrituras nº63, Prego de Parga 1777–1783
Notarial Records
Procolos de Santiago 5.792, 5.987
Protocolos de Padrón, Francisco Antonio Baltar, 1792

Secondary Studies

Blanc, Jérôme, 'La complexité monétaire en France sous l'Ancien régime: étendue et modes de gestion', *De Pecunia*, VI.3 (1994), 81–111

Burgo López, María Concepción, 'Niveles sociales y relaciones matrimoniales en Santiago y su comarca (1640–1750) : A través de las escrituras de dote', in *La Documentación notarial y la Historia: Actas del II Coloquio de Metodología Histórica Aplicada*, ed. by

Antonio Eiras Roel (Santiago de Compostela: Universidad de Santiago de Compostela, 1984), pp. 177–200

Carmona Badía, Xoán, *El atraso industrial de Galicia: auge y liquidación de las manufacturas textiles (1750–1900)* (Barcelona: Ariel, 1992)

Cebreiro Ares, Francisco, 'Las contabilidades nobiliares como fuente para la historia monetaria: La documentación de la casa de Amarante en el siglo XVIII', in *Escritura y scoiedad: la nobleza*, ed. by, A Suárez González (Santiago de Compostela: Universidade de Santiago de Compostela, 2017, pp. 173–88.

———, 'El Registro de Hipotecas y sus posibilidades para la historia urbana', in *Familia, cultura material y formas de poder en la España moderna. III Encuentro de jóvenes investigadores en Historia Moderna*, ed. by Máximo García Fernández (Madrid: Fundación Española de Historia Moderna, 2016), pp. 613–25

Dehouve, Danièle, 'La réglementation du crédit: quelques définitions', in *Prêter et Emprunter: Pratiques de crédit au Mexique*, ed. by Marie-Noëlle Chamoux(Paris: Maison des Sciences de l'homme, 1993), pp. 3–8.

Dermineur, Elise, 'Single Women and the Rural Credit Market in Eighteenth-Century France', *Journal of Social History*, 48.1 (2014), 175–99

Dubert, Isidro, *Los comportamientos de la familia urbana en la Galicia del Antiguo Régimen: El ejemplo de Santiago de Compostela en el siglo XVIII* (Santiago de Compostela: Universidad de Santiago de Compostela, 1987)

Eiras Roel, Antonio, 'Mecanismos autoreguladores, evolución demográfica y diversificación intrarregional: El ejemplo de la población de Galicia a finales del siglo XVIII', *Revista de Demografía Histórica*, 8.2 (1990), 51–72

———, *La población de Galicia, 1700–1860: crecimiento, distribución y estructura de la población de Galicia* (La Coruña: Fundación Caixa Galicia, 1996)

Fernández Cortizo, Camilo, 'Matrimonio y régimen dotal en la Galicia de transición al interior en el siglo XVIII', in *Tomar Estado: Dotes e Casamentos (séculos XVI–XIX)*, ed. by M. Lobo de Araújo and A. Esteves (Braga: CITCEM, 2009), pp. 33–55

Fernández Vega, Laura, *La Real Audiencia de Galicia, órgano de gobierno en el Antiguo Régimen: (1480–1808)* (A Coruña: Diputación Provincial A Coruña, 1982)

Ferreiro Porto, José, 'Fuentes para el estudio de las formas del crédito popular en el Antiguo Régimen: obligaciones-préstamo, ventas de renta y ventas de censos', *Las fuentes y los métodos. 15 trabajos de historia cuantitativa serial de Galicia*, ed. by Antonio Eiras Roel (Santiago de Compostela: Universidad de Santiago de Compostela, 1977), pp. 289–306

Fontaine, Laurence, *The Moral Economy: Poverty, Credit, and Trust in Early Modern Europe* (New York: Cambridge University Press, 2014)

Fontaine, Laurence, and others, *Des Personnes aux Institutions: Réseaux et culture du crédit du XVIe au XXe siècle en Europe* (Louvaine-la-Neuve: Academia Bruylant, 1997)

Greenow, Linda, *Credit and Socioeconomic Change in Colonial Mexico: Loans and Mortgages in Gudalajara, 1720–1820* (Colorado: Bouler, 1983)

Hufton, Olwen, 'Women without Men: Widows and Spinsters in Britain and France in the Eighteenth Century', *Journal of Family History*, 9 (1984), 355–76

Jordan, William C., *Women and Credit in Pre-Industrial and Developing Societies* (Philadelphia: University of Pennsylvania Press, 1993)

Lemire, Beverly, *The Business of Everyday Life: Gender, Practice and Social Politics in England, c. 1600–1900* (Manchester: Manchester University Press, 2012)

Lemire, Beverly, Ruth Pearson, and Gail Grace Campbell, eds, *Women and Credit: Researching the Past, Refiguring the Future* (New York: Berg, 2001)

Pascua Sánchez, María José de la, 'Los Gallegos en el Cádiz de la carrera de Indias: Balance Secular de un proceso migratorio (1682–1778)', in *1st European Conference of the International Comission on Historical Demography*, ed. by Antonio Eiras Roel and Ofelia Rey Castelao (Santiago de Compostela: Universidad de Santiago de Compostela, 1993), pp. 845–57

Poska, Allyson M., *Women and Authority in Early Modern Spain: The Peasants of Galicia* (Oxford: Oxford University Press, 2005)

Rey Castelao, Ofelia, *Aproximación a la historia rural en la comarca de la Ulla (siglos XVII y XVIII)* (Santiago de Compostela: Universidad de Santiago de Compostela, 1981)

———, Movimientos migratorios en Galicia, siglos XVI–XIX' in *1st European Conference of the International Comission on Historical Demography*, ed. by Antonio Eiras Roel and Ofelia Rey Castelao (Santiago de Compostela: Universidad de Santiago de Compostela, 1993), pp. 85–130

Rey Castelao, Ofelia, and Serrana M. Rial García, *Historia das mulleres en Galicia: Idade Moderna* (Santiago de Compostela: Nigra Trea, 2010)

Rial García, Serrana M., *Las Mujeres en la economía urbana del Antiguo Régimen: Santiago durante el siglo XVIII*, Sada (A Coruña: Ediciós do Castro, D.L., 1995)

———, 'Las mujeres "solas" en la sociedad semi-urbana gallega del siglo XVIII', *Obradoiro de Historia Moderna*, 8 (1999), 169–97

———, 'Mujer y actividad económica en la Galicia Moderna: La inserción de las mujeres en la producción económica rural y urbana' (Doctoral thesis, University of Santiago de Compostela, 2002)

Saavedra Fernández, Pegerto, 'Mecanismos informáis de crédito na Galicia Rural a fins do Antigo Réxime', in *Entre nós: estudios de arte, xeografía e historia en homenaxe ó profesor Xosé Manuel Antelo*, ed. by Xesús Balboa López and others (Santiago de Compostela: Universidad de Santiago de Compostela, 2001), pp. 439–56

Sobrado Correa, Hortensio, 'El sistema dotal en tierras de mejora en la Galicia del Antiguo Régimen', in *Tomar Estado: Dotes e Casamentos (séculos* XVI–XIX*)*, ed. by M. Lobo de Araújo and A. Esteves (Braga: CITCEM, 2010), pp. 11–31

Von Wobeser, Gisela, *El crédito eclesiástico en la Nueva España: Siglo XVIII* (Fondo de Cultura Económica: México, 2010)

Wall, Richard, 'Women Alone in English Society', *Annales de Démographie Historique*, 1 (1981), 303–17

Wall, Richard, Jean Robin, and Peter Laslett, eds, *Family Forms in Historic Europe* (Cambridge: Cambridge University Press, 1983)

Concluding Remarks

Laurence Fontaine

Historians have shown long ago that in early modern Europe, credit was evident throughout society. It existed in the most elementary economic exchanges. It could be found in the widest commercial enterprises, in the smallest trades as well as in the most minuscule loans. It weighed upon the peasantry and their land. It circulated at the King's court. It was useful in sustaining the early modern State. Credit was ubiquitous. But few scholars have wondered if men and women used credit in the same fashion.

As this book is far too rich to draw together all the threads that go from article to article, I will content myself with underlining the most important questions this book tackles, with special reference to the change it prompts in our way of thinking about the history of gender, but also regarding more general areas of research. I will highlight what the book says about the relationship between law and practice, about the way people have tried to deal with an uncertain future, the booming informal economy that came with it, about the construction of trust, and about the relation between emotions and economic practices. I shall conclude with an

Laurence Fontaine is a director of research at the Centre National de la Recherche Scientifique (CNRS) and at the Ecole des Hautes Etudes en Sciences Sociales (EHESS) in Paris. She was Professor at the History and Civilisation department at the European University Institute (Florence-Italy) from 1995 to 2003. She has published numerous articles and books. Among her most important contributions: *History of Pedlars in Europe*, 1996; with Jürgen Schlumbohm, *Household Strategies for Survival, 1600–2000: Fission, Faction and Cooperation*; *Alternative Exchanges: Second-Hand Circulations from the Sixteenth Century to The Present*, 2008, and *The Moral Economy*, 2014. She has worked on migrations, mountain societies, poverty, and on the economic, social, and cultural dimensions of credit. Her most recent book is *Le Marché. Histoire et Usages d'une Conquête Sociale*, 2014.

Women and Credit in Pre-Industrial Europe, ed. by Elise M. Dermineur, EER 12 (Turnhout: Brepols, 2018), pp. 345–360.
BREPOLS PUBLISHERS DOI 10.1484/M.EER-EB.5.115760

issue of particular current importance: have changes in inheritance patterns in the seventeenth century resulted in the empowerment of women?

The Relations between Law and Practice

Before tackling these issues, it should be stressed that one cannot speak of women in general. Even if all women can experience the same life cycle, one needs constantly to differentiate women of the aristocracy and the 'middling sort' (to use the term for the bourgeoisie coined by Margaret Hunt) from working class women. The former could count on properties and a comfortable social standing status — they did not work. The latter, in contrast, had no other assets than objects and, like their masculine counterparts, had to work with their hands.

The subordination of women was grounded both in the different patterns of inheritance and in the laws restricting their capacity of action according to their life cycle. Spinsters and widows were everywhere freer than married women. This book offers the reassessment that, if the juridical domination over married women was a reality everywhere in Europe, the laws of inheritance were more or less favourable to them. Roman law recognized the juridical personality of a woman, contrary to English law which placed her under the *coverture* of her husband.

In addition to this diversity, two other dynamics were at work when considering the capacity of women to manage their wealth.

Migration was one of these dynamics. In Galicia, as Francisco Cebreiro Ares shows in this volume, the high rate of male migration led to a new inheritance regime that gave a larger share of the inheritance-goods to a single daughter — or a son — who remained in the parental home, and who in turn took care of the parents and the property. There, just as in any other society of male migration, mothers and wives managed the monetary remittances, acquired land, and granted credit while the men were working abroad. The marketplace constituted another dynamic, primarily in urban areas. Since the Middle Ages, the development of trading had always been accompanied by an expansion of women's legal autonomy, which was visible in Flanders, the Low Countries, France,[1] Sweden,[2] and German speaking regions.[3] In England, customary courts adapted the handling of women's commercial action, circumventing the law of coverture.[4]

[1] Fontaine, *The Moral Economy*, pp. 138–44.

[2] Maria Ågren, in this volume.

[3] Eve Rosenhaft, in this volume.

[4] Teresa Phipps, in this volume.

Besides these dynamics, the book shows that the capacity of women's actions was not so clear cut as the study of law would suggest. The book underlines the difference between law and practice as well as the great diversity of practices. Looking at the late Middle Ages, Richard Goddard has found evidence of married women who used the high-value credit transactions enrolled in staple court, despite the fact that it was rare for women, other than widows, to transact staple debts by themselves. In town courts, the ability of married woman to access justice was in fact determined by a local interpretation of *coverture*. At the end of the Middle Ages, some town courts permitted married couples to enforce credit arrangements made either by the wife or by both spouses in a joint manner. These pleas suggested that wives played a significant role throughout the litigation process. However, as Teresa Phipps reminds us with the example of Chester, nothing was guaranteed forever. In Chester, couples disappeared from the court records in the commercial pleas in the later period, thus suggesting a shift toward a stricter respect of *coverture*.

These shifting borders between law and practice therefore raise questions about the nature of women's inclusion in the credit economy. How did women experience the contradictions between their reduced capacity of action and the necessity to enter financial markets as their wealth was more and more in the form of money? This trend can be observed in most parts of Europe throughout the seventeenth century. It took three forms. First, there was a growing tendency for fathers to leave money to their daughters, rather than moveable goods. Then, daughters became more and more able to access their capital before marriage. Fathers with available capital would also give part of it to their daughters during their lifetime. Finally, as the aristocrats and the middling sort were not supposed to work, they needed to invest in the financial market to protect their capital, raise income, and provide for their old age, if necessary, after the death of their husband.[5] The book brings two different kinds of answer to the crucial question raised above: an institutional one and an emotional one.

The institutional answer tackles the question of women's use of credit instruments according to their social status. As creditors, elite women tended to use more and more institutionalized credit instruments. This secured their returns even if it was to be at a lower rate than more risky operations would have brought to them. In the Italian mercantile cities, James E. Shaw shows, women would invest in business ventures until less risky credit instruments became available, such as *censi* contracts in the fifteenth century and public debt in the early modern period. In the English

[5] See the articles in this volume by Jaco Zuijderduijn, Juliet Gayton, James E. Shaw, Judith M. Spicksley, and Francisco Cebreiro Ares.

countryside, women very much favoured the copyhold tenure. It was referred to as a 'customary tenure' because the landholders were tenants of the lord of the manor, and their rights to hold their property were 'according to the custom of the manor'. Juliet Gayton shows that a married woman could become a copyholder jointly with her husband. These copyholder mortgages were particularly attractive as the manor court carefully recorded the agreements without fee for legal services. These courts could deal with default without asking for further expenses. They were, at least until the foundation of the Bank of England, an institution very much used by women of the middling sort. The pattern of formal lending with the requirement of mortgage expanded from the sixteenth century in Italy,[6] the seventeenth century in England,[7] and is clearly visible in eighteenth-century Alsace where many unmarried women took the precaution to register their transactions before the notary, asking a piece of land to be mortgaged even for loans to family members.[8]

This quest for security means that *everywhere, women tended to give credit to people they knew* whether within kinship relations or within their community.[9] This trend was recurrent, as Elise M. Dermineur shows, among servants in the villages of Alsace in the eighteenth century.

Protecting Oneself Against Life's Uncertainties

Every individual and family had to protect themselves against life's uncertainties, sickness, and old age, moments where they would not be able to rely on work to make a living. This book provides a better understanding of the specific strategies women resorted to in order to face hard times. The first variation was social. Aristocratic and bourgeois women did not invest their money in the same places as women from the lower orders. The wealthiest tended to invest in official institutions that gave a small but secure return. In order to be sure of getting an income, widows and single women were accustomed to invest their money in annuities arranged with institutions such as hospitals, pious associations, churches, guilds, and so forth. In Italy, as in France, widows invested their money in convents in exchange for a life annuity.[10]

[6] James E. Shaw, in this volume.

[7] Judith Spicksley, in this volume.

[8] Elise M. Dermineur, in this volume.

[9] Articles by Juliet Gayton, Judith M. Spicksley, Elise M. Dermineur.

[10] James E. Shaw, in this volume, and also Beauvalais-Boutouyrie, *Être veuve sous l'Ancien Régime*, pp. 305–06.

In the Netherlands, as early as the fifteenth century, women from the elite, the clergy and the urban middling groups were prominent investors in life annuities. But they also showed a preference for joint and survivor annuities which were less profitable but may have provided them with a secure income in old age, or to support a child in the event the older annuitant passed away. Jaco Zuijderduijn shows that these women used life annuities as an insurance.

Comparing the late eighteenth-century creditors of the hospitals and the *Mont de Piété* of Marseille, it is clear that women invested far more in the pawnshop than in the hospitals. A social division was at work here. Widows of merchants or nobles invested predominantly in hospitals, as their husbands had done before them, whereas the pawnshop received deposits of money from the wives of sailors and day labourers, and from the wives and partners of small traders and workers.[11] In Beauvais, at the end of the seventeenth and the beginning of the eighteenth century, widows and unmarried daughters from the bourgeoisie invested in commercial ventures as annuitants because there was no risk involved. Just like officers and bourgeois, they put their available funds in the business of a merchant who instilled trust. These women were satisfied with a fixed interest, often fairly low. They did not ask for a share of the profits.[12]

Studies on England confirm this social distinction among women making financial investments. After 1680, the number of aristocrat and bourgeois *rentières* who lived comfortably off money invested in government loans did increase. On the whole, though, the source of widows' income was not specific.[13] We should not forget that, in order to protect women's standard of living, the law required families to employ professionals in order to manage women's inheritance. In addition, a husband had to leave his wife the necessary means to live in a manner consistent with the woman's social status.[14]

In Italy, since the Middle Ages, married women as well as widows invested small sums in the hospital of their cities to obtain residency rights as well as a modest pension to support them for the rest of their lives.[15] In Florence, people favoured investing their wives' dowries in pawnshops. From 1574 onwards, pawnshops kept two kinds of books: one for ordinary deposits, *depositi libri*, which could be withdrawn at any time, and another for deposits subject to restrictions, *depositi*

[11] Coudurie, *La Dette des collectivités publiques de Marseille*, pp. 239, 248.

[12] See for instance Goubert, *Beauvais et le Beauvaisis*, p. 314.

[13] Holderness, 'Widows in Pre-Industrial Society', pp. 423–42.

[14] Joüon des Longrais, 'Le statut de la femme en Angleterre', pp. 145–46.

[15] James E. Shaw, in this volume.

condizionati, such as dowry money.[16] This culture of savings is also found in Barcelona, as Monserrat Carbonnell-Esteller has shown. There, widows deposited small sums to be accumulated for their old age. Young unmarried women did the same to form their dowries.

An analysis of the composition of the meagre wealth left by parents who died leaving their minor children in the care of the municipality of Amsterdam in the second half of the eighteenth century substantiates the fact that men and women did not share the same monetary circuits and that working-class women depended mainly on the informal sector. In this case we are dealing with the middle and lower classes of the crafts industry and trade. It shows that widows possessed more gold, coins, and jewels than any other groups.[17] Admittedly, these assets were traditional forms of monetary investment, but they stood in contrast with the changes observed in the eighteenth century when people invested increasingly in financial instruments proposed by large companies and by the State.[18] Widows did not follow these changes and preferred, when they could, to have coins in hand. Conversely, married women owned annuities rather than cash.[19] If we study their debt, we find that not only did women not borrow as much as the others from shopkeepers and craftsmen, but that they also made much less use of the more official credit markets. On the other hand, they were used to pawnshops and to pawning cheaper objects.

The example of Amsterdam highlights again the heterogeneity of widows. While some widows were rich and used the help of professionals in their financial dealings, others were among the most vulnerable to poverty. Between the two, one could find widows who owned a few assets, the fruit of their labour or inheritance, and who invested heavily in neighbourhood loans and pawnshops. These widows had experience with these forms of credit, especially when they found themselves in need. Furthermore, information was readily available to them. This explains why, in less well-off milieus, widows and single women (and many servants among them) played a central role in loans within communities — to relatives, neighbours, and other villagers.[20]

To conclude, only a few working-class women resorted to institutions. They tended to convert their earnings into objects, with a dual purpose: (1) to avoid

[16] Carol Bresnahan Menning, 'Loans and Favors', pp. 503–06.

[17] McCants, 'Petty Debts and Family Networks'.

[18] Wijsenbeek-Olthuis, *Achter de Gevels von Delft*, pp. 306–07, 341.

[19] McCants, 'Petty Debts'.

[20] Judith M. Spicksley and Elise M. Dermineur, in this volume.

having to lend their money to their kin in search for money, and (2) to be able to pawn or sell these items if needed.[21] Only when inexpensive ways of securing their credit existed would they register the debts that were owed to them.[22] The insecurity regarding the capacity of the borrowers to pay back their debts, coupled with the lack of properties to mortgage in order to secure the transaction, and the role of objects in the wealth of the working class, explain why pawn broking was exceedingly common in premodern Europe. Pawn broking was indeed the credit instrument of poor economies because, in reality, pawn broking was a sale, not a loan. It was a buy-back contract. An individual in need of money sold a good for a sum lower than its value and was given time to buy it back, having to pay both principal and interest at the time of repurchase. The duration of the transaction was calculated according to the value of the security. But in general, the duration was short: one to six months. This suited the agents of poor economies perfectly. Such loans, it goes without saying, did not involve expensive legal procedures (registration fee, notary fee, mortgages, etc.). It placed the risk upon the creditor, who might not give the object back, and not on the lender as was the case in institutionalized credit transactions.

Women in the Informal Financial Economy

Pawn broking gave rise to an informal economy in which linen, clothes, and small jewellery were sold and resold. The second-hand clothes market was undoubtedly one of the largest markets in premodern Europe.[23] It is difficult to bring to light and study these circuits as we lack the documentation to do so. This informal economy, unless it turned into crime, almost never entered any written record. Written accounts, pamphlets, and criminal records are the only sources shedding light on the underground world of financial circulations. And this is why, thanks to the detailed analysis of urban informal petty credit in Venice by James E. Shaw and in seventeenth-century Swedish cities by Maria Ågren, one can generalize about research on Paris.[24]

These studies show that these women worked in collaboration with other lenders, regardless of the size and the scope of their business. Women took on

[21] Fontaine, *The Moral Economy*, pp. 180–81.

[22] Juliet Gayton, in this volume.

[23] Fontaine, *Alternative Exchanges*.

[24] Fontaine, *The Moral Economy*, pp. 104–11.

responsibility for a loan and paid it back. They represented one of the links in the business of finance and of resale, which was a driving force in the urban economy, whereby money, goods, clothes, and other objects changed hands in a long chain of intermediaries. These women knew whom to approach in order to borrow money or to sell second-hand goods. Shopkeepers came to them when one of their female customers needed money. It was not unusual for three or four intermediaries to be involved in one transaction. More generally, in this scheme of petty credit, women would provide information about possible lenders and borrowers, act as intermediaries, and sometimes even stand as surety. Another notable feature was that, apart from some women who managed to deal with the aristocracy in need of money to pay back their gambling debts, most female brokers dealt with the poorest.[25] They were so ubiquitous that their activity bore a name: in Sweden the female intermediaries were called pawn-women;[26] in Paris, 'revendeuse à la toilette' when they dealt with the aristocracy, 'courtières' and 'prêteuses sur gage' when they worked with ordinary people;[27] in Italy, 'montiste' was the name given to those who advanced money to clients and pawned items on their behalf.[28]

Entering this petty financial market was part of the economic strategies of the working class to make ends meet. Some categories of artisans became very well known for their supplemental role as pawn brokers — jewellers, second hand clothes dealers, and alehouse keepers for instance.[29] This latter specialization was already visible in the fourteenth century when Joan Brailsford from Nottingham brought a suit in 1394–1395 against Richard Brasse in order to recover 3s. 11d. from a loan made to him, as well as a debt of 71/2d. for ale.[30] Whenever it was documented, one can discover that the moneylenders used to arrange loans were primarily women, like the loan in England obtained by the haberdasher and moneylender John Pope[31] or in Paris with the jeweller Aubourg.[32] In Italian cities, Jewish women were frequently involved in small-scale moneylending, operating in partnership with their husbands or under their own name when they became widows. Christian women also acted as brokers to connect clients throughout the

[25] Fontaine, *The Moral Economy*, pp. 95–127.

[26] Maria Ågren, in this volume.

[27] Fontaine, *The Moral Economy*, pp. 104–06.

[28] James E. Shaw, in this volume.

[29] Tebbutt, *Making Ends Meet*, pp. 112–13.

[30] Teresa Phipps, in this volume.

[31] Beverly Lemire, 'Petty Pawns'.

[32] Fontaine, *The Moral Economy*, pp. 115–17.

city's parishes.[33] Another common feature lay in the fact that everywhere elite men and women invested their money in pawnbroking via well-established usurers who in turn could rent out the goods that they received in deposit.

The first pawnshops were created in Italy as early as the fifteenth century. They multiplied in Italy and in Spain in the fifteenth and sixteenth centuries. They became widespread from the seventeenth century onward in other countries, except in England which had to wait until the nineteenth century, the country favouring private initiative instead. The situation in France was more ambiguous. On the one hand, the early creation of pawnshops can be seen in Paris, where the resort to such institutions became well established. But on the other hand, these pawnshops had difficulty settling elsewhere.[34] In general, however, these institutions had an immediate success everywhere among the population and especially among women, as in Barcelona and France.[35] In Northern Europe, as banks started to proliferate, the Bank of Sweden, established in 1668, decided to implement a policy to lend money against pawn 'to poor people who need money'.[36]

What Does This Research Say about the Construction of Trust?

The degree of trust given to the debtor can be seen in the history of debt from oral to written agreements, from informal to institutionalized transactions. The more institutionalized the debt was, the more the lack of trust.[37] Considering gendered patterns in credit transactions, one can note that a greater number of women were asked to register their debt by official means. This is what happened to Eva König, the widow of a well-known merchant. The Jewish moneylender Popert had agreed to write off 40 per cent of her debt. He had to wait for the remaining payment on condition she could find a guarantor. This attitude upset her a great deal. She perceived this as a form of discrimination; 'the Jew has to be punished for his lack of trust', she wrote.[38] Though she acknowledged that he had always been generous to her, this sign of mistrust did hurt her. But asking more guarantees from women was a standard process. The study of debt in the high Dauphiné in France reveals

[33] James E. Shaw, in this volume.

[34] Fontaine, *The Moral Economy*, pp. 156–82.

[35] See Carbonell-Esteller, this volume, and Ferrières, *Le Bien des pauvres*.

[36] Maria Ågren, in this volume.

[37] Fontaine, *The Moral Economy*, pp. 49–51.

[38] Eve Rosenhaft, in this volume.

that among merchants, oral and private arrangements were dominant as a sign of trust. This was why Eva König expected the same attitude towards her as towards her late husband. But she had forgotten that the less powerful the debtors were, the more they were requested to have their debt registered officially and/or have someone else to stand surety. These requests were frequent for female borrowers in general.[39]

On the other hand, due to their reduced capacity of action, women also asked their clients to register their debt officially more frequently than men. The credit given by unmarried women of lower gentry status in the seventeenth century in Herefordshire consisted mainly on loans secured on bills, bonds, state debts and mortgages. There was also evidence of the use of named sureties.[40] It was visible in the urban courts of late medieval England in Nottingham, Chester, and Winchester, as Teresa Phipps notices in this volume. Women brought their debtors to court in order to secure repayment of debt as small as 3d. for milk.[41] An analysis of the instruments of credit is a good way to understand the signs of trust and distrust, as Francesco Cebreiro Ares shows in the context of Galicia, showing the weakness of the peasant women in the census credit market.

Emotions and Economic Practices

Another important element brought to light by the book is a consideration of the emotional consequences of women's activities in credit exchanges and relations. The various stages of one's life cycle, the transition from one status to another, involved emotional experience, which differed according to social status. It is very difficult for historians to reconstruct the inner life of women who went through these changes and had to step into the shoes of their deceased husbands, despite their juridical incapacity. Sources are simply lacking. Thanks to the letters that Eva König, the young widow of a wealthy merchant, wrote between 1770 and 1776 to the dramatist Gotthold Ephraim Lessing, Eve Rosenhaft can uncover the emotional registers that come with König's new status and the economic arrangements the widow had to deal with. The principal asset she inherited was two manufacturers set up in Vienna, one specialized in introducing new luxury textiles to the Austrian market and the other an 'English style' wallpaper factory. But the factories came with debt. The

39 Fontaine, *The Moral Economy*, pp. 49–51 and 61–65.

40 Judith M. Spicksley, in this volume.

41 Teresa Phipps and Eve Rosenhaft, in this volume.

creditors were very powerful since they had a right on the widow's own properties. König decided to move to Vienna and managed to sell both factories to pay back the creditors. In her letters, she always made a distinction between those creditors who were family members, and outsiders, expecting her relatives to accept more delay for payment. And, as Eve Rosenhaft points out, this attitude, namely mixing business and emotions, might not be typically gender-specific. Indeed, economic matters were deeply embedded in social relationships. Everyone in need of credit turned first to his or her family. If a person had no family, or if the family was unable to help, he or she turned next to friends who belonged to the same social group. The last to be approached were foreigners who, depending on the region, could be Jews, Italians, or Savoyards. These successive circles can be seen as a spectrum in which credit relationships were initially made within the various interpersonal relationships of the individual, and then gradually moved outward, ending as a relationship that was more obviously economic and impersonal.[42]

The need of a woman to find an independent adviser in order to overcome the weakness of her social and institutional position, which meant that she was considered as a less trustful manager, was gender specific. This situation, as we have seen, made Eva König angry with Popert, who asked someone to stand surety for her. It drove her to deep anxiety and anger. In order to face the stress of her situation, she finally decided to find an external adviser who was not a family member. But her range of possibility was limited because she was not connected intimately to the business milieu of the city. She even thought that choosing an adviser was comparable to gambling, because the uncertainties were so high. She chose Schubach. When it turned out that he was indeed the person she needed, kind and generous, she was overwhelmed. Confronted by these difficult and crucial matters, which affected both her and her children, the violence of Eva's changing emotions was a measure of the anxiety caused by her feelings of insecurity and weakness.

Clearly, to be a successful entrepreneur, one needed to be entirely devoted to the factory. Schubach understood that Eva, with four young children and with the prospect of remarrying Lessing, would not be able to entirely devote herself to the management of such risky enterprises. He therefore advised her to sell the factories. She agreed and added that her temper 'inclined to worry and ponder' was not appropriated to manage these factories. And, indeed, what she had to do to solve the complex debt problems exhausted her physically and morally. Through her story, one can realize the discrepancy between what was expected from a woman and a woman's limited capacity to reach these expectations.

[42] Fontaine, *The Moral Economy*, p. 26.

But emotions were also part of all economic relations. They were — and still are — behind mental accounts that we use in our daily lives to frame our spending. The fact that poor women acted, and in developing countries are still acting, as money keepers for other individuals or families, is part of this emotional economy. It prevents impulsive spending and secures money for hard times or big family events. From the late Middle Ages and in the early modern period, never-married women were important figures in day-to-day finances. But it is not so easy to shed light on this. Thanks to Judith M. Spicksley, one gets to know Sarah Fell of Swarthmoor Hall, daughter of the Quaker Margaret Fell Fox. She regularly recorded lending a few shillings to named local individuals for a short period of time. Sometimes, she also turned into a borrower herself for short periods of time. In addition to her financial activities, she also accepted small sums 'to lay by' for safekeeping, until the owners required the deposit to be returned.[43]

Given that emotions are dynamic and evolve over time, Margaret Hunt analyses how unmarried women coped with the shifting of their emotional equilibrium when, for instance, the man they loved and who had promised to marry them changed his mind. Hunt has uncovered many examples from the financially accessible Court of Exchequer of such situations. An unmarried woman in love often accepted gifts from the man she was hoping to marry. In exchange, apart from granting him sexual favours, she sewed and mended his clothes, and lent him money. But when she realized that the man was not going to marry her, she recast her gifts from the gift economy to the market economy, giving precise valuations to the labour offered to the fiancé (thus the work done freely during the engagement was no longer considered as a gift, and a bill for services was sent instead). Some women went so far as to place a price on their chastity. The reframing into the market economy of emotional contracts that were not fulfilled was the first step to restore a woman's emotional equilibrium.[44] Doing this, women recast their relations into another kind of mental account; the one they were practising with clients since the status of their lover had changed.

Has the Protection of Women's Financial Interests Led to their Empowerment?

Between the sixteenth and eighteenth centuries, women's legal incapacity became progressively more widespread and their financial interests became more protected

[43] Judith M. Spicksley, in this volume.

[44] Margaret Hunt, in this volume.

everywhere. Clients dealing with a married man, either including the wife's assets or including property that was jointly acquired during marriage, now took the precaution of asking the wife to waive her legal right to the property affected. It was one of the consequences of hypothecation, as a way of protecting a married woman's rights in case of her husband's poor management. Therefore, a married woman, despite her legal incapacity, had control over how her husband disposed of her property.[45] One can then raise with Elise Dermineur the question: have these changes led to a better empowerment of women?

Three key points should be noted. First, this new protection of the wife's lineage property was everywhere met with stiff resistance. Husbands fought to continue enjoying their wives' dowries. Creditors exerted a great deal of pressure to ensure that their loans were secured against women's dowries. The outcome was that the inalienability of a dowry was frequently contravened, for women did not always have the capacity — or the requisite knowledge — to protect it in its entirety. In practice, women frequently signed contracts alienating their property to meet the needs of their family or their husbands. As for creditors, they constantly attempted to change the new law in order to legally secure that a wife's property would serve as a guarantee for the debts of men; a demand which was met with success at the end of the nineteenth century in Germany and in Spain.[46] Earlier, in German mercantile communities like Hamburg, while it was possible in most jurisdictions for women to enter into credit relations under their own name or as co-signatories with their husband, the price was the explicit renunciation of the immunity from claims on their personal property.[47]

In Italy, the roman law tradition recognized a married woman's legal personhood. She was her husband's first creditor because of her dowry. Despite the law, reclaiming her dowry could involve bitter struggles with the husband's kin and even with the children. Frequently the husband had chosen her as guardian of their children, generally on condition that she did not reclaim her dowry and did not remarry.[48]

In Sweden, like in England, a married woman was more protected. A wife and her relatives had to give prior consent to the sale of any piece of land. This right came from the previous right of first refusal whenever a piece of land was offered for sale to someone outside the kin group. It was a well established legal principle.

[45] See articles by Maria Ågren and Elise M. Dermineur in this volume; and also Petot, 'Le statut de la femme', pp. 251.

[46] Sabean, *Property, Production, and Family*, Chapter 13.

[47] Eve Rosenhaft, in this volume.

[48] James E. Shaw, in this volume.

But with the development of the market economy, the kin veto came to be seen as an obstacle to credit. It disappeared from the new national legal code promulgated in 1734. The husband needed the consent of only his wife if he wanted to sell her lineage property. However, the judge could have a private conversation with her to make sure that the husband had not use coercion to obtain her consent.[49] In England, secular Lords Chancellor, such as Francis Bacon, introduced the system of trusts, which meant that a woman handed over all what she owned to trustees — in most cases professionals — through whose mediation she had use of her property and could sell, give, bequeath, or otherwise dispose of it as she saw fit. Moreover, the Court of Chancery imposed the famous 'settlements' on recalcitrant husbands, whereby a woman was assured of the equivalent of a dowry and income in keeping with her social standing during her lifetime.[50] Yet by the end of the Middle Ages, a widow in London was expected to continue or to maintain their late husband business, or even to establish new business enterprises on her own. If she was given to join the economic and social life of guilds and merchant companies, she was denied their political participation.[51]

Facing men and creditors pressures — pressures certainly hard to resist for a woman — what margin to manoeuvre did women possess? It has been shown that in general, women tended to act in conjunction with their fathers, fathers in-law, sons, uncles or grandsons.[52] In England, one of their responses was to increase their use of legal council. This is shown by Matthew Frank Stevens, when he noted that in late medieval England the decline in women's capacity to access courts directly coincided with an increase in the availability of legal counsel which represented them. Women did use counsel to handle pleas concerning land, which were complex cases to defend.[53] Eva König from Hamburg appointed an advisor to finally escape the pressure of her creditors.[54] And others, less wealthy, tended to make bequests to monastic and charitable institutions in order to gain institutional support outside their family, even appointing them as their executors.[55]

In patriarchal premodern societies, the poverty of widows was so widespread that they were counted among the structural poor. This was why the English state

[49] Maria Ågren, in this volume.

[50] Joüon des Longrais, 'Le statut de la femme', pp. 145–46.

[51] Richard Goddard, in this volume.

[52] Francisco Cebreiro Ares, in this volume.

[53] Matthew Frank Stevens, in this volume.

[54] Eve Rosenhaft, in this volume.

[55] James E. Shaw, in this volume.

and the Swedish courts were vigilant. But the more efficient answer came from the Netherlands. There, already by the fifteenth century, family members endowed their daughters with single life annuities, a marriage gift which would protect a woman against mismanagement or even misappropriation by her husband.[56] It was also adopted in other countries like in France. In the eighteenth century, aristocratic families favoured annuities on public institutions to endow their daughters and to invest their wives' money.[57]

These strategies were not so easily available for working class women. In Catalonia, they turned to the bishop who used his power to undo oaths to free those who, under the pressure of their husbands (as they explained to him) were forced to give them their money. Each year, mainly in the seventeenth century and to a lesser extent in the eighteenth century, many contracts of husbands and parents, who profited unduly from the money of minors and married women, were cancelled by the bishop.[58]

Overall, men tried to keep women under political domination to keep them in a state of dependency. This explains why women who could develop important business on their own remained exceptional. But as this volume has shown, despite the constraints and limitations, women did nonetheless experience autonomy. They had agency of their own, fully taking part in the market economy. Throughout Europe, their experience was diverse and varied. Their key role in credit transactions is undisputable.

Works Cited

Secondary Studies

Beauvalais-Boutouyrie, Scarlett, *Être Veuve sous l'Ancien Régime* (Paris: Belin, 2001)

Bresnahan, Menning Carol, 'Loans and Favors, Kin and Clients: Cosimo de' Medici and the Monte di Pietà', *Journal of Modern History*, 61 (1989), 487–511

Coudurie, Marcel, *La Dette des Collectivités Publiques de Marseille au XVIIIe Siècle: Du Débat sur le Prêt à Intérêt au Financement par l'Emprunt* (Marseille: Institut historique de Provence, 1974)

Ferrières, Madeleine, *Le Bien des pauvres: La consommation populaire en Avignon (1600–1800)* (Paris: Éditions Champ Vallon, 2004)

[56] Jaco Zuijderduijn, in this volume.

[57] Forster, *The Nobility of Toulouse in the Eighteenth Century*, pp. 115–16.

[58] Archives of the cathedral, Barcelona. I thank Montserrat Carbonnell-Esteller who was my precious guide in the archives of Barcelona.

Fontaine, Laurence, *Alternative Exchanges: Second-Hand Circulations from the Sixteenth Century to the Present* (Oxford: Longham, 2008)

———, *The Moral Economy: Poverty, Credit, and Trust in Early Modern Europe* (Cambridge: Cambridge University Press, 2014)

Forster, Robert, *The Nobility of Toulouse in the Eighteenth Century: A Social and Economic Study* (New York: Octagon Books, 1971)

Goubert, Pierre, *Beauvais et le Beauvaisis de 1600 à 1730: Contribution à l'Histoire Sociale de la France du XVIIe Siècle* (Paris: SEVPEN, 1960)

Holderness, B. A., 'Widows in Pre-Industrial Society: An Essay upon their Economic Functions', in *Land, Kinship and Life-Cycle*, ed. by Richard M. Smith (Cambridge: Cambridge University Press, 1984), pp. 423–42

Joüon des Longrais F., 'Le statut de la femme en Angleterre dans le droit commun médiéval', *La Femme, Recueil de la société Jean Bodin* (Bruxelles: Éditions de la librairie encyclopédique, 1962), pp. 135–241

Lemire, Beverly, 'Petty Pawns and Informal Lending: Gender and the Transformation of Small-Scale Credit in England, Circa 1600–1800', in *From Family Firms to Corporate Capitalism: Essay in Business and Industrial History in Honour of Peter Mathias*, ed. by Kristine Bruland and Patrick O'Brien (Oxford: Clarendon Press, 1998), pp. 112–38

McCants, Anne, 'Petty Debts and Family Networks: The Credit Markets of Widows and Wives in Eighteenth-Century Amsterdam', in *Women and Credit: Researching the Past, Refiguring the Future*, ed. by Beverly Lemire and others (Oxford: Berg Publishers, 2002), pp. 33–50

Petot, Pierre, 'Le statut de la femme dans les pays coutumiers français du XIIIe au XVIIe siècle', in *La Femme: Recueils de la société Jean Bodin* (Bruxelles: Éditions de la librairie encyclopédique, 1962)

Sabean, David, *Property, Production, and Family in Neckarhausen, 1700–1870* (Cambridge: Cambridge University Press, 1990)

Tebbutt, Melanie, *Making Ends Meet: Pawnbroking and Working-Class Credit* (London: Methuen, 1984)

Wijsenbeek-Olthuis, Thera, *Achter de Gevels von Delft* (Hilversum: Verloren, 1987)

Index

Early European Research

All volumes in this series are evaluated by an Editorial Board, strictly on academic grounds, based on reports prepared by referees who have been commissioned by virtue of their specialism in the appropriate field. The Board ensures that the screening is done independently and without conflicts of interest. The definitive texts supplied by authors are also subject to review by the Board before being approved for publication. Further, the volumes are copyedited to conform to the publisher's stylebook and to the best international academic standards in the field.

Titles in Series

Sociability and its Discontents: Civil Society, Social Capital, and their Alternatives in Late Medieval and Early Modern Europe, ed. by Nicholas Eckstein and Nicholas Terpstra (2009)

Diseases of the Imagination and Imaginary Disease in the Early Modern Period, ed. by Yasmin Haskell (2011)

Writing Royal Entries in Early Modern Europe, ed. by Marie-Claude Canova-Green and Jean Andrews with Marie-France Wagner (2013)

Giovanni Tarantino, *Republicanism, Sinophilia, and Historical Writing : Thomas Gordon (c.1691–1750) and his 'History of England'* (2012)

Friendship and Social Networks in Scandinavia c.1000–1800, ed. by Jón Viðar Sigurðsson and Thomas Småberg (2013)

Identities in Early Modern English Writing : Religion, Gender, Nation, ed. by Lorna Fitzsimmons (2014)

Fama and her Sisters: Gossip and Rumour in Early Modern Europe, ed. by Heather Kerr and Claire Walker (2015)

Understanding Emotions in Early Europe, ed. by Michael Champion and Andrew Lynch (2015)

Raphaële Garrod, *Cosmographical Novelties in French Renaissance Prose (1550–1630): Dialectic and Discovery* (2016)

Languages of Power in Italy (1300–1600), ed. by Daniel Bornstein, Laura Gaffuri, and Brian Jeffrey Maxson (2017)

Performing Emotions in Early Europe, ed. by Philippa Maddern, Joanne McEwan, and Anne M. Scott (2018)

In Preparation

Emotion and Medieval Textual Media, ed. by Mary C. Flannery

Luxury and the Ethics of Greed in Early Modern Italy, ed. by Catherine Kovesi